G-6

All About Gardening

DUTCH IRIS

WEDGWOOD

From a painting by Emily Sartain

All About Gardening

J. COUTTS, A.H.R.H.S., V.M.H.

*Formerly Curator of the Royal Botanic
Gardens, Kew*

Revised and Edited by

G. H. PRESTON, F.L.S.

*Assistant Curator
Royal Botanic Gardens, Kew*

WARD LOCK LIMITED · LONDON

© *Ward Lock & Co., Limited 1954*
Second impression . . *1960*
Third impression (Revised) . *1961*
Fourth impression . . *1963*
Fifth impression . . *1967*
Sixth impression . . *1970*

7063 1109 4

Reproduced and printed in Great Britain by
Redwood Press Limited, Trowbridge and London

Contents

Colour Plates

Photographic Plates

Diagrams

The Nature of Soils

Soils are composed of two groups of compounds: inorganic matter, i.e. material derived from the decay of rocks; and organic matter, i.e. material derived from the decay of vegetable and animal matter. The organic matter is termed humus.

Practically all soils contain sand, clay, limestone, and humus, but in very differing proportions. The preponderating ingredient determines the nature of the soil.

Calcareous soils contain upwards of 20 per cent of lime in their composition. They are formed largely of lime with clay loam or sand, and humus in very small proportion.

Clay soils contain 50 per cent of stiff unctuous clay. They are composed chiefly of clay with a little sand, and are lacking in lime and humus.

Loamy soils are soils in which the proportion of clay varies from 20 to 40 per cent, sand and various kinds of alluvium making up the remainder, with a little lime and humus. When the loam contains a large proportion of sand, it is known as *Sandy Loam*; when it contains a large proportion of lime, it is called a *Calcareous Loam*. A gravel loam and a chalk loam are loams in which there is a considerable proportion of gravel and chalk respectively.

Marly soils are the debris of limestone rock decomposed and reduced to a paste. They contain from 5 to 20 per cent of carbonate of lime, and humus is found in them. They are distinguished as *Argillaceous, Loamy,* and *Sandy* Marls, according to the predominance of clay, loam, or sand among their constituents.

Peaty soils, or vegetable mould, the richest of all garden soils, contain from 5 to 12 per cent of humus, that is, decomposed vegetable and animal matter. *Peat* and *Bog Soil* is composed of fibrous insoluble vegetable matter, mixed with sand and humus.

Sandy soils contain 80 per cent. or thereabouts, of *silica*, that is, the crumbling debris of granite or sandstone rock. In other words, they consist chiefly of sand, with a little clay and lime, and a small proportion of humus.

Good and Poor Soils

A good soil is indicated by gentle slopes; strong woodlands, but no birch or fir; good strong hedges; rich green pasture with an abundance of white clover; deep soil of a good brown or reddish colour; and strong healthy weeds.

A poor soil is indicated by prevalence of birch and fir trees; stunted hedges and trees; sedges plentiful; thin soil, wet and spongy; and the presence of various weeds, such as quaking grass, Yorkshire fog, broom, heath and moss.

Perfect Garden Soil

The perfect soil for general garden use should be composed of the various elements in the following proportions: $\frac{1}{2}$ lime, $\frac{1}{8}$ humus, $\frac{1}{4}$ clay, and $\frac{1}{2}$ sand. Soil containing constituents in these ratios will rarely be found, but many loams will not be far from the ideal, and a little judicious improvement will, in many cases, furnish a compost in which most plants will thrive beyond expectation. Where facilities are available for improving the soil by the addition of other constituents as clay, sand, lime, or humus (which must be well decayed), these should be evenly spread over the soil in autumn and then be dug in in the spring.

SOIL AND DRAINAGE

To some extent different soils naturally need different treatment if they are to be rendered fertile, but there are certain general principles which are more or less applicable to all. In relation to a plant's life the soil can be considered from various standpoints. In the first place it furnishes root-hold by means of which the plant is able to fix itself in space. Then, again, it acts as a storehouse from which the plant absorbs, as required, the greater part of the nourishment on which its continued life depends. Clearly, therefore, we must see to it that if our garden soil is to be fertile it must be of such a texture as shall be compatible with the healthy life and development of the roots and rootlets, and shall contain within reach of those rootlets in an assimilable form the necessary food elements of the plant's growth, and a sufficient supply of moisture at all seasons to present those elements in a dissolved form for absorption.

Water-logged soil will not allow the continual life of the majority of plants. Very sandy soil so unretentive of moisture as rarely to contain enough water for dissolving plant foods is equally hopeless. What most plants require is a soil which, while efficiently drained and containing within a few feet of the surface no body of stagnant water, shall yet be of such a texture and shall include a sufficient proportion of organic material as to retain for an appreciable time a moderate degree of water. If the soil is naturally very heavy, that is to say, if it consists very largely of clay, and especially if it rests at a comparatively shallow depth below the surface on an almost impervious layer, it is almost certain to be more or less water-logged. And it is necessary in such a case to dig it deeply and to provide adequate drainage, in bad cases by means of pipes, in less bad cases by means of stones and broken bricks, and at the same time to lighten the upper layers of the soil by the addition of sand, leaf-mould, organic manures such as stable manure, and the like (*see chapter on* Drainage, p. 31). In a similar way very light, sandy soils should be improved by the liberal addition of clay, fibrous loam

14

such as is obtained from the top spit of meadow land, leaf-mould, and cow or pig manure. These latter, which in the case of the heavy soils, serve to keep open the clay which would tend otherwise to form a solid block, help, in the case of sandy soils, to bind them together, and enable them to retain a greatly increased volume of water.

In the case of practically all soils one of the first things to do, over and above such special measures as have been suggested above, is to trench the ground or to dig it deeply. The processes of trenching, though extremely simple, are not always well understood by amateur gardeners. They essentially aim at the breaking-up of the soil.

For the methods of digging, trenching, etc., *see* pages 18 and 26.

FUMIGATION AND STERILIZATION

Newly-broken land is nearly always infested with wireworms, leather-jackets, and other pests, and a dressing with some soil fumigant such as naphthalene, or carbide refuse is sometimes necessary before successful crops can be obtained.

Soils that have been under cultivation for some time also frequently become pest-ridden. The presence of these pests is indicated by the poor-ness of crops and by the weak and sickly state of individual plants.

It is in the autumn that most of these pests will be present in the soil; at this time not only those that dwell in the earth all the year round will be found, but those that descend from plants and trees to pass the winter in the soil can also be here destroyed at this period, if properly treated.

For this reason soil fumigants should be used in the autumn or early winter; another reason for application at this time is that seeds and plants cannot be inserted until most of the fumigants have lain in the soil for at least three months, or they will be damaged. Use the fumi-gants in December at the latest, therefore, so that crops may be sown in March. Where bushes and herbaceous perennials are left standing in or near the soil to be treated, naphthalene will be found the safest fumigant to use, as it can be employed with impunity quite near the stems of plants. Other chemicals must be kept well away from the roots.

Most of the chemicals used are very poisonous and give off gases when exposed to the air and moisture. The fumigant should be applied to the surface of the soil either as a powder or a liquid, as the case may be, and must be dug in at once so that the fumes may be retained in the soil, as they are the chief agencies in destroying the pests. Fumigants left lying about for one day even, soon lose their strength and efficiency.

Sterilization consists in burning, or heating the soil to such a degree that all pests and seeds of weeds are destroyed and plant growth is stimulated. This process cannot, save the process of burning to be described later, be applied to any great extent to ground in the open, and is generally confined to soil used in pots and borders under glass.

Plants in sterilized soil will at first be slow in growth, as numbers of the bacteria which promote this are destroyed with the pests. Those remaining, however, are free from the influence of pests and quickly multiply, so that after a time the growth of the plants become sur-

15

prisingly vigorous. There are several methods of effecting sterilization; that by which the largest area can most easily be treated is by:

Burning—In this method, all available combustible garden refuse, such as straw, hard and fibrous vegetable matter, and leaves are collected and spread evenly over the soil to be treated. This refuse is set fire to and encouraged to smoulder, rather than to burn fast, so that the process of burning is spread over the longest possible period. This method is best pursued in the late autumn or early winter, at which time the pests will be nearest the surface of the soil. Apart from the sterilization effected by the heat, the ashes will greatly benefit the soil.

Where small quantities of sterilized soil for potting or seed sowing are required other methods can be used.

Portable Equipment—Several types of small portable sterilizing machines are now available or may sometimes be hired from contractors or local horticultural societies. There are various reliable makes using electricity, oil or solid fuel; they are easily controlled and give entirely satisfactory results.

Baking—Here the soil is placed in a shovel, or is spread thinly on a metal sheet over an open fire, and is heated uniformly to 212° F. and maintained at that temperature for a considerable time. The moisture will evaporate in steam, but the soil must be removed from the fire before actual smoke appears. After baking, the soil should be well mixed and allowed to remain 4 to 5 weeks before being used.

Steaming—This is undoubtedly the best and most effective method of sterilizing soil. It consists of passing quantities of steam into the soil until the temperature rises to 212° F. and retaining this temperature in every part of the soil. There are several well-known methods in operation as used in greenhouses both by private and commercial growers. They are the "Small Grid", the "Harrow", the "Tray" and the "Spike" methods. For the amateur who requires a small but effective outfit, portable steam sterilizing plants can be obtained to take from a bushel of soil upwards, while for those who prefer to make their own plant, a wooden box can be constructed with several parallel pipes running at intervals across the bottom; these pipes are provided with holes. The box is filled with soil and covered over the top, and steam at the pressure of 70 lb. to the square inch is forced along the pipes and up through the soil until it is heated to a temperature of 210° F. or as near that as possible. This temperature should be maintained for about 20-30 minutes.

Chemical Sterilization—The two chemicals most commonly used are formaldehyde and cresylic acid. Both are applied in liquid form and both control diseases as well as pests. Cresylic acid is less effective against diseases but more effective against pests. The soil in the glasshouse border should be double dug, brought to a fine condition and if dry, watered 2 or 3 days before being treated. The chemicals should be applied at the correct dilution and quantity and all parts of the house should be washed down with the solution at the same time. The house must be empty of plants and remain empty for 6-8 weeks after treatment.

16

Table of Soil Fumigants

On a large scale in the open, fumigation is preferable to sterilization.

RECOMMENDED SOIL FUMIGANTS

Chemical.	Rate of Application.	Remarks.
Carbide Refuse .	15 oz. per square yard.	Applied as powder. Useful for small pests.
Carbolic Acid .	Mix 2 oz. concentrated acid with each gallon of water. Apply 5/6ths of a gallon of mixture to each square yard of soil.	Applied as liquid from watering-can. Poison; all liquid should, therefore, be used up.
Formalin . .	Mix 2 oz. with each gallon of water. Apply 5/6ths of a gallon of mixture to each square yard of soil.	Stir the mixture just before application and use in can. Containers of formalin should be opened in open air, or the operator may be gassed. It is advisable to use a gas-mask during application.
Naphthalene .	¾ oz. per square yard.	Store in air-tight containers. Harmless to plants.
Salt . . .	12¼ oz. per square yard.	Effective for pests at surface only.
Soot . . .	12¼ oz. per square yard.	Should be fresh. Must not touch leaves of plants. Effective for pests at surface only.

NOTE.—30¼ square yards = 1 square rod.

CHAPTER 2

The Technique of Gardening

Single Digging

In digging with the fork, little can be done beyond breaking and turning over the ground and reducing the clods thus turned up. In digging with the spade the soil can be transferred more readily from one position to another. Shallow digging is of very little value, and to enable the soil to be deeply worked the spade should be inserted in as nearly an upright position as possible. The digger should stand well over his spade, and must not try to dig out more than 5 to 6 inches of soil each time—that is to say in width—he must always dig to the full depth of the spade. The first thing to be done is to mark the ground out into strips each some 10 feet wide; if trenches longer than this are dug it will be found difficult to keep the soil level. Next take out a trench about a spade deep and a spade wide, or, in other words, about 12 inches in depth, the same in width, and the full width of the strip. The sides of this trench must be cut straight and square, and all loose earth must be removed from the bottom, which must be flat and even. The soil from this trench should be removed to the other end of the ground to be dug over. Another trench of the same size is now taken out, and the soil is transferred into the first trench and is left as rough as possible, thus exposing as large a surface as may be to the action of the weather during the winter months. This process is carried on until the whole ground has been dug over and the last trench taken out is filled with the soil taken from the first trench.

Digging should be completed before the soil becomes too wet. If left over-late, the ground may become quite unworkable and the digging may have to be deferred until the early spring —a very bad policy, as the soil is thereby deprived of the beneficial action of air, rain, and frost through the long winter. Digging when the soil is very wet does more harm than good as the earth becomes trodden down and compressed and loses all its porosity, which is the very characteristic that digging is meant to increase. Two-thirds of the cultivated soil in a garden should be dug over each year; the other third should be bastard trenched (*see* p. 19).

In digging, all roots of perennial weeds should be carefully picked out, but vegetable stems and leaves and all annual weeds can be dug in as manure, provided they are deeply buried. In manuring during digging, the manure should be thrown with the fork along the bottom of the trench, and the earth from the next trench must be thrown on top of it. (*See also* Trenching, p. 26.)

18

Mulching

Earthing-up

A term employed to describe the drawing up of soil about the stems or stalks of any growing plant, as, for example, peas, beans, potatoes, celery, leeks, and many other plants. It induces the growth of rootlets from the stem in some cases, and affords greater shelter for the roots. In the case of the potato, it facilitates the formation of tubers, which are found below and round the bottom part of the haulm and near the surface. If these are exposed to the light and air, they turn green and are unfit for food. It is desirable also to draw up the soil round the stalks of cabbages of all kinds. (*See* Blanching *below*.)

Blanching

Several vegetables require blanching to be made tender and prevent the development of the green colouring matter and reduce bitterness —celery, leeks, seakale, cardoons, chicory, endive, lettuces. The first two of these are blanched by the process of earthing-up, which is dealt with above. Seakale is blanched under pots prepared for this purpose, and covered over with litter, sand, ashes or leaves.

The best plan with endive is to place over each plant, when full-grown, a large tile or slate, which will effectually exclude all light and blanch the endive in a few days. With lettuces there is no better plan than tying. (*See also the culture of* Vegetables, chapter 17.)

"Double Digging"

Trenching to three spades' depth, as described in the article on *Trenching*, is not often performed, as unless the top soil is very deep and good there is always the danger of bringing dead, useless subsoil to the top. On only moderately deep ground double digging, that is, to two spades' depth, is usually adopted. The process is the same except that the second spit is not removed but is broken up in the same way as the third spit in trenching proper. The top spit of the second portion of ground is not wheeled away, but is placed over the first trench.

Mulching

This operation, which saves much watering in dry weather, consists in spreading a 3-inch layer of half-decayed stable manure, well-decayed vegetable refuse, leaf-mould, coconut fibre, hop manure, or other material over the soil occupied by the roots of plants, especially those which have been recently transplanted, and in times of drought watering thoroughly before the mulch is laid down. The mulch will then prevent the water from evaporating too quickly. During very dry weather the lawn may also be well watered in the evening, the following day the mower is run over without the grass-box; the cut grass will act as a mulch and preserve the moisture. Rain falling or water applied on a mulch soaks through and carries nourishment through to the roots and thus performs an additional service. Where a mulch of manure or other matter is unsightly and unpleasant, as on some flower borders, coconut fibre can be used as a mulch or can be sifted over to hide the mulch used. **A** mulch is of little benefit unless it is at least 2 inches in thickness; if deeper it is liable to make the roots too cold. After a time the material used, whatever it may be, may be forked into the soil; a new mulch should then be applied. It is, however, seldom necessary to apply more than one mulch during an ordinary summer.

A mulch should be very retentive of moisture; certain mulches are more suitable to one soil than another. For instance, rich loamy or clayey soils are best mulched with well-decayed leaf-mould, freshly-mown grass, or with well-rotted horse manure; on light sandy soils a mulch of vegetable matter should always be well decayed and cow or pig manure should be used in preference to horse manure. The mulch must not be placed close up to the stems of the plants, as it is apt to damage them and cause them to rot, besides it is the roots that benefit by the mulching and these are often found on examination to extend a considerable way out from the stem.

A word of caution is, however, necessary as there are several materials that should not be used as mulches; some because they soon "cake" and form a hard crust, others because of chemical properties they would impart to the soil, or because they encourage insect pests. The following are a few substances that should not be used: mud from the bottom of ponds and streams, road-sweepings, pine needles, and newly-fallen leaves. Such materials as soot and wood-ashes should not be employed as they soon sink into the soil and are useless as mulches. Mulching is usually carried out during the months of May, June and July; it should not be confused with top-dressing (which see), which only aims at providing nourishment to the roots, and does not prevent evaporation in hot weather. Every newly-planted tree, and all wall fruit trees, should have a mulching of some sort spread around them. Plants whose roots lie near the surface of the soil, such as beans, cauliflowers, peas, raspberries, and roses, are those that suffer first in a drought, and these are the ones that most require mulching. With plants of this nature a mulch is put down in the spring; with other plants many gardeners wait until the drought has arrived. Where mulching is impossible, hoeing will go a long way towards making up for it.

Nailing-up Plants

This is a rather difficult operation, for a nail is no ornament, and the less it shows itself the better. The gardener's skill must be exerted to conceal his nails and shreds as much as possible. For use in brick or stonework cast-iron nails are best, as these will pierce very hard substances without bending. Cloth list or shreds of old cloth are generally used; but strips of leather or black tape are preferred by some, under the supposition that they not only have a neater appearance, but afford less harbour for insects. The shreds vary from $\frac{1}{2}$ to $\frac{3}{4}$ of an inch in width and from 4 to 6 inches in length, according to the size of the twig or branch on which they are to be used. Fruit trees should be nailed close in to the wall, but ornamental shrubs, etc., should be merely fastened in for the sake of support.

Planting
Unless well planted the tree, shrub, vegetable, or flower cannot thrive. Firm planting is essential in almost all cases; another vital matter is the preparation of the soil and the site for planting.

Detailed instructions will be found in the chapters on *Bedding Plants, The Herbaceous Border, Climbing Plants, Ornamental and Flowering Shrubs and Trees Bulbs Vegetables, and Potting*, and to these we refer the reader.

Pointing
This consists in thrusting the garden fork some 5 or 6 inches into the soil, which is lifted and turned over. The process is useful in beds and borders filled with plants whose roots run near the surface and where it would be harmful to dig to a spade's depth. By pointing, manure is worked into the herbaceous and shrub borders in the autumn, the manure being first laid evenly over the surface, and then worked in around the plants. The surface of a bed or border is usually pointed over when it has become unduly caked and hard.

Protection from Weather
If the garden is very much exposed to certain prevalent winds, belts of trees or dense-growing shrubs must be planted to break its force, and to protect the tenderer plants in the borders. (*See chapters on* Hedges, p. 42, *and* Trees and Shrubs, p. 300.) Where the garden is walled this protection is, of course, not needed, as the walls, as well as helping to ripen the fruit grown on them, will make a most efficient protection against wind. For protecting early spring flowers, such as tulips, in very exposed positions temporary screens of coarse canvas, scrim, or coconut matting can be erected on poles 3 to 4 feet high or straw or wattle hurdles can be used to break the force of the wind. If branches of fir or other evergreens are available these can be stuck into the ground on the windward side of the plants, and make an excellent screen. Against cold weather and frosts individual protection of the more tender plants will be required, and there are many ways of affording this, varying with the plant. In exposed localities dwarf roses, especially teas, are best protected by a small mound of clean dry straw, bracken, coconut fibre or some similar material heaped round them for a few inches above the ground. The taller roses, standards and half-standards, should have dry bracken fronds tied in among their heads. The ordinary garden mat is the most useful thing for tying round other tender shrubs and for covering frames during hard weather. It may be tied into a cone shape, and supported on small sticks like a " wigwam " over small plants, or spread over trees trained against walls. The more tender herbaceous perennials in the open borders may need protection from frost in severe winters. The means by which this is supplied is described in the chapter on *The Herbaceous Border* (p. 276), to which the reader is referred. The thing is to keep the plants dry during cold weather; it is when a plant gets wet and is subsequently frozen that the damage occurs. In the early spring

protection is chiefly needed for the blossoms of early-flowering fruit trees, such as the peach and apricot, during the period when there is risk of night frosts. This is best given by means of cheap calico, netting or garden tiffany suspended by means of hooks or rings attached to nails in the wall.

Many plants in the greenhouse will need shading from the sun during the summer months, and the reader is referred to the chapter on the Greenhouse where this is fully discussed.

Where individual blooms in the open require shading from the sun, or protecting from the weather, the gardener may either make or purchase a cone-shaped shade of calico from 6 to 12 inches in diameter, stiffened and supported by a galvanized wire framework and mounted by a clip on a wooden stake so that it can be moved up and down until at the right height to give the necessary protection. Such a shade is especially useful for protecting roses from the sun and thus enabling them to keep their colour. Where sweet peas for exhibition have to be protected these individual shades are not practicable, and in this case large strips of cheap calico, canvas, or scrim should be arranged on poles over the rows of peas to protect the blooms from the sun.

Shading and Sheltering Plants
(*See article on* Protecting Plants *on previous page, also the section on* Shading *in the chapter dealing with* Gardening under Glass.)

Staking and Tying-up Plants
As the plants in the beds and borders begin to grow, all that attain a height of over, say, $2\frac{1}{2}$ feet and many more of a less robust nature will require staking, otherwise wind and rain will soon break them down. Rather than use one large stake, to which all the stems of the plant are tied in a tight bush, quite spoiling its natural shrubbiness and contour, it is better to support each of the stronger shoots of the plant with a separate stick and so preserve the natural contour of the plant. Bamboo canes are excellent for this work.

Time will, however, rarely be available for this treatment to be given to smaller plants; with these it will usually suffice if three or four sticks are driven in round the plant and bass or string is tied from stick to stick to support the flower stems. The stakes should slope slightly outwards and away from the plant and the string must not be drawn too tight. This is a good method of supporting plants with delicate stems that would be damaged if individually tied to stakes. As an alternative method, a stake may be driven into the ground at the centre of the plant and the chief stems can be tied to this with bass, not so that they are drawn tightly round the stake, but so that they may resume their natural positions.

The stakes must be hidden as much as possible, and should be placed behind the stems and foliage, and where natural branches and twigs of hazel or birch, which are the least unsightly, are not used, they should be stained green or brown. Stakes will be very unsightly if allowed to overtop the flower stems; they should, on an average, be three-quarters of the length of the stem to be supported, excluding, of course, the portion of the stake thrust into the ground. It must not, however, be forgotten that this refers to when one is staking the mature stalk, and that when supporting young flower-spikes allowance must be made for growth. It must not be forgotten that the plants continue to grow and that further tying and staking will be necessary at intervals.

The tying material naturally varies with the plant and the weather conditions to which it will be subjected. For trees in the open, tarred cord of thickness to suit the size of the trees is used. Perennial border plants are tied up with soft tarred string if it is to last for more than a season. For annuals in the open, for most greenhouse plants, for all tying, in fact, that need not last for more than a year, raffia or bass, worsted, or soft string, will be found most suitable and convenient.

Whatever the method of staking adopted, the material should always be first tied securely round the stake and is then looped round the stem sufficiently tightly to hold it in position, but not tightly enough to cut into the bark or stem, due allowance being made for the future growth of the branches. Stems should be so tied that they maintain their natural distances apart; if bunched tightly together they will be deprived of a large amount of sun and air and will suffer heavily in consequence. They should be able to sway naturally with the wind; if they cannot the blooms will offer resistance and may be torn and damaged.

The Neat Garden

The primary object of tidying-up may be to keep the garden neat, but it is most beneficial to the plants. Firstly the collecting and burning of waste materials, such as dead leaves and twigs, does much to stop the propagation of fungoid diseases and insect pests. Secondly, the hoeing and pointing-in of the soil does untold good. These processes, together with the benefits they confer, are fully explained in other paragraphs in this chapter. But it is more with the removal of dead shoots after flowering and the picking off of dead flowers and seed-pods that we have to deal here. Many think that these things are done purely to make the beds appear tidier; this is certainly a useful function, but the main reason is a far more important one. To reproduce its species is the foremost aim of every plant, and as a rule once this has been ensured, the plant ceases to bear more flowers, and in the case of an annual, dies down altogether. For this reason all annuals should have their dead blooms and seed-pods picked off as soon as possible to encourage the production of fresh flowers; this will greatly extend the period of blooming. With early-flowering herbaceous perennials, such as delphiniums and lupins, the same process should be carried out, except that the whole of the stem supporting the dead blooms should be cut away; this will enable the plants to put forth a second crop of bloom in the early autumn.

About mid-summer, or slightly later, it will be found that border plants will require additional treatment to that mentioned above. Many of them will have grown unwieldy and may be suffocating less vigorous plants; these must be trimmed back. Plants of a trailing and creeping nature will require pegging down to lead them into the way they should go and to make them cover their allotted space. (*See* Staking and Tying-up *in this chapter.*)

Top-Dressing the Soil

Although some mulches are at the same time top-dressings, these two preparations are applied for entirely different purposes. Mulches are used primarily to prevent over-rapid evaporation and to keep the roots warm, the aim of the top-dressing is to enrich the soil and furnish new food for the roots.

Most of the organic manures and artificial fertilizers mentioned in the chapter on *Manures* may be used as top-dressings; those most generally employed for this purpose are bonemeal, potash, leaf-mould, old lawn mowings, old hot-bed manure, nitrate of soda, sulphate of ammonia, superphosphate of lime and wood-ashes. For flower beds and borders a dressing of 75 per cent old hot-bed manure, or if this cannot be obtained the same proportion of well-decayed farmyard manure, and 25 per cent leaf-mould or other well-rotted vegetable matter is excellent. Rock plants will need an additional 25 per cent of leaf-mould and a liberal sprinkling of coarse sharp sand; granite or limestone chippings may also be used. The reader is referred to the table showing the *Application and Uses of Manures*, p. 50, and to the sections on *Manuring Vegetables*, p. 274, p. 313, where the manures, either organic or artificial, most suitable to each fruit or vegetable are shown, together with the amount to give and the season of application.

Top-dressings are used to augment the plant food supplied by the manure dug in at planting time or when it is not feasible to disturb plants so that manure may be dug in, as in the case of the herbaceous border or the rock garden. They are usually employed in spring or early summer, or in the autumn; the coarser organic manures are generally applied in even layers an inch or two thick and are then forked into the soil. Artificial fertilizers are usually very fine in texture and must be well raked into the soil.

In the case of pot plants that occupy the same pot for some time the top inch or two of soil may be removed so that a fresh top-dressing of compost may be added, usually without any stimulant, or in the case of plants known to be " gross-feeders " sufficient room is left in the pot at potting time, to enable one or more top-dressings of fresh soil and fertilizer to be given as the roots fill the old soil and seek nourishment on the surface. Where stimulants are required, one of the artificial fertilizers will be found more suitable than the more bulky organic manures, and is best applied in three or four dressings at intervals.

Training

It is necessary in the case of flowers, climbers, and ornamental shrubs

Transplanting

to train them in order to produce the greatest number of really good blooms; to keep the plants neat and within bounds; and, as far as possible, to make them cover a required space while still retaining a natural habit of growth and appearance. The habits and growth of each plant are described in the paragraphs dealing individually with them (chapter 16), and the reader is advised to study these before starting to train his plants. (*See also* Pruning and Training Shrubs, p. 302.)

Fruit and vegetables are, of course, trained and pruned with a view to quality and quantity in production.

Ornamental trees should be carefully trained from the outset; it is very difficult to recast the shape of a tree badly trained or neglected when young. Keep the tree well balanced by trimming and lopping equally on all sides, and where it is necessary to let in more air cut out a complete branch here and there rather than shorten a number. A clean straight stem should always be encouraged, and the supporting stakes must be inserted where necessary.

A brick wall is by no means improved by having a mass of nails driven into it; other means of supporting a climber are, therefore, often used. Wires can be stretched horizontally in staples across the wall at intervals of, say, 18 inches, and to these the climbers are loosely tied by means of tarred string. A better plan, however, is to make a wooden trellis, with square meshes, which can be fastened against the wall, and the climber is tied to this. Climbers should be trained regularly and not be allowed to run rampant, when the stems will become weak and will be unable to support the heads in future years. Especially is it necessary to cut back the growths of young and newly-planted climbers to encourage the formation of strong sturdy stems; it is a wise plan to cut all new growth on young climbers back to two-thirds each year.

Transplanting
Most of the remarks on planting in this chapter refer equally well to the process of transplanting.

In transplanting—whatever the subject may be—the great thing is to keep the roots out of the ground for as short a time as possible, and for this reason, when transplanting trees and large plants, it is advisable to prepare the sites and dig the holes they are to occupy in advance. Keep the roots " heeled-in " if possible, but if they *must* remain out of the soil for some little time moisten and cover them with litter and matting to keep them from the frost and from becoming dried up, as once the small fibrous roots dry up they perish and the plant must form new ones before it can again take up nourishment from the soil. It, therefore, takes a long time to become established and receives a severe check. If the roots have become dry, soak them well before planting. The " ball " of earth round the roots should be kept intact, although this is not feasible with large shrubs and trees, in view of the weight of the soil that would have to be moved with it.

Every care must be taken not to damage the roots. Seedlings should
25

not be roughly pulled up with the hand, a trowel or hand-fork should be used; herbaceous plants and small shrubs are best lifted by inserting two garden forks to their full depth vertically one on each side and close in to the plant, and then levering the handles gently downwards and away from the plant. This method will lift the plant from the soil with the roots intact. Large shrubs and trees are a more difficult matter; the best way is to dig a trench round the tree and from 2 to 3 feet from it, then dig inwards towards the tree until the roots are reached, next dig downwards under the tree, and it will be found possible to remove it without much damage to the roots. Trees and shrubs should be well watered after transplanting, and if the weather becomes dry before they are thoroughly established evergreens should have their foliage thoroughly syringed every evening as long as the drought lasts.

The method of setting the plants in their new sites is fully set forth in the chapters devoted to the various kinds of plants.

(*See also* Thinning-out and Transplanting *in the chapter on* Propagation, p. 64.)

Trenching

The immediate object of trenching is to deepen the soil and prepare the subsoil to nourish the fibres of deep-rooting plants; the subsoil is not brought to the surface. The operation is commenced by digging a trench 2 to $2\frac{1}{2}$ feet wide and a foot deep, throwing out the top spit, and wheeling it to the farther end of the bed, the second spit is treated in the same manner if the trenching is to be three spades deep. This done, the bottom of the trench is dug over to the full depth of the fork, well broken up and is left level. The top spit of a second portion of the ground is now removed and placed alongside the first, and the second spit of this portion is dug up and placed roughly over the first trench. The first spit of a third portion is now removed and placed in as large masses as possible over the first trench; the bottom of the second trench is then dug up in the same manner as the first, and so on till the whole is finished. Heavy soils are best trenched in the autumn, throwing the soil up in ridges, thus exposing a large surface to the action of frost and air during the winter. Treated in this way, the ridges should in the spring break down to a fine tilth. Light soils may be trenched in the early winter or dug at almost any time.

Water and Watering

Rainwater is by far the best for plants, because the carbonic acid and the nitrates that it contains make it a soil fertilizer. Even pump water, apparently clear, is often far too hard to do well for watering plants, but this hardness may be removed by keeping it in shallow tanks and exposed to the air for some time before use. Plants under glass should always be watered from tanks kept at the same temperature as the plants are growing in, therefore, some vessel must always be kept in the house. Nothing does much greater mischief to plants than chilling them with water of lower temperature than the atmosphere they are in.

26

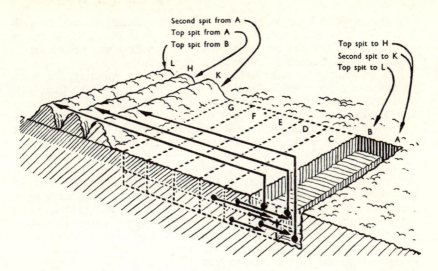

FIG. 1. First stages in trenching. Move the top spit of trench A to H and the lower or second spit to K. The top spit of trench B is then moved to L. Now, move lower or second spit of trench B to space previously occupied by second spit of A, and the second spit of C to that of B and top spit of C to that of top A.

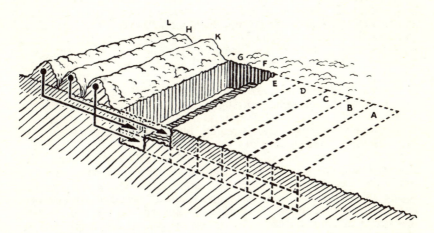

FIG. 2. Final stages in trenching. The second spit from A previously moved to K now fills the second spit of the last trench. The top spit from A (moved to H) fills the top spit of the last but one trench, and the top spit from B (moved to L) takes the place of the top spit of the last trench.

27

Water supplied by pipe from the main is not usually so cold as well-water, but it is often equally hard. If possible it should be stored in a tank, exposed to the air for at least twenty-four hours before use to soften it and to raise it to the required temperature.

It is impossible to make hard and fast rules for watering, for many points have to be considered; first the nature of the plants, then their situation, whether in sun or shade, on a high well-drained spot or in a low-lying and damp locality; plants on light soils on a well-drained sub-soil, such as gravel or chalk, will suffer from drought far sooner than those growing on heavy loams with retentive clay beneath them. Watering is best done when the sun has gone down; if watering is done while the sun is up and hot the flowers and foliage will be scorched, as some moisture is sure to find its way on to them, and the globules will act as microscopes to magnify the power of the sun's rays. This leads us to make the point that watering is best done with the uncapped spout of the hose or can and not through a rose, which tends to cause the surface of the soil to " cake ". A rose should only be used when watering seeds, seedlings, newly-potted plants to settle the soil, and when spraying the foliage. Hold the hose or can so that the spout is close to the ground; if water is given from a height the soil will be disturbed overmuch or washed away.

Watering in the open should never be undertaken until essential. When commenced, sufficient must be given thoroughly to moisten the top 10 inches of the soil; this takes a good deal more water and longer than most people imagine. A little water over the surface merely chills the soil, and draws the roots to the surface where they are quickly scorched unless water is frequently given, which soon " cakes " the surface, and prevents the air from penetrating to the roots. It pays to give a thorough watering once a week rather than a daily sprinkling. Constant hoeing, or better still mulching (*see* p. 19), will eliminate the need for frequent watering.

If a bed is thoroughly forked up and is then well watered one evening, and mulched the following morning with well-rotted dung, decayed vegetable material, or coconut fibre refuse, or well hoed—the latter is, of course, not so effective—it will require little further moisture for a considerable time, even in very dry weather.

There are several classes of plants that are often overlooked as far as the question of watering goes, and among these are: pot-plants stood out in the open during the summer; a large surface of the soil is exposed to the air and heat so that the compost quickly becomes dry and needs frequent attention, unless the pots are " plunged " in the soil, in ashes, or in coconut fibre; the leaves of evergreens perpetually keep much rain from reaching the roots even in winter when other plants receive a good store of moisture; in the same way climbers, shrubs, and trees trained on a wall often suffer during the summer, unless watered and mulched, as the position of the wall will frequently keep off much rain and prevent the plants obtaining moisture.

In watering newly-potted plants, it is important that the whole of the soil shall be thoroughly and evenly moistened all through, which can only be accomplished by filling up two or three times with water, or by soaking thoroughly by immersing the pot to above the brim in a pail of water and then standing it to drain in the shade. This process of watering is especially useful in the case of hard-wooded plants, such as azaleas, deutzias, heaths, and myrtles, which have fine fibrous roots and are very firmly potted in light sandy soil or peat. If at any time allowed to become too dry the inner " ball " round the roots will not readily absorb water which will flow round the " ball " leaving it unmoistened, although the surface soil may seem to be sufficiently moist. Such plants will need a thorough soaking, and to prevent them from getting into such a state it is a wise policy to immerse them in a pail of water for five or ten minutes every week or ten days. No fear need be entertained of over-watering; if the plants have been rightly potted (*see chapter on* Potting, (p. 127), all surplus water, beyond what the soil can conveniently retain, will drain away.

Irregular watering is frequently the cause of failure in plant-culture, even with experienced growers.

Water each individual plant as it requires it; because one plant in a batch needs water it does not mean that all are too dry. Plants in full growth and coming into bloom always require more water than plants past their prime and "going-off". It is of immense importance to bear in mind that the lower the temperature in which greenhouse plants are placed the less *water* they require, and *vice versa*. Cold, which stimulates man's digestive organs to the utmost, paralyses those of plants in the exact ratio of its intensity. Hence the necessity of a stinted supply of water in cold weather if plant life is to be preserved in full vigour.

Plants should never be watered overhead when in bloom or in cold weather, or, rather, while they are in a cold atmosphere; and never, except to wash off dust, should those having a soft or woolly foliage be so treated; but some plants, as azaleas, myrtles, heaths, and others with hard leaves, may be plentifully syringed, or watered overhead from a fine rose, in warm weather, especially when in full growth. or to soften the bark and encourage the formation of new shoots. Syringing should not be over-done, as it tends to weaken the plants; if a moist atmosphere is required this is better obtained by keeping the walls and floor well damped rather than by excessive overhead watering. The best time to syringe is in the early morning before the sun is up and again after the sun has lost its strength in the late afternoon and after the house has been closed. (*See also* Watering *in the chapter on* Gardening under Glass, Watering Seeds *in the chapter on* Propagation, *and* Watering the Lawn, p. 58.)

Weeding
The hoe is undoubtedly the best implement with which to control weeds on beds, and if this is used early in the season and is kept in constant use, weeds will get little chance to multiply; by its aid annual weeds will be destroyed, and biennial and perennial weeds. owing to the frequent

cutting down, will be so weakened that in the course of two, three, or more years they will die.

All weeds that have flowered or seeded, likewise all those with "runner" roots with "eyes" on them, which will grow again if they come into contact with the soil, must be burned, and must not be used, unburned, as a vegetable manure. This latter procedure would surely spread the weeds; the ashes may safely be used as a manure. Other weeds can be put on the refuse heap and can later safely be used as manure.

In hot dry weather, if the weeding is done fairly early in the day, this class of weed may be left lying on the soil to wither and die, but in damp weather and when the soil is wet they must be removed to the rubbish heap, as there is danger of their again taking root.

Hand-weeding—gripping the weeds as near the soil as possible and twisting them with as many of their roots as one can—must be resorted to where the plants are too close to permit of the use of the hoe. If this method is adopted shortly after a good shower of rain, many perennial weeds may be destroyed.

As weeds spread so readily, it is most necessary to keep all rough grass near the garden cut, especially before it has time to seed. The weeds in grass-paths, grass-edgings and on the lawn must also be kept well in check for the same reason; this also applies to all neighbouring banks and hedgerows, which must be kept clean and weed-free.

It is a mistake to hoe up weeds on paths, they may be banished temporarily, but the turned-up gravel is in a more favourable condition for their increase later on. The best method of destroying weeds on paths is to apply a suitable weed-killer.

Weed-Killers

There are two main groups of weed-killers. Those such as sodium chlorate, which act upon all forms of vegetation, and those that are selective and affect certain groups of plants only and do not harm others. The former can be used only on paths and drives or on land that is to remain vacant for some time, the latter on particular crops such as a lawn. In a few cases a pre-emergence treatment may be given; sulphuric acid may be used if seed has been sown but must be applied before the seedlings begin active growth.

Such specialized operations as "grafting", "pruning", etc., are dealt with fully in the relevant chapters, and the reader, when requiring detailed information on these, should refer to the "index".

CHAPTER 3

Garden Drainage

Artificial Drainage

If your land has a good slope, artificial draining will probably be unnecessary, and there is rarely any need to drain lands with gravelly, sandy or stony subsoils. Where this consists of a stiff clay, and in low-lying situations, artificial drainage is almost always essential. The following are two simple tests for ascertaining whether drainage is required. Dig a hole 3 to 3½ feet deep in winter; if water percolates quickly into the cavity the land must be drained. Soil, where the water hangs about in pools on the surface for more than a couple of hours after the cessation of heavy rain, will also require attention.

Trench-Drainage

There are some lands that have a thin stratum of material impermeable to water some 18 inches below the surface. It is obvious that such land cannot be drained by a system of land-drains and trenches, as the water, over the greater part of the surface, would not be able to percolate into the drains. It is here that trenching shows up in its true value. By digging to a depth of 2 to 3 feet over the whole surface the hard crust is thoroughly broken up and the water from the top-soil is enabled to sink down through it. This may be found to provide adequate drainage; if it does not, pipe- or trench-drainage must be installed.

Small-Garden Drainage

This is often a very difficult problem—at least the carrying away of the surplus water is no easy matter, as the natural slope is probably towards a neighbour's garden, and the small garden rarely has a ditch into which the drains can run. Pipe-drainage is also a somewhat expensive and laborious matter; the cost and difficulties, therefore, often lead to the small garden not being drained at all, which is, of course, the worst possible policy, as nothing save a few sickly-looking specimens will thrive in saturated and water-logged land. Some attempt must, therefore, be made at drainage, where necessary, and when cost makes the use of pipes prohibitive, quite efficient drainage can be effected by cutting parallel trenches about 3 feet deep and 1 foot wide across the ground to be drained. Into the bottom of these trenches should be thrown 9 inches of broken bricks, old rubble, and ballast—in fact any hard material that will keep the soil open and allow the water to percolate through. Brush-

31

wood and heather may be used, but are not so lasting as clinkers and rubble. Over this drainage material place turves bottom-side-up to prevent the finer soil from silting through and clogging up the drainage. The remaining 18 inches or so should be filled in with the excavated soil; this must not be rammed down, but should be allowed to sink naturally, otherwise the drain will be rendered useless and might as well not be there.

These drains must either empty themselves into a ditch that will carry off the water, or, where this is not possible, a large sump must be dug in the lowest part of the garden and filled in with drainage material in the same way as the drains. Into this the water will flow and be gradually disposed through the soil.

Sinking Drains

There are various ways of laying out the drains in ground, according to the configuration of the surface. If the ground has a clay subsoil and has a uniform slope, as is often the case with garden ground, it will be sufficient to lay parallel lines of 2- or 3-inch pipes at a distance of from 15 feet to 20 feet apart, provided always that pipes are used in making the drains. When the land slopes slightly on either side to a depression in the middle, a main drain of 3- or 4-inch pipes should be laid along this depression from the head to the outfall, and lateral drains of 3-inch pipes entering the main drain and connected with it by junction-sockets and elbow joints. No precise directions can be given in this matter as the construction and disposition of the drains, must in every case depend on the nature of the soil and the contour of the surface. The depth, too, will also depend upon circumstances, but a main drain will vary in depth from 2½ feet to 4½ feet, being shallowest at the head and deepest at the outfall. The depth of lateral drains will of course depend upon that of the main drain. All lateral drains should enter a main drain obliquely and not at right angles, and the fall should be greater when the lateral approaches the main drain than at any other portion of its course. From 15 feet to 20 feet should be allowed between the feeders to a main drain on clay soils. The fall of a main drain should never be less than 1 in 200.

Laying Drain-pipes

Sometimes the drain-pipes are laid with collars, that is, short pieces of piping sufficiently large to receive the ends of two pipes, thus keeping them firmly in their place. In other cases the pipes are joined together by bands of tempered clay, which answer very well, but when this method is adopted the upper sides of the pipes should be perforated with holes for the reception of the water, so that the solid junction of the pipes is no detriment. It is not usual, however, to do more than lay the pipes end to end in a straight line, or just fit the end of one pipe into the socket made for its reception at the end of the pipe that comes next to it, if pipes of this construction are used. In this case no clay or cement must be used to bind the pipes together, but at the junction of any feeder

32

PLATE 1 DIGGING *Above left*, single digging. *Above right*, forking over the second spit. *Below left*, forking manure into the second spit. *Below right*, double digging. Note the correct angle at which the spade should be held.

PLATE 2 GARDEN TOOLS *Above, left to right,* Dutch hoe, mattock hoe (or draw-hoe), three tined cultivator, double-sided cultivator, French cultivator and hoe. *Below, left to right,* border spade, shovel, potting spade and turf cutter.

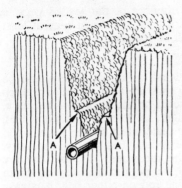

FIG. 3. Drainage pipes are best laid in V-shaped trenches and below the shoulder **A**.

with the main drain the union should be carefully made by clay or cement where permanent dainage is expected.

A straight-edge and spirit-level should always be used to ensure that the pipes are laid truly. This will save many clogged or ineffective drains in future years.

Cover the pipes for a few inches with rough porous rubbish or broken crockery, heather, or gorse, or any such material, and the drains will be effective and permanent: this is especially necessary in heavy clay soils. An excellent plan is to lay soles or flat tiles, and on these to set half-pipes or bridge-pipes which are of a tunnel shape, the rough stuff is then laid over these and the trench is filled in with earth, which should not be rammed or trodden very tight, but merely allowed to settle. (*See also* Selecting the Site, p. 52, *and* Paths and Drainage, p. 36.)

Levelling

In view of the work entailed and the cost, levelling should not be undertaken on anything but a very small scale, unless the scheme has been carefully considered and the site very thoroughly reconnoitred with reference to the probable effect on the drainage system. Where the surface is raised there will be little need for hesitation, but when the levelling consists largely in excavating a considerable portion of soil in the lower part of the garden, the site, if the soil is a heavy and retentive clay, may quite possibly become water-logged and may require extensive draining, which might not be easy in comparatively low-lying sections of the garden. As levelling is to a great extent carried out in the autumn and winter, the gardener may not have long to wait for a few heavy showers of rain, which will soon prove

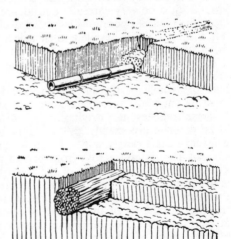

FIG. 4. *Above,* drain pipes must fit closely and evenly. *Below,* drain made of lengths of brushwood and laid lengthwise; this system is not very lasting.

what drainage, if any, is necessary. A number of flat-headed pegs, a garden line. a rake, a heavy roller, a spirit-level, a straight-edge at least 10 feet long, and a set of boning rods will be required.

Boning Rods

In laying drains over long distances where a straight-edge would be too short and take too much time, boning rods are used. There are three of these rods in a set. They are constructed on the lines of a T-square, the uprights being essentially the same length, i.e. 3 feet 6 inches or 4 feet, and the cross-piece 1 foot in length. The material should be white wood measuring 3 inches by ¾ inch, the joint being morticed to ensure security. The over-all length of the three must be the same. In use they are simple, if the pegs at either end are fixed, i.e. pegs to the required depth of the pipes, for by holding erect a boning rod on either peg, it is easy to find the correct depth for intermediate pegs by merely sighting across the top of one and just catching a glimpse of the ridge on the other. The intermediate pegs should be driven in so that when the third boning rod is held erect on them, the upper edges of the three cross-pieces are in line when sighted across from either end. Similarly if two pegs are put in level with the straight-edge and spirit-level, one may get a third by sighting across the two already in. To obtain sufficient fall, knock in this end peg to allow for drop, and put in the intermediates as described above.

Sequence of Operations

As has already been said, the contour, texture, and situation of the ground must be very carefully considered before any work is undertaken. Once the plan of operations has been decided upon, commence by staking out the area to be levelled, then select one corner as a starting-point, drive in a peg so that its head lies at the level to be worked to, and, if the ground is undulating, from it dig trenches, the bottoms of which are all in the same horizontal plane. These trenches should radiate over the whole of the surface to be levelled and will show where soil must be cut away and where it should be added, also in what quantities. In these trenches start driving in pegs 6 to 9 feet apart, so that the heads of all of them are exactly level with the top of the first peg in the corner whence a start was made. To make sure that the pegs are level the straight-edge is laid across from peg to peg, and the last inserted peg is knocked in until the bubble of the spirit-level resting on the straight-edge is in the centre of its run. Where a depression is to be filled in, or where the slope is even and not undulating, there is no need to dig these " trial " trenches, as the lie of the ground is obvious and the pegs can be put in at once, still working, of course, from one guiding peg.

If the slope is considerable such rough masses or materials as can be got out of the higher portion of the ground should be piled in a line along the lower end so as to furnish something in the shape of a containing wall to hold in the earth afterwards thrown into the intervening space. If there are no stones or rough earth that can be utilized, a few rows of short stakes may be driven in to sustain the earth, which must be dug out and thrown if the distance is short enough, or wheeled if it is too far to throw, until the hollow has been filled and all the earth removed from the higher portion. Before the so-called rough levelling is commenced, however, all the top-soil should be re-moved and piled clear of the field of operations, other-wise the subsoil will, in some places, get thrown on top of the top-soil, in other parts the subsoil will be left uncovered and will be of little use in growing either flowers or turf.

Fig. 5. Section diagram showing how to level a site. The earth is made up to the tops of the wooden pegs. It is essential that the tops of the pegs are level. To ensure this a straight-edge and spirit-level should be used as shown on the left of the diagram.

As the earth is gradually cut away more pegs can be driven in, all with their heads on the same level, until the site to be levelled is studded with pegs. The earth thrown between the stakes should be rammed with the rammer to give consistency to it and prevent it from falling out. The rough levelling completed, the garden-line should be tightly stretched from post to post—from the very tops, of course—and then the top-soil can be brought back and spread evenly over the surface and raked fine and levelled up to the level of the line between the pegs. The surface should then be rolled firm. When the soil has settled sufficiently, trial must be made by means of a level to see that the surface is true.

CHAPTER 4

Construction of Paths and Edgings

The essential features of a good path are that it should harmonize with the rest of the garden, and afford a flat dry walking surface in wet weather. Cement, concrete, ashes, brick-dust, and asphalt are sometimes employed for the purpose, but in general we may say that the three most suitable surfaces for garden paths are afforded by gravel, bricks, and broken paving stones.

It will be sufficient to describe the construction of the gravel path, the crazy path and the grass walk. Save for the different materials used, the principles of construction are the same for the ash, brick, concrete, or asphalt path as those described for gravel paths.

Width of Paths

A path must never be less than 2 feet in width, even if it is of quite secondary importance. A good average width is 4 feet; this allows for the easy passage of the barrow and other garden implements, and for two people to walk abreast, an amenity often overlooked. Entrance drives and tracks which must bear motor traffic should be 8 feet wide, at least; rather should they be considerably more.

Paths and Drainage

Let the path be well designed and carefully made; if so constructed it will last many years, and will not only serve its purpose as a means of communication, but will also be a great help in draining the garden.

Whether it will be necessary to lay a pipe-drain or not depends upon the nature of the soil and the lie of the land. In light, porous soils the rough stones, bricks, or clinkers used as a foundation will provide sufficient drainage, but in heavy, retentive clays a pipe-drain will invariably be advisable; this may run directly below the centre of the path, or else on either side of the path; on the lower side when the path is on a side slope, and always at the lowest point below the clinker or brick foundation, and resting on a firm base. Where there is any doubt as to the porosity of the soil, always lay a drain. As has been said above, a single drain down the centre or down one side will be found adequate for ordinary paths of 4 feet in width; but paths wider than this and drives should have drains down each side. The pipes used for draining should be 3 to 4 inches in diameter and must be laid from $1\frac{1}{2}$ to 2 feet deep, according to the nature of the soil and the width of the path. (*See* *chapter on* Draining Land, p. 31.) The drains must slope gently towards

36

the outlet, which may be into a garden main drain or into a ditch or pond. The pipes being in position, cover them with 12 to 15 inches of broken bricks or rough stones through which the water can trickle.

Path Foundations

The chief thing to be done in every case is to provide a solid, but still porous substratum, which will afford sufficient support to the materials of which the upper part of the walk, or rather its surface, is made, and yet allow of the rapid passing away of the water that may fall on the path in the form of rain. Of course, we are now supposing that the walk is to be made in the ordinary way, and coated—if a road, with broken stones, technically called "metalling"— and if a garden path, with gravel.

Gravel Paths

The course of the path or road must be marked out with stakes, and the surface soil removed to the depth of 6 to 10 inches if there is no lack of materials to fill it; the wider the path the deeper the excavations necessary.

The nature of the soil also affects the depth of excavation necessary; in heavy clay at least 9 inches should be removed, in light soil 6 inches will suffice.

There is a point that must be stressed here, and that is the importance of eradicating all perennial weeds, especially those with long creeping roots, from the soil at the bottom and sides of the path. If this is not done, all kinds of weeds will soon make their appearance through the new path, and will be very difficult to get rid of.

Weed-killer *will* kill these perennial weeds, but it takes three or four years to effect a thorough clearance. From one-third to one-half the depth must then be filled up with rough stones, brickbats, clinkers from the brickfields, slag and scoriæ from the ironworks, or any coarse, hard rubbish that can be gathered together; the greater part of the remainder must then be filled up with coarse gravel, shingle, etc., which may be mixed with a little earth to give consistency to the whole, and finally coated with gravel to the depth of 2 or 3 inches, which must be raked level and be constantly rolled with a heavy garden roller until the path is hard and solid. The gravel must not be made too wet or it will adhere to the roller, and any large stones should be screened out of the gravel and used in the foundation. The correct level for the crown of the path can be marked by wooden pegs driven in to the right depth. (*See* Levelling, p. 33.) Allow the path to set for a few days before using it and then fill up any hollows with gravel and roll again. Gravel taken from the beach should not be used if other is obtainable, as it does not bind and always remains loose. If, however, it must be used, mix a quarter-part of clean dry clay with the gravel before it is laid; when moistened the mixture will bind well. Supposing, as is sometimes the case, that the ground is of a loose porous character, or wet and marshy, and, therefore, not calculated to afford a solid basis to the pathway; it is then a

37

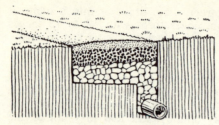

Fig. 6. Section diagram showing the construction of a gravel path.

good plan to make the trench deeper, and to lay brushwood at the bottom before throwing in the rough rubbish.

Gutters and Drainage—In some cases it is desirable to have a solid facing to a garden path so that it may be impervious to rain, and in this case it is of importance that the surface of the walk should be rounded—higher in the centre and sloping down on either side. The water will escape into the earth or turf by which the walk is bordered, or, if desired, gutters can be formed to carry the water to a tank formed for its reception in some part of the garden. The gutters may either be moulded in the material of which the path is made or they may be constructed below the surface, like a drain, and hidden from view. In this case catch-pits with iron gratings should be made on each side of the path at distances of about 30 feet apart. In no case, however, should these gratings communicate directly with the drains, as the sand soon chokes them up. They should consist of a well, formed of brick, a foot or 18 inches square, and of sufficient depth to leave a space of 1 foot or 18 inches (for a 4-foot path) below the level of the drain, which should be directly below the grating and at the top of the pit. This allows ample space for collecting the sediment.

The main drain, into which these side drains empty, usually runs down the centre of the path below the hard core.

Where the path lies on a steep slope, a heavy shower of rain may soon cause havoc with the gravel, the surface-water rushing down and ploughing great furrows in the path. This can be prevented by constructing brick, tile, or cement gutters, 6 inches to a foot in width, down both sides of the path, and by inserting catch-pits at regular intervals to carry away the water.

Large bricks or pieces of rock placed in the gutter just below the catch-pits will do much to impede the rush of water and will enable the drains to carry it off more easily.

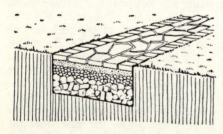

Fig. 7. Section diagram showing the construction of a crazy paving path.

Another way of getting over this "washing-out" trouble is to mix cement with the gravel when laying it down in the proportion of six parts of gravel to one of cement. Add water and mix until the consistency of a thick paste is obtained, then immediately lay the mixture down over the path, flatten out with the back of the spade, and level off with a

38

lath of wood or with the back of a rake, and allow it to set thoroughly.

Crazy Paving
Crazy paving must be well and evenly laid, otherwise it is very unpleasant to walk on and will always be giving trouble by the loosening and rising of the stones. In the initial stage of construction the procedure is the same as for a gravel path, so that is to say, the same remarks apply as to drainage: the foundation of large stones or broken bricks is laid down in the same way, but need not be quite so deep, likewise the layer of clinkers or smaller stones. The one great aim is to afford a sound and level surface for the paving, and the straight-edge and spirit-level will therefore be constantly in use with a view to this. The foundations must be rammed and rolled absolutely firm: if there is the slightest fear of any settlement in the base, as may well happen in clay, an inch layer of cement in which to lay the paving had better be laid down. Over the hard core spread a 2-inch layer of sand or ashes, if cement is not used; make this quite level and then lay down the paving, fitting the pieces carefully together so that small pieces are not required, as these always tend to work loose. No crevices of much more than an inch in width should be left between the stones or the path will be uncomfortable to walk on and will not remain firm. Where there is likely to be much traffic, the main stones, and all those at the sides of the walk, should be set in mortar. This will tie the whole together and keep it firm. Fill the interstices with sandy loam, so that rock plants, such as saxifrages, thymes, and other creepers and trailers, may be planted. (*See* The Paved Garden, chapter 20.)

Grass Walks
Grass walks running between gay borders are a delight, but ought never to be depended upon as necessary routes to or from any given place. When of great length, and 12 or 18 feet wide, they are most imposing. They should never be less than 2 feet in width, otherwise there will be difficulty in handling the mowing machine; rather should they be well over 6 feet wide: the wider they are, within reason, of course, the more imposing they will be. Where there is likely to be much traffic on grass walks, their foundations should be formed and drained as if for gravel; but it will be more satisfactory to make good gravel walks for the general traffic, and to reserve the grass walks and keep them closely cut for occasional use only, their beauty providing ample justification for their existence.

Where these grass walks are likely to be much used a single row of flag-stones, either edge to edge or some 2 feet apart, sunk in level with the surface of the turf, will not only make the walk more substantial and lasting, but will also, in many cases, greatly enhance its charm. Equally pleasing and more useful, because the borders can be approached in wet weather, will be two paved walks, 18 inches to 2 feet wide, one down each side of the grass way.

In newly-laid-out gardens the grass walks are usually formed of the

39

existing turf, and it is surprising what consistent weeding, rolling and cutting will accomplish. Where, however, the walks are to be seeded, a variety of seed that will stand much wear should be chosen. If the barrow is to be used on turf walks in winter, boards must be laid down to prevent the wheel from sinking into and ruining the turf.

For details as to the upkeep of grass walks, *see the chapter on* The Lawn.

Types of Edging

Edgings to paths resolve themselves into two classifications, formal and informal. As formal we include edgings of stone, bricks, tiles, and wood, also grass verges, and miniature hedges of box. Edgings made of plants (*see* list, p. 41) are, of course, informal. Where suitable stones can be obtained the most interesting borders of all are afforded by irregular blocks of stone, bedded in cement if large, with alpines growing between and over them. The stones must never project more than 6 inches from the border.

Formal Edgings

In the following paragraphs will be found brief descriptions of the best formal edgings.

Tiles—This word seems to conjure up the exceedingly ugly borders of fancy tiles seen in some gardens. A tile border, however, need not be ugly; it should be severely plain and nondescript in colour, and must never attract the eye, its function being utility pure and simple. The tiles must be firmly set in the soil and should be even and regular. Some have hollow heads through which canes or wires may be inserted to keep the tiles straight and in line. To lay the tiles dig a straight-sided trench to the required depth and with its bottom cut level with the incline of the path. On the inner (border) side of the trench place a long and straight board and against it set the tiles evenly. Now fill in the earth and gravel on the path side of the tiles, ram it very firm, then remove the board, fill the space with soil and carefully firm the tiles from that side.

Bricks make excellent border edgings, but they must be of a good hard variety; those that will crumble under the action of frost, when lying in the damp ground, are worse than useless and soon become ragged and unsightly. The bricks should be laid on edge, that is to say, with one of the shorter sides in the ground, and sloping slightly inwards towards the border and away from the path. If they are set vertically, or incline outwards over the path, they are more liable to be damaged by the passage of the barrow or roller.

Nearly half the brick should be buried in the soil, or it may be set in a 2-inch layer of mortar, when only one-third of the brick need be below the surface level.

Concrete makes a good edging, and is easily constructed. Two boards of wood one-half to an inch in thickness, a foot high, and of any length, are set up 4 inches apart, with 6 inches of their height covered by the soil. The soil between them is excavated to the full 12-inch depth of the boards, which are held firm and upright by two stout pegs driven into the soil on the outer sides and nailed into the board. A series of boards of similar size are laid in this way, in line, where the edging is required. Now mix the concrete and fill up the space between the boards, making the top flat and neat with a trowel. When the concrete has set (four to five days) remove the boards and a neat permanent edging will remain. An iron rod is often laid in the centre of the concrete edging, while in the course of construction, to reinforce it.

Wood edgings are neat and last a considerable time if creosoted or tarred. They should be made of planks 1 inch thick and 6–9 inches wide. About half the width should lie in the soil and they must be kept firm and upright by strong wooden pegs, about 2 inches square and some 2 feet in length, driven in on the inner (border) side till they are flush with the top of the board. The pegs should be driven in about every yard, and should be fixed to the planks with long galvanized iron nails.

Grass Edgings or verges are the neatest and most pleasing of all the formal edgings. They entail a good deal of labour if they are to be kept properly trimmed and cut, but if time can be spent on them they will repay the gardener for it. They are out of place in the small garden and should only be used as edgings to large beds or borders, as they must be at least 2 feet wide to enable the mower to work properly on them. If they are too small to cut with the mower, the gardener must then have ample time and patience to spare to keep them in anything like good order.

EDGING PLANTS

NOTE.—For details as to Colour, Height, Season of Flowering and Culture, *see* the Alphabetical List of Flowering Plants and Shrubs, p. 147.

Achillea umbellata (H.P.)
Ageratum Houstonianum (H.H.A.)
Alyssum saxatile var. compactum (H.P.)
Antirrhinums (dwarf, vars.) (H.P.)
Arabis caucasica and var. fl. pl. (H.P.)
Aubrieta deltoides vars. (H.P.)
Bellis perennis vars. (Daisy) (H.P.)
Brunnera macrophylla (H.P.)
Campanula (dwarf species) (H.P.)
Cerastium Biebersteinii (H.P.)
Cheiranthus Allionii (Siberian Wallflower) (H.P.)

Dianthus deltoides (H.P.)
Dianthus (Pinks) (H.P.)
Dianthus squarrosus (H.P.)
Dryas octopetala (H.P.)
Erica darleyensis, E. carnea vars. E. vagans vars. (H.S.)
Genista pilosa (H.P.)
Geum (dwarf species) (H.P.)
Gypsophila repens (H.P.)
Hypericum olympicum (H.S.)
Iberis sempervirens (H.P.)
Lavendula Spica (H.S.)
Linum salsaloides (H.P.)
Lobelia Erinus vars. (H.H.A.)
Lysimachia Nummularia (Creeping Jenny) (H.P.)
Malcolmia maritima (Virginia Stock) (H.A.)

Myosotis Royal Blue (Forget-Me-Not) (H.H.A.)
Phlox subulata vars. (H.P.)
Portulaca grandiflora (H.H.A.)
Primula variabilis var. (polyanthus) (H.P.)
Primulas Juliana (vars.) (H.P.)
Saponaria ocymoides (H.P.)
Saxifraga (dwarf vars.) (H.P.)
Silene pendula compacta (H.A.)
Tagetes (dwarf) (H.H.A.)
Verbena (hybrid vars.) (H.H.A.)
Zephyranthes candida (H.P.)

NOTE.—H.A.=Hardy Annual; H.H.A.=Half-Hardy Annual; H.P.=Hardy Perennial; H.S.=Hardy Shrub.

CHAPTER 5

Hedges, Fences and Walls

Hedges play an important role in most gardens, and it is because they do that it is wise to give some thought to the siting and methods of planting and to the type of plant to form the hedge. Until quite recently it was the custom to plant the inevitable and monotonous privet or laurel, but of late years it has been realized that there are better subjects for the hedge. Of deciduous hedges, the beech, the hornbeam, cherry, plum, briar, and thorn are the most general, while the box, cypress, *Cupressus macrocarpa*, *Lonicera nitida*, evergreen oak, holly, thuja and yew are all evergreen.

To What Purpose?
Whether the hedge is required as a shelter from the wind, as a screen, as a barrier, or purely as an ornament, are points which must be taken into consideration, and shrubs suited to the soil and aspect should also be chosen. Evergreens like holly, laurel, or yew, and leafy, quick-growing deciduous shrubs like the elder or privet, are excellent for shelter from cold winds. As a screen, cypress, holly, laurel, *Lonicera nitida*, or yew are undoubtedly the best; while flowering shrubs such as *Berberis stenophylla* and *B. Darwinii*, guelder rose, double gorse, lilac, or *Viburnum Tinus*, make an excellent ornamental hedge. Nothing is so suitable for a barrier as beech, hornbeam, myrobalan plum, or quickthorn.

Factors that must be Considered
In forming any hedge it is necessary to take into consideration the aspect, the quality of the soil, and many other particulars. All plants will not suit all climates, all situations, and all soils. It is wise, therefore, to consider that though there are many ornamental plants and shrubs that will make good hedges, it is not all of these that may choose to flourish where we wish our hedge to grow. As a general rule the knife may be used unsparingly on all things suitable for hedges, and the hedge itself will be greatly improved. All hedges, especially those that bear the shears or clippers, should be cut upwards to a narrow ridge, for by this means the lower part, not being overshadowed by the upper, will be kept thick, and the hedge will last much longer. After they have been planted several years, hedges of most materials will require to be cut down, the soil renovated, and, perhaps, new plants introduced.

Flowering Shrubs
Many flowering shrubs make excellent hedges. The best of these

are *Berberis Darwinii, B. stenophylla*, flowering currant, *Chænomeles lagenaria*, double gorse, guelder rose, lilac, and the shrubby honeysuckle. The hedge need not necessarily be composed entirely of one species; a very ornamental hedge, sections of which will be in blossom almost the entire year through if the plants are carefully selected, can be made up of various species of flowering shrubs. Evergreens may be interspersed among the flowering shrubs, and the hedge will be all the firmer if a thorn or a cherry plum is inserted fairly frequently as a stiffener. The Sweet Briar and the Penzance Briars make a splendid hedge.

Methods of Planting

Many seem to think that a hedge will grow anywhere and however it is planted; but it must be borne in mind that a hedge, once planted, is usually in position for many years, and that if it is to do well every care should be taken in its planting. A strip of ground 3 feet wide, in which the hedge is to be planted, should be trenched to a depth of at least 2 feet, and vegetable refuse, leaf-mould, and well-decayed manure should be forked in. Most hedge shrubs are best planted when from 2 to 3 feet in height, they then more easily establish themselves, are easier to train, and are also cheaper. The larger the shrub the more care necessary in planting. With the exception of the quicker or larger-growing shrubs, such as the evergreen oak or cupressus, most hedge shrubs are best planted out 10 to 15 inches apart; if a very thick hedge is required two rows may be planted some 10 inches apart, the plants, as before, being 10 to 15 inches apart in the rows, but planted so that those of one row come opposite the middle of the gaps between those in the other row thus: · . · ·

Long tap roots should always be shortened back before planting, and to ensure bush plants, in the case of deciduous shrubs, 6 to 10 inches must be trimmed from the top of the newly-planted hedge when the buds begin to swell in spring. Evergreens are best cut back at planting time. Water well after putting the shrubs in, and once a week in dry weather, until the roots are established. Should a very dry season follow, syringe the foliage of evergreens every evening if the plants do not appear to be thriving. In late April or early May, during its first year, the hedge should be well watered and then mulched with a 2- to 3-inch layer of well-decayed manure and well-rotted leaf-mould. Severe frosts during the first winter after planting will probably raise the bushes somewhat from the soil. After frosts, therefore, newly-planted shrubs should be firmed back with the foot. We refer the reader to the chapter on *Shrubs*, p. 300, and to the tables at the end of that chapter, where will be found a wide choice of hedge shrubs, together with details as to the method and time of planting, and the manner of trimming.

For individual cultural details and particulars as to species and varieties, *see* chapter 16.

Care of Hedges

Most hedges are best trimmed twice a year, in May and again in August or September; few shrubs will make much growth after the autumn trimming and will remain tidy all the winter. All hedges, especially evergreen hedges, are best cut to a point pyramidically; for if the top is allowed to overhang the bottom, the lower shoots will invariably die off. If carefully trimmed they may be cut square at the top, as is necessary in the rose garden and some of the more formal parts of the garden, but the top must not overhang the bottom. With hollies and laurels use the knife in pruning, to avoid the rusty appearance of the withering of half-cut leaves. Privet, box, thorn, and all small-leaved shrubs may be clipped with the garden shears.

In winter the hedge and the soil around it should be thoroughly cleaned; all dead wood should be cut out and any brambles and climbers should be removed. The weeds must be taken out from the hedge bottom and the soil should be turned up. Where insect pests and disease have been prevalent, the hedge should be sprayed with an appropriate solution, which must not be too strong in the case of shrubs flowering in the early spring, or the blossom may be damaged.

Although hedges are delightful and useful features in a garden, since they help to produce the much desired "element of surprise", and are useful as screens, shelters or barriers, too many should not be planted in a small garden, as they take up a deal of room, keep sun and air from other plants and, worst of all, make a great demand upon the soil.

Types of Fences

Fences may be constructed of various materials and of many different patterns.

Close Wooden Fencing—This type of fencing is strong and will last a considerable time. Split oak makes a more durable fence than sawn oak. The usual heights are from 3½ to 7 feet. Fir, larch, pine or deal are sometimes used in lieu of oak. They are, of course, by no means so durable and lasting and should be creosoted to preserve them from the weather.

Wattle Hurdles make effective and quite artistic fences; they are easy to set up and are comparatively cheap.

Split Chestnut Fencing, in which the palings are wired together with strong strands of wire so that there is an interval of about 3 inches between each, makes an efficient and economical fencing, although it affords no shelter from the weather and no privacy. It forms a useful boundary fence of a temporary nature; and is itself quite durable as a protection to a newly-planted hedge. The fencing is stretched to posts some 10 feet apart. The footings of these posts should be charred and tarred.

Rustic Fences are much used to separate one part of the garden from another. They can be made of hazel, larch, spruce, and indeed of any young trees. The bark should always be left on, and the more numerous and rougher the knots, the more rustic the fence will be. The bars of rustic trellis-work should be slightly notched one into another at the points at which they cross, so that they may have a better bearing one

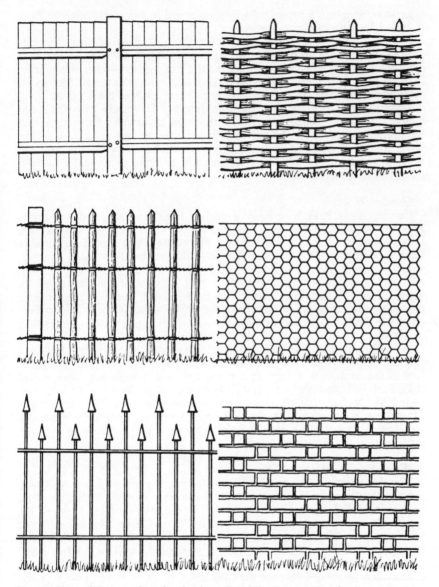

FIG. 8. Six useful types of garden fencing. *Top left*, close wooden fencing; *top right*, wattle hurdles; *centre left*, split chestnut fencing; *centre right*, wire netting; *bottom left*, iron palings; *bottom right*, two-brick wall.

45

against another and a firmer holding than round stocks could possibly have if nailed together without notching.

Wire Netting—There are many patterns and sizes of this "rabbit-netting" to choose from, and the size of the mesh and the strength of the wire used should be regulated by the purpose to which the netting is to be put. It is stretched on posts planted on an average 10 feet apart. Straining-posts will be needed every 100 feet and at each corner.

Iron Palings form a very durable fence. There are two favourite types: the park fencing, usually with three horizontal bars supported by uprights every 3 or 4 feet; or upright iron spiked palings, 4 inches apart and held in position by two horizontal bars, one at the top, the other at the bottom. These palings require painting periodically to keep them in good condition.

Garden Walls

Garden walls have long been a subject for discussion, and will probably always remain so; like everything else connected with gardening, they depend on local circumstances. The walls which would be suitable for a moderate-sized kitchen garden, in a flat or thickly-wooded country, would be very unsuitable for a loftier site, on the side of a hill, or in an open, undulating country; while a plot of small extent, enclosed by walls 14 or 16 feet high, would be inadmissible both on artistic and physiological grounds; on the first, the walls would appear prison-like; on the second, they would exclude the air which is essential to the growth of plants.

A walled garden is usually designed as a parallelogram and not as a square. Besides the fact that the former shape is more pleasing, there is also the utilitarian reason that north and south walls are more useful than east and west walls and are, therefore, made longer. In addition, owing to the fact that the power of the sun in these colder latitudes is greatest an hour or so after noon, the south wall of a garden is generally so situated that the sun strikes it fully about 1 p.m.; that is to say, the wall faces slightly west of south.

What Size Wall?

For this reason it is considered that for small gardens 8-feet walls are most suitable, provided the trees on them are planted so far apart as to admit of full horizontal extension. For gardens of larger size, 10-feet walls, and for an extensive garden 12, and even 14 feet, will not be too great. Where an acre of ground, in the form of a parallelogram is enclosed, on a gentle slope, a north wall might well be 14 feet high, and the east, west and south walls only 10 feet; if the slope of the ground is considerable, the difference may be less. In gardens of greater extent —enclosures of four acres for instance—the walls may be higher, but in no instances more than 18 feet high for a north wall, 15 feet for east and west walls, and 12 feet for a south wall.

(*See also* Forms of Fruit Trees, p. 308.)

CHAPTER 6

Manures—Organic and Artificial

Manures serve a two-fold purpose and both of equal importance to the promotion of plant life. Firstly, it contributes directly to plant food, and secondly, by virtue of chemical reactions with the soil, produces healthy humus.

Organic manures—It is because it fulfils both these functions that farmyard manure, or its equivalent, is so especially valuable. Not only does it directly add to the soil constituents needed for the healthy life of plants, but also through the fermentation which it undergoes, and the acids produced thereby, it liberates from the soil itself plant foods which would not otherwise be available. By its texture, and by the gases produced in the process of its fermentation, moreover, it tends to lighten the soil and keep its texture open.

For similar reasons there is considerable value in garden compost made from such substances as leaves, lawn cuttings, road sweepings, and all vegetable refuse. All organic waste, indeed, has some manurial value. It is very great in the case of such substances as cow manure, fowl manure, pig manure, and night soil. Wood-ashes and soot are also useful, the former largely on account of the potash it contains, the latter for its ammonia.

Artificial manures—It is, however, not always convenient to obtain a sufficiency of stable or farmyard and organic manure for the requirements of one's garden. In such cases resort must be had to various so-called artificial manures, most of which provide plant food in a highly concentrated form. These, for the most part, have but little effect—at any rate directly—on the structure or chemical activity of the soil itself. They add no humus to the soil and do not affect the tilth, and for this reason, if for no other, they cannot entirely replace organic manures.

The three elements which it is generally necessary to add to soil in the form of manure if crops, whether vegetable, fruit or flowers, are to be raised year after year on the same ground, are phosphates, potash and nitrogen. And it must be remembered that these have not only to be added to the soil, but to be added in such a form that they are, or readily become, soluble and so capable of being absorbed by the fine rootlets of plants.

Nitrogenous manures—The most expensive of these elements is nitrogen, that is to say, nitrogen in a form available for plant food. Apart from guano and other mixed-elements manures, the most useful nitrogenous manures are nitrate of soda and sulphate of ammonia; the

47

latter should be applied early in spring at the rate of 2 oz. to the sq. yard. The former is often applied at the rate of $\frac{1}{2}$ oz. to the sq. yard as a top-dressing during the growing season. Nitrate of potash is also good, but is much more expensive. In well-drained soils certain bacteria exist, especially round the roots of leguminous plants such as peas, beans, and clover, which, by their activity, collect nitrates from the air and add them to the soil. Thus it is often possible to furnish a soil with both humus and nitrates by growing a crop of clover and lucerne and digging it in. Nitrogenous manures act very rapidly and appreciable growth is often visible a few days after application. The plants become noticeably greener and more vigorous. Nitrates must, however, not be added to excess, or rank growth will follow, accompanied by lack of flowers and fruit and susceptibility to attack by fungus.

Potash manures help the development of sugar and starch in seeds, tubers, and fruit, and improve the colour and size of the blooms. Of potash manures, kainit is, on the whole, the cheapest and most useful; it should be dug well into the soil at the rate of $1\frac{1}{4}$ oz. to the sq. yard in the spring. On heavy soils, sulphate of potash applied at the rate of $\frac{3}{4}$ oz. to the sq. yard in the spring is also valuable. A simple way of providing potash for a small plot of ground is to add wood-ashes and the ashes from burnt weeds in generous quantities.

Phosphatic manures—These assist the correct development of the plant, its fruit or seed, and its roots. The three commonest forms of phosphatic manure are superphosphate of lime, bone meal, and basic slag. Superphosphate is the quickest acting, whilst basic slag is the cheapest, slowest acting, and therefore most enduring. It is best applied in autumn. Superphosphate is usually applied just before the plants are mature at the rate of $2\frac{1}{2}$ oz. to the sq. yard, and should be thoroughly mixed with the top 4 inches of the soil.

Basic slag is a chemical manure much used of late years, consisting largely of lime, phosphoric acid, and various iron oxides. It contains other constituents as well as these, but in small proportions. Its effects are much those of superphosphate, but almost twice the quantity is required to produce a given result. It does not succeed mixed with ammonia salts, as it sets free the ammonia and wastes valuable material, but is useful with nitrates. It is most useful on medium or heavy soils which are deficient in lime, or are too wet and stiff; but to obtain the full advantage the soil must already be fairly well provided with organic matter. As a manure it is good for flowering shrubs, roses, fruit trees, lawns, and pastures. It should be applied and well dug in in the autumn at the rate of $7\frac{1}{2}$ oz. to the sq. yard.

Phosphates encourage the formation of fibrous roots, cause earlier development of the plants, and counteract rank, sappy growth caused by excess of nitrogen in the soil. They should be applied every third year.

Where chemical manures are applied to trees and plants which have made full root growth, so that the soil is filled with roots, the best plan, in order to avoid injury to the plants, is to scatter the manure where

PLATE 3 LAYING CRAZY PAVING A wooden frame is constructed and filled with rubble over which a layer of cement is laid. The crazy paving is placed on this cement and tapped down level with the edge of the frame, *above*.

As the stone will vary in thickness each piece must be bedded down separately, *above*, to give a uniform surface. To complete the path the crevices are pointed with a stronger mixture of cement, *below*.

PLATE 4 MAKING LIQUID MANURE A sack should be filled with well rotted manure, *above left*, and the neck of the sack securely tied with string, *above right*. It is then placed in the bottom of a tank, *below left*, and the tank filled with water. After being left to stand for six weeks or more the mixture can be diluted by putting two inches in the bottom of a 2-gallon watering can *below right*, before use.

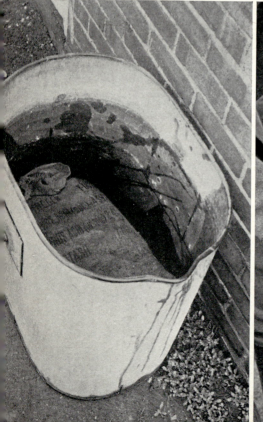

it is required, and then lightly to "point it in" with a small fork, only placing the manure just under the surface of the ground. In this way the manure is protected from loss by wind or rain, while the delicate roots of growing plants are not liable to suffer, as they are if the manure is dug in with a spade.

Requirements of different crops and soils—Different crops have naturally different manurial requirements. Thus potatoes and tomatoes, for example, have special need of potash, whilst leguminous plants, such as peas and beans, and certain roots such as turnips, are particularly influenced by the addition of phosphates.

The requirements of each soil can only be ascertained after individual consideration, experiment, and possibly analysis. But there are certain rough rules. Farmyard manure in reasonable quantities improves almost all soils, heavy or light. It is usually unnecessary to add potash to clay soils, and usually necessary to add it to sandy soils. At the same time it may be necessary, in order to liberate the potash in the clay soil, to add lime. Gravelly and sandy soils are nearly always deficient in nitrogen, and are much less retentive of manures generally. Soils that are peaty, or that have become sour from excessive humus from constant year-by-year manuring with organic manure, are much improved by the addition of quicklime applied frequently in small doses and dug in at once.

Then again, different manures in each class differ in their action; nitrate of soda, for instance, works more rapidly than sulphate of ammonia. Some fertilizers suit one crop, others another. The requirements of both soil and crops must be studied when applying manures. (*See* Manuring Vegetables, p. 274.)

The Compost Heap—All waste vegetable matter that is not diseased should be used for making compost, a valuable means of adding to the store of humus and plant food and improving soil texture. The heap should be made up of alternate layers, one of vegetable refuse about 9 inches thick, and one of animal manure about 2 inches thick or a sprinkling of sulphate of ammonia or a proprietary "accelerator". If the material is dry it should be well soaked, and if sulphate of ammonia is used, a sprinkling of chalk or powdered lime (not quick-lime) should also be added. Heaps can be any length, but should not be more than 6 ft. wide and 5 ft. high. They soon warm up as decomposition begins and after 6 to 8 weeks should be turned by forking over from one end and turning the outside unrotted material into the centre. After another 8 weeks or so, the compost should be made and ready for digging in.

Stable manure and, indeed, all animal manures, should not be left exposed to rain and air. They are best mixed with a little soil, and covered with about another 6 inches of soil until they are required for use.

Amount of manure required—As a guide to the amount of various artificial manures to apply in average cases, it may be said that it is safe to add to a square yard of ground needing that particular manure, 1¼ oz. of kainit or ¾ oz. of sulphate of potash, 2½ oz. of superphosphate, 2 oz. of dissolved bones, 2½ oz. of steamed bone flour, 6 to 7½ oz. of basic slag, 1 oz. of guano, a good dressing of stable manure, 5 oz. of fowl manure, ½ oz. of nitrate of soda, 1 oz. of sulphate of ammonia.

The fertilizers must be spread evenly over the soil and must be crushed fine and be free from lumps, so that every inch of soil receives its proportion of the fertilizer. If this is not done parts of the ground will receive an excessive amount, which may kill the plants. The manure should be well worked into the soil.

When to apply the various manures—Slow-acting manures, such as bonemeal, basic slag, farmyard manure and compost, are best applied while the digging is being done in the autumn and early winter. Quicker-acting fertilizers, such as dissolved bones, guano, nitrate of soda, sulphate of ammonia, sulphate of potash, must be applied in the spring or when the crops are growing. It is quite useless to apply quick-acting manures in autumn or winter as the rain would wash away all their properties before the plants were ready to assimilate them. Conversely, slow-acting fertilizers would provide little benefit if applied while the plants were growing.

Lime as a plant food—The nitrates, phosphates, and potash supplied by manures are quite inaccessible to plants in a soil deficient in lime. Lime, too, assists the bacteria which render organic matter in the soil available to crops, and is itself an essential plant food. It makes heavy soils more porous and, therefore, better drained and warmer, cleanses the soil of insect and fungoid pests, and sweetens soil which has become deficient in lime.

APPLICATION AND USES OF MANURES

SHOWING THE SOILS TO WHICH THEY ARE MOST SUITABLE AND THE TIME AND QUANTITY TO APPLY. NOTE.—A Dressing of 2¼ cwt. per Acre is equal to 2 lb. to the Square Rod, or 1 oz. per Square Yard.

Manure.	Soil to which best Suited.	When to Apply.	Rate per Sq. Yard.	Remarks.
Ammonia, Nitrate of	Any.	Growing Season.	1 oz.	Fruit and Vegetables.
Ammonia, Phosphate of	Clay and Chalk.	Spring and Early Summer.	1 oz.	Cabbage Tribe, Cucumbers, etc. Never on soil deficient in Lime.
Ammonia, Sulphate of				
Basic Slag	Heavy or Light.	Autumn (Heavy) Spring (Light).	7½ oz.	Best for slow-growing plants. Do not use on Chalk or Sand.
Blood, Dried	Any.	Growing Season.	3 oz.	Good for Flowers and Vegetables.
Bone Meal	Light.	Autumn.	2¼ oz.	Excellent for Lawn, Fruit, Shrubs and Herbaceous Plants.
Bones, Dissolved	Chalk.	Spring or Summer as Top-dressing.	2 oz.	Never on soil deficient in Lime. Good for all plants.

APPLICATION AND USES OF MANURES (*Continued*)

Manure	Soil to which best Suited	When to Apply	Rate per Sq. Yard	Remarks
Farmyard Manure .	(Horse) Heavy (Cow) Light	Autumn or Winter Spring	A Good Dressing	All crops
Fish Meal . . .	Light or Medium	Autumn and Winter	1½ oz.	Good for nearly all plants, especially Potatoes, Turnips, etc.
Guano . . .	Any	Growing Season	1 oz.	Never on soil deficient in Lime
Hop Manure .	Clay, Chalk, Gravel and Sand	Autumn	15 oz.	Good for all Fruit Trees, Shrubs and Herbaceous plants
Horn Shavings, Feathers, Hair, etc.	Any	Autumn	15 oz.	Useful only for slow-growing plants
Kainit Salts . . .	Heavy or Light	Autumn (Heavy) Spring (Light)	1½ oz.	All Vegetables and Fruit
Leaf-Mould . . .	Heavy Clay	Winter or Early Spring	A Good Dressing	Add Humus to the soil
Lime, Nitrate of . .	Any	Growing Season	1 oz.	Especially good for Cabbage Tribe, but suitable to all crops
Lime, Sulphate of .	Clay or Medium	Spring or Early Summer	6 oz.	Fruit and Vegetables
Nitrate of Potash . .	Any	Spring	1 oz.	All Plants
Nitrate of Soda .	Light and Dry	Spring or Early Summer	½ oz.	Helps on leaf growth in cold weather or after attack by insect pests
Potash, Muriate of .	Light and Medium	Spring or Early Summer	1½ oz.	Fruit and Vegetables
Potash, Phosphate of .	Light	Spring or Early Summer	1½ oz.	All Flowers and Vegetables, and all Fruit under glass
Potash, Sulphate of .	Light or Heavy	Spring or Early Summer	¾ oz.	All Flowers; Asparagus, Carrots, Cauliflowers, Onions, Potatoes
Poultry Manure .	Any	Growing Crops or Autumn	5 oz.	All plants, especially Root Crops
Salt	Light	Spring or Early Summer	1 oz.	Salt-loving plants such as Asparagus, Beet, Cabbage Tribe, Celery, Leeks, Onions, etc.
Seaweed (fresh) . .	Light	Spring or Autumn	A Good Dressing	All salt-loving plants as above
Soot	Sandy or Light	Summer	A Dusting	All young plants
Superphosphate of Lime	Medium or Light	Autumn (Medium) Spring (Light)	2½ oz.	Never on soil deficient in Lime
Vegetable Ashes .	Any	Spring	5 oz.	Beans, Carrots, Onions, Peas, Potatoes, etc.
Vegetable Refuse .	Medium to Light	Winter	A Good Dressing	Adds Humus to the soil
Wood Ashes . . .	Heavy and Rich	Autumn or as Top-dressing in Spring, Summer and Autumn	5 oz.	Excellent for Beans, Carrots, Onions, Peas, Potatoes and Fruit Trees
Wool Waste (Shoddy)	Any	Winter	7 oz.	Slow-growing crops. Manurial value lasts over three years

CHAPTER 7

The Lawn and its Construction

The construction of a lawn is no twelve-months' job, but, rather, one taking years of careful and patient work. It is, of course, possible to obtain a covering of grass in a single season, but anything that could reasonably be called a lawn is a work of years. Of course, a grass plot on which one may walk almost at once may be prepared by transplanting blocks of turf from a neighbouring field, common or hillside, and rolling it into place. But more and more gardeners have come to the conclusion that a perfect lawn of uniform colour and even surface, free from plantain and other weeds, can only be obtained by careful preparation of the soil, and by sowing carefully selected grass seed mixture. The seeded lawn is cheaper than one laid down with good turves, but cannot be used—as a tennis-court, for instance—during the first year after sowing as the turved lawn can be.

Selecting the Site

Where there is any choice of situation a northern aspect is to be preferred to a southern one, especially where the water supply is limited. A fairly moist soil is indeed essential to a good lawn, though it is equally necessary that the soil should be well drained, and must not remain soft and spongy for long after a shower of rain. Deep drainage is not necessary, seeing that the roots of grasses do not penetrate far below the surface; but on heavy clay, pipe-drains are usually necessary, and a 4- to 5-inch layer of ashes must be placed immediately below the top-soil, which should be from 6 to 9 inches in thickness. Whatever the nature of the soil the whole surface should be trenched over to a depth of 18 inches to 2 feet, the best soil being kept on top. A point to remember is that the final dressing of soil over the drains must be much poorer than that covering other parts, otherwise the grass will grow better and greener over the drains than elsewhere and a patchy lawn will result. (*See chapter on* Garden Drainage, p. 31.)

Levelling

It is more than likely that it will be necessary to level the lawn; this is, of course, essential in the case of the tennis-lawn. Levelling should be commenced as early as possible so that the land may have ample time to settle before the sowing or turfing is done. Unless the soil is very porous a lawn should not be dead level, or the water may hang on it after rain; even a tennis-court should be from 3 to 4 inches higher on one side than the other; this will not be apparent and will in no way affect the play. Where levelling is necessary, *see* p. 33.

Treatment of Soil

The soil itself should be a good fibrous loam, rich in humus, the ordinary soil excavated in making the foundations of a house, which it is often desired to employ for a lawn, being altogether unsuitable. Where suitable soil, from 18 inches to 2 feet in depth, is not already *in situ* it should be obtained, and used to replace, at any rate, the top foot of the existing earth. A deep root-run like this will assist the drainage of the lawn and will prevent the grass from becoming scorched up in hot, dry weather. In introducing soil from outside it is, however, important to remember that it is likely to contain the seeds of many weeds which would be fatal to a satisfactory lawn. A certain time should therefore be allowed to elapse in order to afford opportunity for these seeds to germinate, and the resulting weeds to be destroyed before any grass seed is sown. As an alternative, the introduced soil may be burned, and then enriched with a liberal dressing of manure. If fresh mould cannot be introduced the top-soil, if heavy, must be well broken up, weeds and stones must be removed, and with it should be incorporated plenty of finely-sifted ashes or coarse sand and grit, to render the soil porous and enable the roots to work through it. If the soil is too light, well-decayed manure and leaf-mould should be added, until the top 10 inches of the compost consists of one part of these ingredients to four parts of soil. In any event, a good dressing of farmyard manure, say twenty cartloads to the acre, should be incorporated with the top-spit of soil and should not lie more than 4 inches below the surface. Where lime is found to be lacking, powdered lime must be dug in at the rate of 6 oz. to the square yard. If this preparation is made in the autumn, the ground should be allowed to lie fallow through the winter. In the spring the surface should be again carefully tested for level with a straight-edge and spirit-level, so that any inequalities may be made up; the upper 4 inches of the soil is then made as fine as possible by repeated rakings and thorough rollings, until the surface is so firm that it scarcely shows the mark of a foot when trodden on and is entirely devoid of stones and weed-free.

Sowing Grass Seed

Seed can be sown early in April or about the end of August or the beginning of September. Spring-sown seed will take between a fortnight and three weeks to germinate, but in autumn—the better time to sow—the soil is warm and the seed may be expected to show above the ground in a week or ten days. Seed should be sown on a day when there is no wind and when the soil is dry enough not to stick to the boots or the rake, and great evenness should be aimed at, two sowings being made at right angles to one another. This even distribution of seed is best obtained by marking the lawn out into squares whose sides are from a yard to 2 yards in length. The seed, which should have been mixed with twice its quantity of fine mould, is then divided into as many portions as there are squares so that each square may receive an equal amount.

53

From 2 to 4 oz. per square yard is the quantity of seed to sow, and special seed should be obtained for the purpose from a first-rate firm of seedsmen. No economy should be attempted in this important matter, as the seed must be good; and it is difficult to sow too thickly, as the thicker the sowing the less chance weeds will have of growing through, and the young seedlings, when closely massed together, are not so liable to damage by frost or scorching sun. When autumn sowing is practised, the lawn should, if possible, be drained, levelled and should have the surface prepared in spring. Then if the soil is thoroughly and consistently weeded throughout the summer, there should be an absolutely weed-free seed bed for sowing in August or September.

When sowing a lawn care should be taken to see that the seed sown is suitable for the soil, the situation, and for the use to which the lawn is to be put. Grasses vary just as other plants do in their tastes and careful selection will do much to secure a permanently satisfactory lawn.

Seeds for Different Situations
The following list will enable the reader to choose seed suitable for sowing on a lawn in practically any situation that he is likely to encounter:

General use:
Festuca tenuifolia
Cynosurus cristatus
Poa nemoralis var. sempervirens
Poa pratensis
Poa trivialis

Light soil:
Cynosurus cristatus
Festuca longifolia (duriuscula)
Festuca tenuifolia
Festuca rubra
Poa pratensis

Dry soil:
Festuca rubra

Poor and shallow soil:
Festuca longifolia (duriuscula)

Under trees or moist, shady situations:
Poa trivialis

Town gardens:
Poa annua
Poa nemoralis

Sports grounds:
Festuca rubra

Near sea:
Festuca rubra

Large areas:
Lolium perenne

Care after Sowing
A very light raking is then desirable, just cover with a $\frac{1}{4}$ of an inch of finely-sifted soil, and afterwards the ground should be rolled over, lengthwise and across, provided the soil is not damp enough to stick to the roller. To protect the seeds from the birds, black cotton should be stretched on short sticks, or old netting can be thrown over small tree branches spread over the seeded surface. As soon as the grass is an inch or so high roll it with a light wooden roller—in fine, dry weather—and when it has grown to 2 to 3 inches above the ground weeds must be removed and regular cutting with the scythe and rolling must be begun. A top-dressing of an ounce of guano to the square yard will help on the young grass. The scythe must continue to be used until the time

The Turf Lawn

when the grass is sufficiently secure in the ground to bear the mowing machine, which has a tendency to pull young grass up by the roots. It should be possible to use the mower in June, but the blades must be raised an inch above the normal level for the first two or three cuttings. That is to say, the grass should be cut so that it is from 1 to 2 inches in length, instead of the ½ to ¾ of an inch necessary for mature grass.

The Turf Lawn

The turves laid down should be of good quality, that is to say, the texture of the grass must be fine and the turves moderately weed-free. Turves of coarse grass and full of weeds will give endless trouble and never make a good lawn; if really good turf cannot be obtained it is far better to sow seed. Cumberland turf is among the best, but the cost of carriage makes it expensive and out of reach of most pockets. The best possible turves, however, should be obtained and all the largest weeds should be removed before laying down. In preparing a piece of ground for turfing, the soil should be well dug to a depth of about 9 inches, and a light dressing of well-rotted manure may, with advantage, be incorporated with it. The soil should then be well rolled and levelled, any hollows being filled with soil and again rolled. Immediately before the turves are laid down the top ½ inch of the soil should be raked up so that the roots of the grass may work into it and bind the turf to the soil. The turves are usually cut in slabs 3 feet long, 1 foot wide, and 1½ or 2 inches thick. In this form they are easily torn and will require to be very carefully laid if the lawn is to be level and even. Turves 1 foot square and the same thickness as the above are often used, as they are far more easy to handle and give much better results. They should be placed turf side down in a wooden frame or gauge-box 1½ inches deep, made so that they lie tightly in position. A two-handed knife with a long curved blade, or an old scythe, is then passed straight across the frame to cut off any inequalities, so that the turf shall be exactly 1½ inches thick all through. If the turves are not to be laid down immediately they should be stacked in a sheltered position out of the sun. They should not, however, be stacked for longer than is necessary, and should be laid down while the grass is still green and bright in colour. When put down they should be fitted very close together, should be laid diagonally across the lawn, and must be " bonded " as bricks are in a wall, that is to say, the junction between two in one row must come opposite the middle of a turf in the rows before and after it. Finely sifted soil must be worked in to fill the crevices and the turf should at once be watered well and then thoroughly and evenly pounded with the turf-beater and rolled, a spirit-level and straight-edge being used to ensure evenness. Water should be given daily for some time, and rolling both across and up and down the lawn with a light roller should be almost constant, provided the soil is not too wet. A dressing, ½ an inch thick, of fine sharp sand, after the rolling has been completed, will be found to improve the texture of the grass and should be well brushed in. Turves may be laid in fine weather, either in spring or autumn, the latter being

55

perhaps the better time. Turf must never be laid later in the spring than April, otherwise it is liable to suffer from drought. For the first three weeks the grass should be cut twice a week with the scythe, after that time it should be cut at least once a week with the machine, being rolled after each cutting during the first year. Lawns laid down in turf wear better than a seeded lawn during the first two or three years.

Care of the Lawn

In the autumn the lawn should be well swept and raked to drag out all possible moss, weeds and dead grass. It should then be rolled with a spiked roller, or the prongs of a garden fork should be thrust perpendicularly into the turf to a depth of 6 inches, to aerate it and help to surface-drain it through the winter. The holes made by the fork should not be more than 3 to 4 inches apart, and should stud the whole surface of the lawn. If the grass, from the nature of the soil, is inclined to grow rank and coarse, it will be much improved by a good dressing early in February of clean sharp sand all over it; if, on the other hand, it has a tendency to scald and burn up, it will receive great benefit from a dressing of equal parts of leaf-mould and fibrous loam together with a sprinkling of good guano, soot, or finely-powdered horn-meal. The loam must be free of fungi, the eggs of insect pests, and of the seeds of weeds; if there is room this may be ensured by spreading out the soil for six months or so before use, so that any seeds may have time to germinate. A sprinkling of naphthalene will invariably dispose of insect pests.

Methods of Mowing

The two methods of lawn-mowing—mowing by machine and with the scythe—are best done at different times in the day. The mechanical lawn-mower works best and most quickly when the grass is dry, but for cutting with the scythe the early morning, when the dew is still on the grass, is the best and easiest time. In the cool of the morning the grass is fuller of moisture and stiffer in the stem, thus standing up more firmly against the scythe. The exact times of the year at which mowing should be commenced and ended vary, of course, with seasons, but as a general rule mowing is necessary from March until about the middle of November. The lawn should be well swept before the first mowing of the season to clear it of all stones, twigs, and worm casts that would otherwise injure the machine. Mowing should be commenced as soon as the ground will stand it, and the grass, unless newly sown, should not be allowed to grow so long that the first cutting has to be by the scythe. In spring and autumn it will be sufficient to mow the lawn once in ten days; in summer it will be necessary once a week and even twice a week when the weather is warm and showery. In very hot, dry weather, the knives should be raised and the collecting box should be left off so that the cut grass may act as a mulch to the roots. If during the winter the weather is very mild the grass may start growing, and should it become over 2 inches in length the mower should be run over it if the ground is firm enough, otherwise the grass will tend to become thin and straggly.

The Roller and its Use

Great mistakes are made in rolling, and lawns otherwise in excellent condition are often ruined through ignorance of the proper methods of doing this. The roller should be used periodically from September to May, when the lawn is not too wet and sodden; if rolled with a heavy roller when in the latter condition, a hard crust is formed on the surface, surface-drainage is impeded and the air is prevented from reaching the roots of the grass. Roll, therefore, when the lawn is rather on the dry side, and not directly after rain, and remember that two rollings with a light roller are far more beneficial than one with a heavy roller. Rolling is intended to keep the surface even and to spread the roots of the grass, but it is *not* intended, and cannot, make the lawn level; this should have been done when the lawn was laid out. Never, therefore, use a heavy roller in wet weather. Rolling should be more frequent on a newly-laid lawn than on an older one, when a few rollings in the early autumn and another three or four in the spring just before mowing commences should be sufficient. The roller should never be used directly after frost; allow the turf to become thoroughly thawed out before either rolling or even walking on the grass.

Care of Edgings

These should be kept neat and must be cut regularly with the edging shears; if they are neglected an edging iron has to be used. This implement requires great skill in its manipulation and often results, in amateur hands, in ragged and uneven edges. Do not, therefore, neglect the edgings. During the summer the edgings may, in places, be trodden down; in autumn, therefore, as soon as the ground becomes softer, a spade should be driven under them to raise them to the correct level.

Feeding the Lawn

No lawn, however good the soil, can go on looking its best year after year unless it receives occasional stimulant in one form or another. In the natural state the grass remains long, and in the autumn dies down to form plant-food in the soil. This natural process does not occur in the lawn, as the grass is cut weekly, if not more often, and the cuttings are caught in the cutting-box and removed from the lawn, which is deprived of their nourishment.

Lawns must, therefore, be fed every two or three years or the grass will become weak and thin and will gradually give place to moss and weeds, which are always ready to force their way even into the best-kept lawn. The grass should, therefore, be carefully watched, and when it becomes off-colour it should be dressed three or four times in one season with intervals of three weeks between the feedings. *Little and often* should be the motto in dressing the lawn. Too heavy a dressing at one time may scorch up the grass, and it must be remembered that the fertilizer must be chosen to suit the condition of the grass and the nature of the soil. Fertilizers must not be applied indiscriminately; a chemical good for one lawn may ruin another. All fertilizers are best applied in showery weather and the lawn should afterwards be well brushed with a hard birch broom to work the dressing well into the roots. If no rain is likely, give the lawn a good soaking with the sprinkler or the hose. Mix the fertilizers with twice the quantity of finely-sifted loam if dressing a lawn on a sandy and rather poor soil, and with the same amount of sand when working on a clay soil; this makes even distribution of the fertilizer more easy. Stimulants are, as a rule, applied at any time from April to September, two or three dressings being applied during that period. (For rates to apply the various fertilizers, *see* table, p. 61.) Dressings of freshly-slaked lime or powdered chalk, used to sweeten a sour soil and to keep down moss, can be given in November or December, at the rate of 10 oz. to the square yard. These dressings should not be rolled into the lawn, as they would form a hard covering and would exclude air from the roots. They must not be allowed to lie about on the lawn, but must be raked and swept backwards and forwards, first in one direction and then in another, with a stiff broom, so that they are worked well down into the roots, and any dressing left lying on the surface after three weeks or so should be cleared away before a subsequent one is put on. If farmyard manure is used as a dressing it must be well decayed, finely sieved, and must not be applied too thickly or it will smother and kill the fine grass. It should be mixed with twice its bulk of finely-sieved loam, which must be absolutely weed-free. About twenty-five barrow-loads would be required for a full-size tennis-lawn, and it should be applied in December or January. Any dressing remaining in March or early April should be swept off the lawn, as it will hinder the growth of young grass.

Many advise the use of road-sweepings, but these are, in most cases, undesirable, since they are bound to contain seeds of weeds, in addition to being contaminated with tar and oil in these days when most of the roads are tarred.

Watering

Water should never be applied unless necessary. To begin with, grass seed should not be watered after sowing, and the established lawn should not receive water until a long drought makes this necessary, as once begun, watering must be continued, at least once a week, as long as the dry weather lasts. Watering seems to encourage the increase of weeds and clover rather than grass; at the same time grass seems to stand dry weather better than the weeds. Brown, scorched and apparently dead grass recovers remarkably quickly after a shower or two of rain, and as the weeds do not make so quick a recovery, many lawns are greatly benefited by a drought, if the burnt-up appearance can be countenanced for a short time. If the drought becomes serious, and the top-soil is thin and sandy, watering will become essential, and must then be applied liberally by means of the garden hose or sprinkler. The ideal way is to apply water through a fine spray over a long period so that it can permeate several inches into the ground, rather than to flood the area in a short time by using a coarse nozzle; in the latter case the water soon runs off, much of it being of little value to the grass. When mowing during the period that water must be applied, the machine should be run over the grass the day after watering, and the collecting-box should be left off so that the cut grass may form a mulch to preserve the moisture at the roots.

Weeds and Weeding

Before regular mowing commences, it will be well to go over all grass and carefully remove rank and unsightly weeds, such as daisies, plantains and dandelions. There is only one way of doing this thoroughly, and that is to stretch two garden lines across the lawn parallel to each other and from 3 to 4 feet apart, and to work steadily along between these lines until every weed is out. The worker should have a bucket of fine soil with which grass seed has been mixed, and should fill up any large holes left by the removal of the weeds. He must ram the soil down hard, so that a cup or depression is not left when the soil settles, and should roll each strip thoroughly as soon as weeding has been completed. This can be done at any time in autumn or spring, provided it is possible to get on the lawn without damaging it: the autumn is perhaps the better time, as the grass has longer to recover before the following summer.

Removing Worms

There is a very general opinion that worms are beneficial to the lawn in that the burrowings provide natural drainage. This may to some extent be true, but they do far more harm than good; they make the surface muddy and soft to walk upon, the grass becomes weakly and easily wears out if much used, and their evil-smelling casts, with which they cover the ground in autumn, winter, and spring, stifle fine grass and encourage the growth of coarse grasses and weeds. Worm casts should always be swept off the lawn before the roller is used—never roll them in. On an ordinary lawn as many as one thousand worms to the square yard may be found. Every effort must, therefore, be made to exterminate them.

The only way to get rid of worms on a lawn is to use a worm-killing solution. Watering the soil with potassium permanganate at the rate of $\frac{1}{2}$ oz. to 1 gallon of water can be very effective. This also applies to worms in pots and pans. A ready-made mixture can be obtained from any seedsman; full instructions for use are sent with the mixture and these should be closely followed.

DRESSINGS FOR KILLING WEEDS ON LAWNS

Type of Weed.	Dressing to be Used.	Quantity applied per square yard.	When to Apply.	Remarks.
Clover	Nitrate of Soda or Anti-clover Mixture.	¼ oz. ½ oz.	March. Repeat Dressing in 3 Weeks.	Besides discouraging clover, this fertilizer encourages the growth of grass in cold weather. Clover may also be raked out and is weakened by very close cutting with the machine in dry weather. Most seedsmen sell a special anti-clover mixture with full directions on the container.
Daisies	3 parts Ammonium Sulphate, 1 part Sulphate of Iron, and 30 parts Fine Sharp Sand	2½ oz.	September in Dry Weather, with a Second Dressing early in April.	Mix the ingredients of this lawn-sand thoroughly together.
	or Weed-killer.		Spring or Autumn.	Apply on a dry, still day.
Dandelions	Weed-killer or Carbolic Acid (1 oz. to a gallon of water) in a weed-killer ejector or on a skewer.		October and November.	Pierce the heart of each weed and apply weed-killer.
Moss	2 parts Kainit to 3 parts Superphosphate of Lime	2½ oz.	January.	Give this dressing two or three years running.
	or Sulphate of Iron.	¼ oz.	October.	Rake out all possible moss before applying the weed-killer, which must be mixed with twenty times its bulk of sand or fine mould and well raked into the surface. Ten days after application again rake out all dead moss.
Plantains	See Daisies.			

NOTE.—There are various good weed-killers on the market. They should be used according to makers' instructions.

FERTILIZERS AND DRESSINGS FOR THE LAWN

State of Lawn.	Nature of Soil.	Fertilizer or Top-Dressing Required.	Amount to Apply per Sq. Yard.	When to Apply.	Remarks.
Grass Poor and Weak.	Light.	Sulphate of Potash, or Kainit.	1 oz.	March.	
„ „	Heavy.	Bone Meal, or equal parts of Bone Meal and Superphosphate of lime.	2 oz.	October or February.	Bone Meal should not be used too freely as it encourages the growth of clover. Superphosphate is more suitable to a medium soil than to a heavy clay and is best applied in autumn, but never on soils deficient in lime.
„ „	Damp and Sour.	Slaked Lime (fresh), or Pulverized Chalk.	10 oz.	November or December.	This dressing sweetens the soil. Ten days after application thrust the prongs of the fork vertically 6 inches into the surface, all over, to let the air into the soil.
Grass Rank and Coarse.	Heavy.	Clean Sharp Sand (well-screened Sea or River Sand is best, never use soft-binding Sand).	Dressing ¼ in. Thick.	Early February.	
Grass Scorched.	Light Sandy or Gravelly.	Equal parts of well-sieved fibrous Loam and Leaf-mould with a sprinkling of good guano, soot or horn-meal finely powdered.	Dressing ¼ in. Thick.	February.	The compost should be very finely sifted. If well-sieved the compost soon works down into the roots and allows the fine grass to grow.
„ „	Heavy.	Nitrate of Soda.	¼ oz.	March.	Discourages clover, but encourages growth of grass in cold weather.
Young Seedling Grass.	Any.	Guano.	1 oz.	May.	Never apply guano on soils deficient in lime.
Lawn, Mossy.	Any.	Soot.	Sufficient just to Blacken Grass.	October and November. Before rain if possible.	The soot should have been exposed to the atmosphere for six months before application. Encourages growth of young grass. Wood-ashes applied in December also help towards the elimination of moss.

CHAPTER 8

Plant Propagation

Propagation of cultivated plants can be effected from seed, cuttings, layering, root division, root cuttings, leaf cuttings, budding and grafting.

SOWING SEED

Generally speaking, seeds retain full vitality for one or two years only in ordinary circumstances. From this we gather it is better to sow seed saved during the previous year, or, at the utmost, not more than two seasons old.

Conditions for Sowing

Never sow in a cold, wet soil. Wait until the ground has dried sufficiently and until the weather really bids fair to be mild. It is false economy to sow before one feels sure of the weather, just on the off-chance of getting an extra early crop. Dry, calm weather should, therefore, be chosen for seed sowing, and if seed can be sown just before a gentle shower, or when the weather is likely to be showery, so much the better. Of course, there is a proper time for sowing for every kind of seed (*see* chapters 16 and 17), but this cannot be specified in a series of general instructions which apply equally to all. The smaller the seed, the finer should be the soil in which it is grown. The soil in which seed is sown should be tolerably dry—dry enough to crumble lightly when worked with the hand. It must not clot together in a pasty mass. Place or position—that is to say, whether in the open air or under protection— also forms an important factor with regard to time.

Storing Seeds

Seed should be stored in a dark, cool place; it should be kept dry and above all in an even temperature. It is best placed in tins with tightly-fitting lids, in thoroughly clean glass bottles, if kept in the dark, or in glazed paper impermeable to moisture. Soft absorbent paper is bad, as the seeds will either dry and shrivel up or, if kept in too moist a place, will get damp and will rot. Do not leave the seeds in their pods, as the pods dry up and draw both moisture and vitality from the seeds.

When saving seeds from the garden, they should not be gathered too early, but must be allowed ample time to ripen.

Site, Soil and Treatment of Seed-bed

The seed-bed should be situated in partial shade and should be sheltered from the north and east. The soil should be made as fine as possible, first by breaking up the lumps with a fork and then by raking it thoroughly until the earth is well pulverized. It should contain 10 per cent to 20 per cent of sand—this will make it porous and will enable the air to penetrate freely through it. If the soil is not made fine in this way many of the seeds will fall down in between the clods and will not germinate; those that do come up may have their tiny roots parched up, as there will be no fine soil through which they can work and so obtain nourishment and moisture. Too rich a soil must not be used, as the seedlings would become tall and straggly, instead of short and sturdy, which is the ideal at which to aim. The bed must be pressed down firmly and left to settle for a few days before seeding. Water the bed thoroughly, if dry, and sow the seed thinly in drills running north and south, if possible, and about 6 inches apart (for times, depth to sow, and distances apart for the different flowers, vegetables, etc., *see* chapters 16 and 17).

Depth to Sow
Cover the seeds lightly with fine, sandy soil; the depth of covering required depends on the size of the seed. Minute seeds hardly need any covering at all, a mere sprinkling of sand is sufficient; medium-sized seeds must have a covering a little less than half an inch thick; and large seeds, such as those of the iris or pæony, and also those like the seeds of the anemone and phlox, which quite often do not germinate the first year after sowing, can do with $\frac{1}{2}$ to 1 inch of soil over them. Few seeds require a covering of more than 1 inch. Seeds may be sown slightly deeper out of doors than under glass, as the rain is liable to wash out any with too sparse a covering. A good rule is to cover the seeds with a layer of earth twice their own thickness. Do not pat down the soil after the seeds have been planted. Seeds sown in heavy soil must not be placed so deep as those planted in sandy loam, while in sandy soil a covering of nearly twice that given in a heavy soil will be all that is required.

Do not plant the seeds too deep, however, as if so planted and they ever reach the surface at all, they will have used up most of their strength and energy and will make weak, straggly seedlings. Should the soil of the seed-bed be very dry it should be watered overnight until sufficiently moist.

Methods of Watering
As soon as the seeds have been covered, give them a good watering from a can with a very fine rose; the rose must be very fine or the seeds may be uncovered and washed away. Keep the soil uniformly moist but not too wet; over-watering causes the seeds to rot and is the most frequent cause of failure. A few strands of black cotton, supported on small sticks, should be stretched across the bed to keep the birds away. If, before planting, the seeds are steeped for a short time in a weak solution of paraffin, neither mice nor birds will trouble much about them.

Thinning-out and Transplanting

In a month or so the seedlings should be about 2 inches high and will be large enough to be handled between finger and thumb and pricked-off. This should always be done at the earliest possible moment. Delay in thinning and transplanting means that the seedlings become drawn-up and weakly; when they are eventually moved the fibrous roots may become torn and the seedlings take much longer to become established. They will, in fact, never make such sturdy plants as those transplanted at the right time. In order that the roots shall not be torn the seed-bed should be watered the evening before the day on which thinning is to take place.

The seedlings should be raised from the seed-bed by means of a small fork, each seedling may then be lifted without any damage to its roots, and should be planted very firmly, by means of a small trowel, in a hole just large enough to receive the roots without cramping them or doubling them up, and care must be taken not to leave an air-pocket below the roots or they will soon be parched. Sturdy seedlings should be transplanted about 10 inches apart, smaller ones 6 inches apart. If, as in the case of carrots or onions, the seedlings are to be thinned and not transplanted, the fork is not used to raise them, but the unwanted seedlings are pulled up between the finger and thumb, a finger of the other hand being pressed upon the soil to keep the roots of the other seedlings in place. The soil should be firmly pressed back around those seedlings left in the seed-bed or they will be likely to die off. If transplanting is done in the evening, the seedlings will have the cool night in which to recover, and will not be so liable to be scorched as when transplanted in the heat of the day. The reserve garden into which the seeds are transplanted must possess a sunny aspect, should have been well dug and the soil, if poor, will be all the better for having had good, well-rotted manure mixed with the top 3 inches of its surface, which must be dressed with just sufficient soot to blacken the surface of the soil in order to ward off slugs. A further dressing of vegetable ashes will help to lighten the soil and furnish nourishment for the seedlings. In dry weather the reserve bed should be well watered the day before it is to receive the seedlings, but it must not be made too wet, as the seedlings will not grow if it is made to "cake". The bed should be again watered after the transplanting has been done. If transplanting can be carried out in showery weather, so much the better.

Care of the Seedlings

In dry weather, the seedlings should be watered (but not when the hot sun is on them) and the bed must be well hoed. Tepid water is far more congenial to them than cold water from the tap or a deep tank, and provided the soil is fairly rich the seedlings should receive no manure until they approach maturity. A dressing of soot-water is a sufficient stimulant and a protection from slugs.

In warm and sheltered districts the young plants may be left in the open all winter (annuals will, of course, have attained maturity, flowered

PLATE 1
Above, two modern varieties of rhododendron and *below*,
two varieties of large-flowered gladioli

Pricking-off

and died down), but in colder districts it is safer to winter them in a
frame, where they should be placed in October. Light, sandy soil and
a southerly aspect best suit most seedlings. As much air as possible
should be given, but care must be taken to exclude damp.

In November of the second season or in March of the third year the
plants can be put out in their permanent positions; tender plants receiving
protection during the second winter as afforded in the first. Slugs are
the great enemy of young seedlings and some good slug bait should be
used to keep these at bay. *See* p. 105.

Sowing Seeds Under Glass

The less hardy plants must be raised under glass preferably in " John
Innes " seed compost or a mixture of two-thirds good loam and one-
third leaf-mould, together with a good sprinkling of sharp silver sand.
The compost should be sieved through a quarter-inch mesh and the
soil for covering the seeds through a sieve even finer. Mix the compost thoroughly, press it gently into the pot or box, and make a level
surface just below the rim of the pot. The seed pans or boxes should
be drained by means of "crocks" or broken pots, an inch of crocks
being required in a box or pot 5 inches in depth. Earthenware pots or
pans are preferable, as the earthenware keeps the soil more evenly moist
than the wooden box. The seeds must be sown thinly in February or
March, and then be watered, not with a can but by immersing the pots
or pans nearly to their brims, thus allowing the water to soak up from
the bottom. Place the seed pans in a frame or greenhouse in moderate
but steady heat (about 60° F.). A sheet of glass should be placed over
the boxes and the glass in turn be covered with a sheet of brown paper
to keep out the light. Each day the glass must be lifted so that the
condensation may be wiped off, or the seeds will be kept too moist. No
further water need, as a rule, be given until the seeds have germinated.
As soon as the seeds are up (in about three weeks, according to the type
of seed) the glass and paper may be removed, and the boxes must be
lifted by gradual steps up to within 6 inches of the lights. If the box
is left some distance from the glass, weak straggling seedlings will result.
In warm weather it is wise to water the seedlings in the evening, but in
the colder weather the watering must be done before lunch-time or there
may be danger of the seedlings "damping-off".

Seeds in a Frame

The seeds may be sown in a frame in exactly the same way as described
for sowing in pans or boxes; the frame should be in a sheltered position,
as it is essential to ventilate as much as possible when the weather is
sunny and sufficiently calm.

Pricking-off

When the seedlings are from 2 to 3 inches high, they must be pricked-
off, using a wooden label in place of a small hand-fork, from 1 to 3
inches apart so that the leaves do not touch (strong-growing kinds 6 inches

apart), and should be transplanted into boxes of light sandy soil and again put in a position some 6 inches from the lights. The wooden label should be inserted in the soil an inch or so from the seedling, whose roots may then be gently levered up without damage—never should seedlings be pulled up between the finger and thumb, as this will sorely damage the roots. The seedlings should be planted so that the first pair of leaves show just above the soil. They must be planted firmly and should have the soil pressed tightly down round the roots and stems, though care must be taken not to injure any part of the seedling. A thin dibble about the size of a pencil should be used to make the holes for the seedlings, and these must not be made too deep or the roots of the seedlings will not reach the bottom and the air-pockets left under them will wither their roots. Do not "firm" the seedlings by pressing the earth round the stems with the fingers, but use the dibble, inserting it into the soil, in three or four places round the seedlings, about half an inch from them, and to the same depth as when preparing the holes. This will firm the soil all round the seedlings, right down to the bottom of the roots; the fingers would only press in the top and the roots would be left loose in the soil. Strongly-growing seedlings can be potted up at once, the process of pricking-off being unnecessary. In the case of seeds that germinate irregularly, the first batch of seedlings should be pricked-off as soon as they can be handled, and the seed boxes should then be replaced so that the remaining seeds may germinate.

Such treatment is necessary with plants like the anemone, auricula, polyanthus and other primulas. After pricking-off keep the seedlings in a close atmosphere and shade from the sun for a few days until they are established in their new pots.

Hardening-off and Damping-off

In March or April the seedlings should be transplanted into the cold frame which should contain soil similar to that in the seed boxes. There they are hardened off by gradually allowing them more and more air until they are planted out very firmly in the reserve garden in May or at the beginning of June. Annuals will, of course, be placed in their flowering position if not sown there.

Half-hardy biennial and perennial seedlings, however, will require protection during the coming winter, and in early October must be lifted, then replanted close together in light sandy soil in boxes, to be stored in the greenhouse in a temperature of about 50° F., or in a cold frame. Give as much air as possible when the weather is fine and dry to prevent the plants from "damping-off". Should there be any signs of this, take every opportunity of thoroughly ventilating on dry warm days and sprinkle the soil very finely with powdered charcoal, or better still, water with Cheshunt Compound. The following May the biennials should be set out in their flowering positions and the perennials must again be placed in the reserve garden. Half-hardy perennials will require protection during each winter and will again have to be lifted in October and wintered under glass. It is as well to look at the thermometer at night and to cover the lights with sacking if frost threatens. The mats should not be removed too early in the morning.

Half-hardy perennials or biennials can, of course, be sown in the open in May or June and wintered as stated above. Hardy plants are frequently sown under glass to procure early and sturdy plants for bedding-out in the spring.

PROPAGATION BY CUTTINGS

Soil for Cuttings

Coarse sand is, perhaps, the best medium in which to strike cuttings. A light soil through which the air can pass freely is essential to the well-being of all cuttings. That aeration is necessary is proved by the fact that cuttings will strike readily in coconut fibre, a material that is extremely pervious to air and which retains moisture for a considerable period. Powdered charcoal also forms a good medium. In recent years a number of chemical hormones which have the property of stimulating root-formation on cuttings have become available.

Taking Cuttings

Cuttings should be taken of shoots that have ripened or which are beginning to ripen, because in wood which is attaining or has attained maturity the callus so necessary to root formation is more readily induced to show itself. The side shoots of plants, low down on the stem, are the best for cuttings, and should be taken when the sap is in full motion, because its return by the bark tends to form the callus, or ring, of granular matter from which the roots proceed. The leaves of a cutting must never be cut off, except in so far as may be necessary at its base in order that it may be inserted in the soil. The leaves are the lungs of the plant, and if they are cut the sap that they contain will be lost to the cutting and prevented from passing downwards to form the callus. Cuttings of plants that are difficult to strike may frequently be induced to do so by making a ring round them, or by tying a piece of string round them for a short time before they are taken from the parent plant. The downward flow of the sap is arrested by the tightened ligature and a swelling is caused, which forms a callus from which roots are soon emitted. The cutting must be severed from the parent plant just below the ring or band, and the callus formed should be covered when the cutting is inserted. Growth-promoting substances are easier to use.

In taking cuttings strong sturdy shoots varying from 3 to 12 inches in length should be removed from the plant, with a very sharp knife, by a clean, straight cut just below a joint. If it is possible to take a " heel " or small wedge-shaped portion of the old wood and bark with it, so much the better, and it is then not essential to cut immediately below a joint. The joint need not necessarily be the junction of two stems; it may equally well be the " eye " from which a pair of leaves have sprung. When no " heel " is taken, the cut must be especially clean and just below a joint, but the joint itself must be left intact; in fact, about an eighth of an inch of wood should be left below the joint. The " heel ", from which all

67

ragged edges should be trimmed, when placed in contact with the ground provides a large surface on which roots can form. The length of cuttings is decided by the distance between the joints; when these are, say, an inch apart, the cuttings must be 12 inches long and over half this length must be buried in the soil. Where the distance between joints is less, the cuttings may be shorter, but all hard-wooded cuttings should have at least 6 inches in the ground, and all cuttings must be inserted right to the bottom of the hole prepared for them.

Types of Cuttings

Cuttings of hard-wooded shrubs, such as the heath or myrtle, are more difficult to strike than those of soft-wooded plants, such as the geranium, and for this reason on hard-wooded cuttings the "eyes" on the part of the stem that will be placed underground should be carefully cut out; this will encourage the formation of roots at these places. Cuttings of free-growing hardy plants, such as the gooseberry, and the willow, strike freely without care or attention after being inserted in the soil. The position for all cuttings should, of course, be sheltered and shaded from full sun, and although not necessary with hardy plants, most cuttings when planted in the open do better if covered by a hand-light until the roots have formed. The less hardy and less vigorous plants should be struck in pots or boxes in a cold frame or under hand-lights, while the more delicate still require artificial heat or the bottom-heat of a propagating box. It may be taken as a general rule that cuttings of soft-wooded plants require more heat than those of hard-wooded plants. "Soft" cuttings, as a rule, should not be struck in the open as, apart from a little heat being desirable, the wind and sun would dry the moisture from their leaves and the roots would never form. A glass covering is, therefore, necessary. Cuttings of soft-wooded plants, such as the pelargonium, strike best when they have not too much foliage to bear, and should have the stems shortened to two or three joints beneath the point from which the foliage springs. Never make the cuttings longer than necessary. In the case of the less hardy plants the soil should be stored in a warm greenhouse for a few days before the cuttings are inserted, and rooting will be more certain and prompt if the cuttings are watered with lukewarm water.

There are several plants like the pansy or the honeysuckle whose stems, when mature, are hollow and useless for ordinary cuttings. In such cases the young shoots must be struck, or with the honeysuckle both ends of the cutting may be inserted in the soil. There are other plants, such as dahlias and lupins, whose cuttings must be taken at the junction of the stems and the roots. These require a glass covering.

Cuttings of nearly all the less hardy and greenhouse plants require a propagating case, placed over the hot-water pipes. With the more hardy kinds no artificial heat is needed, except that provided by the glass, but the soil must be kept uniformly warm and moist.

Shrub cuttings may be taken at three distinct periods, firstly in autumn when the wood has hardened and is quite mature; secondly in September or August when the shoots have half matured; and thirdly when the shoots are beginning to ripen in early summer; the latter time is perhaps the best of the three. With many of the hardier shrubs the cuttings may be struck in sandy soil in a sheltered bed in the open, and, of course, provided the wood is fully ripe. Half-matured cuttings, even of hardy shrubs, must, however, be treated like those of the less hardy natures and be struck under glass. Cuttings of hardy evergreen shrubs are also best struck under glass, not because they need heat, but because a close, steady and fairly moist atmosphere is required (*see* Propagation from Cuttings, p. 303).

When cuttings are struck in pots or boxes the latter should be well drained by an inch layer of crocks at the bottom, and must be clean. If they are dirty the mould will be likely to stick to them when the cuttings are turned out for transplanting and the tender new root fibres may be torn.

Compost for Cuttings

A good compost for striking the cuttings of most plants can be made by mixing equal quantities of leaf-mould and well-sieved loam and by adding to this a good proportion of sharp silver sand, and then sieving the whole through a quarter-inch mesh. It is always well to sprinkle the surface of the soil which is to receive the cuttings with a layer of coarse sand about 1 inch thick, so that when the dibble is pressed down to form the hole for the cuttings, some of the sand will trickle into it and be ready to encourage the production of roots. The sand keeps the soil porous and prevents the base of the cutting from rotting. The soil should be firmed down and the slips inserted at least 1½ inches apart; they must not be placed too close together or they may " damp-off ". Press the earth well down round the cuttings, as they will not root if standing loosely in the soil. If the cuttings can be fairly easily pulled from the compost it may be taken as an indication that they are not planted sufficiently firmly.

Inserting the Slips

As has been said, cuttings strike more readily when placed at the side of a pot than when inserted in its centre. Of ordinary plants about seven cuttings can be placed in a 4-inch pot. No cutting should be set too deeply, but as in the case of seeds, the depth will depend mainly on the size of the cutting; a good general rule is to set about two-thirds of the length of hard-wooded cuttings in the soil, with soft-wooded cuttings only one-third or one-half should be inserted. Leaves should not be permitted to touch the soil; if they do they will " damp-off ". Water well after insertion.

When using pots or boxes, it is better, but not necessary, to sink these nearly to their brims in ashes or coconut fibre, which will keep the soil at an even temperature. Whether the cuttings are covered by plates of glass, glass bells or the lights of a frame, the condensation must be wiped off each morning.

Once the cuttings have struck, ventilation must be given whenever possible, and decaying leaves must be removed to avoid any possibility of "damping-off". The great thing is to keep the soil at the same temperature as the surrounding air.

Too much light, air, water, heat, or cold are alike injurious to cuttings freshly inserted under glass. A close equable temperature and a moderate degree of moisture should be maintained until the cuttings have "rooted". This condition is best attained by covering them with a bell glass or hand-light and by shading them if not placed in a shady situation.

Once they have struck, which will be in about three weeks, the cuttings should be gradually given more ventilation and hardened-off until they can be potted up singly for the greenhouse, or planted out into the open.

Soft-wooded cuttings soon form roots, and can often be potted-off within a few weeks; cuttings of hard-wooded shrubs, however, take root less quickly and should not be disturbed for at least a year (sometimes 18 months) after being struck. To give the cuttings ample room to grow they are usually planted at least 6 inches from each other in rows 10 inches to a foot apart.

PROPAGATION BY LAYERS

This is an easy and very sure method of propagation, usually effected about July, though it may be effected at any season of the year. It consists in the production of roots on one or more of the lower shoots of the plant to be produced. An upward cut, just below a joint, is made in the layer or shoot; the incision passes from the underside through to the centre of the shoot, and is from about 1 inch to 3 inches in length, according to the size and nature of the plant to be propagated. The aim is to produce a "tongue" of bark and wood that can be wedged open and pegged down into the soil; the more the tongue is kept open when placed in contact with the earth the better the chance of rooting. The shoots chosen for layering must be perfectly healthy, and should be semi-matured. It is usual to layer several shoots at a time, and when the cuts have been made, as described above, the earth all round the plant is stirred up to a depth of 3 inches and the layers are pegged down firmly, so that the open tongues come well in contact with the soil. Little mounds of earth some 6 inches high are then piled up over the layers, which are pressed firmly down into the earth, and well watered. An addition of coarse sand to the soil (often in the proportion of 50 per cent of its volume) as in the case of cuttings, helps the layers to root. The outer end of the shoot, beyond the cut, should be turned upwards to check the flow of the sap, and all buds not required to form shoots in the new plant should be removed. When the layers have rooted firmly, they may be cut away from the parent plant, potted up or planted out, preferably in autumn. The layers of soft-wooded plants, such as the carnation, will be found to root in six weeks or so, shrubs like the laurel or hebe will take two or three months to form roots; while with hard-wooded shrubs, like the daphne, magnolia or rhododendron, it will be a year or more before the layers can be severed from the parent plant.

Root Division

AIR LAYERING

Air layering, Chinese layering or marcotting, as it is variously called, is a system of layering whereby the moist material is brought to the stem, the latter being left in its original position. It is a useful method for propagating rare and valuable plants which are difficult or impossible from cuttings, and where ordinary methods of layering is not practicable. Clean young shoots are best for air layering. They are prepared by making an upward cut about 2 inches long at or about the stem centre. Alternatively the stem may be girdled by removing a ring of bark about ½ inch wide. The wound may be dusted with a growth-promoting substance, and a handful of moist sphagnum moss is packed between the cut surfaces and all round it so as to give complete cover. Polythene film is wrapped round the moss to prevent its drying out.

PROPAGATION BY RUNNERS

This is, perhaps, the most simple method of propagation, though only possible with certain plants, namely those that throw out long thin stems or runners which grow out over the surface of the ground. The strawberry is a well-known example of the runner-producing plant. At intervals along the stems will be found joints, and wherever one of these joints comes in contact with the soil and so remains for some time, roots form and foliage is thrown up.

To assist in this method of propagation, the earth should be stirred up to a depth of 2 or 3 inches all round the plant and the runners must be firmly pegged down into it, at the required number of joints. Young roots will form and after a few weeks they will be strong enough to support the new plant which may be cut away from its parent, and potted up or transplanted. A better method, but one entailing a little more work, is to sink to their brims pots of good sandy soil exactly under the joints of the runners and to peg the latter down firmly to the soil in the pots. This operation provides an easier way of transplanting and one beneficial to the young plant, as the roots are not so easily injured when replanting.

PROPAGATION BY OFFSETS

Offsets afford yet another means of propagation suitable to many herbaceous perennials and to many rock plants. These offsets are growths forming young crowns round the older central crown, and may be carefully separated from the parent crown with some roots when large enough and can be potted up into small pots or transplanted in the open. About a month after the plant has flowered will be found the best time to accomplish the operation.

PROPAGATION BY ROOT DIVISION

Plants are best divided in October and November, or in March and April. The clumps should be lifted with their roots as entire as possible, that is, with a good "ball" of earth round the fibres. This is done by inserting two forks vertically downwards, one on either side of the plant

71

and backs facing each other, and then by levering the clump and its roots gently upwards. When the plant has been lifted, don't, as is so often done, use a spade to cut the roots apart, but carefully divide the plants up into as many crowns as possible by means of a sharp knife which will do the minimum injury to the roots. The strong new outer crowns are those that should be retained and replanted; the old inner roots being removed.

The stems that have already borne flowers should be cut away from the new crowns, so that only the young and vigorous shoots from the base remain. Replant as described in chapter 18, devoted to *The Herbaceous Border*.

PROPAGATION BY ROOT-CUTTINGS

This is another and easy method of propagation eminently suitable in the case of plants with fleshy roots and those that sucker freely. If the roots are examined in the early spring, they will be found to be covered with small whitish knobs or shoots; these are the "eyes" from which the new growth will spring. Cuttings of these roots from 2 to 8 inches in length, in accordance with the virility of the plant, and each having an "eye", are taken. They are planted 1 inch deep and 8 inches apart in light sandy soil in partial shade, or in a cold frame with a warm close atmosphere. The cuttings are inserted vertically with that part of the root which was nearest the stem uppermost.

In propagating plants whose roots are fleshy, but rather more fibrous in nature, the larger root-stems should be cut away from the crowns with as many of the smaller fibrous roots as possible adhering, and should be planted as advised above, but should be left intact and not be cut up into small pieces. In the case of plants whose roots creep horizontally just below the surface of the soil, cut the roots into pieces from 1 to 6 inches in length, each piece having an "eye" or bud from which shoots can spring, and plant horizontally in the soil at the same depth as they were before being dug up.

The root-cuttings will require frequent watering during the following few months, and will be benefited by the ocasional application of a little weak manure water. It is essential to keep the surface of the soil loose. The cuttings can be planted out in the autumn or in the following March or April.

PROPAGATION BY LEAF-CUTTINGS

Propagation by leaf-cuttings is a very interesting method not often resorted to, and then only in the case of plants with succulent or thick spongy leaves, and soft veins.

A perfectly healthy leaf must be selected; it is then taken and planted, stalk downwards, and with the leaf proper just clear of the soil, in a propagating case in equal parts of sandy loam and leaf-mould. Roots will soon form and a young plant will grow from them. Haberlea, Ramonda and Saintpaulia may be so treated. In the case of a large and thick leaf, the veins on the back may be slit at their junctions. The stalk is then planted in sandy soil, and the whole leaf is pinned firmly backside-down, so that it cannot move, on to the mould in the propagating case (temperature 70° F.) and allowed plenty of moisture, though the bed must be well drained and not be permitted to become stagnant, or the leaves will rot. In a short time plants will grow wherever the veins have been slit.

The little plants can be transplanted or potted up just as soon as they have roots strong enough to support them. This method of propagation, which may be resorted to at any season when fully matured leaves are available, is particularly suitable in the case of such plants as the achimenes, begonia, and the gloxinia.

RINGING

Hard-wooded plants which are difficult to propagate by other methods may be increased by a process known as *ringing*, and which consists in removing a small narrow ring of bark all round the stem in the place in which the formation of roots is desired to take place. Care must be taken not to cut deeply into the stem—indeed, it is better to peel off the outer bark only, and not to cut into the inner wood at all; no hindrance is then offered to the ascent of the sap. A callus is formed on the bark which forms the upper edge of the ring, and this thickens as times goes on, and ultimately emits roots. Branches and trailing stems operated on in this way should be firmly pegged down, and earth should be drawn over the incision. Layers should be brought into as erect a position as possible, and they may be shortened back. (*See also* paragraph on layering, p. 70.)

THE USES OF GRAFTING

Grafting has been spoken of as "ennobling", the branch which is transferred being spoken of as the "scion", and the tree to which it is attached as the "stock". The scion becomes, as it were, parasitic upon the stock, and by carefully removing all branches which spring from the stock below the point of union, gardeners are enabled to divert to the scion all the energy produced by the roots of the stock. It is only possible to graft a scion on to a stock of nearly allied species. Thus quinces, apples, pears, and medlars can all be mutually grafted on to one another, as also can plums, peaches, apricots, and almonds, but it would be impossible to graft an apple on to an oak or a plum on to a willow.

Much valuable time may be saved by grafting; it might take some fifteen or twenty years before a tree raised from seed would bear fruit, whereas by grafting fruit might be had in three or four years. Better results are also often obtained by grafting a tree on to a stock and roots other than its own.

Another purpose for which grafting is employed is for the altering of the habit of a tree. Thus, pears and apples are dwarfed by grafting them respectively on the quince and the paradise stock, and dwarfed weeping trees are converted into tall standards by attaching a scion from the weeping variety to a tree with a tall, upright trunk.

73

Suitable Soil

In the selection of a suitable stock attention should be paid not only to the readiness with which connection is able to be established between the scion and the stock, but to the soil in which the trees are to be grown. Thus, for example, in light soil, plums grown on their own roots rarely do well, but when grafted on the peach they usually thrive. *Vice versa*, peaches on their own roots rarely do well in heavy soils, and may often be made to succeed by grafting them on the plum. Again, on chalky soil, where the peach usually does badly, it can often be made to grow and fruit by grafting it on the plum. It is certain, also, that in some cases the flavour of fruit can be modified by the stock on which the variety is grafted. For some years now research work has revealed the importance of using the right type of stock for various fruit trees if the best results are to be obtained.

Development and Restoration

Grafting is also occasionally employed to bring about the development of flowers or fruit from parts of a tree otherwise lacking in them. Sometimes, again, it is made use of for the purpose of restoring an exhausted tree: and lastly it is employed to bring together on one stock the two sexes of monœcious plants—that is to say, plants which bear their male and female flowers on different trees—and so to facilitate their fertilization and consequent fructification.

THE PRINCIPLES OF GRAFTING

Time to Graft

In order to effect a successful union by grafting it is necessary that the sap should be flowing in the portions of the wood used for the operation, and it is therefore possible to graft in the open between the first signs of growth in the buds at the beginning of spring until about midsummer, when the sap has risen fully. Under glass the time is somewhat earlier, being possible any time from January to March, and again from July till September. The operations of budding and grafting are not unlike, being, indeed, identical in theory, but whereas in budding a bud only of the current year's growth is employed, in grafting whole branches are used, while their buds are still dormant or nearly so. The time for grafting trees will, therefore, vary with the time of their breaking into leaf, those kinds which bud early being the first to be dealt with. Plums are generally the first to be ready in late March, then come quinces and pears, followed by cherries and apples in this order; but as the time of leafing varies with certain varieties the order is not without exceptions. To ascertain whether the stock is ready for grafting, the bark should be slit and if it is easily raised to expose the polished surface of the wood beneath, the stock is ready. If the bark tends to tear, the stock must be left for a week or so longer.

Initial Preparations

Grafting needs a certain amount of previous preparation. The stock or tree which is to receive the graft should be cut back or beheaded at about the end of January. Where the frosts are still very hard it is well to defer the operation till the weather loosens a little, but no risk must be run of movement having begun in the sap. The object of the preparation of the grafts and scions beforehand is that the last year's ripened sap should still be in them, to supply life to the severed scion until union has been effected, and to this end the scions, which must be well ripened one-year-old wood and taken from prolific and healthy trees only, should be cut in winter before there is any chance of movement, while the buds are still absolutely dormant. Grafting must be carried out when the scion is in the same state of vegetation as the intended stock. It is necessary, therefore, where the grafts selected are in a more advanced state of vegetation, to detach them from the parent stems and to lay them with their stems three-parts buried in moist soil under a north wall until stocks and grafts are in a similar state. In this position the grafts will remain stationary while the stocks are advancing. When the weather is so mild as to appear likely to cause movement of the sap the scions should be pulled up occasionally, and left exposed to the air for a little while in order to check growth. The scions should be cut at about the same time as the stock is cut off. This latter process consists in removing from the stocks, which should be three-year-old plants, planted at least a year before grafting, all the side branches together with the tops, and cutting down the main stock to just above a bud within about 7 or 8 inches of the soil. Where older plants are used as stocks, as in the case of grafting on mature trees, these should be cut back throughout to within from 3 to 6 feet from the stock, according to the size of the tree. Enough wood should always be left to allow for removal of a further portion, as this will be necessary when the actual grafting is proceeded with. If this cutting back is not done until the actual time of grafting the junction is seldom so good, and where the trees employed are stone-fruit trees—particularly liable to this accident—gumming is very likely to result, with consequent weakening of the trees. Stocks to be used as standards must be allowed to grow to the height required. The time of grafting varies according to the stock used. It should be ascertained with accuracy that the sap is really rising, and it is better for that reason to be a little too late than too early, when there is a chance that it has not yet begun to move. Usually May will be found the best time for grafting on mature trees, and April for those which are only in their third year.

THE PROCESS OF GRAFTING

The stock should be grafted, as in the case of budding, as near to the ground as possible. To effect a union the inner edges of the inner bark of the two parts must meet and remain in contact, this inner layer of bark being the only portion of the wood which is capable of uniting. The process consists in cutting the bark of the two portions so that this inner layer shall be in contact when the two pieces are pressed together, and in keeping them together and excluding air, which might dry the tissues, by means of wax or clay and raffia.

Grafting Tools and Materials

When grafting is to be undertaken, all materials should be got in readiness beforehand. The stocks and grafts should be prepared and at hand, together with a few tools such as a strong knife for cutting back the stocks, a saw, chisel, and mallet, a small knife with a narrow blade for fine operations, raffia or soft string for tying, and the wax or clay required. The clay needs careful preparation, and should be obtained some weeks before it is required for use, and beaten up into the consistency of mortar with water. This moistening and beating should be repeated every day for a fortnight, and a day before it is to be used it should be mixed with one-third of its own bulk of cow manure and about the same amount of hay. The hay should be cut up into lengths of about 3 inches, and thoroughly mixed into the other ingredients, and will prevent the clay from cracking off as it hardens, as well as materially assisting in keeping it moist.

It is simpler for the amateur to buy a good grafting wax than to prepare it for himself, and he is advised to obtain one of the many good proprietary materials that are now on the market. A good substitute for grafting wax is the quick-drying varnish called "knotting". This is very quickly dry, and is impervious to wet and weather. It is applied with a brush over the part to be protected.

Whip- and Tongue-Grafting

The method of grafting employed depends largely on the size and other conditions of stock and scion. Where the stock is young and about the size of the finger, the kind known as whip- and tongue-grafting is most suitable. With this method of grafting the stock must be more advanced in its state of growth than the scion. The scion is prepared by taking a well-ripened one-year-old shoot some 6 inches long, and selecting a place on it where two good buds come on opposite sides of the shoot, one a little higher than the other. Beginning just below the upper of the buds, make a clean cut at one sweep through the wood in a downward slope, coming out just below the lower bud. It is essential that there should be a good bud just above the cut at each end. Now, beginning at the top of the cut just under the top bud, with a perfectly sharp knife, cut a hollow curve in the wood, sloping the cut from the inner end of the curve down in a straight line to the tip of the cut by the lower bud. The bottom of the shoot, seen sideways, should now have a section like the letter J turned upside down. It is important that these cuts should be made firmly and without unevennesses, or the scion will not fit closely to the stock, and its chance of a perfect union will be lessened. Having prepared the scion, attention should be turned to the stock. This, as will be remembered, was cut back late in January to about 8 inches from the soil. Remove all side growth from the base and selecting a good smooth place about 3 or 4 inches from the surface of the ground, cut the stock cleanly off just above a good healthy bud. This bud's chief function will be to draw up the sap into the top of the cut parts while they are healing together, just as do the buds on the scion, but while the latter are allowed to grow and, indeed, become the real tree, the former should not be allowed to outlive its utility, and when perfect union has taken place it should only be allowed to grow two or three leaves, and then should be stopped out. Having cut down the stock, its top should be carefully measured against the scion, and cut in a curve corresponding with the curve on the scion. Where the scion has a long " tail ", the tail of the " J " shape, a strip of wood and bark should be peeled from the side of the stock, with the greatest care to fit it, so that the stock and scion, when placed together, may fit with accuracy. The tail of the scion will be found to fit on to the peeled strip of the outside of the stock, though, owing to the different angle of the section, a narrow strip of the inner bark of the stock will show round the edge of the scion when applied. The important thing to arrive at is that the cut surfaces of the inner bark of both stock and scion should touch as much as possible. If it is found impossible to make these layers of bark meet on both edges, make them meet perfectly on the one. The tail of the scion should not in any case come below the end of the peeled piece of the stock; if anything it should err on the other side.

When both scion and stock fit perfectly, a further security should be obtained by making a small upward cut in the tail of the scion, in order, to obtain a slip projecting towards the stock. In the stock itself, opposite this slip, should be made an incision into which the slip will exactly fit, thus holding stock and scion together during the operations of tying and covering with wax. This slip should be thin, or it may cause the junction to bulge and the scion to be pushed away from the stock. When these two latter are fitted closely together, and it is found that their layers of inner bark are fitting closely and neatly, the junction should be made firm by tying with raffia, woollen thread, or soft string, the ligature being made firm enough to prevent movement but not tight enough to prevent the proper circulation of the sap beneath the bark. The last process is the secure covering of the whole junction—scion, stock and ligature— with grafting wax or clay, and the graft is complete. The label should always be attached to the stock, not to the scion, as otherwise there would be an added risk of the scion being caught accidentally and pulled off before a union has been effected.

Saddle-Grafting

Saddle-grafting is a kind much used for stocks of about the thickness of a broom-handle, the scion in this case being about the same thickness as the stock and cut with two tails, the one below the upper bud being shorter than that below the lower bud. The whole of the inner part of the wood below the buds is removed, and at the top the cuts are ended by a cross-cut beginning just behind the upper bud and sloping slightly upwards. The scion will now have two tails of unequal length, the shorter one having a bud at its upper extremity, and the longer one having a bud midway up its length. The stock should then be taken, and its top cut to slope slightly, at an angle corresponding with that of the cross-cut of the scion. A slip should be peeled corresponding with the long tail of the scion, and the latter laid over the stock, saddlewise, the long tail fitting its peeled slip, and the top angle of the stock fitting into the top angle of the cross-cut. The short tail of the scion will be found to cross the top of the stock and project a little. A slip should be cut off the side of the stock to fit this projecting piece of the tail, which should then be bent down on to it, and the graft is ready for tying and waxing. This system has the advantage that the scion unites on both sides of the stock, and is therefore not so liable to an accidental break during the healing process.

These methods of grafting are both employed for young stocks, but others must be used in the case of mature trees, where the branches are usually too large for either of the systems described—Cleft-grafting, Crown- or Rind-grafting, and Notch-grafting. The first system is not to be recommended, as it results in a crack being left right across the top of the stock, in which rain, insects, and fungi are apt to lodge and injure the tree.

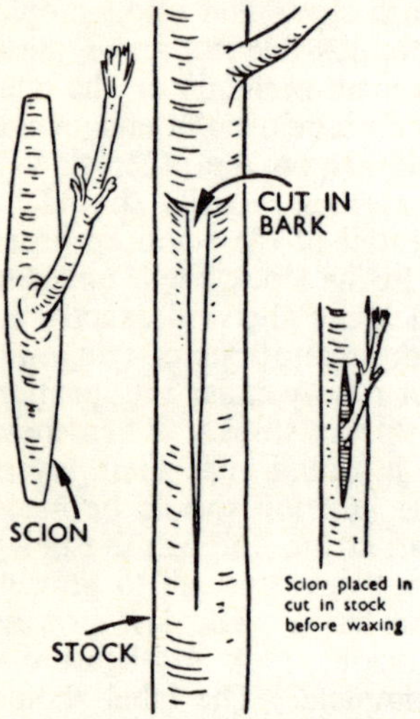

Notch- or Slit-Grafting

Notch-grafting is rather difficult, but is excellent when well done, and is used when the diameter of the stock is some four times greater than that of the graft. In this method the stock is first cut clean across, as in the other ways, and then pointed, wedge-shaped incisions are made in the bark and wood, beginning at the cut edge of the bark and sloping downwards and outwards. The scions are prepared by making sloping cuts on two sides of the wood, making an angle corresponding with that of the wedge-shaped incision in the stock, so that the scion, when fitted into the stock, fills the space closely, the outer layer of the bark of the scion being slightly lower—because thinner—than that of the stock. The best way of doing this is to make the first cut in the stock with a widely-set saw, and then sloping the sides of the cut slightly outwards with a sharp knife. The angle of the cut in the stock should not be quite so wide as that of the scion, as the latter will in this way be held tighter in the slit. The scion, when properly shaped, should be set into the cut and hammered lightly down into position with a small wooden mallet. It should then be tied and waxed as described.

Fig. 9. Crown- or rind-grafting. The scion and cut in stock, and the position of former before waxing.

Crown- or Rind-Grafting

is the most popular and the easiest method of grafting on to mature trees when the stock is comparatively large, especially when renovating old fruit trees. In this system the scion is prepared much as for whip- and tongue-grafting, but the curve at the top is replaced by a sloping cut about $1\frac{1}{2}$ inches in length.

The tail is quite thin, too much wood often being left by beginners when preparing scions for grafting.

The stock should be cut off cleanly, and with a sharp knife a slit should be made in the bark of the same length as the tail of the scion.

While the knife is still in the cut the blade should be gently pressed from side to side so as to loosen the bark in the immediate neighbourhood of the cut, and on withdrawing the knife the scion is slipped in between the wood and the bark, and pressed down until the surface left by the cross-cut at its head lies on the top of the stock.

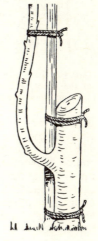

Any number of scions from two to four should be placed on each branch over 4 inches in diameter so treated, as the more scions there are the better and more strongly will the sap be drawn up, and the quicker and better will the stock heal and effect a junction. When the grafts are growing well they should be supported by being tied to sticks fastened securely to the branches of the stock.

Until the grafted tree has developed a good head of new grafted wood it is a great mistake to remove all the shoots and twigs of the old stock. A number of these should be allowed to grow for a long time, or the circulation of the tree will be impaired and its health affected.

After-care of the Graft

In May the grafts should have begun to make growth, and if this is the case the clay or grafting wax should be removed so that the binding may be undone before it "throttles" the new growth, which it will do if left in position.

Fig. 10. Supporting a graft by means of a rigid stake.

If the graft is not yet secure the binding must be replaced immediately, but more loosely. The clay or wax should not be replaced. The graft should also be supported by a stake firmly bound to the stock. Laterals that form on the graft should be pinched off to encourage a good straight single shoot from the graft, and any shoots forming on the stock below the point of grafting must be rubbed off, once they have served their purpose in drawing sap up to the graft.

The wax may be found difficult of removal and in such a case care is required in order to get it off without damaging the junction. It is best done by placing a block of wood or some other firm thing on one side of the lump of wax, and lightly hitting the other side with a hammer, no unnecessary force being employed. The wax will crack off and may be removed with ease.

BUDDING

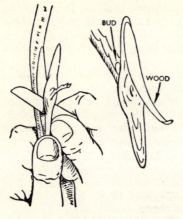

FIG. 11. *Left,* cutting the bud out of the shoot, and *right,* separating the wood from the bark.

Budding is another method of improving or altering the nature of the fruit and flowers borne by a given tree, and it is based on the same principles as those which govern grafting. It is superior to the latter inasmuch as it produces a more perfect union, a proportionately larger surface of the inner bark coming in contact with that of the stock. In budding no wood at all is left on the bud employed, only the bud itself and a surrounding surface of bark being left on the "bud" when prepared.

Time to Bud

A spell of showery or dull weather should be chosen for the operation of budding, as then the bark separates freely and easily from the wood, but if the year is very dry and hot, the stocks to be budded should be given a good soaking of water for a day or two before the operation. The best time for budding is between the early part of July and the end of September, and if the buds do not start until the next spring so much the better. New wood of the current year's growth is usually the best for budding upon, but young growths up to two or three years may be used, if otherwise more suitable. Fruit trees are best budded in July and August, while roses do best from the middle of July till early in September.

Budding Operations

In this operation, unlike grafting, the bud and stock are prepared on the spot, not beforehand, and a time should be chosen when the sap is rising freely both in stock and bud. The tree should be looked over, and the best shoot selected for the cutting of the buds. If they are not to be used at once the shoots should be put in water, or the bark will dry slightly and be more difficult to work. A good half-matured shoot of current year's growth having been chosen, the leaves should all be removed from it close to the leaf-stalk, only a piece of the latter being left on. If the leaves are left on they will draw and pass out the moisture from the bark and the bud, shrinking the latter. With a sharp knife the bud is then cut out of the wood, the knife making a curve behind it, leaving the bud midway on a thin strip of bark and wood. The knife should enter the wood some half an inch above the bud, and leave it an equal distance below it, leaving a piece of bark of the shape of a long shield, whence the name of "shield-budding" sometimes given to the operation. The woody part of this must now be removed, and in order to do this

80

the piece is held by the leaf-stalk and bud, starting the bark away from the wood at the top end with the tip of the knife, and then giving a sharp pull, when the bark should peel cleanly off the slip of wood. Occasionally, and generally when the bud is too forward when cut, the wood, when it pulls away, will leave a small hole in the bark behind the bud, as if it had pulled out a little bit of the inside of the bud with it. When this has occurred the bud is spoilt, and will shrivel and die before it has time to build up new cells to

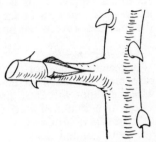

FIG. 12. Position of the cut in the side shoot of a standard rose.

replace the missing ones. Such a bud should be thrown away and a fresh one, less developed, taken.

The bud being ready, the stock must be dealt with. A clean, smooth spot on the stem is chosen, and with a budding knife a cut about 1½ inches long is made, only just sufficient pressure being employed as will pierce the bark without penetrating the wood beneath. At the top of this a cross-cut half an inch long should be made with equal precaution, and the bark on either side of the first cut raised from the wood by means of the blade of the knife, or its thin handle slipped in between bark and wood. The point of the "shield" containing the bud is then inserted at the cross-cut, and gently pushed under the bark until the bud

FIG. 13. Cut with the bud inserted and the bark cut off level.

is well down below the level of the cross-cut. The easiest way to do this is to hold the shield between the finger and thumb of the left hand, by the leaf-stalk, while holding the bark open with the knife held in the other hand. When the bud is well down, the projecting tip of the shield should be cut off with a cut exactly on a level with the cross-cut in the stock, so that the top of the shield fits inside the bark. Afterwards bandage lightly with soft material—raffia, worsted or matting— above and below the eye, bringing the lips of the bark of the stock together again over the bud by means of the ligature in such a manner that no opening remains between them. Above all, take

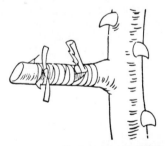

FIG. 14. Bud bandaged lightly with soft material, such as raffia.

care that the base of the eye is in free contact with the bark of the stock. As much rapidity as is consistent with thoroughness should be used, as much of the success of the operation depends on the moist condition of the bud and stock when brought into contact.

Selecting the Buds

In selecting buds for this purpose, particularly in the case of fruit trees, care must be taken to make sure that the buds are wood buds, from which a shoot will start, and not fruit buds, which will not make wood. These two kinds of bud are more easily distinguished in some kinds than in others, but as a general rule it may be taken that the wood buds are more pointed than are the fruit buds. The buds of some fruit trees, most usually in dry seasons, are troublesome to peel away from their wood, the wood very frequently pulling out the middle of the bud with it, as already described. When this is very marked, it is a good plan to pierce the wood just behind the bud with the point of the knife, so as actually to cut it away from the bud at that point, before beginning to peel it from the bark. The shoots selected for budding, whether for fruit or rose trees, should be plump, firm and well ripened. Watery shoots or buds are valueless.

After the budding process is completed the stock should be left untouched, neither leaves nor any other part being cut away until about November, when the binding must also be cut to allow the stock to grow. At this time the top of the stem which bears the bud may be cut back to about 3 inches above it. When the bud shoots in the spring —or possibly before—this three inches should be reduced to one, and all shoots springing from the stock should be cut away periodically through the summer. In autumn the " snag " above the bud may be cut away completely.

When the buds begin to grow they require to be protected from strong winds; otherwise they would be detached from the stem. This is done by driving a stake (Fig. 10) firmly into the ground, attaching it by a strong cord to the stem of the stock above and below the junction, as in the illustration, and tying the shoot of the young scion firmly to the stake above, protecting it by a bandage of hay or other substance to prevent the bark being injured.

These are general principles applicable to the majority of plants; for individual cultural details, *see* the Alphabetical List of Flowering Plants and Shrubs, chapter 16.

CHAPTER 9

Garden Diseases and Pests

The volume of damage to garden crops caused by diseases and pests can be, and sometimes is, very considerable. This being so it becomes every gardener to gain some knowledge of how to identify them and, more particularly, how to treat plants affected by them.

The words diseases and pests are here used in their broadest sense. Diseases may conveniently be divided into two main groups, those of a physical character due to poor growing conditions or lack of some essential plant-food and those caused by parasitic agents such as fungi, bacteria or viruses. The second group is the more important and the organisms concerned are among the simplest forms of vegetable life, minute or microscopic, with the viruses beyond microscopic recognition. Fungi may live on or inside the plant and many of them go through well-defined phases of development, finishing in a fruiting stage which produces spores that spread the disease further. Bacteria multiply by simple cell-division and with the viruses are usually spread through some intermediary such as a sucking insect, the gardener's hands, boots, or tools, by taking cuttings or dividing the roots of an infected plant, or less commonly by using infected seed.

Among pests, the gardener includes all those animals which attack plants: insects, mites, slugs, snails, birds, etc. But many are beneficial and these should be carefully preserved. Ladybirds, lacewings, hover flies, centipedes and some of the ground beetles live on other insects. Shrewmice and hedge-hogs are also good friends and birds do much more good than harm, particularly if seedlings and fruiting crops are protected by netting or cotton or a suitable bird-scarer is used. The largest group of pests is formed by insects, most of which develop in four stages, egg, larva or grub, pupa or chrysalis and adult. The grub stage is generally the most damaging for it is then that the insect needs the most food and the adult stage is usually the most infective when the females seek new quarters for egg-laying. Many insects produce more than one generation a year and some, like aphides, produce living young as well as eggs.

From the gardener's point of view, insects are of two kinds, those that bite and eat the tissues of the plant and those that pierce the tissues with their tongues and suck the sap. The first are generally controlled by applying a poison on to their food, the second by applying a toxic substance on to the insects themselves or, in greenhouses, by using a fumigant. A sucking insect cannot be controlled by using a spray or dust designed to act only as a surface poison.

Up to fifty years ago there were very few sprays or dusts capable of controlling diseases and pests satisfactorily, but modern research has given an effective answer in all but a very few cases. A few of the most-recently discovered methods which are highly successful on a commercial scale are however unsuitable for private gardens. Some require the operator to wear special protective clothing and a respirator and others may damage adjoining crops if the spray drifts in the wind. Such remedies are quite safe on farms and market gardens, but may be extremely dangerous in a residential area with its children and domestic pets and where fruit, flowers and vegetables are grown together in a small area and there is always the risk of causing damage to plants in a neighbour's garden. For these reasons, only the safest of the effective treatments are here recommended, but even so, this involves the use of several poisonous or harmful substances and the most sensible plan is to regard them all as dangerous and store them under lock and key.

The mixtures recommended can be made up by the gardener or bought in convenient sizes under various proprietary names. In addition, many other preparations are available. They are carefully manufactured and tested and can be used with every confidence. But since different active principles may be used and the strengths of the concentrate vary, it is most important that the manufacturer's instructions are properly carried out.

Spraying and Dusting Equipment
Even the smallest garden will require some form of equipment for applying spray fluids or dusts, and here again manufacturers nowadays offer a very wide choice.

For large gardens or where there are fruit trees a knapsack-type of sprayer which is strapped to the shoulders and has its own " one-hand " pump and flexible hose and lance is perhaps the most suitable. Smaller machines of the stirrup-pump type are available in many forms and for the small garden there are various types of syringes and "atomisers" which blow the fluid out as a misty spray. All machines and syringes should have a fine as well as a coarse nozzle.

Dusting machines are smaller and lighter. The larger kinds are generally carried on the shoulder and have a " one-hand " bellows and a flexible spout which can be directed up to a tree or down to a ground-level crop. For small-scale work there are many kinds of hand "puffers", some of them being incorporated in the container as bought from the shop.

But whatever method is used the principal aim must be to cover the whole plant thoroughly, including the undersides of the leaves. This can best be done by putting on the spray or the dust in the finest particles possible and for this reason it is important to buy good quality dusts which use a very fine base powder as a carrier or to add a spreading agent to the fluids and use a fine nozzle on the sprayer. The work should be carried out on calm, dry days and dusting should preferably be done in the early morning or evening when the normal dampness on the leaves will help the dust to cling. Once the spray or dust has dried on, only heavy rain will wash it off. Dusts are of course washed off more easily and therefore have to be applied more frequently than sprays, but against this, the job is lighter and quicker.

Essential Precautions
There is no short cut to the control of diseases and pests and since most of them appear at different times of the season on a wide variety of crops and develop in various ways with their most vulnerable stages occurring at different times there is, as yet, no cure-all or once-for-all magic available. With the inevitable but few exceptions, fungicides have no effect on insects, nor insecticides on fungi. Some of the soil fumigants will, however, control many soil insects as well as fungi and it is sometimes possible to incorporate an insecticide with a fungicide when spraying a particular crop, e.g. apples attacked by aphis and scab at the same time.

Soil Sterilization

In the average garden where fruit, flowers, shrubs and vegetables are generally grown close to each other, the control of diseases and pests is not always a straightforward job and certain fundamental precautions are necessary.

1. Winter washes, e.g. tar oils, must be used only in the dormant period and should not be applied to fruit trees if leafy vegetables or herbaceous plants are growing underneath. Spring spraying, e.g. with nicotine, should be done instead.
2. Fruit and ornamental trees or shrubs should never be sprayed with an insecticide while the blossom is open owing to the danger to bees and other pollinating insects.
3. Non-volatile surface poisons such as arsenate of lead must never be applied to a food crop nearing its harvesting time.
4. Insecticides containing BHC (benzene hexachloride) should not be applied to black currants, potatoes or root vegetables nor to trees growing above them as they may taint the crops.
5. DDT and derris should not be used where they may contaminate a stream or ornamental pond containing fish.
6. Boxes or sheds used for storing fruit or vegetables should be cleaned every year with hot water and soda and not with any disinfectant which may affect the flavour of the stored produce.

Fumigants for the Greenhouse

Fumigation is the most convenient way of controlling the more serious pests and diseases in greenhouses, particularly red spider and white fly. Various substances are used, the active principles being nicotine, hydrocyanic acid gas, azobenzene, tetrachlorethane, sulphur, BHC or DDT. They can all be bought as proprietary articles, many of them in the convenient form of "smokes". But as most of them are exceedingly poisonous the maker's instructions must be followed precisely and on no account should a greenhouse or conservatory leading into a dwelling-house be fumigated in this way.

The best time to do the job is in the evening when the plants are dry. Tender plants and those in full flower should be removed and treated separately. The house must be made as airtight as possible and the work done quickly. starting from the far end, and moving towards the door. When finished, the door should be locked. In the morning when the house is opened up ample time must be allowed before going inside.

Soil Fumigants

A different type of fumigation is sometimes used in the open. It is rarely necessary in well-managed gardens, but may be the best way of dealing with the heavy infestations of leather-jackets and wireworms which often occur when old, rough turf or neglected land is broken up. Naphthalene is used in powdered form and raked in. and as it does not harm growing plants (except very young seedlings) it can be used at any time of the year. Formalin and cresylic acid are used as liquids, but as they are harmful to plants when freshly applied they should only be used when the land is uncropped. Both of them, particularly formalin, will control a number of soil fungi.

Soil Sterilization

In greenhouses where plants are grown in beds or borders the soil may become infected with certain serious root diseases or pests like eelworms. It must then either be replaced with fresh clean soil or sterilized. The best sterilization is by steaming, but in a private garden the second best, formalin or cresylic acid, has to be used in the same way as for soil in the open. After sterilizing the house should be well aired for 10–14 days.

Small quantities of soil for potting can be sterilized at home by baking or steaming. Thin layers can be placed on a shovel held over a fire until the soil is just too hot to hold. It must not be overbaked. Alternatively, a bucketful of soil can be suspended for one hour in a copper of boiling water so that the steam envelops it. The copper must be covered over and no water allowed to get into the bucket.

Essential Hygiene

Plants that are well grown and well managed are much less liable to be attacked by diseases or pests than those which are unhappy in their surroundings. But even the strongest are by no means immune and everything possible must be done to prevent trouble or to act as soon as it is seen. General tidiness does much to remove potential sources of infection. Weeds should be kept down, hedges trimmed and cleared of rubbish at their base, and boxes, pots, stakes, etc., kept clean and stacked tidily instead of being left lying about the garden.

Very often, the prompt removal and burning of an attacked shoot or plant will prevent any further spread, and sometimes it may pay to scrap an unhealthy crop entirely and buy in fresh, clean plants or follow with a different crop altogether. Broken branches on trees and shrubs or accidental wounds should be pared off smoothly and covered with white lead paint or grafting wax, and as soon as flowers or vegetables are finished the remnants should be taken up and composted. Anything showing signs of rotting, such as rotten fruit or slimy growth, should be collected and burned.

Pests and Diseases
(*Arranged in Alphabetical Order*)

Ants

Ants do not attack plants themselves but cause damage by helping to spread aphids which they often " nurse " for the honeydew, and they may tunnel among the roots of young seedlings.

Treatment—The nests must be destroyed with boiling water, liquid derris, paraffin, sodium cyanide or a proprietary " ant killer ". If the nest cannot be discovered, a little sugar should be sprinkled about; the ants will carry this away to their homes.

Aphides

These are the well-known Greenfly or Blackfly, which attack a wide range of both outdoor and greenhouse plants. They may be black, green, reddish, almost white or bluish. There are several generations a year, with or without wings. They feed by sucking the sap and in so doing frequently spread virus diseases. They occur on the roots of some plants, e.g. lettuces and brassicas, as well as above ground. Most of them exude a sticky " honeydew " on which sooty moulds frequently grow, further spoiling the appearance of the plant. The Woolly Aphis, commonly seen on apple trees, exudes a white fluffy covering.

Apple and Pear Scab

Symptoms—Attacks generally start on the undersides of the leaves or tips of the shoots. Curling and malformation follow, making spraying difficult. Prompt attention is therefore essential.

Treatment—Spray or dust with nicotine, derris or malathion. Several applications may be necessary. On fruit trees the routine winter-washing must not be missed, and in greenhouses annual fumigation should be carried out.

Apple Blossom Weevil

A dark-coloured weevil about ¼ in. long, covered with greyish hairs with a yellowish V-shaped mark across the wing cases. The insect has a long snout which the female uses to bore a hole in the flower bud ready for laying an egg. Usually only one egg is laid in each bud. Pears, quinces, and medlars are sometimes attacked but apples suffer the most.

Symptoms—When the grub hatches it feeds on the growing flower which wilts, turns brown and fails to develop a fruit. The brown petals form a " cap " under which a grub is usually found.

Treatment—Spray with DDT just before buds begin to burst, or dust with a 5% DDT dust when the flower buds are " breaking " and again just before bursting. An alternative method is to tie bands of sacking or corrugated paper around the trunks in June, to offer shelter for the adults. Remove and burn the bands in Oct.

Apple Sawfly

The adult insect is about ¼ in. long, black, with legs and underside yellowish red. It appears at blossom time, laying its eggs, one to a flower. The grub is creamy white with a black head which later becomes brown.

Symptoms—The grub tunnels into the developing fruit which often shows the tunnelling as a ribbon-like scar. By June the attacked fruits show a hole from which dirty brown "frass" exudes. One grub may attack several fruits. When fully fed it drops to the ground and pupates in the soil.

Treatment—In small gardens, affected fruits should be picked or gathered up and burned. On a larger scale, nicotine or B.H.C. should be used at petal fall or within the next few days.

Note—The damage done by Apple Sawfly must be distinguished from that of Codling Moth (*see* p. 92) because the control measures are different.

Apple and Pear Scab

Two species of fungi are concerned, each confined to its own host. Infection can occur at any time during the growing season, the winter stage being passed under the bark or on fallen leaves. Many of the best varieties suffer the worst.

Symptoms—As the leaves develop, dark olive-green patches appear and later become brownish or black. Blister-like swellings and cracks occur on the shoots. Later the fruits are attacked, the skin becoming cracked or covered with scattered dark or black spots.

Treatment—Diseased material should be collected and burned, and the trees sprayed with lime-sulphur or captan at the following stages of growth:

1. When the flower buds are fully developed but still green, lime-sulphur 1 gallon to 40 gallons of water.

2. When the flower buds are showing pink but have not opened, lime-sulphur 1 gallon to 50 gallons of water.

3. When most of the petals have fallen, lime-sulphur 1 gallon to 100 gallons of water.

As far as possible, the sprayings should be spaced at intervals of 14 days, and on no account must heavier concentrations be used otherwise damage will be done to some varieties. Doyenne du Comice pears must not be sprayed with lime-sulphur but with colloidal sulphur.

Apple Sucker

Small flattened yellowish insects which are often seen around the young leaves and blossoms. They excrete a sticky fluid and white waxy threads. Later they become green and when adult have wings. Small, oval, creamy eggs are laid in the autumn on the fruit spurs.

Symptoms—Flower buds die or fail to set fruit. A badly-attacked tree looks as though it had been damaged by frost.

Treatment—The best control is obtained by routine spraying with a winter wash. If this has been missed spray in spring just before the blossoms burst, with nicotine, malathion or B.H.C.

Asparagus Beetle

The beetle is about ⅛ in. long and has a greenish-black head and orange wings with black bars. The eggs are greenish black and and laid in rows on the shoots of asparagus.

Symptoms—The beetles eat the buds and later the grubs feed on the foliage.

Treatment—Spray or dust with derris or pyrethrum. After cutting is finished malathion can be used. As the beetles hibernate in old stems or surrounding rubbish, the beds and the garden around must be kept tidy.

Bacterial Rots

Most of the more common bacterial diseases of plants cause varying forms of wet or slimy rot. The first visible sign may be a sudden wilting, and at this stage discoloured tissues are usually seen if the affected part is cut across. Many herbaceous plants and vegetables are attacked, especially potatoes (Blackleg), cucumbers under glass (Wilt), rhubarb (Crown Rot), French beans (Halo Blight), carrots, onions, iris and other bulbs. The "drier" forms of bacterial diseases produce typical cankers on trees and shrubs (*see* Die-back) or gall on the roots of fruit and other trees, roses and certain root vegetables such as beetroot (Crown Gall).

Treatment—The only satisfactory method is to remove and burn infected plants. After completing the work, the hands and any tools used should be disinfected in formalin (2%).

Bean Weevil

The beetles are small, about ¼ in. long, generally yellowish-brown with striped wing-cases, and the short snout characteristic of weevils. They attack peas as well as beans, but are only serious on seedling plants.

Symptoms—The beetles eat circular patches from the edges of the leaves which take on a scalloped appearance.

Treatment—Good cultivation and manuring to help the crop grow away quickly is generally sufficient. In cold, slow-growing weather, the plants should be sprayed or dusted with DDT.

Beet Fly

A greyish-black fly about ¼ in. long lays its eggs on the underside of the leaves of beetroot in the seedling or young stages. There are two or three generations a year.

Brown Rot

Symptoms—Pale blotches appear on the leaves caused by the grubs burrowing in between the surfaces. The plants wither and may die.

Treatment—Hoe regularly and top-dress with nitrate of soda to help the plants grow away quickly.

Big Bud
This is caused by the Black Currant Gall Mite which is widespread throughout the country. It is minute, just too small to be visible to the naked eye, and its main host is black currants. Red and white currants and gooseberries are occasionally attacked.

Symptoms—The mites live in the buds which swell to about twice the normal size and fail to open normally. In the following spring, the infested buds dry up and die and the mites move on to fresh buds.

Treatment—On a small scale hand-picking of all infested buds if done in good time will reduce attacks, but the best control is by spraying with lime-sulphur (1% solution) when the leaves are about as big as a two-shilling piece and before the flowers open. The mites are then exposed as they begin to move to fresh buds. Some scorching may result and the crop be reduced, but in the following year spraying should be unnecessary and a full crop be obtained. In severe cases the bushes should be grubbed and burned and replaced by healthy stock.

See Reversion, a virus disease which can be spread by these mites.

Black Spot
Roses may sometimes be seriously affected. Some varieties are more resistant than others.

Symptoms—Black spots or blotches appear on the leaves and sometimes on the shoots.

Treatment—Spray with Bordeaux or captan. Remove and burn affected shoots and all fallen leaves.

Blossom Wilt
The many separate strains of this disease affect cherries, plums, apricots, peaches, pears and apples including many of the ornamental varieties. They are closely related to the fungi causing Wither Tip in plums and Brown Rot, and their severity varies widely from year to year. The most important is the Blossom Wilt of apples.

Symptoms—The fungus enters the flower and soon the surrounding leaves wilt and droop. The fruiting spurs become infected and may be killed. In bad attacks the disease may spread along the whole shoot. Spores develop on the infected areas and spread the disease.

Treatment—Cut out and burn all infected parts, cutting back to sound healthy wood.

Routine spraying with winter wash and lime-sulphur also has some control.

Brown Rot
Different species and strains of the fungi causing Blossom Wilt attack the fruits of apples, pears, plums and cherries and less frequently peaches, nectarines, almonds and quinces.

Symptoms—Whitish, yellow or grey pustules appear on the fruits, generally in rings. The infected fruits drop off or shrivel and remain on the trees as "mummied" fruits, to act as the source of infection in the following year. The disease also occurs among apples in store, the fruits showing the characteristic rotting or turning black.

Treatment—Collect or cut out and burn all diseased material. Examine fruit in store regularly every two or three weeks.

Bulb Mite
These small, round, shiny, yellowish mites often occur as a secondary pest, attacking hyacinths, lilies, narcissi and tulips which have first been damaged in some other way.
Symptoms—The mites swarm between the scales of the bulbs either in store or when growing, often causing serious rotting.
Treatment—Infested bulbs should be burned and where possible all others which may have been in contact should be fumigated in an air-tight container with paradichlorbenzene or immersed in hot water kept at 110° F. for one hour. All bulbs must be treated carefully to avoid damage.

Cabbage Caterpillar
These are the well-known larvæ of the Cabbage White butterflies and the Cabbage moth. They are found on all brassicas and are common on nasturtiums (Tropæolum).
Symptoms—The eggs are laid on the leaves, and the caterpillars not only eat the leaves but also spoil the crop with their excreta.
Treatment—Early action is essential before the caterpillars get into the hearts. The eggs and larvæ may be crushed or picked off by hand or the plants sprayed or dusted with nicotine, derris or pyrethrum. (Nicotine should not be used near harvest time.)

Cabbage Root Fly
This is a serious pest of all brassicas, especially cabbage and cauliflower. The fly is ashy-grey, about ¼ in. long and like a small house-fly. There are two or three generations a year.
Symptoms—Attacked plants look blue and stop growing. The leaves flag. If the plant is taken up white, legless maggots about ⅓ in. long will be found around the root or inside. The root may be partly eaten or tunnelled, or almost severed.
Treatment—Sprinkle calomel dust around the stem of each plant in a ring about 1 in. wide. Any later-planted crops should be treated in this way at planting time.

Cabbage White Fly
In warm sheltered gardens a small white fly often occurs on brassica crops, the eggs and larvæ being found on the undersides of the leaves. Usually no harm is done, except when the larvæ get into the hearts.
Treatment—Spraying is rarely satisfactory as it is difficult to hit the flies. Generally a good control can be obtained by pulling off and burning the lower leaves. Stumps from an infested crop should be burnt.

Canker
The word canker is loosely used to cover any kind of wound surrounded by swollen bark or callus. It may be caused by mechanical injury when the wound usually heals naturally or by certain fungi or Woolly Aphis. Cankers due to fungi occur on cabbages and turnips and on fruit trees, principally apples and pears. The so-called canker of parsnips is a physiological disorder common on wet soils deficient in lime.
Symptoms—Small depressed areas occur in the bark and extend to form a ragged wound which often encircles the branch or twig. Whitish pustules appear followed by small, round, red bodies.

Chafer Beetles

Treatment—As the fungus enters through wounds, any breakages in the branches and the cut surfaces made by pruning should be coated with grafting wax or white lead paint. Insects, especially Woolly Aphis, must be kept down. Poor growing conditions, such as bad drainage, appear to favour the disease.

Where the infected branches are small they should be cut well back to healthy wood. On large branches the infected areas may be cut out with a chisel. Badly attacked trees should be grubbed. All infected material must be burned.

Capsid Bugs

Several species of capsids, all about ¼ in. long but varying in colour from green to reddish-brown, attack many garden plants.

Symptoms—In most cases rusty-looking pin-prick holes occur on the leaves. On apples rough scars also appear on the surface of the fruit. Frequently the growing point of a plant is damaged and poor or malformed growth follows.

Treatment—Spray or dust with nicotine, covering also the soil around the plants as the capsids are very active and usually drop off the plants when disturbed. On fruit trees winter spraying will help by controlling the egg stage.

Carrot Fly

A shiny, greenish-black fly about ¼ in. long, with yellowish legs appears in May and again in Aug. when the second generation occurs. It lays its eggs on or near carrots.

Symptoms—The foliage wilts and turns reddish in colour. A lifted root will show a number of small colourless maggots burrowing into the flesh.

Treatment—In badly-infested areas the crop should not be sown before the end of May. This will avoid the first generation. Seed should be sown thinly so as to avoid or reduce singling which bruises the seedlings and sets free the smell of carrots which attracts the flies. Burn any thinnings. Aldrin or naphthalene sprinkled along the rows at fortnightly intervals to the end of June, or frequent dusting with soot will act as repellents.

Celery Beetle

A small steel-blue beetle about ⅛ in. long which normally feeds on weeds may attack celery and occasionally carrots and parsnips during July and Aug.

Symptoms—The leaves and the stems are eaten.

Treatment—Dust with derris. (Lead arsenate may be used on young plants.)

Celery Fly—*See* Leaf-miners.

Centipedes—*See* Millepedes.

Chafer Beetles

There are four species. The adults vary from ½ to 1 in. long. All have hard brownish wing-cases except the Rose Chafer which is green. The beetles feed on the leaves of many trees and shrubs and the fleshy, white, curved brown-headed grubs feed on the roots of many plants.

Symptoms—The plant suddenly wilts and on being dug up a grub is often found. The root is often cut right through.

91

Treatment—The grubs should be collected whenever possible. In bad "chafer years" naphthalene should be dusted around the crops.

Cherry Sawfly—See Slugworms.

Chocolate Spot
Occasionally this disease is serious on broad beans, if the season is wet.
Symptoms—Chocolate-coloured spots appear on the leaves and sometimes on the stems and pods. The flowers may fall.
Treatment—Top-dress with sulphate of potash and burn the haulm after harvesting.

Chrysanthemum Midge
A small brownish fly, about $\frac{1}{10}$ in. long, with a red abdomen, may attack chrysanthemums in greenhouses where it breeds all the year round. Occasionally in dry summers it may be found out of doors.
Symptoms—The larvæ burrow into the leaves or shoots and as they grow cause cone-shaped swellings which lead to malformation of the buds and flowers.
Treatment—Remove galls and spray every week with nicotine or BHC.

Club Root
Sometimes called Finger and Toe, this is a common and generally well-known disease, favoured by an acid condition of the soil. The cabbage family, turnips, swedes and radishes are the most important of the susceptible crops, but any cruciferous plant is liable to attack. Many weeds such as charlock and shepherd's purse can also become infected and occasionally the disease is found on wallflowers, stocks, candytuft, etc.
Symptoms—The plants look stunted and unhappy. Swellings of various shapes occur on the roots or on the stems at ground level, later becoming slimy as they decay. If cut through the swelling is solid and often has a marbled appearance, thus differing from the swelling caused by Gall Weevils which is hollow and usually has a maggot inside.
Treatment—The lime content of the soil must be kept up by regular dressings, and susceptible crops should be spaced as far apart as possible in the rotation. In severe cases plants should be dipped in a paste of calomel before being planted out.

Codling Moth
The moth is brown-grey with a coppery tip to the wings. Eggs are laid in June and July and the grub enters the fruit through the side or the eye, and burrows into the core. Apples, including the ornamental species, are most generally attacked, but pears, quince and walnut may occasionally suffer.
Symptoms—When fully fed the larva burrows its way out of the fruit which may stay on the tree or fall. It leaves a characteristic hole with no "frass" showing.
Treatment—As the larva hibernates in cracks in the bark or in rubbish such as dead leaves on the ground, general tidiness is essential. Trees with rough, moss-covered bark should be sprayed with tar oil in winter. In bad attacks lead arsenate should be sprayed on to the blossoms 14 days after petal-fall. (*Note*—Codling Moth should be compared with Apple Sawfly. Codling Moth occurs later and its grub has eight pairs of legs while that of the Sawfly has ten. Fruits attacked by Codling Moth do not show frass

Deficiency Diseases

exuding from the hole in the flesh and if cut across the destroyed part will be mainly in the centre around the core.)

Coral Spot
The disease attacks a wide range of ornamental, forest and fruit trees and shrubs. It is particularly common on red currants, and often enters through wounds or breakage of branches.

Symptoms—Branches often wilt suddenly and die. When the wood is dead, pink to red pustules appear. These are full of spores which are later released and so spread infection.

Treatment—All wilting and dead branches should be cut out as soon as possible and burned. As the fungus can also live on dead twigs, or old stakes and posts, tidiness in the garden is essential. New stakes and posts should be treated with a preservative.

Cuckoo Spit
The small, pale greenish-yellow larva of the Frog-hopper attacks many plants, especially herbaceous plants, sucking the sap and surrounding itself with a white froth. Not usually serious.

Symptoms—The froth is generally seen towards the top of the shoots.

Treatment—Spray forcibly with nicotine or B.H.C.

Currant Moths
The Currant Clearwing and the Currant Shoot Borer are two moths which sometimes cause appreciable loss but are generally of little importance. The life histories are different but the caterpillars of both tunnel into the young shoots causing them to wilt and die.

Treatment—Cut off and burn infested shoots.

Cutworms or Surface Caterpillars
This heading covers the caterpillars of several different moths. They are mostly grey to black and generally feed at night on a wide range of plants.

Symptoms—Seedlings and young plants suddenly wilt and are found to be eaten at or just below ground level.

Treatment—Collect the caterpillars to be found around any wilted plant and set baits of Paris Green and bran or dust with Aldrin.

Damping-off
Several different fungi are concerned and a wide range of plants in the seedling stage may be affected.

Symptoms—The fungi attack the seedlings at ground level and a sudden collapse of the stem follows.

Treatment—Good growing and general hygiene are essential. Under glass ample ventilation must be given and excessive moisture avoided. Seeds should be sown in sterilized soil or watered with Cheshunt Compound or captan.

Deficiency Diseases
This term is used to cover a wide range of non-parasitic disorders due to the lack of any one essential plant food leading to unnatural or malformed growth. Among the most common are:

Leaf-scorch. Many trees and shrubs may show dry, yellow to reddish-brown leaves due to lack of potash.

Blotchy Ripening in tomatoes may be due to lack of potash or less commonly of nitrogen.

93

Brown Heart of turnips and swedes due to lack of boron may cause the roots to be tough and bitter after being cooked. Beetroot may suffer in a similar way.

Chlorosis or patchiness in the leaves may be due to lack of lime or iron.

Whiptail of cauliflowers may be due to lack of molybdenum causing the young plants to go blind and show malformed leaves.

Treatment—A proper system of manuring must be carried out. The trace elements, such as boron, are required only in minute quantities and are best applied in the form of good farmyard manure and organic fertilizers, e.g. hoof and horn, shoddy, blood, bonemeal, etc.

Die-back

This term is used to describe various kinds of sudden die-back in the young shoots of many trees and shrubs. They may be due to poor soil or cultivation or caused by certain bacteria and fungi. The effects often resemble those of canker.

Treatment—Cut out and burn affected shoots and branches.

Dry Rot of Potatoes

The early varieties are the more susceptible and the disease is most noticeable during the storage period.

Symptoms—Infected tubers shrink and shrivel, the sunken areas showing white or pinkish pustules.

Treatment—All tubers in store should be examined regularly and infected ones removed and burned. Suspected tubers should never be used for seed as the rot is progressive and will lead to misses in the rows. Potatoes should always be handled carefully as infection easily enters through wounds.

Earthworms

Earthworms are entirely beneficial. Their burrowing helps to drain and aerate the soil and they pull down large quantities of decaying vegetable matter for their food. But their cases can sometimes spoil the appearance of a lawn or interfere with games.

Treatment—Regular brushing is generally sufficient, but where large numbers are present the lawn should be dressed with a proprietary worm-killer or potassium permangate ¼ oz. to 1 gal. of water for every square yard. Poisons such as lead arsenate or copper sulphate should be avoided as the dead worms will be poisonous to birds or poultry.

Earwigs

Earwigs feed at night and hide during the day under leaves, in canes, boxes or rubbish. They are generally most troublesome on greenhouse plants, but also attack many plants grown out-of-doors.

Symptoms—The leaves show holes and eaten areas and the flowers become ragged or malformed.

Treatment—All dead leaves and rubbish should be cleared up and the plants sprayed or dusted with DDT. Large numbers of earwigs may be trapped in pieces of sacking or crumpled paper or in plant pots loosely stuffed with straw and set up on canes.

Eelworms

There are many different species and strains of eelworms and several of them cause serious damage to cultivated plants. Generally speaking, they keep to their own host-plants or groups of plants, and if in the course of rotational cropping these are not grown in the infested soil the eelworms

Greenhouse White Fly

can still exist as dormant cysts for a few years. All species are minute, the largest being just visible to the naked eye. They can live within the plant tissue or encysted in the soil, so that they are easily and quickly spread.

Symptoms—The Stem and Bulb Eelworm causes stunted, malformed growth in a large number of herbaceous and bulbous plants. The leaves are often narrow and twisted and the stems split or wiry-looking. The Leaf Blotch Eelworm causes brown or black areas in the leaves of many greenhouse plants, including ferns, and a related species causes similar and often very serious damage to chrysanthemums which generally also show malformed flowers. The Root-knot Eelworm causes galls on the roots of many plants, particularly tomatoes, cucumbers and flowers grown in greenhouses. In bad attacks the whole root system is affected, the plant wilts and may even die. Another species attacks the buds of currants and yet another may be extremely serious on potatoes by stunting the growth so much that little or no crop is obtained. In this case the females can often be seen as minute whitish to brownish spherical bodies on the roots or tubers.

Treatment—There is no known cure. All plants bought in should be purchased from reliable sources. Susceptible crops should not be planted in infested soil for 3–5 years and in the vegetable garden a long rotation should be strictly followed. Greenhouse borders should be sterilized.

Flea Beetles
Several species of small, black or blue-black beetles about $\frac{1}{16}$ in. long, with yellowish stripes on the wing-cases, attack many plants especially the cabbage family, turnips, beetroot and several herbaceous plants. They are most destructive to seedlings.

Symptoms—The leaves show small holes as well as eaten areas. The plants look blue.

Treatment—As the beetles hibernate in rubbish, hedges, etc., a clean, tidy garden is essential. Seedlings should be sprayed or dusted with derris, B.H.C. or DDT once a fortnight for as long as necessary.

Gooseberry Sawfly
This is a common pest which may be very destructive if not controlled in the early stages. It occasionally attacks currants also. The fly is typical of many sawflies, black and yellowish in colour and $\frac{1}{4}$ in. long. The caterpillars are green at first with black spots. Later the spots disappear and small orange-coloured areas develop at both ends. There are generally three generations a year.

Symptoms—The caterpillars feed on the leaves and shoots and if unchecked may strip the whole bush of its foliage.

Treatment—Spray or dust with derris or DDT. On a small scale the caterpillars can be picked off by hand.

Note—It is important to distinguish the caterpillars of this sawfly from those of the Magpie Moth which are black, white and yellow, for although the control measures are the same, there is only one generation of Magpie Moths a year, whereas the sawflies will continue to demand attention.

Grease Banding—See Winter Moth.

Greenfly—See Aphides.

Greenhouse White Fly
This white waxy-looking fly about $\frac{1}{25}$ in. long attacks many greenhouse

95

plants. It is distinct from the Cabbage White Fly and cannot survive the winter out of doors.

Symptoms—The larvæ suck the sap, causing the leaves to lose colour and look spotted. The flies fly readily when disturbed.

Treatment—Fumigate the greenhouse with hydrocyanic acid gas or tetra-chlorethane.

Grey Mould

Although a number of outdoor plants, particularly lettuce, are attacked the greatest amount of damage is done to fruit, flowers and vegetables growing under glass.

Symptoms—A greyish velvety fungus develops and leads to decay.

Treatment—Infected material should be removed and burned. Under glass ample ventilation must be given and humidity reduced.

Lackey Moth

Although always present, especially in the south, this yellowish to reddish-brown moth with a wing-span of 1¼ in., does little harm until a year comes when it assumes epidemic proportions. Most kinds of fruit trees and several kinds of forest and ornamental trees are attacked.

Symptoms—The eggs, which are easily seen, are laid on young shoots in the form of a bracelet made up of 100–150 eggs. When hatched, the caterpillars keep together spinning a web to form a tent in which they live. As they eat the foliage they move on, spinning another tent. The caterpillars are bluish-grey with white and orange stripes.

Treatment—The best control is to break-up the "tents" and destroy the caterpillars by hand. Spraying with lead arsenate or DDT must be done early to be effective. In winter the egg-bracelets should be cut off and destroyed.

Leaf Galls

Many different kinds of galls and swellings may often be seen on the leaves of a number of ornamental trees and shrubs. They are caused by various species of Gall-wasps, Gall-midges and Gall-mites, but only very rarely does any harm result.

Treatment—If a young and valuable tree is seriously attacked by gall-wasps or gall-midges, it should be sprayed with nicotine. If the galls are caused by gall-mites it should be sprayed with 5% lime-sulphur.

Leaf-miners

The larvæ of many different species of moths, weevils and flies are loosely but conveniently classed as Leaf-miners. They attack a wide range of plants, among them apples, roses, shrubs, herbaceous plants and vegetables. Chrysanthemum, cineraria, azalea, celery and beetroot are probably the most important.

Symptoms—The larvæ live on the inner tissue of the leaf between the upper and lower surfaces, making characteristic tunnels or mines as they move along.

Treatment—Weeds must be kept down since many of them can act as host plants. On a small scale the larvæ can be crushed in their mines with the finger and thumb or affected leaves can be picked off and burned. A quick-acting top-dressing can be applied to help the crop along and soot can be dusted over to repel the egg-laying adults. On a larger scale or when the attack is severe the crop should be sprayed with nicotine or malathion.

96

PLATE 5 LAYING TURF To enable the soil to be levelled with accuracy pegs of uniform height should be hammered into the ground, *above left*. The soil may then be raked up to the level of the pegs, *above right*.

The pegs should be checked with a spirit level, *above left*. See that the ground is firm, with a fine tilth on top, before the turves are laid, *above right*. The edge of each row of turves should be straightened, *below left*, and firmed down lightly with the back of a spade, *below right*.

PLATE 6 ROOT DIVISION
Left, the clumps should be lifted with as much root as possible in late autumn or in early spring. Care must be taken not to damage the fibrous roots unnecessarily.

Below, the roots are then cut or preferably levered apart by means of two forks.

Above, with certain plants the roots may be further separated by hand, but the roots must not be left exposed to the air for long or they will become dry and useless.

Magpie Moth

Leaf Mould of Tomatoes
The fungus often causes severe losses in tomatoes under glass. It is rarely seen on the outdoor crop.

Symptoms—Yellowish spots which later take on a purplish tinge, appear on the leaves in June or July. On the undersides a grey mould appears. The affected parts dry out and the leaves shrivel or die.

Treatment—The atmosphere must not get too warm or too humid. Ventilation should always be given and as soon as the disease appears must be increased. Overhead spraying must be stopped and watering reduced. The lower leaves should be stripped. If necessary a colloidal copper spray should be used at intervals of 10–14 days. At the end of the season the house should be washed down with formalin or fumigated with sulphur. Resistant varieties are obtainable.

Leaf Roller—*See* Slugworms and Tortrix.

Leaf Spots
Several different fungi attack different crops, including many herbaceous plants, but the disease is not generally serious. Celery and chrysanthemums are perhaps the most important.

Symptoms—Brown, round spots appear on the leaves and occasionally on the stems.

Treatment—With most plants good growing is generally a sufficient control. In severe attacks Bordeaux Mixture should be used. With celery the disease is carried in the seed, and care should be taken to buy from a reputable source.

Leather Jackets
These are the well-known dirty-brown or greyish-black legless grubs of the Daddy Longlegs or Crane Flies. They have a tough, leathery skin, are about 1 to 1½ in. long, and feed on the roots of a wide range of plants.

Symptoms—The plant suddenly wilts and if dug up a grub can often be found or it may have moved on to the next plant.

Treatment—General cleanliness and regular hoeing is normally sufficient. Bad attacks often follow the breaking up of old or neglected turf when baits of Paris Green should be used or aldrin applied.

Leopard Moth
The wings are white with bluish-black spots and have a span of 2½ in. The moths appear in June and July and lay eggs on fruit trees, especially apples, and many ornamental and forest trees. The caterpillars are yellowish-white with black spots and grow to 2 in. long. They tunnel into the shoots and branches where they stay for 2 or 3 years.

Symptoms—The foliage turns yellow and wilts and on young trees sawdust or frass may be seen. On cutting open infested branches the tunnels may be seen.

Treatment—Cut out and burn infested branches. In severe attacks it may be necessary to grub and burn the whole tree.

Magpie Moth
The caterpillars of this well-known black, white and yellow moth feed on the leaves of currants, gooseberries, laurels, apricots, nuts and other plants and if neglected may cause serious defoliation. There is one generation a year beginning in July or Aug. when the eggs are laid.

Symptoms—The caterpillars are at first small and black. They feed till the autumn, then hibernate on the bark or dead leaves and emerge again in the spring when they feed on the young growth, become much larger and black and white with a yellow stripe. They pupate generally on the tree and the moth emerges in July.

Treatment—As soon as the caterpillars are seen, spray or dust with derris or DDT. On a small scale the caterpillars may be picked off by hand.

Mealy Bug

These small, scale-like insects have a white, waxy covering, are fairly active and breed throughout the year. They occur principally in glasshouses, especially on vines, but are also found out of doors on Ribes, Ceanothus, Robinia, Laburnum and less commonly on other shrubs. They feed by sucking the sap and may occur on the roots as well as the foliage.

Treatment—Repeated spraying with nicotine or malathion. In addition glasshouses should be fumigated with hydrocyanic acid gas at the end of the season.

Mildew

The mildews which occur on a great number of trees, shrubs and plants can be very broadly divided into two types: the Powdery mildews where the fungi live on the surface of the foliage, spoiling the appearance rather than causing serious harm, and the Downy mildews, which are more deep-seated, live within the tissues and as a rule are far more serious. Powdery mildews are found on roses, vines, apples, gooseberries, marrows, turnips, strawberries, chrysanthemums, asters, calendulas and many other plants. Downy mildews appear on brassica seedlings, lettuce, onions, spinach, vines, wallflowers, stocks, etc.

Symptoms—The Powdery mildews generally produce a whitish to greyish powdery effect on the foliage while the Downy mildews cause yellowish patches on the leaves with (generally) a greyish or purplish downy growth on the underside.

Treatment—For Powdery mildews dust with sulphur and remove any badly-infected shoots. For Downy mildews remove all infected plants and shoots and spray with Bordeaux Mixture or dust with a copper-lime dust. In both cases, avoid overcrowding and under glass give ample ventilation and reduce humidity.

Millepedes

Millepedes attack the leaves of seedlings and the roots of a large number of plants and frequently eat into bulbs. They often extend the damage caused by wounds or other insects and generally set up decay. They must be distinguished from centipedes which are beneficial. (Centipedes are flat in appearance, have one pair of legs to each body segment and are very active; millepedes have two pairs of legs to each segment, are more rounded and usually curl up when disturbed.)

Treatment—Regular hoeing and good cultivation is generally sufficient. In bad attacks the soil should be dressed with aldrin dust or seedlings may be dusted with DDT. Large numbers may be trapped in pieces of potato or carrot buried in the soil. These baits should be marked and examined every few days.

Mosquitoes

Mosquitoes, particularly the blood-sucking females, are a pest of the gardener and not of the plants he grows. In some gardens where there are ponds, streams or exposed water and liquid-manure tanks they can be a great nuisance. The larvæ, sometimes called "wrigglers", live and feed in the water, continually rising to the surface to breathe through their tails.

Treatment—Fish in ponds will readily eat all the eggs and larvæ they can reach, and they should be helped by preventing plants from spreading over the surface of the water and providing hiding-places for the pest. DDT may be sprayed on to the water *only* where there is no danger of its coming into contact with fish.

Mushroom Flies

Several species of small black flies about ¼ in. long, which normally live on decaying vegetable matter, will attack mushrooms.

Symptoms—The larvæ eat into the stems and set up decay.

Treatment—Doors and ventilators should be screened with fine gauze or muslin and the beds sprayed or dusted with derris, pyrethrum or DDT. In severe attacks it may be necessary to fumigate with hydrocyanic acid gas.

Mushroom Mites

Several species of mites often occur on mushroom beds, usually introduced in the manure. Slow-moving grey or white mites are the most harmful, but they have their own enemies—the more active brown mites which are therefore beneficial.

Symptoms—The mites tunnel into the stalks and caps and the mushrooms turn brown.

Treatment—Fumigation is of doubtful value. Derris or pyrethrum dust gives some control but the best method is to clean the shed and equipment thoroughly with boiling water.

Mushroom Moulds

The White Plaster mould may appear as a whitish powder on the surface of the bed at spawning time and the Brown Plaster mould may occur on the compost as a white fluff which later turns brown. Both these fungi rob the crop of its nutriment but neither is usually serious, and good growing is normally a sufficient control.

But there is another White mould or Mycogone which grows vigorously, completely covering the mushrooms and ruining the crop. The only control is to remove and burn all infected material and when the crop is finished to disinfect the house, boxes, trays, etc., with formalin or cresylic acid.

Narcissus Flies

There are three kinds: the large Narcissus fly which confines its attacks to narcissi (which include daffodils) and two smaller ones, known as Small Bulb flies which may also attack other bulbs and occasionally some of the root vegetables.

The Large Fly resembles a small "bumble" bee. It lays eggs in May and June singly on or near a bulb. The larva burrows in and eats out the centre of the bulb. The Small flies appear earlier, are more like Hover flies and lay several eggs to each bulb.

Symptoms—Bulbs which show weak or distorted growth in spring should be lifted. If soft they will probably contain the larva or chrysalis of the Large fly or if rotten they may show the presence of the Small flies. At the planting time the bulbs should be pressed gently; those which feel soft and springy may contain the hibernating larva of the Large fly.

Treatment—Discard all suspicious bulbs. In bad attacks, dust with BHC or DDT dusts every fortnight from end Apr. to end June. Where possible suspected stocks may be given the hot-water treatment before planting, by being immersed for 1 hour in water kept at 110° F.

Onion Fly
A small grey fly with black and brown markings, resembling a house-fly, may attack onions, leeks and shallots from spring onwards. The eggs are laid on the young leaves and stems. There are three generations.
Symptoms—Dirty-white maggots about ¼ in. long burrow into the bulb. The leaves and stems turn yellow, seedlings may be killed and the bulbs begin to rot.
Treatment—Remove and burn infected plants, taking care not to leave any maggots in the soil. Dust with calomel or aldrin and grow the next crop as far away from the site as possible.

Onion Smut
Onions, leeks, shallots and chives are attacked in the seedling stages and serious losses may occur. The disease is not general.
Symptoms—Dark, greyish stripes occur on leaves, which begin to wilt.
Treatment—Remove and burn infected plants. Susceptible crops should not be grown on the same site again, as infection remains in the soil for many years.

Pea Moth
A grey-brown moth about ¼ in. long may be seen fluttering over the crop from mid-June to mid-Aug.
Symptoms—The caterpillars eat into the pods and feed on the developing peas, causing the damage that is so well known.
Treatment—Regular hoeing will destroy many of the larvæ which, when fully fed, leave the plant to pupate in the soil. In bad areas damage can be largely avoided by sowing only early and late crops and missing out mid-season varieties. Spraying with DDT or nicotine gives only a partial control.

Pea Weevil—*See* Bean Weevil.

Peach Leaf Curl
Sometimes called Peach Leaf Blister, this disease is caused by a fungus which attacks peaches, nectarines, almonds and occasionally other species of Prunus.
Symptoms—The leaves become swollen, curled or malformed, look blistered and change to a reddish colour. The flowers and fruits may sometimes be affected.
Treatment—Spray with Captan or Bordeaux mixture in Feb. or Mar. as soon as the buds begin to swell.

Pear Leaf Blister Mite
This may be a troublesome pest in the south of the country especially on cordons or trees trained against a wall. Apples, cotoneaster and some other trees may also be attacked. The mite is microscopic, hibernates at the base of a bud and begins to feed as the new growth develops. There are several generations a year.
Symptoms—The mite burrows into the leaf, causing green or reddish

Potato Scab

blisters, which later turn brown or black. Young fruits and stalks may also be attacked.

Treatment—Lime-sulphur (5% solution) should be sprayed on just before the buds open' (usually in early Mar.). Slight attacks can be controlled by the early removal and burning of affected leaves.

Pear Midge

The minute black adults, typical of "midges", lay their eggs at blossom time. The maggots burrow into the developing fruits. Mid-season varieties suffer most.

Symptoms—Attacked fruitlets have a flattened appearance. Most of them fall to the ground. If cut open they generally show the maggots inside.

Treatment—As the maggots pupate in the soil regular hoeing will destroy most of them. All infested fruits should be collected and burned. Alternatively, the soil may be sprayed with tar-oil wash, covering an area a little greater than the spread of the tree, or the tree may be sprayed with DDT. (Tar oil must not be applied to the trees at this time of year.)

Physiological Disorders

Poor conditions, lack of air or water, unsuitable temperatures in greenhouses or an abnormal climate out of doors, will produce certain well-recognized disorders in many plants. None of them is infectious.

Tomatoes seem particularly subject: irregular watering and excess of nitrogen often causes a premature Blossom Drop, and too much heat and humidity may cause a blister-like oedema on the leaves and sometimes on the fruit. Potato tubers may show various forms of cracking or malformation, generally due to excessive moisture after a dry spell, or the flesh may show a discoloration which is probably caused by lack of humus. Many fruits may suffer from sun-scald, causing discoloration of the skin or glassy patches. Apples are subject to various kinds of breakdown, particularly in store, one of the commonest being Bitter-pit, which causes spongy brown spots in the flesh.

Treatment—What little can be done must be of a preventive nature and consists mainly of good and careful growing.

Potato Blight

This disease may cause very serious losses among potatoes and outdoor tomatoes, especially in warm, moist summers when infection spreads rapidly. The damage done to the leaves prevents a normal crop being produced.

Symptoms—Patches appear on the leaves, generally near the edges at first. They are brown to black on top and greyish underneath. In potatoes the spores may be washed down through the soil to the tubers and cause a brownish colour on the flesh under the skin. The infected tubers may rot in store and affect sound tubers. In tomatoes the fruits shrivel, crack and rot.

Treatment—Immediately the first sign is seen the crop must be sprayed with Bordeaux or Burgundy Mixture or a proprietary copper spray. The spraying must be repeated every fortnight as necessary. Dusts may also be used (as often as once a week in a wet season). When lifting the potatoes the haulm should first be cut and burned and only sound tubers should be put into store and none saved for seed.

Potato Scab

There are two forms of scab caused by different fungi, Common Scab and Corky Scab.

101

Symptoms—Common Scab causes the well-known rough, dry, scabby patches on the skin of potatoes. Sometimes the patches are deep and sunken, but generally they are only skin deep and are removed in peeling. The seriousness of the disease is that it spoils the appearance of the crop.

Corky Scab also causes scabby areas which at first resemble raised swelling and later break to form a canker. It is the more serious but less common of the two.

Treatment—Common Scab is worst on dry, gravelly or overlimed soils and can be reduced by good dressings of farmyard manure or compost. Lime should never be applied to a potato crop.

For Corky Scab the best remedy is to space the crop as far apart as possible in the rotation. Tubers from an infected crop should not be saved for seed.

Raspberry Beetle
The beetles are about 1⅛ in. long, golden-brown to greyish brown. They attack the buds and flowers and the yellowish larvæ burrow into the fruits, causing the well-known "maggoty raspberries". Loganberries and black-berries are also attacked. Severe infestation will render the crop useless and even slight attacks will spoil the appearance of the fruit.

Symptoms—These are not generally noticed until the grubs are found inside the ripe fruit. Eradication is then impossible, but the warning is given that control measures will be essential for the following crop.

Treatment—Spray or dust with derris 10 days after flowering and again 12–14 days later.

Raspberry Fungus Diseases
Several different fungi attack raspberries. The leaves may suffer from rust or mildew and the canes from several forms of spotting or wilting. As a rule none of these is serious, and good growing, removal of infected canes, tidiness and the avoidance of overcrowding keep the crop healthy.

Raspberry Moth
The moth is dark purplish-brown, small, with a wing-span of ¼ in. The eggs are laid on the flowers in June and for a time the tiny larvæ live inside the plug of the fruit but they do no harm. They leave the fruit to hibernate and the following spring crawl up the canes and enter the shoots, tunnelling inside. They are then pink to red.

Symptoms—The new shoots begin to wither and die. If cut open, the caterpillars may be found.

Treatment—Cut off and burn wilted shoots and keep the bed tidy and regularly hoed.

Red Spider Mites
Three species are of importance to gardeners, the Greenhouse Red Spider which attacks a wide range of greenhouse plants, including fruits like grapes and peaches, the Fruit Tree Red Spider found on fruit trees growing out-of-doors and the Gooseberry Red Spider which not only attacks gooseberries but also many alpine plants in the open and under glass. In hot, dry summers other outdoor plants may also be attacked. The mites are small, just visible, and are usually greenish-grey to pale red, becoming more red as they mature. They generally feed on the underside of the leaves, sucking the sap, and often spin a fine webbing which acts as a protection.

Symptoms—Attacked leaves lose their fresh green colour and look dry.

Rusts

Later they take on a rusty colour with a silvery effect and begin to fall. The mites and their webs may be seen on the undersides.

Treatment—Outdoor trees should be sprayed with a petroleum wash in winter or with lime-sulphur and malathion in spring. Greenhouses should be fumigated with azobenzene but tender-leaved plants should be sprayed with nicotine.

Reversion

This is a serious virus disease of black currants. As infection spreads in the bush the blossoms become affected and the crop is progressively reduced. The disease is spread by the Currant Gall Mite and possibly by aphids and capsids. It can also be carried on pruning knives.

Symptoms—The leaves become smaller and narrower and the marginal teeth and main veins become fewer. A healthy leaf has 5 to 8 veins on each side of the main (middle) vein, a reverted leaf has less than 5. These symptoms are only reliable if seen during June on strong-growing shoots. They can also arise from mechanical or other damage, but in such cases later growth quickly becomes normal.

Treatment—Once infected, a bush cannot be cured. The only safe course is to grub and replant with healthy stock. Cuttings should never be taken from an apparently healthy branch on a bush which also shows one or more infected branches.

Rhododendron Bug

The adult is about ⅛ in. long, shiny and black with netted wings. The eggs are laid in the lower surface of the leaves in late summer and the larvæ hatch in the following spring.

Symptoms—The leaves become spotted with rusty-looking spots on the underside and mottled on the upper surface.

Treatment—Nicotine should be sprayed on to the undersides of the leaves about mid-June and again 2–3 weeks later. After bad attacks careful cutting back of all shoots should be done in Mar. These should be burned to destroy the eggs which are generally laid on the top leaves.

Rhododendron White Fly

The small white mealy fly may be seen in June and July on the undersides of the leaves. Eggs are laid on the leaves and the larvæ feed until the following spring.

Symptoms—The larvæ excrete honeydew which falls on to the leaves below. These become black owing to the growth of a "Sooty Mould". Where flies are suspected, shaking of the branches may dislodge the flies which at once fly upward but quickly resettle.

Treatment—Spray or dust with nicotine in Sept. and Apr., taking care to cover the undersides of the leaves. In bad attacks prune hard in Mar.

Rose Sawfly—See Slugworms.

Rusts

Several different species of fungi cause rusts on the foliage of a number of plants. The most important are antirrhinums, asparagus, carnations under glass, chrysanthemums, hollyhocks and mint.

Symptoms—Small brown, reddish or orange-coloured spots occur, often giving a dry, rusty appearance. The spots contain the spores which may sometimes be released as a dust when the plant is shaken. Defoliation and death may follow.

Treatment—General hygiene and good, careful growing are usually a sufficient control on chrysanthemums, carnations and hollyhocks, especially if the first leaves to be attacked are removed and burned. Asparagus should be dusted with sulphur, and resistant varieties of antirrhinum should be used. Infected beds of mint should be destroyed and replaced with healthy stock, although a partial control can be obtained by burning off the bed with straw in the autumn.

Sawflies—See Slugworms.

Scale Insects
There are many different species, varying in colour and shape, but all are what may be called " stationary pests ". When young the larvæ move about on the host-plant, but later they develop a protective covering (which may be hard or soft) under which they live by sucking the sap from the plant. Some species attack outdoor plants, including fruit trees, forest trees and ornamental trees and shrubs, the most important being apples, beech, ceanothus, cotoneaster, yew, peach, currant, ivy, holly, camellias, etc. Others are found on a wide range of greenhouse plants, particularly vines, figs, ferns, orchids and palms. In numbers, scale insects can be very serious.

Symptoms—The stationary oval to round scale appears to be stuck on to the plant. Many species excrete a honeydew which falls on to other leaves and often becomes covered with a " Sooty Mould ". Ants are frequently present, attracted by the honeydew.

Treatment—Tender plants should be sponged with nicotine wash. Single scales should be prised off with a pointed stick. In more serious cases malathion should be sprayed on and deciduous trees sprayed with tar oil in winter. Greenhouses should be fumigated with hydrocyanic acid when possible.

Silver Leaf
This disease is due to a fungus which invades the branches of trees and in some way interferes with the normal growth of the leaves by allowing air to enter between the top and bottom surfaces. This produces the characteristic silvery or leaden sheen. It is a serious disease of plums, but also occurs on apples, poplars, Portugal laurel, cherries, various thorns and peaches.

Symptoms—In addition to the silvering of the leaves, dead branches are usually present. On the dead wood the fruiting stage of the fungus may be seen in the form of purplish crusts several inches long or as bracket-shaped projections up to an inch wide.

Treatment—Since infection can only come from the spores in the fruiting bodies, all dead wood should be cut out and burned. This should be done early in the summer when natural healing takes place most readily. The work must be finished by 15th July (Silver Leaf Order 1923). The fruiting bodies also occur on wooden posts or stakes which should not therefore be left lying about. As the spores can only enter through wounds any broken branches should be cut clean and all pruning wounds should be covered over with white lead paint or grafting wax.

Slugworms or Sawflies
The name is given to a large group of sawflies, the larvæ of which resemble small slugs, although they are usually white when young and become dark-green to black later, and have ten pairs of legs which is a characteristic of

all sawflies. The most important species are those which attack cherries and pears, various shrubs and roses. The adult flies are generally dark in colour, about ¼ in. long, appearing in May and June and again in Aug. when a second generation occurs.

Symptoms—The slugworms feed on the leaves, often eating the upper surface completely away. Some roll the leaves into a rough cylinder and others, particularly the Rose Shoot-borer, burrow down the stem.

Treatment—Since most sawflies pupate in the soil, good and continuous cultivation helps to reduce numbers considerably. In severe attacks spraying with D.D.T. or nicotine should be carried out. Lead arsenate may also be used except where an edible crop is being produced.

Slugs and Snails

Enormous damage is done by slugs and snails, much of it never visible. Some species feed at or above ground level, others below. Most of the feeding is done at night or on moist warm evenings and whole rows of germinating seedlings may be eaten off in a very short time. Slugs feed all the year round, snails hibernate generally in groups, especially in rockeries.

Treatment—Continual attention is necessary and one of the many proprietary " slug-killers " should be used or a bait can be made up at home using 1 oz. metaldehyde to 3 lbs. of bran. This should be dotted about in small heaps about a foot apart.

Small Ermine Moths

The caterpillars of several species of Ermine moths feed on the foliage of apples, hawthorn and spindle. Other fruit trees and shrubs are less commonly attacked.

Symptoms—From May to July greyish caterpillars up to ¼ in. long, with black spots, may be seen eating the leaves and living in webs spun between the leaves or twigs.

Treatment—Spray with lead arsenate. Tar-oil washes may be used in winter on deciduous trees.

Storage Rots

All forms of rotting which occur among fruit, vegetables, bulbs or roots in store are not necessarily serious, apart from the loss they cause. But those due to fungi and bacteria must be regarded very differently because they are generally infectious, may spread very quickly, and contaminate the store.

Treatment—Stores must be kept clean and should be washed down every year with boiling water and soda. The crops in store must be regularly examined. In bad cases the store should be cleaned with formalin, but other disinfectants with characteristic odours should be avoided as many fruits and vegetables will become tainted.

Thrips or Thunder Flies

Small black flies about ₁₆ in. long are often seen on many plants both out of doors and in greenhouses. As a rule they appear to do little serious damage outside, but they act as carriers of certain virus diseases. In greenhouses they may become a serious pest of many flowering plants. They breed more or less continuously.

Symptoms—Thrips feed by scraping away the surface tissue and sucking the sap, causing mottled, spotted areas. In greenhouses flowers of carnations, cyclamen and many other plants may become distorted.

Treatment—Spray with malathion or, in greenhouses, fumigate.

105

Tortrix Moths

There are a number of species which attack a wide range of plants in various ways. The larvæ appear in spring, most of them active and having the characteristic of wriggling backwards when disturbed or hanging from the leaf by a thread.

Symptoms—The larvæ feed on the leaves, shoots or buds, most of them rolling or spinning the leaves together. They are very common on oak trees. In apples the surface of the fruit is also scarred, in some herbaceous plants the flowers may be eaten, and in some shrubs the centre of the shoots may be eaten out.

Treatment—The larvæ may be crushed in the rolled leaves. In severe attacks nicotine spray or dust should be used as soon as possible (in the case of apples a few days before the blossom opens).

(*See also* Codling Moth and Pea Moth which belong to the Tortricidæ.)

Tulip Fire

This can be a very serious fungus disease of tulips. It is generally worst in cold, wet seasons.

Symptoms—Specks and streaks occur on the leaves and flowers and the tips of the leaves become brown and scorched.

Treatment—The bulbs should be lifted every year and all unsound ones destroyed. Tulips should not be planted in the same soil for four or five years.

Turnip Flea Beetle or Turnip Fly—See Flea Beetles.

Virus Diseases

This group of diseases attacks a great number of plants. All are carried in the sap and so are frequently spread by sucking insects or other means of contact. Many have been proved to be highly infectious.

Symptoms—The general symptoms are an unhappy or stunted appearance about the plant. Growth is frequently checked and there may be malformation of the foliage or the production of a bad colour. In some cases parts of the foliage may dry up and die.

The most common types are as follows:

Mosaic. Many plants are attacked, showing a mottling or spotting of the leaves. Raspberries, potatoes, dahlias, marrows, cucumbers and lettuce are but a few.

Leaf-roll is often found in potatoes. The lower leaves curl upwards and feel dry and papery. The plant looks stunted and spiky.

Strawberries suffer from several virus diseases which cause a yellowing of the edges of the leaves, a crinkling or the production of many small leaves and few if any flowering stems instead of normal growth.

The " breaking " of tulips is due to infection by virus.

Treatment—The greatest control is effected by keeping down insects, especially aphides, and by buying-in only healthy stocks of plants from reliable sources. Seed, including seed potatoes, cuttings or any other form of propagating material should never be used from an infected crop.

Wart Disease of Potatoes

This disease, sometimes called Black Scab, can be very serious, resulting in a crop which rots in store. Only certain varieties known as " susceptible " or " non-immune " are affected.

Symptoms—Crinkled warts appear on the stems at ground level and on the tubers.

Treatment—Under the " Wart Disease of Potatoes Order " outbreaks must be notified to the Ministry of Agriculture and Fisheries, London, S.W.1, and only immune varieties may be grown in infected soil.

Water-plant Pests
Some of the plants grown in ornamental pools, particularly water lilies, may be attacked by Aphis, the larvæ of the Water Lily Beetle.
Symptoms—The Water Moth larva is a caterpillar living in a tubular case, it feeds on the submerged part of the plant. The Water Lily Beetle is brown and feeds on the leaves and petals.
Treatment—None of the usual sprays containing arsenic, derris or DDT can be used because of the risk of poisoning fish. Pyrethrum is reasonably safe but the best plan is to help the fish reach the insects by syringing the plant forcibly to knock the insects into the water or by submerging the whole plant for a day at intervals as required.

Weevils
Weevils are a type of beetle distinguished by their snout-like heads and legless grubs. There are several important species varying from brown to black, most of them about $\frac{1}{2}$ in. long. The adults generally hide by day and feed at night, eating the leaves of many trees, bushes and plants while the grubs live on the roots. The bark of young trees is often attacked.
The Vine Weevil may become a serious pest both out of doors and under glass, especially to alpines and plants in pots.
Symptoms—In addition to the visible damage the plants may also show a poor colour and look unhappy. The grubs may often be seen on the roots of pot-plants if the plants are knocked out of their pots.
Treatment—The adults may be trapped in small heaps of rolled leaves, pieces of sacking or corrugated paper. The grubs may be picked off the roots of pot plants. Infected plants should be repotted in fresh or sterilized soil to which DDT dust has been added (8 oz. per bushel of soil).

Wilts
Various forms of wilts occur on a number of plants grown out-of-doors and under glass. Many of them are due to fungi which generally cause a sudden collapse of the plant.
Treatment—In the open the cropping should be changed and in the vegetable garden a long rotation introduced. Under glass the soil should be sterilized or replaced by fresh clean soil.

Winter Moths
Three different species of moths give rise to caterpillars which attack fruit trees and many ornamental trees and shrubs. The caterpillars move with a characteristic " looping " movement.
Symptoms—The caterpillars hatch in spring and can be seen feeding on the buds and young leaves. In June they let themselves down on a silken thread to pupate in the soil.
Treatment—Since the females are wingless and crawl up the trees to lay their eggs, many can be trapped by grease bands. These should be made of grease-proof paper, 6 in. wide, put round the trunk as high as possible, both the top and bottom edges of the paper being tied with string. The paper should then be smeared with a proprietary brand of grease.

Wireworms

These are the well-known shiny, yellowish-brown grubs found in many soils, particularly when turf has been newly broken up. They are the larvæ of the Click Beetles which are brown to black, ½ in. long, and often jump with a click when disturbed. Wireworms take up to five years to reach maturity and are then about ¾ in. long. They feed voraciously on the roots of most plants and burrow into bulbs, potatoes and other roots, and occasionally into the stems of tomatoes and chrysanthemums.

Symptoms—Seedlings and young plants wilt and die and when dug up often show the grub around the roots. Larger, stronger plants generally show less visible signs of attack, and in some cases, e.g. tuberous or bulbous plants and root vegetables, the presence of wireworms may not be suspected until the roots are lifted.

Treatment—Thorough cultivation and tidiness are very important. The grubs should be collected whenever they are seen. They may also be trapped in pieces of potato or carrot put into the soil on pointed sticks or in the flower garden, controlled with BHC.

Wither Tip—*See* Blossom Wilt.

Woodlice

Though living principally on decaying vegetable matter, woodlice will often attack plants especially in frames and greenhouses. They feed at night and hide during the day.

Treatment—Rubbish should always be cleared away. In bad attacks the woodlice may be trapped in potatoes or orange peel or killed with baits of Paris Green and bran, D.D.T. or B.H.C.

PREPARATION AND USES OF
INSECTICIDES AND FUNGICIDES

Preparation.	How to Make.	Principal Use.
Aldrin		General insecticide
Arsenate of lead	Mix ¼ lb. lead arsenate paste *or* 4 oz. lead arsenate powder with a little water. Make up to 10 gals., stirring all the time. Add a spreader (not soft soap).	Leaf-eating caterpillars, Codling Moth and larvæ of sawflies, beetles and weevils. Must not be used on edible crops near to harvesting nor on open blossom.
BHC (Benzene hexachloride)	Buy ready for use.	General insecticide, for aphis, caterpillars, weevils, capsid, sawfly, codling moth, leaf-miners, red spider and wireworm. Must not be used on open blossom nor on vegetable root crops.
Bordeaux Mixture	Put 1 gal. water into a wooden, earthenware or china vessel, add 1 lb. of powdered copper sulphate and stir. Into another vessel put 9 gals. of water; add slowly 1¼ lb. hydrated lime and stir. When dissolved add the copper sulphate solution to the lime solution. Stir and use as soon as possible. Lead arsenate, nicotine, BHC or other insecticides can be added when necessary. A spreader (not soft soap) should be used.	Downy mildews, potato blight and scab on some varieties of apples and pears.
Burgundy Mixture	Mix as above, using 1¼ lb. washing soda instead of lime.	As above.
Calomel (mercurous chloride)	Sold as a 4% powder.	Root flies and club-root.
Captan		General fungicide
Cheshunt compound	Mix 1 oz. powdered copper sulphate with 5½ oz. ammonium carbonate. Dissolve 1 oz. of the mixture in a little water and make up to 2 gals. Use a wooden receptacle. Can also be bought ready for use.	To control fungi causing " damping off " of seedlings. Apply with fine rose.
Colloidal copper Colloidal sulphur Copper-lime dust	Can be bought under various proprietary names.	General fungicide for use in place of Bordeaux or Burgundy Mixtures.
Cresylic acid	Mix 1 gal. cresylic acid with 39 gals. water. Use 4 gals. per sq. yd. and dig in.	Soil insects and certain soil fungi.
DDT	Can be bought ready for using as spray, dust or smoke.	Ants, woodlice, capsids, caterpillars, carrot fly and greenhouse pests. Dangerous to fish.
Derris	Can be bought ready for using as spray or dust.	For flea-beetles and as a non-poisonous substitute for nicotine. Dangerous to fish.

Preparation.	How to Make.	Principal Use.
Formalin	1 pint Formalin to 49 gals. water. Dig the soil and sprinkle on 3 gals. per sq. yd.	For soil insects and soil fungi.
Greenhouse fumigants	Buy proprietary fumigants ready for use as liquids or smokes containing BHC, azobenzene, DDT, tetrachlorethane, nicotine or hydrogen cyanide.	For aphis, thrips, white fly, red spider, scale, mealy bug, leaf-miners, etc.
Lime sulphur	Buy ready for mixing. Use at 2% before blossoming and 1% after. Arsenate of lead or nicotine may be added if desired, using a spreader (not soft soap).	Apple and pear scab, also red spider and other mites.
Malathion		General insecticide
Meta (Metaldehyde)	1 oz. Meta to 3 lb. bran. Set in small heaps, 1-2 ft. apart or scattered thinly.	Slugs and snails. Cover heaps to safeguard birds and pets.
Naphthalene powder	Sprinkle on the soil 3-4 oz. per sq. yd. Rake in. (Up to 6 or 8 oz. if infestation is heavy.)	Wireworms, leather-jackets, mille-pedes, soil caterpillars.
Nicotine	Dissolve ¼ lb. soft soap in a little warm water. When cool add ¼ oz. nicotine and make up to 10 gals. with water. A proprietary spreader may be used instead of soft soap.	Aphis, capsids, thrips, leaf-miners, leaf-hoppers, scale mealy bug and small young caterpillars.
Nicotine dust	Buy ready for use. Frequent applications necessary.	As above, also for leaf-curling insects if applied in warm weather.
Paris Green	1 oz. Paris Green to 2 lb. bran, slightly moistened. 1 oz. Paris Green to 4 lb. dried blood.	Leather-jackets, cutworms. Woodlice. Cover baits to safe-guard birds and pets.
Pyrethrum	Buy ready for use.	As for nicotine.
Sulphur	Buy ready for use as: (1) a very finely-ground powder (2) a fumigant in greenhouses.	For Powdery mildews. As above, and for Leaf Mould.
White oil	Buy ready for using.	Mealy bug, red spider and scale.
Winter washes	Buy proprietary brands ready for using.	For use on trees and shrubs when dormant to destroy eggs of aphis, winter moths, red spider, scale, apple sucker, etc.

CHAPTER 10

Gardening Under Glass

Many plants, particularly the more exotic flowers and fruits, need to be grown in a greenhouse. The enthusiastic gardener should, therefore, make every effort to buy or build one—however small—for it is truly the "open sesame" to the successful propagation of cultivated plants.

Siting the Greenhouse

If the greenhouse can be placed only in a shaded corner of the garden it is clearly hopeless to attempt to grow plants and flowers which need much sunshine. It is better to devote the space to growing ferns to which shade is not only not harmful, but absolutely necessary. If the greenhouse is to be used for fruit and flowers it should stand in full sunlight. Daylight and shelter from north and east winds are essentials.

Ventilation and Heat Regulation

Upon the proper ventilation and regulation of the heat and moisture of the greenhouse much of its success depends. It is very easy to kill, or at least gravely to injure, a house full of plants by injudicious opening or closing of all ventilators. Only in summer, when the temperature is too high, should top and side ventilators be opened simultaneously and then only in moderation, as a chilly draught between the two openings may cripple the less hardy plants. Only ventilators on the side opposite to that from which the wind is blowing should be opened, except in summer, when a mild wind can do little harm provided a draught is not caused.

The amount of air admitted, of course, depends on the nature of the plants; young growing plants and seedlings require a warm and moist atmosphere, while plants in bloom require the air to be drier; the moisture would, in many cases, injure the bloom. Where there is ample top ventilation there is far less need of side ventilation as well, indeed many experts now discontinue the use of side ventilators altogether, as they are held to make the atmosphere over-dry. In cases in which this dryness is desired,· as it may be in a few houses built for particular plants, side ventilation may be employed by means of small sliding shutters placed in the side of the house and below the hot-water pipes. This latter position will ensure the slight warming of the air as it passes over the pipes and before it circulates in the house. It is important that the temperature of the house should be carefully watched, especially in the morning—the sun will often come out suddenly with surprising power, and unless the ventilation is regulated in time the heat will become intense. In order to avoid the risk of scorching, the ventilators, in mild weather, should be opened early, beginning with a little opening, which is gradually increased as the sun becomes more powerful, reversing the process towards evening as the temperature falls. Violent changes of temperature are as harmful to plants as to people, and the sudden check given to foliage which is in a state of great heat and transpiration on the sudden lowering of the temperature of the surrounding atmosphere will almost certainly give rise to mildew. If this occurs, dry flowers of sulphur should be sprinkled over the plants affected.

Methods of Watering

Plants will need most water in the spring and summer, both because the air is then drier, and because the plant is in full activity and is using up water at a great rate. Water at least once a day, sometimes twice, will be needed at this season, and it is permissible in very hot weather to stand moisture-loving plants in saucers of water. Dormant plants and freshly-potted plants are best kept rather dry until growth begins. A watering once a week will suffice for most plants in winter time; the soil must be prevented from becoming dust-dry. In the greenhouse, watering is often as useful for keeping the air in a proper state of moisture as for anything else, and in hot weather the walls, staging, and floor should be frequently syringed. When the air is very hot and dry, the floor may with advantage be absolutely swilled with water, which will evaporate into the air and keep it moist. This is better than too much overhead watering with a rose, which tends to produce weak, insipid foliage.

In the summer, the watering of the plants themselves should be done when the sun's heat is at its lowest, early in the morning or in the early evening, but in spring, late autumn, and in winter it is essential to water in the morning so that excessive moisture may have drained off before the evening, otherwise there is great liability to " damping-off ". Plants should never be allowed to become so dry as to droop, as this may cause irreparable damage, but if this has occurred, the whole plant, pot and all, should be stood in water deep enough to cover the pot. When thoroughly soaked, it should not at once be replaced on the staging, but put in the shade for an hour or two to recover. Nearly all plants, and especially those that have not recently been re-potted, will be the better for a watering with liquid manure every ten days while the buds are forming. The manure water must be discontinued as soon as the flowers are out.

Shading the Greenhouse

During the summer, from about March to the end of September, the house will require shading from the strongest sunshine, or there is great risk of the plants being scorched and dried-up. No definite dates or hours when shading should be commenced can be given, as everything depends upon the weather prevailing. The cool house, however, usually needs shading from about the end of February and should be shaded each day as soon as the direct rays fall on the house. The blinds may

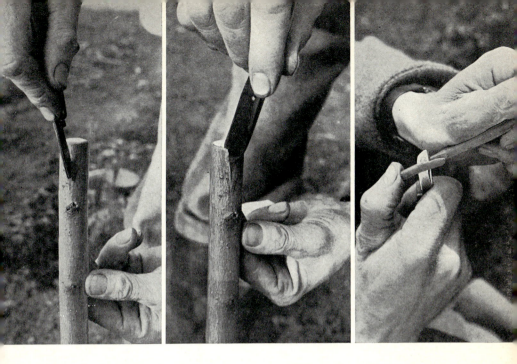

PLATE 7 CROWN GRAFTING The top of the stock is cut off level and the bark cut and peeled back on either side, *above*. The scion is then correctly cut and prepared, *above right*, so that it will fit under the bark of the stock, *below left*. The graft is then bound tight with bass and completed with a covering of grafting wax, *below right*. To ensure clean and accurate cuts a really sharp knife is indispensable.

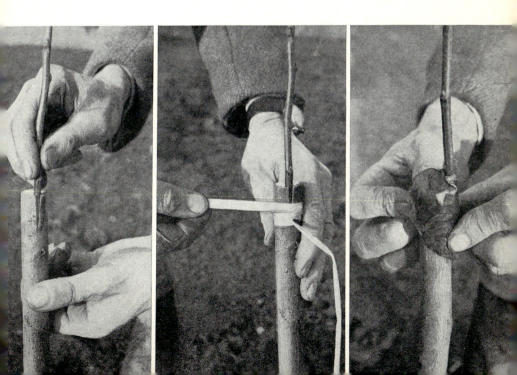

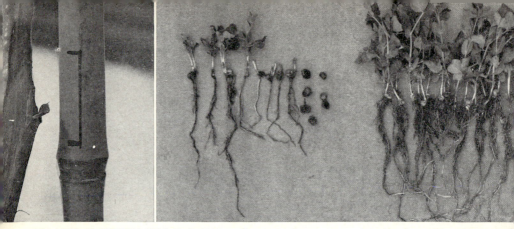

PLATE 8 DISEASES *Left*, Didymella on a plant stem and *right*, effect of Foot Rot on pea seedlings.

[*Plant Protection Ltd. and Shell Photo.*

Left to right, above, Tomato Leaf Mould, Onion White Spot and its effect on an onion. *Below*, Silver Leaf Spotted Wilt on a tomato plant and Verticilium on mushroom.

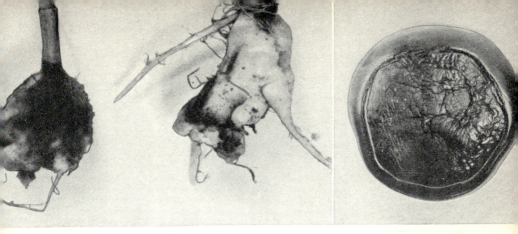

PLATE 9 DISEASES *Left*, Brussels sprouts affected with Clubroot, and *right*, Blossom End Rot on a tomato.

[*Plant Protection Ltd. & Shell Photo.*

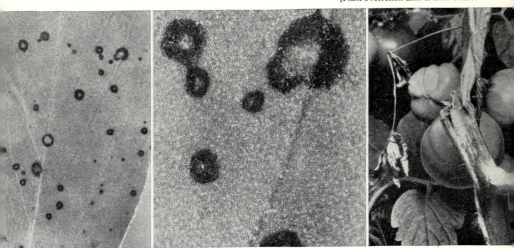

Left to right, above, Bean Chocolate Spot and close-up of the spots (X), and Botrytis of a tomato stem. *Below*, Buck Eye Rot on a tomato (X), Papery Bark Canker and Coral Spot. The sign (X) indicates that the subject is magnified.

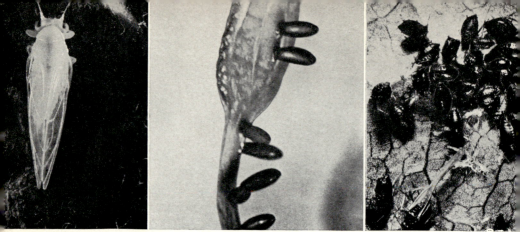

PLATE 10 PESTS *Reading left to right:* Apple Sucker (X), eggs of the Asparagus Beetle (X), and Bean Aphis (X). The sign (X) indicates that the subject is magnified.

[*Shell Photo and Plant Protection Ltd.*]

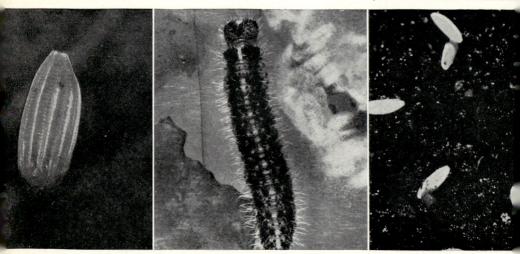

Reading left to right, above, egg and caterpillar of a Cabbage White Butterfly (X), eggs of the Cabbage Root Fly (X); *below,* Cutworms (X), Flea Beetle (X) and Hover Fly (X) and egg.

be removed as soon as the rays are passed. The plants in the warm house can do with more sun and heat. Let the rays play for half an hour or so on the house before shading it and remove the shading about half an hour before the sun's rays leave the glass, in order that the heat of the house may be maintained. Protection from the direct rays of the sun only should be given. Where constant attention can be given, an arrangement of roller blinds is, of course, the best, as the amount of light can be better regulated, and the blinds can be left up on dull and sunless days. Where, however, as is often the case, the greenhouse must of necessity be left to look after itself for a good part of the day, some other plan must be adopted. The simplest, and on the whole the most satisfactory method is to wash the glass over with a mixture of whiting and milk. It is far better to risk losing a little sun than to court damage from burning. The whiting solution is easily washed off when cloudy weather sets in and more light is necessary.

An Essential Note

Cleanliness inside the greenhouse is most essential. Aphides, thrips, red spiders, mealy bugs, scale insects and woodlice are the chief pests met with here. Keeping every corner of the house and the stem of every plant as clean and free from rubbish as possible will do a great deal to keep down insect pests.

GREENHOUSE TEMPERATURES

It is not possible to give any fixed rules for the temperature of the greenhouse. This must of necessity vary with the plants grown and instructions in this matter will be found under the headings of the different plants. Greenhouses are, however, roughly divided into cold, cool, warm or intermediate, and hot houses, and as a rough guide the following may be taken as the mean temperatures of the last three.

	SUMMER.		WINTER.	
	Day.	Night.	Day.	Night.
HOT HOUSE . .	70°–85° F.	65°–75° F.	65°–75° F.	60°–70° F.
WARM HOUSE . . (Intermediate)	65°–75° F.	60°–70° F.	60°–70° F.	55°–65° F.
COOL HOUSE . .	60°–65° F.	55°–60° F.	55°–65° F.	45°–50° F.

Unheated Greenhouse

This type of house depends solely on the heat of the sun for its warmth. thus its temperature varies enormously at different times of the year. It requires no artificial heat even in winter. It must, however, be remembered that glass of itself will not keep out frost and the plants selected for the cold house must necessarily be hardy and able to stand a few degrees of frost. Much may be done by placing sacking and canvas over the glass to keep frost from the more tender plants and such hardy plants as bloom too early in the season to withstand the frost in the open.

Ventilation—The cold house must have ample ventilation, but care must be taken to exclude all draughts. On warm summer nights the ventilators may be kept open all night; in cooler and damper weather it is best to ventilate thoroughly in the morning and to close the ventilators soon after lunch. For shading, the roller type of blind is best, as these may be pulled down as protection against frosts on winter nights.

Watering—Watering requires a good deal of care and is best done in the morning; the foliage and atmosphere will then have time to dry somewhat before the cold night air can cause "damping-off". This applies especially to watering in autumn, winter and spring; in summer the watering may be done in the evening. In hot weather plants may be sprayed overhead and the paths and staging damped, as advised for the warm house, but this should be done with caution and only in the hottest periods, as the majority of cold house subjects are not lovers of a damp and humid atmosphere.

Cool House

The cool house will need artificial heat during the colder periods of the year only. Between October and March a day temperature of 55° F., with a night temperature of 45° F., is necessary. During April and May, in a normal year, a temperature five degrees above that of the outer air, both night and day, will be enough.

The cool house provides a home for a very large number of tender and half-hardy plants, and will generally be found the best all-round house for the amateur.

Warm (Intermediate) House

The warm, or intermediate, greenhouse requires a 55° F. night temperature, and a 65° F. day one all the colder part of the year and from 65° F. to 75° F. in the day all the summer and spring.

The warm greenhouse will give the amateur a very wide range of choice, for many of the plants which have been included amongst those grown in the cold and cool houses can also be had in perfection in the slightly warmer house.

The warm house also allows of very much greater scope in the matter of forced and out-of-season flowers. *See* List of plants, p. 120.

Hot House

The hot house requires considerably more heat. In winter the night temperature should never fall below 65° F., while the day temperature in summer should range between 70° F. and 85° F. The amateur is very prone to give too much heat in winter at a time when most plants

114

are resting. Forcing them at this period will weaken them and impair the beauty and quantity of their flowers. Exposure to the open air and sun matures the wood and strengthens all plants. All except the more tender greenhouse plants should, therefore, be kept in the open from the end of May until early in September, having first been hardened-off for a fortnight in a cold frame and then shaded from the strong sun for their first ten days in the open. On returning the plants to the greenhouse before the first frost, they must be given very free ventilation. The plants are not usually taken out of their pots, but the latter should be plunged to their rims into beds, preferably not of earth, but of ashes or fibre, which will keep them well drained and prevent worms from entering and disturbing the roots.

HEATING THE GREENHOUSE

It is generally recognized that the hot-water system is the best method of heating the greenhouse. Oil and electricity are also being increasingly used, but whichever system is adopted considerable care and experience are required and unless he is himself qualified to supervise the work, the amateur is advised to put the work in the hands of a reliable person.

Fuels and Stoking

Between coke and anthracite there is not much to choose. In the case of small, upright boilers, coke must be used, the anthracite being unsuitable, and the fuel must be broken into pieces of the size of a walnut before being used.

To light the fire open the ash-tray door, pull out the damper and lay the fire with paper or shavings, dry wood and some small coal as for a house fire and close the fire-door. Light it and put on a little more coal as the fire burns up, then add the anthracite or coke and anthracite. Close the ash-tray door and regulate the draught by means of the damper. When the pipes are hot enough, push the damper in further to check the draught; if this does not regulate the fire sufficiently, open the fire-door a little. The more the latter is opened, the less the draught. The fire should remain thus until more heat is wanted in the late afternoon or evening when the final stoking up is given.

For the last stoking before leaving the fire for the night the bars of the furnace should be raked thoroughly clear and the hot coke or anthracite raked down together. The furnace should then be filled with anthracite or with coke which has been slightly moistened, broken up and mixed with breeze or slack. The addition of the latter will help to liven up the coke fire. The door of the ash-tray should be opened and the fire-door closed and the damper drawn out; the fire will now burn up and if properly stoked should go well till next morning. When the fire has burnt up, open the fire-door and leave it so during the night. Should the night be cold and windy push the damper almost right in and nearly close the ash-tray door, but if there is no wind, the damper should be half-way in, and the ash-tray door half open.

In the morning close the fire-door, pull out the damper and open the

115

ash-tray door, then rake out the clinkers after the fire has been stirred and had time to burn up a little. It may then be banked up to burn through the day.

PROPAGATION

Propagating Frame

A propagating frame is a most useful adjunct to the greenhouse, both for the purpose implied in its name and for bringing on plants and bulbs required for forcing and for greenhouse decoration. It saves a great deal of room in the house, as well as giving a home to all kinds of plants, cuttings, and seedlings which do not help the attractive appearance of the house.

Propagating Box

For raising seedlings, propagating cuttings, and such purposes a box within the greenhouse is very useful where a house cannot be set aside for this alone. This box may either be a fixture, in which case it should be built in such a position as to include within it some portion of the heating pipes, or it may be movable, if space is an object, so that it may be cleared out of the house when not wanted. Where the pipes are built in they should be covered with a good depth of coconut fibre, and the pots or boxes containing the plants to be dealt with plunged in the fibre.

The propagating box will need watching carefully while it is in use. The glass should have a sheet of paper thrown over it to shield newly inserted cuttings and seeds from the sun, and this paper should be kept in position until the cuttings have rooted, probably in about three weeks, or until the seeds have germinated. All decayed leaves must be frequently removed as they encourage " damping-off ", and the condensation should be wiped off the glass every morning.

It may be here stated that the cutting or seeds of nearly all cool house plants should be placed under glass in a temperature of 50° to 60° F. Warm house plants require a propagating temperature of from 65° to 75° F.

THE COLD FRAME

Span-roof frames are excellent as the lights can be opened on either side and it is, therefore, possible to ventilate, whatever the direction of the wind. The span-roof frame should be placed so as to run north and south; either side then gets its proportion of sun. Lean-to frames must face due south so that they may get full sun, unless shade and a low temperature are necessary, when the frames should face north.

The substance used to form the bed of the frame will depend upon the uses to which it is to be put. If pots or boxes are to be kept in it, a dry and hard bottom of ashes or shingle, some 3 inches deep, is admirable; this will keep out worms and other pests and will afford good drainage. If a seed-bed is made, support the four corners of the frame with bricks, place a layer of leaves at the bottom and cover with 6 inches of well-sieved compost consisting of loam, leaf-mould and sand. Make

116

the bed firm and sprinkle the surface fairly liberally with coarse sand. (*See* Making a Seed-bed, p. 62.) The bed must, in any case, be made up so that the surface is not more than 6 to 9 inches from the glass, otherwise the plants will soon become weak and drawn-up.

(For Ventilation, Shading, etc., *see* p. 111.)

THE HEATED FRAME

In the heated frame the heat is either supplied by means of 3- or 4-inch hot-water pipes along the front and back of the frame, or through the medium of a hot-bed upon which the frame is placed.

Management is in all respects identical with that of the cold frame, except that even more care must be given to correct ventilation and to the steady maintenance of an even temperature.

With a heated frame and a temperature of from 60° F. to 70° F. it is not only possible to raise plants for early transplanting to the open, but by careful management a sequence of crops of almost any vegetable can be had practically the winter through, until the vegetables from the open are ready to take their place.

THE HOT-BED

A quantity of stable dung not more than three weeks old should be collected and proportioned to the size of the frame; two double loads for a three-light frame are usually allowed. The dung should be thrown up into a heap and be turned over four or five times during a fortnight, and wetted if dry. In order to prevent the material from becoming too hot, and burning the roots of the plants, it is advisable to mix an equal quantity of leaves with the dung.

When the material is ready, measure the frame, length and breadth, and mark out the bed, allowing 18 inches more each way for the bed than the length and breadth of the frame. At each corner of the bed drive a stake firmly into the ground, and perfectly upright, to serve as a

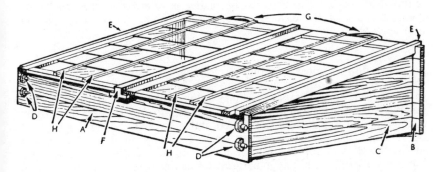

FIG. 15. Example of a two-light frame of wooden construction and quite simple to make. A is the back, B the front, C the side, D mortices, tenons and pegs to hold the frame together, E and F are rebated members in which the frame slides, G two iron handles and H flat iron bars to strengthen the lights.

117

guide by which to build the bed. Then proceed to build the bed, shaking up the dung well and beating it down with a fork. The whole should be equally firm and compact, so that it is not likely to settle more in one part than in another; the bed should be about 4 feet high at the back and 3 feet in front. The frame and lights may now be placed in the centre, but the lights left off, so that the rank steam may escape.

When the rank steam has passed off, which generally takes five or six days, place a 9- to 10-inch layer of good loam under each light. By the next day this will be warmed to the temperature of the hot-bed, and the plants may be planted in it. Such a bed will last up to two months.

Cloches are now available in many forms from the simple tent or barn, consisting of 2 or 4 sheets of glass held in position by galvanized wire to the larger and taller kinds which resemble frames or miniature glass-houses and are made up on a framework of wire or rigid metal. All serve the same purposes; they protect young plants, warm the soil and encourage early growth and final maturity. They are easy to handle and are made so that they can be placed end to end to cover continuous rows. They are particularly useful for covering crops grown for successional harvesting. In winter or early spring they may be used on lettuce, flower seedlings or salads and in March to May put over such crops as narcissus, sweet corn, strawberries or tomatoes. When not in use cloches should be stacked on end nested together on a level piece of ground.

FORCING

Vegetables

Vegetables may be forced in a heated frame, or in borders and boxes in the warm greenhouse. For forcing fruit a greenhouse is necessary; cucumbers, figs, grapes, nectarines, peaches and tomatoes require a warm greenhouse, most other fruit can be forced in a cool greenhouse and is generally grown in pots. For cultural details and for the temperature required at the various seasons the reader is referred to the articles on the cultivation of the different vegetables in the chapter on *The Culture of Vegetables*.

Flowers

Of the flowers most suitable for forcing are those of a woody and shrubby nature and those with bulbous or large, fleshy roots. All plants to be forced must be vigorous and fully matured or no blooms will result. Bulbs for forcing must be firm and plump and are best of medium size. For cultural details, *see* Potted Bulbs, p. 143. After forcing, the bulbs should be placed in a cold frame for a fortnight or three weeks to harden-off and for the foliage to die down. Bulbs are useless for forcing a second year, but if naturalized in the wild garden or in grass, they will soon regain their vigour and will bloom for many years. Lilies, however, can be forced year after year and will show little sign of deterioration.

The following are most usually forced: *Alliums, crocuses, freesias,*
118

hyacinths, lilies, narcissus, scillas, snowdrops, tuberoses, and *tulips.*

Flowering Shrubs
Shrubs for forcing must, above all things, be vigorous and the shoots should be firm, well ripened and must show plenty of flower buds. Heat must be applied gradually, and too little rather than over much should be given. The shrubs are usually potted up in September and early in October and are placed in a cold frame until November. Early potting is essential. About the middle of the latter month transfer them to the greenhouse and place them in a temperature of about 45° F. for the first fortnight; during this period syringing overhead twice a day will be necessary in fine weather. After the first couple of weeks the temperature may be raised to 60° F., and as soon as the plants break into active growth the temperature can be raised another ten degrees. When the colour of the buds begins to show, lower the temperature by five or ten degrees and maintain this level while the plants are flowering. After forcing, some of the old wood that has borne flowers should be cut away and weak shoots should be cut right back; the aim being to let air and light into the centre of the plant so that the shoots shall become thoroughly ripened and be able to produce buds for the following season. After trimming, let the plants remain in the warm for three weeks or so and syringe overhead in fine weather with tepid water and feed once a week with weak liquid manure. Following this treatment they should be stood in the cold house or cold frame for a fortnight or three weeks to be gradually hardened-off and set out in the open for the summer early in June.

Nearly all shrubs are the better if forced every alternate year only, and with lilacs this is essential. Roses, however, can quite successfully be forced for several years in succession.

For details as to the pruning and special cultural requirements of individual shrubs, *see* the Alphabetical List of Flowering Plants, p. 147.

The following is a selection of hardy shrubs for forcing:

Acer japonicum and vars.
Acer Negundo var. variegatum
Amelanchier canadensis
Azalea mollis
Ceanothus species
Chimonanthus praecox
Choisya ternata
Clematis Jackmannii types
Cytisus Dallimorei hybrids
Daphne Mezereum
Deutzia gracilis and Lemoinei

Forsythia intermedia spectabilis
Hydrangea paniculata grandiflora, etc.
Jasmine nudiflorum
Kalmia latifola
Kerria japonica florepleno
Laburnum anagyroides
Lonicera Standishii
Magnolia stellata
Malus floribunda var. atrosanguinea
M. purpurea and M. spectabilis
Philadelphus coronarius and hybrids

Prunus, subhirtella and triloba fl. pl.
Pyrus, see Malus
Rhododendron vars.
Ribes sanguineum
Roses (various)
Spiraea arguta, media and Thunbergii
Staphylea colchica
Syringa Charles the Tenth or Marie Legraye
Viburnum Carlesii, tomentosum, var. plicatum and Opulus
Wisteria sinensis

119

The treatment of roses differs slightly from that of other shrubs in that they must be established in their pots at least twelve months before forcing is to take place; that is to say, they must not be lifted straight from the open ground to be forced. They can, however, be re-potted in October if need be. Early in November they must be placed in a cold frame, pruned about the middle of December, and transferred to the greenhouse; about a fortnight later the forcing heat should gradually be applied.

Other plants for forcing are: *Astilbe japonica, Convallaria majalis, Dicentra spectabilis,* and *Polygonatum multiflorum.*

These roots should be potted-up at the end of October or early in November and kept in a cold but frost-proof frame to be transferred to the greenhouse, in batches as required, at any time from December to March or April. This will ensure a good show of bloom all through the winter from December until the end of May. The plants should be kept near the glass for some time after being taken into the house and ample water must be given. Gradually remove the pots farther from the glass as the days become longer, and shade the plants while in bloom.

SELECTION OF GREENHOUSE PLANTS

NOTE.—For Cultural Details, for Colour of Flowers, Time of Blooming, Height and the best Species and Varieties, *see* the Alphabetical List of Flowering Plants and Shrubs, p. 147.

THE COLD HOUSE

Aquilegia cærulea
Astilbe japonica
Begonia (tuberous vars.)
Calceolaria (shrubby types)
Campanula pyramidalis
Chrysanthemum (large decorative types)
Clarkia elegans
Convallaria majalis

Dianthus Heddewigii
Dicentra spectabilis
Fuchsias species and vars.
Godetia grandiflora and vars.
Lobelia cardinalis
Matthiola annua and vars. (Intermediate Stock)
Myosotis sylvatica
Pelargoniums

Phlox divaricata
Polygonatum multiflorum
Primula vulgaris (Primrose)
P. Auricula hybrids
P. variabilis (Polyanthus)
P. stellata
Schizanthus retusus and types
Trollius asiaticus
T. europæus
Violo odorata (Violet)

BULBS

Anemone blanda
A. fulgens
*Chionodoxa Luciliæ, var. sardensis
Crinum Moorei and C. Powellii
*Crocus vernus var.
*Cyclamen coum
*C. neapolitanum, etc.
Erythronium Dens-canis

*Fritillaria latifolia, F. Meleagris
Galanthus nivalis (Snowdrop)
Hyacinthus orientalis
Iris alata
Iris reticulata and vars.
*Iris unguicularis
Ixia
Kniphofia Macowanii
Lilium auratum, L. candidum, L. regale, etc.

*Muscari botryoides
*Narcissus Bulbocodium
*Narcissus cyclamineus
*N. asturiensis
Ornithogalum arabicum
*Scilla sibirica
Trillium grandiflorum
Tritonia crocosmæflora
Tulip vars.
Watsonia Meriana var. Ardernei

* Denotes bulbs suitable for culture in the Alpine House. All small bulbs are best grown in shallow pans 5 to 6 inches in diameter; not in pots.

FLOWERING SHRUBS

Azalea mollis
Berberis Darwinii
Camellia japonica and vars.
Ceanothus rigidus
Chænomeles japonica
Choisya ternata
Clematis Jackmanii
Cytisus kewensis (Broom)
Daphne Cneorum

Deutzia gracilis
D. Lemoinei
Erica carnea
E. mediterranea
Forsythia intermedia, var. spectabilis, F. suspensa
Hydrangea macrophylla vars.
Jasminum nudiflorum
Magnolia stellata

Pernettya mucronata
Prunus japonica fl. pl.
P. tenella (nana)
Ribes sanguineum
Spiræa arguta
Syringa vulgaris (Lilac)
Veronica speciosa
Viburnum Tinus (Laurustinus)
Wisteria sinensis

THE WARM HOUSE

Summer Temperature, 60°—70° F.; Winter Temperature, 55°—60° F.

FLOWERING IN EARLY SPRING

Acacia armata (Mimosa)
Azalea mollis
Camellia japonica and vars.
Cineraria all types
Convallaria majalis
Cytisus canariensis
Diervilla florida
Erica hyemalis

Freesia refracta, alba, etc.
Kerria japonica fl. pl.
Laburnum anagyroides
Lachenalia aloids (Nelsonii)
Malus spectabilis, etc.
Olearia stellulata
Philadelphus Lemoinei
Primula stellata, etc.
Prunus serrulata, etc.

Ribes aureum
Ribes sanguineum
Spiræa Vanhouttei
Syringa vulgaris (Lilac)
Viburnum tomentosum, var. plicatum (Snowball Tree)
Wisteria sinensis

FLOWERING IN LATE SPRING

Calceolaria herbeohybrida
Cineraria all types
Deutzia gracilis
Dicentra spectabilis

Eupatorium Purpusii
Hippeastrum equestre hybrids

Kalmia polifolia
Lilium longiflorum
Pelargonium zonale and regal

FLOWERING IN SUMMER

Abutilon striatum var. Thompsonii
Achimenes vars.
Agapanthus orientalis
Begonia species and vars.
Campanula isophylla
Campanula pyramidalis
Canna indica and hybrids
Celsia Arcturus
Cobæa scandens

Cotyledon glauca
Crinum Powellii and C. Moorei
Dianthus (Malmaison Carnation)
Fuchsia species and vars.
Gloxinia hybrids
Heliotropium peruvianum and vars.
Hydrangea macrophylla

Impatiens Balsamina
Lilium auratum
Lilium speciosum
Mimulus moschatus
Nerium Oleander
Oxalis species [regal
Pelargonium zonale and
Petunia violacea
Plumbago capensis
Schizanthus retusus
Verbena hybrids

FLOWERING IN AUTUMN

Begonia species and tuberous rooted
Bouvardia hybrids
Chrysanthemum indicum, etc.

Nerine Bowdenii
Polianthes tuberosa [ette)
Reseda odorata (Mignon-Salvia rutilans, S. involucrata var. Bethelii, etc.

Salvia patens and S. splendens vars., etc.
Streptocarpus hybrids
Vallota speciosa (Scarborough Lily)

FLOWERING IN WINTER

Begonia (Fibrous-rooted)
Bouvardia Humboldtii, etc.
Chrysanthemum indicum etc
Cineraria all types
Cyclamen persicum and hybrids

Daphne odora
Erica hyemalis, etc.
Euphorbia fulgens
Freesia refracta alba papyraceus
Narcissus Tazetta vars.

Pelargonium zonal vars.
Primula stellata, etc.
Solanum Capsicastrum
Sparrmania africana
Tropæolum peltophorum
Zantedeschia æthiopica

121

CHAPTER 11

The Flower Garden

Situation and Design

The flower garden should, whenever possible, be situated so that it is sheltered from the cold, biting north and east winds. Such shelter, whether natural or artificial, should be sufficient to protect quite tall-growing shrubs without excluding light and air. It is an almost hopeless enterprise to attempt very much in the way of flower culture in a soil that is heavy and impervious, or in an exposed situation, unless shrubs can be grown to afford shelter, and the impervious soil either replaced by one of light texture or so improved by the addition of some element, such as sand, leaf-mould, lime, chalk, or charred garden debris that the tender roots may be able to penetrate it easily.

Drainage of Site

A very important consideration is drainage and one which such a treatment of heavy soil as is recommended above makes doubly necessary. It will be obvious that if certain portions of the soil are broken up and lightened, they become automatically drains for the heavier surrounding land, and all the surface water which such land is unable to absorb will just drain down into the beds that have been rendered pervious, turning them into a sort of natural reservoir. The foundation of such beds must, therefore, be constructed of such loose yet durable ingredients as will permit the accumulation of water to drain through. For this purpose nothing is better than broken bricks or flints, but even this precaution needs support from a drain which will collect and convey the surface water away. It will be seen, therefore, how essential it is that the land to be used for a flower garden should be properly prepared before anything very elaborate in the way of cultivation is begun.

Backgrounds and Settings

An important consideration in the arrangement of the garden is that of form; the selection of plants beautiful in themselves, and their arrangement singly or in groups, as backgrounds for smaller flowers, as screens, boundaries and hedges. When one speaks of form in the matter of plants, one's mind turns instinctively to such outstanding examples as the cypress whose telling silhouette is so beautiful a feature of the Italian landscape, to the tropical palm, to the poplar groves of France, and last but not least to the many beautiful varieties of English trees which at any season of the year present such lovely appearances.

Annuals

Among the plants whose foliage is beautiful and whose presence in the garden is of the utmost value from the point of view of backgrounds are the willow, the acacia, the asparagus, various specimens of bamboo, reeds, pampas grass, the cypress, cedar, yew, and fir, and a host of hardy evergreens and flowering shrubs. Such plants, indeed, lend themselves to a variety of decoration and practical purposes. The larger of them can be used as screens for unsightly corners, and to afford shelter to more delicate specimens; others to break up the monotony of a lawn and to maintain the beauty of the garden through even the most trying winters. Others again require no such practical warrant. Their mere beauty is sufficient reason in itself for their inclusion. The azalea, magnolia, rhododendron (in moderation), broom, Chænomeles lagenaria, to mention but a few, whose flowering periods but crown their common life as elegant shrubs, should need no recommendation. In the use of evergreens discretion should be exercised, and their hardy and enduring qualities must not be favoured to the detriment of more vulnerable plants. In moderation their usefulness cannot be too highly praised, but it must be remembered that most evergreens are greedy feeders; their roots are voracious and spread very widely; and when, as is often the case, they are used to border flower beds, if planted there too generously or allowed to multiply unchecked, they impoverish the soil and weaken the chances of the flowers.

Siting of Flowering Shrubs

The many varieties of beautiful flowering shrubs which grow well in this climate should appeal to the gardener for more than their purely outdoor qualities. Most people who have gardens like to decorate their houses with flowers, and, in this connection, nothing lends itself more charmingly to indoor use than single sprays of some small flowering shrub.

As an immediate setting for the house, also, no form of planting is more satisfactory than groups of flowering evergreens. Here, above all other places in the garden, permanence is a quality to aim at, for this is the view which is most constantly in evidence. In winter weather it may, perhaps, be regretted but not deplored that the remoter places of the garden are not bright with flowers, but if the immediate view from the windows is equally barren then the dreariness of the whole garden will weigh more heavily. For this reason, then, the use of flowering evergreens near the house is to be recommended.

Annuals

The class of plants which flower and fruit in the same year as that in which their seeds are sown, or, at any rate, complete the series of those processes within twelve months of the time of sowing, is known as that of Annuals. In the flower garden it includes some of the most beautiful, as well as undoubtedly the most easily grown of all those things which make up a typical English garden.

Hardy Annuals—Any ordinary garden soil is suitable for hardy annuals, and in fact for annuals generally. It does not require to be at all rich, since this encourages luxuriance of growth, which is incompatible with the production of flowers. Annuals do best, however, in light, sandy soil, and they should have this where possible, though not necessarily. Good drainage is essential.

In almost all cases it is wise to incorporate with the natural earth a very generous allowance of humus or of leaves or other decomposing vegetable matter which will help to create humus. In the process of decomposition of leaves or other organic matter, various acids and other products are created, which tend to liberate from the mineral elements in the soil certain foods essential to the life of plants. Gases also are generated, which help to keep the soil in a porous, spongy condition, which is agreeable to the roots, and which assists in the maintenance of that moist condition so essential to healthy growth.

Very hardy annuals may be sown in autumn, not earlier than the last week in August and not later, even in sheltered spots, than the last week in September. Autumn-sown plants, if they survive the winter's frosts, will bloom early in spring. The situation best suited for autumn sowing is one that is sheltered from strong and cutting winds, but free from shade and well exposed to the sun. Spring sowings for blooming in summer may be made at any time from the middle of March to the middle of April. Later sowings for flowering in autumn should be made from the middle of May to the middle of June. The different conditions and climates prevailing in the various districts make it impossible to give exact times and details.

To raise annuals for transplanting, they may be sown in V-shaped drills about ½ an inch deep and 10 inches apart in the reserve garden or elsewhere, and removed when about half grown to the position in which they are intended to flower; on an average about 9 inches should be left between each plant. They should be firmly planted then well watered to fix the soil round the roots. The transplanting of annuals, unless very carefully done, is always attended with some danger. This may be obviated if they are raised in pots, from which they can be turned out without disturbing the roots, or sown on pieces of turf turned grass downwards, the seeds being covered with a thin coating of mould after they have been sprinkled thinly on the turf. Hardy annuals sown in spring, and some kinds sown in autumn, need no protection from the weather. (*See* Depth to Sow, p. 63, *and* Bedding Plants, p. 132.)

Half-Hardy Annuals—The seeds should be sown in March or April in well-drained pots or pans, in a mixture of loam, leaf-mould, well-decayed manure and silver sand, and sheltered in a frame, or else the pots should be plunged in moderate bottom-heat, such as a hot-bed that is gradually cooling. The temperature should not rise above 75° F. by day or fall below 55° F. at night. (*See* Depth to Sow, p. 63.) Harden-off gradually and remove to flowering quarters about the middle of May, but delay the removal to the end of the month if the weather is cold and unfavourable.

Biennials

The difference between annuals and biennials consists in their nature and habit only. The former grow flowers, yield seeds for their reproduction, and die in the same year; biennials, on the contrary, are sown and grow in the first year, but do not come to maturity until the second, when they flower, seed and die.

Hardy biennials may be sown at a later period of the year than annuals, that is to say in May, June or July, sometimes in August, though not later than the middle or end of September, for plants sown at this time will bloom the following year as freely as those that have been sown at an earlier date. It is wise to sow as early as possible, as this enables the plants to become well established before the colder weather sets in, and to ensure well-developed plants for flowering the next year. If a frame is available early sowing is not so important, as the plants will continue development in the frame at a time when cold and bad weather would impede any growth in the open. Biennials should be raised in drills 8 to 18 inches apart in partially-shaded beds in the reserve garden; as soon as they are tall enough to be handled they should be thinned out to 6 inches apart or transplanted to the same distance between plants. Plant out in moderately good deeply-worked soil in their blooming quarters in the spring, or in October if planted in early summer and sufficiently grown.

Half-hardy biennials should be sown in boxes from March to June. They should be protected during the winter in a frame or in the greenhouse and be planted out in their flowering positions the following spring, from April to June. (*See* Depth to Sow, p. 63.)

SELECTION OF ANNUALS AND BIENNIALS

For Notes on Colour, Height, Season of Flowering, Culture, and the best Species and Varieties, *see* Alphabetical List of Flowering Plants, p. 147.

HALF-HARDY ANNUALS

Ageratum Houstonianum
Alonsoa Warscewiczii
Amaranthus caudatus
   (Love-lies-Bleeding)
Arctotis stoechadifolia
Brachycome iberidifolia
Callistephus chinensis
   (China Aster)
Celosia cristata (Prince of
   Wales' Feathers or
   Cockscomb)
Dianthus Heddewigii and
   D. chinensis
Dimorphotheca aurantiaca
Gaillardia (Single and
   Double)

Helichrysum bracteatum,
   etc.
Helipterum Manglesii and
   roseum
Impatiens Balsamina
Kochia scoparia trichophila
Limonium Bonduellii, L.
   sinuata, L. Suworowii
Lobelia Erinus vars.
Matthiola incanna, var.
   annua (Ten-week Stock)
Mesembryanthemum crys-
   tallinum (Cryophytum)
Nemesia strumosa vars.
Nicotiana affinis (Tobacco
   Plant)

Petunia vars.
Phlox Drummondii vars.
Portulaca grandiflora
Salpiglossis sinuata
Salvia carduacea and S.
   coccinea
Scabiosa atropurpurea
Schizanthus pinnatus, S.
   retusus
Tagetes erecta, T. patula,
   T. tenuitolia (African and
   French Marigolds)
Verbena vars.
Zinnia elegans

SELECTION OF ANNUALS AND BIENNIALS
(*continued*)

HARDY ANNUALS

Alyssum maritimum (Lobu-
laria)
Calendula officinalis (Pot
Marigold)
Centaurea Cyanus (Corn-
flower or Bluebottle)
Centaurea suaveolens
(Sweet Sultan)
Clarkia elegans and vars.
and C. pulchella
Collinsia bicolor   [vars.
Convolvulus tricolor and
Coreopsis tinctoria, etc.
Delphinium Ajacis
Eschscholzia californica
(Californian Poppy)
Gaillardia pulchella, var.
Lorenziana
Gilea lutea, G. multicaulis
and G. tricolor
Godetia Single and Double

Gypsophila elegans
Helianthus annuus and
H. cucumerifolius
Iberis umbellatus (Candy-
tuft)
Ipomoea purpurea
Lathyrus odoratus (Sweet
Pea)
Lavatera trimestris
Limnanthes Douglasii
Linaria maroccana, etc.
Linum grandiflorum var.
rubrum
Lupinus hirsutus L. luteus,
L. mutabilis (Lupins)
Malcomia maritima (Vir-
ginian Stock)
Malope grandiflora
Matthiola bicornis (Night-
Scented Stock)

Nemophila Menziesii, var.
insignis
Nigella damascena and N.
hispanica   (Love - in - a
Mist)
Papaver Rhœas vars. (Shir-
ley Poppy) and P. somni-
ferum (Opium Poppy)
Reseda odorata (Mignon-
ette)
Salvia Horminum and vars.
Senecio elegans
Silene pendula, var. com-
pacta
Statice (*see* Limonium)
Tropæolum aduncum
(Canary Creeper)
T. majus (Climbing Nas-
turtium) and var. nanum
(Dwarf Nasturtium)

BIENNIALS

Althæa rosea (Hollyhock)
Anchusa capensis
Campanula Medium
Campanula pyramidalis
Cheiranthus Cheiri (Wall-
flower)
Coreopsis grandiflora
Dianthus barbatus (Sweet
William)   [glove)
Digitalis purpurea (Fox-

Lavatera arborea
Lunaria biennis (Honesty)
Lychnis Flos-jovis (Rose
Campion)
Matthiola (Intermediate
Stock)
Matthiola (East Lothian
Stock)
Matthiola incana (Giant or
Brompton Stock)

Myosotis sylvatica (Forget-
Me-Not)
Œnothera biennis (Even-
ing Primrose)
Papaver nudicaule (Iceland
Poppy)
Silene compacta
Trachelium cæruleum
Verbascum species

NOTE.—Although some two or three of the species included in this list are not actually
biennials, in a true sense, they are most satisfactory when grown as such.

126

CHAPTER 12

Principles of Potting

Before doing any potting whatsoever it is essential to wash carefully each pot in hot soda water, otherwise any disease or fungus present in the old potting soil will be transferred to the next inhabitant of the pot; besides, a dirty pot will not be porous, as it should be, to allow the air to permeate the soil. Even new pots should be put in water for at least half an hour, for a dry pot will draw away the moisture from the potting soil. The pot, however, must not be actually *wet* when used, as this would be almost as bad as using a dirty pot, for the soil and eventually the roots would stick to it. For the winter always store pots in a dry, frost-proof place: if they are dry the frost will not hurt them; if they are wet, however, when the frost comes it is almost certain that many of them will be ruined.

The following table shows the inside measurements of the pot-sizes in general use.

Sizes.	Diam. Top in Ins.	Depth in Ins.	Sizes.	Diam. Top in Ins.	Depth in Ins.
Thimbles	2	2	Sixteens	9½	9
Thumbs	2½	2½	Twelves	11½	10
Sixties	3	3½	Eights	12	11
Fifty-fours	4	4	Sixes	13	12
Forty-eights	4½	5	Fours	15	13
Thirty-twos	6	6	Twos	18	14
Twenty-fours	8½	8	Ones	20	16

Potting Compost

In our *Alphabetical List of Flowering Plants*, chapter 16, details as to the most suitable individual composts are given. The usual ingredients of potting composts are: loam, which generally forms the greater part; leaf-mould or peat-moss; sand; old mortar rubble; well-rotted manure; and charcoal. The gardener should always have quantities of these ingredients handy on his potting bench, or in bins below it.

Potting Soils

The potting soil must be moderately moist, that is to say, if a handful is taken up and pressed firmly together, it should become moulded to the shape of the hand, but at the same time it should be dry enough to crumble as soon as it is disturbed. Mix the ingredients well together, but do not sieve the compost; this would rob it of much of its plant food and most of its porosity; large lumps must, of course, be broken up.

Only for seeds and cuttings should the compost be sieved, and in this case through a quarter-inch mesh. Young plants with fine fibrous roots need a compost much finer in texture than do mature and vigorous plants being potted-on into their final pots.

As has been said before, the proportions in which the various ingredients are added to the compost vary in accordance with the requirements of individual plants and with the nature of the loam used, but the following may be taken as a suitable compost for the general run of soft-wooded plants.

$\frac{1}{2}$ part Fibrous Loam
$\frac{1}{4}$ part Leaf-mould or Peat-moss
$\frac{1}{8}$ part Well-rotted Manure
$\frac{1}{8}$ part Coarse Silver Sand

The compost should be stored in the potting-shed, and where greenhouse subjects are to be potted-up, the compost should be stored in the warm house for at least twenty-four hours previous to potting, if possible, so that the compost may be warmed up to the temperature of the house.

When to Re-pot

The time at which a plant should be re-potted depends on whether the "ball" is to be broken up, as for instance when a plant from the open ground is to be potted-up or when a plant has to be re-potted because the soil is old and sour, or whether the "ball" is to be left practically intact as when a growing plant is to be "shifted" into a slightly larger pot. In the latter case the operation can be performed at any time when the plant is in fairly active growth, as the roots will at once go ahead and take possession of the new soil. Where the "ball" is to be broken up, however, re-potting can only be undertaken just as the roots are beginning to come into active growth, at which time they will be able to penetrate the new compost; if the "ball" were broken up when the roots were not in their most vigorous state, the young root-matter could not fail to be badly damaged and in consequence would be unable to recuperate in sufficient time to penetrate the new soil before the "resting" period set in, and the new soil would become sour before it could be occupied.

During the growing season a plant or two of each batch of similar flowers, whether they are biennials being grown on for greenhouse use, soft-wooded perennials or hard-wooded plants, should be turned out of their pots so that it may be seen whether re-potting is necessary. As soon as the roots begin to wind round the sides of the pot a larger pot should at once be given unless the "resting" season is approaching when potting should be held over till growth again begins. Plants make most growth in April and May and again in August and September; the best time to re-pot, therefore, is just before this growth commences, that is to say about March and again in August and early September. March is the better time at which to re-pot established plants as the spring

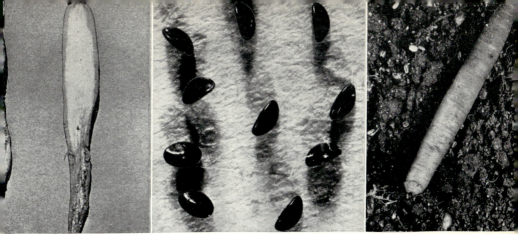

PLATE 11 PESTS *Left*, damage due to Carrot Fly, *centre and right*, eggs (X) and larva of a Leather Jacket.

[*Shell Photo and Plant Protection Ltd.*

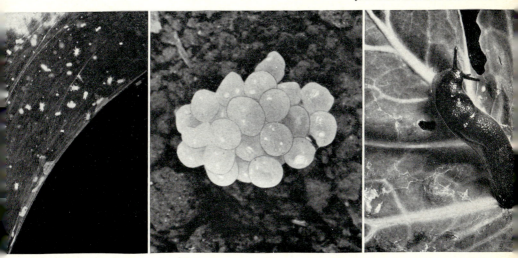

Reading left to right, above, Red Spider Mite on a cucumber, Slug eggs (X) and adult on a cabbage; *below*, Raspberry Beetle (X), White Fly on cucumber and Woolly Aphis.

PLATE 12 CHRYSANTHEMUM CUTTINGS After blooming the stems are cut down to within 6 inches of the base and the pots are placed in a frost-proof frame or house. After a time sturdy shoots will commence to grow from the base of the plant and these will provide material for taking cuttings, *below left*. After preparing, the cuttings are inserted round the edge of the pot, *below right*. Above can be seen, *left*, two unprepared and, *right*, two prepared cuttings.

growth is more vigorous than the autumn growth, and new material will then be of more use to them.

Size of Pot

It is always advisable to put a plant into a pot slightly too small rather than too large. Unless the plant is very pot-bound, or is required to grow very quickly (as in the case of many young and growing plants), put the plant back in the same sized pot if possible. Many gardeners like to have about 1 inch of soil between the "ball" and the sides of the pot.

It is fatal to try to save work or to force a plant on by putting a small subject into a pot too large for it. The small roots will be unable to make use of all the moisture and plant food in the soil; this hangs about in the compost and it is a long time before any fresh air is able to enter, so that the soil becomes clammy and finally sour. For this reason pot-up into small pots, re-potting frequently as the plants grow and the roots become pot-bound. It is rarely necessary to move a plant into a pot more than two, at the most three, sizes larger than the old one. As soft-wooded plants are as a rule vigorous growers, they may usually be put into proportionately larger pots than would be advisable for the slower-growing hard-wooded plants.

Drainage and Crocks

Over the hole at the bottom of the pot should be placed small pieces of broken pots, technically called "crocks". For cuttings, which are not intended to remain in the pot for any length of time after they have rooted, a single piece of crock, convex side uppermost, is sufficient, but when the time of tenancy is likely to be prolonged to months, and perhaps even years, it is necessary to fill one-sixth, and in some cases as much as one-fourth, of the entire depth of the pot with broken potsherds. If possible, a conical form should be given to the crocking.

Finishing Touches

The crocking being done and a little coarse mould thrown over them, some fine mould should be put in and shaken together by gently knocking the edge of the bottom of the pot against the potting-bench, or by striking the sides of the pot gently with the hand. The soil at the bottom of the pot should be just sufficient to lift the plant so that the top of the "ball", when set in the new pot, is within $1\frac{1}{2}$ inches of the rim of the pot—when firmly planted and covered with $\frac{1}{2}$ to 1 inch of new soil, it should be in 1 inch below the rim in a large pot and $\frac{1}{2}$ inch in a small pot.

Re-potting

The most suitable times for re-potting the various kinds of plants will be found in the individual articles in the Alphabetical List of Flowering Plants, chapter 16.

The plants to be re-potted should, if necessary, be watered an hour or so before the work is to take place so that the "ball" of earth round the roots may be just moderately moist; if too wet the fibrous roots may be torn; if over-dry the small roots will find great difficulty in becoming established in the new compost. Now turn the pot upside-down, placing the first and second finger of the left hand so that the stem lies between them while the palm and fingers lie across the top edges of the pot, and grasp the bottom of the pot, which is now uppermost, with the right hand. Next tap the rim of the pot gently on the edge of the potting-bench, and the roots and soil will come out complete, being supported by the left hand, as the pot is removed by the right.

Care must be taken that the plant and soil do not drop from the pot. Should the plant " ball " not come out of the pot, the finger or a small blunt-headed stick should be inserted through the drainage hole at the bottom of the pot, and if gentle pressure is applied, the " ball " will soon be removed from the pot.

Potting-up

The crocks, any sour soil, and dead roots must be carefully removed so that the roots are not bruised, and some of the thickest roots should be drawn out from the " ball " with a pointed stick; these will establish themselves in the new soil round the sides of the larger pot. Now place the " ball " on the soil already in the pot so that the plant will be quite central, and pack the soil with the hand or trowel between the " ball " and the sides of the pot on the bench, consolidating the earth by knocking the pot on the bench, and pressing the compost down round the sides with a potting stick, or the thumb, which is more convenient when dealing with the smaller sizes of pots. Press the new soil firmly about the collar of the plant with the thumbs. Keep the new soil *level* with the top of the old " ball ". The collar should not be raised above the general level, but to depress it beneath is certain death to hard-wooded plants. All plants, however hardy, should be kept warm and moist for a few weeks after re-potting, especially if they have received a large shift. The growth of the roots is thus promoted—a point of great importance at this stage.

Only remove from the " ball " that soil that is really sour; it is a mistake to disturb the roots if the soil is still fresh; if, however, the compost has become very sour, all the soil must be removed and the roots must be well washed through with lukewarm water, any dead or diseased parts being cut away.

Potting-on Seedlings and Cuttings

Cuttings and seedlings are best potted-up in the house in which they have hitherto been grown; they are delicate and if transferred to a cold, draughty shed may receive a set-back. Once established in their new pots, they can gradually be hardened-off to stand the temperature of their new house.

The size of the pot to be used naturally depends on the kind and size of the plant, but as a general rule 3- or 4-inch pots are suitable for the first potting-up of seedlings that have previously been pricked-off into

130

boxes, round the sides of pots, or into thumb pots; the new pots should be just large enough to take the roots without their touching the sides; a larger pot will be needed with each shift as the plants grow. The size of the pot in which the plant is ultimately to be flowered bears closely upon the dimensions of the pot used for the first potting-up. If the ultimate pot is to be 8 inches in diameter, the first pot should usually be a 3½-inch one, the pot for the second shift being a 5-inch one. A 3-inch is generally large enough as a first pot when the eventual size is to be 6 inches, the intermediate shift being into a 4-inch pot. For the general run of biennials potted-on for greenhouse use three pottings in all (excluding the seed or cutting boxes and the pricking-off) are all that the gardener can afford to give, though in some cases more frequent potting is beneficial, if possible. Perennials are potted-on as they increase in size and as they become pot-bound.

The procedure is the same as for the potting-up of maturer plants, but the stem of the seedling must be buried nearly up to the two small seed leaves, or cotyledons. The young roots are very brittle and tender, so that the soil must not be pressed down with the thumbs and fingers as when potting maturer plants; the tapping of the pot on the bench and the watering afterwards should render the compost quite firm enough. Seedlings grown in boxes or close together in pots should be potted-off fairly early, that is, before their roots begin to intertwine.

Potting Shed

The potting shed should be furnished with a shelf or stage of suitable height on which plants can be potted or re-potted, as the case may be, before removal to the greenhouse. This should be large and strong enough to hold sufficient potting soil to complete a good batch of plants, before it is again necessary to mix more compost, and must be of sufficient height to obviate stooping.

How Firm to Pot

With most plants it is desirable to pot firmly, not to ram the earth down too hard, but sufficiently firm for the plant to offer resistance if slight pressure is applied to it to pull it upwards. The degree of firmness necessary varies with the age of the plant, the nature of the roots, and the character of the compost. Young plants, of all kinds, whose roots will expand need planting only moderately firmly, the soil being packed just tight enough to hold the plants in position; each potting must, however, be firmer. When mature, fibrous-rooted plants should be planted very firmly, the more sandy the compost the firmer must the planting be. Plants with large fleshy roots require a much looser compost. Between these two extremes there are roots of varying sizes and characteristics, and in each individual case the gardener must use his discretion. Although it may be necessary to firm the soil firmly round the roots, do not pack the surface down hard or the air will be excluded. Lastly, never fill a pot with soil right up to the edge, but only to about half an inch below the edge of smaller pots, and 1 inch for larger pots.

CHAPTER 13

Bedding Plants

It is not uncommon to hear some gardeners criticize as old-fashioned and dreary summer bedding. Now, it is true that it can be so if the maker displays no imagination. For example, to fill the beds year after year with pelargoniums (geraniums), calceolarias and lobelia. Although these are excellent flowers if used with discretion, and should never be forgotten, there are so many other beautiful flowers that may be used, and which, if tastefully combined and laid out, will give brilliant masses of colour all through the summer.

There need be no monotony, for almost all flowers can be used to furnish beds, and it is now a common practice to use for this purpose such beautiful annuals as saponaria and myosotis (forget-me-nots), or such hardy plants as pansies and violas. Still, the old term of "bedding plants" is commonly used to refer to certain half-hardy or tender flowering plants which are grown under glass during the winter and spring, and are merely planted out during summer to be again lifted as soon as the hot months are over. Pelargoniums or geraniums, as they are commonly called, begonias, verbenas, petunias, calceolarias and lobelias are the plants perhaps most frequently grown in this way.

Construction of Beds. (*See* chapter 14.)

Manuring the Bed

As soon as the summer bedding is cleared away in the autumn some well-rotted manure (old hot-bed manure is excellent), leaf-mould, and thoroughly decayed vegetable refuse should be forked into the beds to a depth of about 12 inches, this will draw the roots well down. In addition to this the plants benefit by a weekly dressing with weak liquid manure made from a diluted solution of phosphate of ammonia or phosphate of potash or from some farmyard manure water. The mixture must not be allowed to touch the foliage.

Bedding Colour Schemes

Great care must be taken in the colour schemes, so as to avoid clashing colours, the colours must harmonize or else the gardener must aim at getting a contrast. Do not use too many colours, two, or at the most three, are best massed together; likewise only two or three kinds of flowers should be used in each bed. It is necessary, too, to remember the height and habit of the plants associated together; some make ideal

132

carpet plants, others are excellent for use as the principal plants or for "dot" plants, while, a point sometimes forgotten, all subjects in a bedding scheme must flower together. Never overcrowd, as this leads to weak, straggly plants with poor and scarce blooms. No plant, unless very small, should be planted nearer than 6 inches to its neighbour, while the average-sized plants need to be some 10 to 15 inches apart. Dot plants are placed about 3 feet apart, while edging plants are best set about 10 inches from the edge of the bed, otherwise they are liable to be damaged when the grass is cut.

For colour schemes, we would refer the reader to the *Colour Schemes for Bedding*, p. 136, and to our remarks as to colour grouping in the chapter on *Herbaceous Borders*, p. 282. The plants used must depend chiefly on individual taste and largely on the glass available to raise them.

As to the bedding designs they should be as simple as possible, especially in small beds, and should aim at providing masses of one colour rather than small patches of highly contrasting shades in a small bed. Where the plants themselves are very small, more complicated designs may be attempted.

Cannas or tall fuchsias make very striking "dot" plants in a large bed of begonias, as do standard heliotropes or kochias in a bed of salmon-pink geraniums. Abutilons and plumbagoes also make excellent "dot" plants. Bear in mind the beauty of pale pink flowers thrown up by a groundwork of mauve, dark blue or purple; a group of dark blue or purple flowers if edged with yellow violas makes a most striking display. Beware of associating colours like magenta or pink with scarlet; these colours need very careful handling. We will content ourselves with these cursory remarks, as the tables of *Colour Schemes for Bedding*, p. 136, will be found to be replete with suggestions.

Summer Bedding

Although it is unwise to bed-out too early, this does not mean that the preparation of the beds should be left until just before it is time to put the plants in. The beds should be prepared as soon as the spring bedding is over. All bulbs used in bedding schemes should be lifted and planted in the reserve garden and watered occasionally until the "grass" has turned yellow. They should then be dried off and stored; if care is taken of them they may be used for three or four years in succession without any appreciable deterioration in the blooms. The amateur is often worried as to what he should do with the spring bedding he takes out; should he save any of it or should he destroy it all? As space is usually a consideration, all plants that are easily raised from seed should be destroyed, but such perennials as arabis, daisies, erysimum, polyanthus or violas should be divided into small plants and placed in the reserve garden where they are shaded from the hottest rays of the sun to be grown on for the next year's spring bedding.

After the beds have been dug over, they should be made thoroughly firm by treading, if the soil is light, and should then be raked over, draw-

133

ing the soil well up towards the centre of the bed. This will not only drain the bed, but will display the plants to better advantage.

Antirrhinums, calceolarias, chrysanthemums (marguerites), and violas are among the most hardy of our summer bedding plants and a start can be made with these as soon as the beds have been cleared of the spring bedding. This will not only help to get the work forward at this heavy time, but will give these plants time to become established before the hot weather comes.

Pot plants make better bedding subjects than those grown in boxes, as the roots are not so liable to be damaged when removed for bedding-out. In planting, use a trowel to scoop out just sufficient earth to make a hole to take the roots without crushing. Do not use a dibble as this is apt to make a hole so deep as to leave an air pocket under the roots, which will be parched and will also not have a hole wide enough to accommodate them. Press the soil *very firmly* round the roots with the hands after planting or the plants will be slow in becoming established and will be greatly handicapped. If the weather is warm, bedding-out should be done in the late afternoon or in the evening, and after planting the bed should receive a thorough soaking with water through a fine rose—which operation should be repeated daily for a week or so if the weather is very dry. If the nights tend to be cold, water should not be applied through a rose, but a little water should be given to the roots of each plant by means of a can with the rose removed. This will save possible chilling of the foliage and consequent checking of growth, or even the death of the plants. Do not bed-out while the soil is very dry either in the case of summer bedding or when planting the spring bedding. Give the bed a good soaking with water the evening previous to the planting, before the final raking down of the soil, and, as stated above, after the bedding-out has been completed. (*See* Mulching, p. 19; *and* Watering, p. 26.) Care must be taken to insert the plant to about the same depth as it stood in its pot or in the box. Keep the "ball" intact and plant so that the top of it is just $\frac{1}{2}$ an inch below the ground level. If the plant is set in too low there is the possibility of it "damping-off". Always remove the crocks at the bottom of the pot before the plants are bedded-out, otherwise the bed, in the course of time, will become littered with these bits of broken pots.

Care of the Bed
For the care of the bed during the summer—that is to say, weeding, removal of dead flowers, staking and training—we would refer the reader to the *Care of the Herbaceous Border*, p. 280.

Spring Bedding
Spring bedding requires much the same treatment as summer bedding. It should be done as early as possible so that the plants may establish themselves before the severe weather sets in. Plant them, therefore, early in October, as soon as the summer bedding has been cleared away; this should be done immediately the flowers are over. The question of what

Spring Bedding

plants to discard and what to save again arises. As summer bedding plants are nearly all either half-hardy or tender they will require the protection of glass through the winter. The amount of glass available, therefore, usually largely decides the question. Glass space is always very valuable, therefore it would be folly to preserve any plants that can easily be raised from seed or from cuttings; such plants as the following can, therefore, be thrown away: alyssums, antirrhinums, asters, calceolarias, coreopsis, gaillardias, geraniums, geums, heliotropes, lobelia, penstemons, petunias, stocks, and verbenas; these, however, must not be discarded until cuttings have been taken from them. Woody plants such as abutilons, fuchsias, standard heliotropes, hydrangeas and plumbagoes; cannas, centaureas, senecios and other foliage plants that take several years to grow to the most effective size should be taken up with as complete a ball of roots as possible and planted in suitably-sized pots, the branches being trimmed if space is at a premium. If the branches are trimmed, the roots may also be reduced. Store the plants in a frost-proof frame or on shelves in the greenhouse and water occasionally. Bulbous and tuberous-rooted plants such as begonias, dahlias and gladioli must, of course, be saved. (*See* paragraphs on individual plants, chapter 16.)

Do not leave the bedding-out until the early spring when bloom is coming and the roots are not in a favourable condition to establish themselves. As soon as the summer bedding has been removed dig over the bed to two spades' depth and manure it as described on p. 132, then put in the plants that are to form the groundwork, and let them be just far enough apart so that, when grown, they will cover the surface of the bed. In the interstices between these insert the bulbs, at the correct depth for the kind planted. (*See* chapter on Bulbs, p. 141.)

Plants for the Spring Bed

At one time bulbs were practically the only plants used by the gardener for spring bedding. This use of bulbs alone had many drawbacks; firstly the beds were plain and bare all through the winter, then as soon as the bulbs had flowered the beds would become untidy and uninteresting. To-day we use a groundwork of alyssum, arabis, aubrieta, daisies, myosotis, polyanthus, silenes, violas, wallflowers, and other dwarf hardy plants, through which the bulbs rise to form a mass of colour over a carpet that is chosen either to harmonize or contrast with them. This groundwork clothes the ground and looks neat all the winter and also keeps the bed tidier and interesting for some time after the bulbs have flowered. Spring bedding is thus rendered less formal and stiff, and the period of bloom is also extended. In addition, small shrubs and dwarf conifers are often used to relieve the bareness of the bed during the winter. These are best sunk into the beds in pots, they are then easily removed when the summer bedding has to be put in. The best time to buy bulbs is in September, and care should be taken to see that they are plump and firm to the touch, of good but not excessive size, and free from disease. No growth should be visible.

COLOUR SCHEMES FOR BEDDING

NOTE.—For details as to Colour, Height, Time of Flowering and Culture, *see* the Alphabetical List of Flowering Plants and Shrubs, p. 147.

SUMMER BEDDING

Principal Plant	Ground, Edging or " Dot " Plant
Ageratum Houstonianum (Pale Blue)	Pelargonium Madame Crousse (Rose-pink)
Ageratum Houstonianum Swanley Blue	Alyssum maritimum minimum (White)
Antirrhinum majus (nanum), Golden Queen, Enchantress, White Queen	Ageratum Houstonianum Swanley Blue
	Browallia viscosa (Blue)
	Gladiolus primulinus Vanessa (Salmon)
Begonia semperflorens Triumph (White)	Lobelia Erinus Cambridge Blue
Begonia tuberous-rooted vars. (Various)	Alyssum maritimum (White)
Calceolaria Camden Hero (Brown)	Phlox Drummondii nana Snowball
Calendula officinalis Orange King	Anchusa capensis (Blue)
Dahlia Coltness Gem (Scarlet)	Viola White Swan (White)
Fuchsia Ballet Girl (Red and White)	Phlox Drummondii nana (Mixed vars.)
Pelargonium Paul Crampel (Scarlet)	Abutilon striatum var. Thompsonii (Yellow)
Pelargonium Madame Crousse (Rose-pink)	
Gladiolus Majuba (Scarlet)	Antirrhinum majus (nanum) White Queen, Golden Queen
Gladiolus Red Charm (Crimson)	
Godetia Rosy Morn (Coral-pink)	Dianthus chinensis Purity (White)
Heliotropium peruvianum Giant vars.	Eucalyptus globulus (Silver-blue Leaves)
Kochia scoparia var. trichophylla (Burning Bush)	
	Tagetes erecta nana Orange Prince
Lobelia fulgens Queen Victoria (Scarlet)	Antirrhinum White Beauty (White)
Nicotiana sylvestris (White)	Polygonum orientale (Crimson)
Nigella damascena Miss Jekyll (Blue)	Verbena Miss Willmott (Rose)
Penstemon Southgate Gem (Carmine)	Phlox Drummondii compacta Snowball
Petunia Countess of Ellesmere (Rose)	Callistephus chinensis Comet (White)
Phlox Drummondii (Rose & Pink Shades)	Gaura Lindheimeri (White, tinted Red)
Salvia patens Cambridge Blue	Calocephalus Brownii (Silvery Leaves)
Senecio—Cineraria Diamond (Grey Leaves)	Gladiolus America (Lilac-rose)
Tagetes erecta (Orange)	Lobelia Erinus Sapphire (Sapphire-blue)
Tropæolum minus Golden King (Yellow)	Penstemon Pink Beauty (Pink)
Verbena Mammoth Firefly (Scarlet)	Antirrhinum majus Yellow King
Verbena venosa (Rosy Purple)	Alyssum maritimum (White)
	Artemisia Purshiana (Grey Leaves)
Zinnia elegans (Scarlet and Yellow vars.)	Gazania longiscapa (Golden Brown)

SPRING BEDDING

Principal Plant	Ground, Edging or " Dot " Plant
Alyssum saxatile compactum (Yellow)	Wallflower Dwarf Blood Red
Anemone St. Brigid (Mixed)	Iris Spanish (Mixed)
Hyacinth City of Haarlem (Yellow)	Myosotis alpestris Victoria (Blue)
Hyacinth Gertrude (Rose-pink)	Aubrieta Lavender
Hyacinth L'Innocence (White)	Primula (Polyanthus) (Red) var.
Hyacinth La Victoire (Rose)	Viola William Robb (Lavender)
Iris Dutch (Mixed)	Violas, Blue, Yellow and White
Iris Spanish (Mixed)	Violas, Blue, Yellow and White
Muscari Heavenly Blue (Blue)	Tulip Early Prince de Ligne (Yellow)
Narcissus Empress (Yellow and White)	Muscari Heavenly Blue (Blue)
Narcissus Seagull (White)	Myosotis dissitiflora Perfection (Blue)
Primula (Polyanthus) var. (White)	Bellis perennis Mammoth Etna (Red)
Primula (Polyanthus) var. (Orange)	Crocus Maximilian (Azure-blue)
Tulip Keizer Kroon (Early) (Scarlet-Yellow)	Arabis caucasica (albida) (White)
Tulip Early Vermilion Brilliant (Scarlet)	Pansy Winter-flowering Winter Sun (Yellow)
Tulip Early Double Van der Holf (Yellow)	Myosotis alpestris Victoria (Blue)

COLOUR SCHEMES FOR BEDDING

SPRING BEDDING (*continued*)

Principal Plant	Ground, Edging or "Dot" Plant
Tulip Darwin Clara Butt (Pink and Rose)	Myosotis dissitiflora Perfection (Sky)
Tulip Darwin King Harold (Blood-red)	Iberis sempervirens (White)
Tulip Darwin Princess Elizabeth (Rose)	Silene pendula Bijou (Salmon-rose)
Tulip Darwin William Pitt (Scarlet)	Narcissus Leedsii White Lady (White)
Tulip Breeder Bacchus (Royal Purple)	Wallflower Golden Monarch
Tulip Breeder Panorama (Chestnut red)	Wallflower Ivory White
Tulip Cottage Inglescombe Pink	Tulip Cottage Arethusa (Primrose)
Tulip Cottage Inglescombe Scarlet	Wallflower Fire King (Orange-scarlet)
Tulip Cottage Picotee (White and Rose)	Viola Kitty Bell (Lavender)
Viola Jersey Gem (Purple)	Tulip Cottage Inglescombe Yellow
Wallflower Vulcan (Crimson)	Tulip Cottage Orange King
Wallflower Ruby Gem (Ruby-Violet)	Tulip Breeder Yellow Perfection (Bronze-Yellow)

NOTE.—For details as to Colour, Height, Time of Flowering and Culture, *see* the Alphabetical List of Flowering Plants and Shrubs, p. 147.

Planting the Bed

Both with spring and summer bedding it is best to mark the positions of each plant by means of stakes and string, before a start is made with the actual planting.

If planting a round bed, a stake should be inserted at the exact centre and to this stake is attached a piece of string; by fixing a peg of wood at different distances down this string, the gardener can trace out circles of different diameter, on which the plants, still in their pots, should be spaced out evenly. The gardener can then see more or less how his scheme will look when planted, also the number of each kind of plant required to fill the bed.

In bedding-out small beds most gardeners find it easiest to work from the edges inwards to the centre; in large beds, however, mark the centre accurately and work outwards from this, using a board to stand on so that the feet do not tread down the soil.

If this plank is long enough to span the bed and rest on two or three bricks on each side, it will be raised above the bed and will save any pressure on the soil.

Carpet Bedding

Carpet bedding consists in arranging masses of low, compact-growing plants with various coloured leaves in such a manner as to show patterns. It is usual to arrange a background of plants of some one colour, and through this to run plants of other colours in masses, stripes or ribbons, so as to produce the artificial result desired. Among the commoner plants used for this purpose are Sempervivum of various colours (grey and green), Echiverias, Sedum glaucum (grey), Cerastium tomentosum (silver), Herniaria glabra (green) and Chrysanthemum Parthenium var. aureum (yellow).

Methods of Propagation

It is advantageous to have bedding plants as well advanced as possible; late and consequently undeveloped plants bear poor flowers. Sow the annuals in heat, if possible, in February or in the open, if hardy, in March or April. Biennials should be sown from May to August and wintered under glass. Annuals, too, may be treated as biennials, sown in September, and wintered under glass.

Cuttings of most half-hardy plants, as pelargoniums and verbenas, are taken in July and August; ageratums, calceolarias and salvias in September, and may be kept in the open till the end of September, when they must be wintered in a cold frame or better still near the glass in a greenhouse in slight heat. For cuttings in early spring old stocks must be placed in gentle heat and induced to grow, and when sufficiently large the young shoots may be taken off as cuttings, to be rooted also in gentle heat. (*See* Plant Propagation, p. 62.) Begonias and similar tuberous-rooted plants need to be "started" in heat early in February and will then be ready for planting out with the other bedding plants at the end of May or early in June.

Hardening-off

Never bring the plants straight out of the frame or warm house into the beds, harden-off by giving gradually more and more air for three weeks to a month before the time for bedding-out, which is usually about the middle of May. Planting out without adequate hardening-off is responsible for much failure and usually results in checked growth, and consequently late and poor flowering, or often complete loss of the more tender plants.

For further information as to the propagation of bedding plants, see chapter 8 on *Plant Propagation,* and for cultural details peculiar to each species, see the *Alphabetical List of Flowering Plants and Shrubs* p. 147. *See also* Beds and Borders, chapter 14.

CHAPTER 14

Beds and Borders

Their Design and Construction

The first and essential purpose of a flower bed is to display flowers and shrubs to their best advantage. The more simple the shape of the flower bed the better it will fulfil its purpose, and at the same time be all the more easy to construct, plant and keep in order. Elaborate geometrical designs have, except in the more formal Dutch and French gardens, gone right out of fashion. Many of these older designs had sharp-pointed extremities, which were very awkward to plant and care for; the most useful shapes are circles, ellipses, squares and rectangles.

Rectilinear beds are generally situated in the more formal parts of the garden, near the house, as they best harmonize with the straight lines of the architecture of the house; if they are laid out on the lawn they should be so placed that their longer sides run parallel with those of a neighbouring straight path, or with the edge of the lawn. Except when they are permanently to accommodate shade-loving plants, the beds should be so placed that they are open to the sun, but should at the same time have shelter from cold or strong prevailing winds. When beds are made on a lawn they must be so designed and placed that the lawn-mower can operate easily; grass verges or walks between beds should never be less than 18 inches or 2 feet wide, otherwise even a small machine will have difficulty in cutting them well.

Making the Beds

Having pegged out the design to the required size and shape, the turf should be removed on a dry day with a turfing-iron in turves 2 inches deep, and the soil should then be bastard-trenched, that is, the surface must be thoroughly dug over to a depth of two spades, the top layer being kept on top, and the subsoil below this being forked over, but left in position. If the soil is very heavy, the top 2 or 3 feet should be removed, the subsoil should be broken up as before, and upon it should be placed 5 to 6 inches of broken bricks or large stones as drainage. When the top-soil is moderately good it may have loam added to it and then be returned to the bed, or if the soil is quite unsuitable, that is clayey or stony, all should be removed and fresh loam must be introduced. In either case, a liberal dressing of well-rotted manure should be dug well into the top-soil. If these beds are being made in a new garden, lime at the rate of 14 oz. per square yard should also be worked into the soil, as insect

139

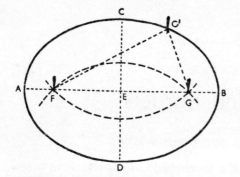

FIG. 16. Method of marking out an elliptical bed. AB and CD equals the length and width respectively of the proposed bed. The points F and G are formed by the intersection of the two arcs of radius AE struck from the points C and D. Drive the stakes at F and G, and around these place a continuous cord of length AB. With a marking stick scribe the ellipse ACBDA; the cord should be held such that it is always taut.

pests and fungi are certain to be present in quantities in any newly-broken grassland.

Each autumn the beds should be dressed with manure, as bedding plants are, as a whole, voracious feeders, like a rich soil, and soon exhaust it when spring and summer bedders are, as is usually the case, grown in the same bed. If manuring cannot be carried out in the autumn it should be done in April or May when the summer bedding is put in. Every three or four years the soil should be thoroughly dug over to a depth of two spades, and if it appears at all sour and greasy should be dressed with lime.

The addition of new soil, manure, and drainage material will raise the bed somewhat above the level of the surrounding ground. The soil should slope neatly up to the centre of the bed, and will thus best display plants of equal height when bedded out, and will provide drainage. A bed 4 feet wide should be about 4 inches higher at the centre than at the edges; beds of other sizes, of course, varying in height at the centre in proportion to their width. If on a lawn, the edging of the bed should be neatly trimmed round with an edging-iron. (*See also* chapter 7.)

FIG. 17. Method of marking out a ser-pentine bed. First divide the length AB into three equal parts and then subdivide AC and DB into equal parts to form the points E and F. From E and F strike semicircles of radius AE and FB as shown, and from C and D the semicircles of radius AC and DB. From the centre M mark a circle of radius AM, thus forming the two serpentine areas AGCLBO and AKDHBN.

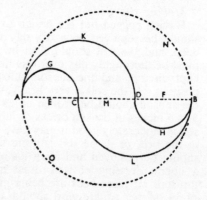

CHAPTER 15

Bulbs and their Culture

Of all flowering plants perhaps the easiest to cultivate are bulbous plants, for they need only to be planted in the early autumn at about two or three times their own depth, in reasonably good and light garden soil, with which a good amount of leaf-mould has been mixed. They should be planted at a uniform depth and should not come into contact with recent manure. Good drainage is essential. If the soil is inclined to be at all heavy it is desirable to lighten it by working in sand at and round each spot in which a clump of bulbs is to be planted. Bulbs, as a rule, should be planted deeply, rather than shallowly, especially crocuses, gladioli and lilies, because the bulbs are then less likely to suffer from the effects of frost.

Fig. 18. *Left*, the wrong way to plant a bulb and, *right*, the correct way, in which the bulb sits firmly and without an air space in hole formed with a trowel.

Plant the bulbs as early in the autumn as possible, especially the spring-flowering ones, they then have ample time to develop their roots before the strain of flowering makes its demands on them. Early planting promotes larger blooms. It is advisable always to plant the bulbs with a trowel and press them firmly, but gently, into the earth before they are covered up. Never plant bulbs with a dibber; this makes a narrow " V "-shaped hole in which it is difficult to set the bulb straight and in which an air space, which will parch the roots, will be left.

Most bulbs, having been planted in suitable soil at a reasonable distance apart, may be allowed to remain for several years without being taken up, divided and replanted. But there are certain exceptions. Tulips and hyacinths, for example, should be lifted when the leaves die down, carefully dried, stored in a cool, dry place, and replanted in October and

141

September respectively. For individual cultural details of the various bulbs, see the *Alphabetical List of Flowering Plants*, p. 147.

Bonemeal is a good artificial manure for bulbs, and should be dusted round the bulbs at the rate of 2 oz. to the square yard and thoroughly forked in in February; an equal amount of superphosphate may, with advantage, be added at the same time.

Various spring bedding schemes for planting bulbs are given on p. 136. Here will be found a list of dwarf plants that will form a suitable ground-work, and that will harmonize in colour with the bulbs forming the main feature.

After-Flowering Treatment

No attempt should be made to remove leaves or flower-stalks until they have withered and decayed to such an extent that they may be removed by a very slight effort. The long swordlike leaves of crocuses, hyacinths, etc., should be neatly plaited together, to obviate untidiness of appearance, and should be allowed to remain until they are quite decayed. The dead flowers ought to be cut off just below the spike of bloom, unless it is wished to save the seed. This holds good for all bulbs that have a woody or strong flower stem.

Lifting and Storing Bulbs

When the leaves have completely died away, but not before, bulbs may be taken up and allowed to dry. When the tops are dry and withered they should be cut off an inch above the bulbs, and the roots should also be cut away; the bulbs should then be kept in a dry, dark and frost-proof place to which the air has free access until the time for planting comes round again, which commences in September for hyacinths, etc., and ends in March for late-flowering varieties of the gladiolus, the period of planting being regulated in a degree by the period of flowering.

Most bulbs may, however, remain where they are from year's end to year's end, provided that the soil is suitable, the drainage sufficient and that they are planted deeply. (*See individual cultural details in* Alphabetical List, chapter 16.) Bulbs have a tendency to rise to the surface, especially corms, for in the crocus and gladiolus, though not in the cyclamen, the new corms are formed every year on the top of the old corms which perish. The continuance of bulbs in the places in which they are first planted leads to the formation of splendid masses, from which at the proper season rise glorious flower spikes.

Naturalizing Bulbs in Grass

Most of our spring bulbs are far more beautiful when viewed in their natural surroundings among the grass and in the meadows, woodlands, or wild garden than when planted, however naturally and artistically, in borders. Most of them, too, especially daffodils, crocuses and scillas, do much better in this natural state than in beds or borders where they are constantly being disturbed.

Do not plant them on lawns, as the grass cannot be cut until the leaves of the bulbs have turned yellow and dried up. Another word of caution: do not plant daffodils in pastureland, as they are somewhat poisonous to cattle.

The bulbs are best planted in long, narrow oval strips some 30 to 40 feet in length, shaped like patches of snow driven by the wind into long slender drifts on the ground. They should be scattered on the grass over an area shaped as above, so that they lie thicker towards the centre of the "drift", and should be planted with a trowel or bulb planter just where they fall. There should be no regular, well-defined margin to the "drift", the edges should be indistinct and gradually merging into the surrounding grass.

August and September is the best planting time; small bulbs like the crocus and scilla should be set some 3 inches apart, while daffodil bulbs should have about 10 inches between them. Bulbs that have been used for beds and borders are equally as good as new bulbs for naturalizing in grass and should be replanted immediately after being lifted from the beds and while their foliage is still green and succulent.

Some seven years, at least, may be allowed to elapse before it is necessary to disturb naturalized bulbs, provided they receive an annual top-dressing of leaf-mould each autumn.

The bulbs most suitable for planting in grass are: Allium moly, Anemone appennina, Chionodoxa Luciliæ, Crocuses, Cyclamen species, Daffodils (Golden Spur, Barri Conspicuus, Poeticus), Erythroniums, Fritillaria species, Irises, Muscari armeniacum, Scillas, Snowdrops, and Winter aconites.

Potted Bulbs

These should be planted in autumn and the crowns should just appear above the surface of the soil, which should come up to within $\frac{3}{4}$ inch of the top of the pot. After planting, the pots should be well soaked in water and placed in the open on boards or slates so that worms cannot get up into the soil. The pots should be surrounded and covered with a layer of 5 inches of fibre or ashes, and left for seven to nine weeks until the roots will have formed and the tops have made an inch of growth, when they may be moved to a frame or a cold greenhouse, if the roots have made sufficient growth, and should be liberally supplied with water but not saturated.

The less forward plants should be put back in the ashes and will furnish a succession of later blooms if brought into the greenhouse at successive intervals.

The darkness encourages growth of the roots, which is so essential to good blooms. Bulbs should never be forced on before their roots have sufficiently developed.

The pots should not be subjected to full light until two or three days after the covering of fibre has been removed, that is, until the pale yellow shoots have turned green. When this has happened the pots should be placed close to the glass and be brought on gradually till the flower buds are well advanced, when liquid manure-water may be used and the plants forced on with moderate heat. A good compost consists of a mixture of equal parts of loam, leaf-mould and well-rooted cow-manure, together with a little sand.

As to the number of bulbs that may be planted in a pot, this, of course, depends on the species of bulb and on the size of pot used. Snowdrops, crocuses and scilla may be planted so that they practically touch one another, that is, about nine bulbs in a 5-inch pot; larger bulbs, such as those of the daffodil and tulip, may be planted six in a 5-inch pot, while only three hyacinths should be grown in a 6-inch pot.

Depth to Plant

The bulbs of the daffodil, hyacinth, tulip, and similar flowers should be potted so that their tips are just above the surface of the soil; a few other bulbs should only be half buried; while others again must be buried one, three or even more inches below the surface. Crocuses and scilla, for instance, should be just covered with soil. For the depth to plant each species of bulb, see the *Alphabetical List of Flowering Plants*, p. 147.

After forcing, which cannot be done for more than one year running, bulbs may be planted out in borders or used for naturalizing; they should be dried off and planted out in July or August. The year after forcing, the bloom may not be very fine, but in subsequent years a wealth of bloom will be provided.

Bulbs in Fibre

When growing bulbs in this way in small numbers it is obvious that it is false economy to buy any but the best bulbs for treatment. It is waste of time, labour and space to grow small weak plants, some of which may not flower at all. In ordering the bulbs it is best to tell the people from whom they are procured that they are required for this form of culture, and they will select suitable bulbs.

At the same time you should order the fibre, which will be found on experiment to be the best material for filling the bulb bowls. These latter should be simple in shape and colour, so that they may not distract attention from or clash with the flowers growing in them, and should be shallow, some 5 inches deep, and glazed; porous bowls are not good. Mixed with the fibre will be found a certain proportion of lumps of charcoal, and a few of them should be placed at the bottom of the bowl. If the fibre is at all lumpy pick it over and rub out the lumps between the fingers, then soak it for a day or so and drain it thoroughly until only a drop or two of water comes out when the fibre is squeezed in the hand. Then fill your bowls to a depth of about one-half for large bulbs, such as the narcissus and hyacinth; three-quarters for the smaller, such as crocuses and scillas. On this layer, which should not be pressed down too tightly, place your bulbs; if the bowl is very large grouping them in small clumps, not spacing them regularly over it; if it is small the bulbs may nearly, but not quite, touch. Then fill the bowl nearly to the top with the fibre, so that the extreme tips of the bulbs just show above it, and the planting process is complete.

Bulbs in Fibre

The bowls should be kept for the first six weeks in a dark place, preferably an airy one, and certainly not near a fire. A cool, airy cupboard or cellar will do. Once a week or so examine the bowls to see whether the fibre is dry, and if it shows signs of dryness plunge them in a tub or basin of lukewarm water, which should cover them completely. When the fibre is well soaked take out the bowls and turn them carefully sideways, so that any superfluous water may drain off. While this is being done care must be taken that the whole of the contents of the bowl do not fall out; the fibre should be supported by the open hand during the operation. The fibre should be just damp, never sodden. When the bulbs have made shoots about an inch long the bowls should be brought out into the light, but they should not be exposed to full air and sunshine until the shoots have turned a healthy green. While this is happening the bowls should be kept in a shady corner of the room. When the shoots are green the more light and air they have the better, but when they are placed in a window they should always be removed to the middle of the room if there is the smallest likelihood of a frost during the night. It should also be remembered that the plants will naturally grow towards the light, so that to ensure good straight plants and flower stalks the bowls should be turned each day. No manure should be used.

Crocuses, daffodils, tulips, hyacinths, chionodoxas, fritillarias and grape hyacinths may all be successfully grown in fibre, as we have described, each kind being raised in a separate bowl.

SELECTION OF BULBS AND TUBERS

NOTE.—For Cultural Details, for Colour, Height, Season of Flowering and the best Species and Varieties, *see* the Alphabetical List of Flowering Plants, p. 147.

*Agapanthus orientalis
Allium species
Alstrœmeria aurantiaca
Amaryllis Belladonna
Anemone (tuberous vars.)
Begonia (tuberous vars.)
Brodiæa species
Bulbocodium vernum
Calochortus species
Camassia species
Chionodoxa Luciliæ and vars.
Colchicum species and vars.
Commelina cœlestis
Convallaria majalis
Corydalis solida
Crinum species
Crocus species
Cyclamen species
Dicentra spectabilis

Eranthis hyemalis
Erythronium species
Fritillaria species
Galanthus (Snowdrop) species
Gladiolus vars.
*Gloxinia vars.
*Habranthus pratensis
Hyacinth vars.
Iris vars.
*Ixia vars.
*Ixiolirion montanum
Lapeyrousia cruenta
Leucojum aestivum
Lilium species
*Mirabilis Jalapa
Muscari species and vars.
Narcissus vars.
Nerine sarniensis (Guernsey Lily)

Ornithogalum species
Oxalis species
Pancratium illyricum
Paradisea Liliastrum
*Phædranassa chloraca
Polygonatum multiflorum
Puschkinia scilloides
Ranunculus vars.
Schizostylis coccinea
Scilla species
*Sparaxis tricolor
Sternbergia lutea
Tigridia vars.
Trillium grandiflorum
Tritonia (Montbretia) vars.
Tulips vars.
*Vallota purpurea eximia
*Watsonia Meriana
Zephyranthes candida

NOTE.—* Denotes half-hardy bulbs or tubers only suitable for growing in the open in warm, sheltered situations or in the greenhouse.

HOUSE PLANTS

In addition to the bulbous plants mentioned above, there are many other kinds of flowering or foliage plants suitable for growing indoors.

Choosing the Positions

The positions for the plants to stand in should be chosen carefully. Good light is essential for encouraging the full colour of flowers and leaves and plants that do not get enough should be changed regularly with others in better positions, or if good light falls on one side only, should be turned around every day. Windows that give the best light may also be draughty or if they face south may be too hot at mid-day when the sun can cause the moisture in the pot to dry out quickly. Above or near a fireplace or radiator the air may be too dry or too hot, and near a door or on the stairs there may be constant or sudden draughts.

Management

Watering is generally the most difficult problem. Some plants need water every day, some not more than once a week, but the majority require attention every two or three days. Some indication can be obtained by tapping the pots with a piece of wood about the size of the handle of a hammer or mallet; a dull sound will show that the soil is moist enough, a ring that it needs watering. Too much water is far more damaging than too little, because the soil may then become waterlogged and lead to the death of the roots. It is important, therefore, that the drainage material in the bottom of the pots is adequate and that the pots are not placed in watertight holders or on deep saucers. If a plant becomes too dry and the soil fails to absorb water, the pot should be put into a bucket with water coming up to the rim of the pot and when soaked through, taken out and allowed to drain thoroughly. Dead or wilting leaves and flowers should be cut off regularly and plants with large or hairy leaves that collect dust easily should be sponged over.

A SELECTION OF FLOWERING PLANTS

Astilbe	Chrysanthemum	Fuchsia
Azalea indica	(pot varieties, Pompon,	Hydrangea
Begonia (winter-flowering)	Charm, Cascade)	Pelargonium
Calceolaria	Cineraria	Primula
Celosia	Erica	Saintpaulia
		Solanum

A SELECTION OF FOLIAGE PLANTS

Araucaria	Dieffenbachia	Monstera
Begonia (ornamental)	Fatsia	Peperomia
Bromelia	Fatshedera	Philodendron
Cacti	Ferns	Rhoicissus
Cissus	Ficus	Sansevieria
Codiaeum (Croton)	Hedera	Scindapsus
Coleus	Impatiens	Tradescantia
Cordyline	Maranta	

NOTE.—For Cultural Details, for Colour, Height, Season of Flowering and the best Species and Varieties, *see* the Alphabetical List of Flowering Plants, p. 147.

CHAPTER 16

Alphabetical List of Flowering Plants, Ornamental and Flowering Trees and Shrubs

RECOMMENDED SPECIES AND VARIETIES TOGETHER WITH DETAILS OF THEIR INDIVIDUAL CULTURE

NOTE.—*The words in the brackets following the varieties indicate first the colour of the flowers, then the time of blooming, and lastly the average height in inches or feet to which the plants may be expected to grow.*

Abelia—Hardy and half-hardy evergreen and deciduous shrubs which in mild, sunny, sheltered positions can be grown out of doors. *Culture*—Take cuttings in late summer and strike in frame or layer in August. Plant out in Mar. or Oct. in well-drained peat, loam and leaf-mould, or pot-up for the cool greenhouse. Trim to keep in shape only, cut off dead blooms and thin old wood after flowering. *Species—A. floribunda* (Purple-rose, June–July, 48 in.); *A. triflora* (Pink-white, Aug.–Sept., 36–96 in.); and the hybrid *A. grandiflora* (Pink-white, Aug.–Sept., 36–48 in.).

Abies (Fir)—Handsome evergreen coniferous trees, which thrive in open positions in good loam. *Culture*—Plant in Apr. or Oct. No pruning is required. To propagate, sow in the open in Mar. or Apr. *Species—A. alba* (Silver Fir); *A. balsamea* (Balsam Fir); *A. homolepis* (Nikko Fir); *A. cephalonica* (Grecian Silver Fir); *A. grandis* (Giant Fir); *A. nobilis* (Noble Fir).

Abronia—Small half-hardy annual trailing plant, thriving in sunny borders, or rock gardens, in light sandy soil. *Culture*—Sow in pots under glass in spring and plant out the following Apr. or May. *A. umbellata* (Pink, Summer, 9 in.) is one of the best species.

Abutilon (Indian Mallow)—Handsome half-hardy shrub for the greenhouse, or sheltered beds and borders. *Culture*—For bedding-out increase by means of cuttings of young wood struck in moderate heat (60° F.) during the previous autumn, or early in Feb., grow on, and, if for summer-bedding, plant out about the end of May. 2 parts fibrous loam to 1 part of peat and sand makes a suitable compost. Trim and cut out old wood in Feb. *Varieties—A. Boule de Neige* (White); *A. Golden Fleece* (Yellow); *A. Red Gauntlet* (Dark Red); *A. Thompsonii* (Mottled Green and Yellow Foliage). All Aug. to Nov., 18 to 24 in.

Acacia (Mimosa)—Most of these evergreen trees and shrubs are greenhouse shrubs, not sufficiently hardy to plant in the open, except in warm sheltered borders during the summer months. *Culture*—Sow seeds when ripe, or take cuttings of half-matured wood with a " heel " and strike in a close frame in July or Aug. In the warm greenhouse *A. armata* will flower in early spring. Pot-up in summer after blooming, in 6 to 10-in. pots, and give liquid manure while growing. Stand in a sheltered position out of doors in summer and take in again in Sept. Cut back straggling shoots after flowering. For Hardy or Rose Acacias *see* Robinia. *Species*—*A. armata* (Yellow, Jan.–Mar. 3–10 ft.); *A. Baileyana* (Yellow, Jan.–May, 3–20 ft.); *A. dealbata* [Mimosa] Yellow, Jan.–May, 3–50 ft.); *A. hastulata* (Pale Yellow, Feb.–Apr., 3-4 ft.).

Acæna (New Zealand Burr)—Genus of trailing plants, the dwarf-growing kinds of which are useful rock plants. They do well in sun or shade in ordinary light sandy soil. *Culture*—Sow under glass in Mar., place cuttings in a cold frame in Aug. or propagate by division in Apr. Plant out in spring or early autumn. *Species*—*A. adscendens* (Purple, June–Aug., 6 in.); *A. Buchananii* (Yellowish-red, Summer, 2–3 in.); *A. microphylla* (Bright Red, June–Aug., 3 in.).

Acantholimon (Prickly Thrift)—Useful little rock plants, which like a warm, dry, sunny position and gritty, well-drained loam. Are best propagated by means of cuttings with a " heel " in July, in a cold frame, or by layering. *Species*—*A. Echinus* (White); *A. glumaceum* (Pale Pink); and *A. venustum* (Pale Pink). All July–Aug., 5 to 6 in.

Acanthus (Bear's Breeches)—Hardy perennial useful for beds, borders and cold greenhouse. It likes a sunny, sheltered side with light soil. For culture, *see* Perennials, p. 281. *Species*—*A. mollis, var. latifolius* (Rose, Summer, 24 in.); *A. mollis* (Lilac, Pink or White, Aug., 40 in.); *A. spinosus* (Purple-pink or White, July and Aug., 40 in.).

Acer (Maple)—Hardy deciduous trees for the pleasure grounds and park in positions with well-drained ordinary soil. *Culture*—Plant in Nov. No pruning is required. Propagate by means of seed, layering and budding in the open in Aug.

Achillea (Milfoil, Yarrow and Double Sneezewort)—This genus includes a number of hardy perennials. The dwarf-growing kinds are useful for the rock garden. They like a sunny situation and light, dry, ordinary soil. For culture, *see* Perennials, p. 281. *Species*—*A. argentea* (White, May and June, 3–4 in.); *A. filipendulina* (Yellow, July–Sept., 36–40 in.); *A. Millefolium* [Cerise Queen] (June–Aug., 24 in.); *A. tomentosa* (Yellow, June–Aug., 6–9 in.).

Achimenes—Genus of tuberous-rooted plants, suitable for the living-room or greenhouse. *Culture*—Use a compost of equal parts of leaf-mould, loam and silver sand. Plant 5 to 6 tubers an inch deep in a 5 or 6-in. pot in Feb., and place in the cool house. Shade from the hot sun and feed with liquid manure. To keep up a succession, commence starting them in heat in Jan. and continue until May. Dry-off after flowering, lift rhizomes and store. Propagate by offsets in Feb., or by cuttings in May under glass. *Species and Varieties*—*A. Admiration* (Red-purple); *A. Celestial* (Pale Mauve); *A. coccinea* (Scarlet); *A. grandiflora* (Violet); *A. longiflora* (Blue); *A. l. alba* (White); *A. Pink Perfection* (Rose-magenta). All July–Sept., 12 to 18 in.

Aconite (Eranthis)—Winter Aconites like a shady position in moist sandy loam and leaf-mould. *Culture*—Plant in Oct. 2 in. apart and 2 in. deep. Do not lift from the ground. Propagate by means of division in Oct. *Species*—*E. cilicica* (Yellow); *E. hyemalis* (Greenish Yellow). Both Jan–Mar., 4 in.

Aconitum (Monkshood or Wolfbane)—Hardy perennial, *poisonous* plants. For culture, *see* Perennials, p. 281. *Species*—*A. Carmichœlii* (Pale Lilac-blue, Sept.–Oct., 36 in.); *A. Lycoctonum* (Yellow, July–Aug., 36 in.); *A. Napellus* (Blue and White, June–Oct., 48 in.).

Acorus (Sweet Flag, Sweet Sedge or Myrtle Grass)—Genus of hardy perennials 6–30 in. high, flowering in July and Aug. *Culture*—Propagate by means of division in Mar. and plant out in sunny, marshy situation or in shallow water.

Adenophora (Gland Bellflower)—Hardy perennials which thrive in sunny borders, in well-drained ordinary soil. For culture, *see* Perennials, p. 281. *Species—A. cœlestis* [Large] (12 in.); *A. ornata* (24 in.); *A. lilifolia* (12–40 in.). All have blue flowers from June–Aug.

Adonis (Pheasant's Eye)—Genus of useful rock plants, annuals and perennials, thriving in shade in a mixture of loam, peat and leaf-mould. For culture, *see* Annuals, p. 123, *and* Rock Plants, p. 283. *Species—A. æstivalis* (Crimson, May–June, 12 in.); *A. annua* (Blood Red, June–Aug., 12 in.); **A. amurensis* (Yellow, Feb.–Apr., 12 in.); **A. vernalis* (Yellow, Mar.–Apr., 10 in.). Perennials marked *.

Æsculus (Horse Chestnut and Buckeye)—One of the most handsome of flowering trees. *Culture*—Plant in Nov. in a sunny position with ordinary soil. Thin out branches when overcrowded only. To propagate, sow in Mar., layer in autumn or graft in the spring. *Species—A. carnea* (Red Horse Chestnut); *A. Hippocastanum fl. pl.* (Double Horse Chestnut); *A. Pavia* (Red Buckeye).

Æthionema (Burnt Candytuft)—Genus of dwarf-growing shrubby perennials that are excellent subjects for the rock garden. They thrive in the sun in gritty or sandy loam. *Culture*—Sow under glass in Mar. or insert cuttings in a cold frame in July. *Species and Varieties—A. cordifolium* (Rose, June–July, 6 in.); *A. grandiflorum* (Rose, May–July, 12 in.); *A. Warley Rose,* hybrid (Carmine-rose, May, 9 in.).

Agapanthus—Beautiful African lilies blooming in Aug. and Sept. They thrive in the open in warm sunny borders in rich sandy loam and leaf-mould, but are more suitable for the cool greenhouse. *Culture*—Pot-up in Mar. using a 9-in. pot and compost of 2 parts loam to 1 part of leaf-mould, rotten manure and sand. A large pot or tub is required for several plants. During summer give abundance of water and liquid manure twice a week. In winter protect from frost and water sparingly. Large plants may be stood out during the summer. Sow seed under glass or propagate by means of division in Mar. *Species—A. orientalis* (Blue); *A. orientalis albus* (White). Both Aug., 18 to 40 in.

Agastache mexicana (*syn. Brittonastrum mexicana*)—Beautiful herbaceous plant which, in the milder districts of the south, has proved quite hardy. It may require protection during the winter months when grown in the less favourable parts of the country. It requires a well-drained soil and a sunny position. Propagation is carried out by means of seed sown in spring or division of rootstock at that time. It bears cerise flowers from June to Aug. Height 2–2½ ft.

Agave—Best known variety is the *Agave americana*, or American Aloe, which, in the cool greenhouse, usually grows from 20 to 40 in. high, though much larger plants are obtainable. *Culture*—Pot-up firmly every 4 or 5 years in a well-drained compost of 2 parts of rich fibrous loam to 1 part of leaf-mould, sand and brick rubble. The plants may be stood out of doors in summer. Propagate by means of seed in heat in Feb. or by offsets in the summer. *Species—A. americana* (Yellowish-green, Aug., 30 in.); *A. americana marginata* (variegated); *A. densiflora* (Green, Sept., 40 in.); *A. filifera* (Aug., 29–36 in.).

Ageratum (Floss Flower)—Useful half-hardy annual for the rock garden, and for edgings to beds or borders. For culture, *see* Annuals, p. 123. *Species—A. Houstonianum* (Blue and White, May–Sept., 6–18 in.). *Named Varieties*—Blue Perfection (Amethyst Blue); Imperial Dwarf (Deep Blue); Lavender Band (Lavender); Little Dorrit (Pale Blue); and Snowflake (White).

Alisma (Water Plantain)—Hardy perennials useful for bog or water margin in ordinary soil. *Culture*—Sow in Mar. in peat, or propagate by means of division in Apr., and plant in sunny position with from 1 to 12 in. of slow-moving water above the crowns.

Allium—Attractive hardy bulbous plants which grow from 6 to 18 in. high and bloom from May to July. They like a sunny position and light loam to which a little sand and leaf-mould have been added. *Culture*—Plant in Sept. or Oct. 3 in. deep and 4 in. apart. Lift from the ground when overcrowded and replant immediately. Propagation is by seed in frame in slight heat in Mar., or by offsets in Oct. *Species*—*A. Beesianum* (Blue); *A. cæruleum* (Blue); *A. Moly* [Lily Leek] (Yellow); *A. neapolitanum* (White); *A. roseum* (Lilac-rose), and many others. All May–July, 6 to 18 in.

Alnus (Alder)—Deciduous tree which grows well in sunny open positions in moist swampy soil. *Culture*—Plant in Nov. No pruning is necessary. Propagate by seed, layering or grafting.

Aloe—Greenhouse evergreen plant, generally in the form of a rosette. Plant firmly in summer in pots or tubs in a compost of sandy loam, peat and well-rotted manure. Stand in a sunny position and water freely in summer, but sparingly in winter (Temp. 45° to 60° F.). Propagate by means of suckers in spring or sow in heat.

Alonsoa (Mask Flower)—Pretty half-hardy dwarf annual suitable for sunny beds, or for pot culture, in the cool greenhouse. *Culture, see* Annuals, p. 123. If " stopped-back " periodically through the summer some can be lifted and potted-up in Sept. for flowering indoors, during autumn and winter. *Pot Culture*—Pot-up in 5 to 6-in. pots, keep close for three weeks, then give ample light and air. Pinch out young shoots occasionally. Water carefully and give weak liquid manure until buds show colour. *Species*—*A. caulialata, A. linifolia,* and *A. Warscewiczii.* All Scarlet, July–Aug., 18 in.

Aloysia—*See* Lippia.

Alstroemeria (Herb Lily or Peruvian Lily)—Tuberous-rooted perennials, some of which are hardy and suitable for sunny borders, in which the soil is well drained, rich and light, with a little old mortar, leaf-mould and sand mixed with it. They are also useful for pot culture. *Culture*—Propagate by means of division in spring or autumn. Plant 4 in. deep and 10 in. apart. Water freely and mulch in summer when growing and protect from severe frost in winter. Do not lift the rhizomes. Seed may also be sown in gentle heat in Jan., and seedlings planted out in May or June. *Species*—*A. aurantiaca* (Orange-red, May–Aug., 30–36 in.); *A. chilensis* (Red, Pink or Yellow, July, 30 in.); *A. Ligtu* (Lilac, Streaked Purple, July, 1½–2 ft.); **A. Pelegrina* (Pinkish with Purple Spots, July, 12–18 in.). Greenhouse species *.

Alyssum (Madwort)—Useful dwarf annuals and perennials for sunny beds, edgings, or rock garden with sandy soil. For culture, *see* Annuals, p. 123, *and* Perennials, p. 281. *Species*—*A. maritimum* [Sweet Alyssum] (White, May–July, 4–6 in.); **A. montanum* (Yellow, May–June, 3 in.); *A. saxatile var. citrinum* (Yellow, May, 6–10 in.). Perennials species marked *.

Amaranthus (Love-lies-bleeding, and The Prince's Feather)—Half-hardy annuals growing from 12 to 36 in. high and flowering from July to Oct. They thrive in sunny beds or borders with shallow, light soil, or in the cool green-house. For culture, *see* Annuals, p. 123. *Species*—*A. caudatus* (Crimson, July–Oct., 10–40 in.); *A. c. var, ruber* (Crimson, with Carmine Foliage, July, 30 in.); *A. c. var. tricolor* (Crimson, with Red, Yellow and Green Foliage, July, 36 in.); *A. hypochondriacus* (Crimson, July–Oct., 36–40 in.).

Amaryllis Belladonna (Belladonna Lily)—This beautiful species is very variable in the size and colour of its flowers, frequently producing flowers variously shaded from white to a reddish or purplish hue. There is only one species. Some of the varieties are *A. Belladonna ruber major, A. Belladonna var. pallida*, and *A. Belladonna Parkeri*, a cross between *A. Belladonna* and *Brunsvigia Josephinæ*. This plant succeeds outdoors in well-drained soil at the foot of warm plant-house walls. The bulbs should be planted during the summer, when they are dormant, being covered with about 6 in. of rich loamy soil mixed with leaf-mould and silver sand. If planted too deep they do not flower freely. The blooms are produced during Aug. and Sept., and the leaves, in common with those of many South African bulbs, during the winter and spring. Leave the bulbs in the ground but protect with fibre in winter. *Greenhouse Culture*—If grown in the greenhouse, they require very large pots or pans. Even so, they do not flower freely.

Amelanchier (June Berry or Service Berry)—Hardy deciduous trees and shrubs that thrive in sunny sheltered positions and in moderately light and moist soil. *Culture*—Plant in Oct. or Nov. Do not prune, but cut out dead wood and thin when necessary after flowering. Propagate by means of seed in Mar., by grafting on the thorn in Mar., by cuttings struck in the open in Oct. or by layering. *Species—A. alnifolia; A. canadensis* (20–30 ft.); *A. rotundifolia* (6–15 ft.). All White, Apr.–May.

Ammobium alatum (Everlasting Sunflower)—Beautiful half-hardy biennial, growing about 18 in. high and blooming from June to Aug. Excellent for warm, sunny borders. For culture, *see* Biennials, p. 125.

Anagallis (Pimpernel)—Half-hardy annuals, suitable for a warm, sunny rock garden or greenhouse. For culture, *see* Annuals, p. 123. *Species—A. arvensis, linifolia*, etc. (Various, Summer, 6 in.); *A. tenella* (Bog Pimpernel), said to be perennial (Pink, July, 3 in.).

Anchusa (Alkanet)—The annuals are unimportant. The half-hardy biennials and perennials like a sunny position, but do not require very rich soil. For culture, *see* Biennials, p. 125, *and* Perennials, p. 281. *Species—A. capensis* (Blue, July, 20 in.); **A. italica var. Dropmore* (Rich Blue, June–Oct., 40–60 in.); **A. sempervirens* (Deep Blue, June, 24 in.). Perennials species marked *.

Andromeda (Marsh or Wild Rosemary)—Hardy, evergreen, heath-like shrubs, which thrive in the sun in boggy or moist peaty soil, and also make good pot plants for the cold greenhouse. *Culture*—Plant in Oct. Propagate by means of ripe seed in pans or boxes under glass in Oct., divide the roots, or layer in Sept. *Species—A. polifolia* (Rose-white, May and June, 20 in.). *Vars. angustifolia* and *major.*

Androsace (Rock Jasmine)—Perennial rock plants which like a moderately sunny position and a mixture of loam, peat and 30 per cent grit. *A. foliosa* and *A. lactea* require some limestone and no peat in the soil. For culture, *see* Perennials, p. 281. *Species—A. carnea* (Rose, May, 3 in.); *A. foliosa* (Rose-lilac, May–June, 6 in.); *A. primuloides* (Rose, White Eye, May–June, 4 in.), and many others.

Anemone (Windflower)—Anemones of both kinds, hardy fibrous-rooted herbaceous perennials and tuberous-rooted, thrive best in semi-shade in a moist, light, rich medium loam, but generally succeed in any which is well drained, well dug and manured. The dwarf-growing kinds are excellent for the rock garden, while *St. Brigid* anemones are favourites for beds and borders. *Culture*—(Tuberous). Plant from Oct. to the end of Mar. Set the tubers about 3 in. deep and 5 in. apart. The roots are best left undisturbed, but may be taken up as soon as the leaves have died down for removal or for drying-off and replanting in the autumn. A change of position is recommended at intervals of two or three years. These anemones may be propagated by means of division of dry rhizomes from Sept. to Mar. (Fibrous-rooted Herbaceous Perennials.) Sow in the reserve garden in Apr., thinly in drills 1 ft. apart and ¼ in. deep. Shade from the sun until the seed is up. Thin-out the seedlings to 3 in. apart and leave them in the reserve garden until the leaves have died down after flowering the following spring, then lift, store, and replant in their flowering positions 8 in. apart early in Sept. *Greenhouse Culture*—Plant in the autumn, using 6-in. pans and a compost of deep, rich sandy loam, and place in the cool greenhouse. Dress annually with fertilizer and lift the tubers when the foliage has died down. *Species*—*A. alpina* (Cream, May–July, 18 in.); *A. Hepatica* and *vars.* (Blue, Red, Pink and White, Mar.–May, 6 in.); *A. hybrida* [*Charmeuse*] (White-Rose, Aug.–Oct., 30 in.); **A. apennina* and *vars.* (Blue or White, Mar.–May, 9 in.); **A. blanda* (Blue, Pink, White, Mar.–Apr., 6 in.); **A. coronaria* (Various, May–June, 12 in.); *A. fulgens* (Scarlet, May–June, 12 in.); *A. hortensis* (Purple-Rose and Whitish, Apr., 10 in.); **A. nemorosa* and *vars.* (Blue or White, Apr., 6 in.). Tuberous species marked *.

Anthemis (Chamomile)—Hardy perennials that like a sunny border or rock garden with sandy loam. For culture, *see* Perennials, p. 281. *Species and Varieties*—*A. montana* (White, June–Aug., 12 in.); *A. Sancti-Johannis* (Orange, June–Aug., 12–18 in.); *A. tinctoria* (Yellow, June–Oct., 18–24 in.); *A. tinctoria var. Kelwayi* (Pale Yellow, June–Oct., 18 in.).

Antherirum Liliago (St. Bernard's Lily)—Hardy tuberous-rooted perennials, which thrive in a warm, sunny border with moist, light, rich soil, or in a 6-in. pot in the cold greenhouse. They grow to a height of 30 in. and carry white flowers in June and July. For culture, *see* Perennials, p. 281.

Antholyza paniculata (African Corn Flag)—Hardy bulbous-rooted perennial, which thrives in a sunny position in well-drained borders with sandy loam and grows to about 30 in. high, carrying scarlet and yellow blooms from June to Aug. *Culture*—Propagate by offsets in Mar. or Oct., and plant 5 in. deep and 6 in. apart.

Anthyllis (Kidney Vetch and Ladies' Fingers)—Pretty little rock plants which like a sunny position and warm, gritty loam. They flower in June and July, and reach a height of 10 in. For culture, *see* Rock Plants, p. 283.

Antirrhinum (Snapdragon)—These are grown both as biennials and perennials. They like a dry, well-drained, well-manured loam, and a sunny position, and are extremely useful for dry beds, borders, wall, rock and wild gardens. For culture, *see* Biennials, p. 125, *and* Perennials, p. 281. *Varieties* —TALL—*Cottage Maid* (Pink and White); *Crimson King; Moonlight* (Apricot); *Primrose King; Scarlet Prince; Snowflake* (White, tinged Yellow); *Torch Light* (Orange-scarlet); and *Yellow King.* All flower from Apr. to Oct., and grow from 30 to 48 in. in height. INTERMEDIATE—*Amber Queen* (Yellow and Pink); *Black Prince* (Deep Crimson); *Bonfire* (Orange-red); *Bronze Queen; Buff Beauty; Coccinea* (Orange-scarlet); *Cottage Maid* (Pale Pink and White); *Mauve Beauty; Pink Perfection; Prima Donna* (Apricot and White); *Rosy Queen; The Fawn* (Apricot); and *Yellow Queen.* All flower from Apr. to Oct., and grow from 15 to 30 in. in height. DWARF—*White Prince, Yellow Queen.* Both these flower from Apr. to Oct., and grow 6–15 in. in height.

Aponogeton distachyus (Cape Water Hawthorn or Pond Weed)—Hardy aquatic plant which produces masses of white flowers from May to Oct. *Culture*—Propagate by means of offsets or division in Mar. Plant in a weighted basket in slowly-moving water with from 6 to 30 in. of water above the crowns.

Aquilegia (Columbine)—Hardy herbaceous perennials and biennials, that thrive in rather shady borders in moist, cool, well-drained, deep loam and leaf-mould. They are also useful for greenhouse culture and the dwarf kinds for the rock garden. For culture, *see* Perennials, p. 281, *and* Rock Plants, p. 283. *Species and Varieties—A. alpina* (Violet-blue, May and June, 10 in.); *A. cærulea* (Pale Blue and White, May–July, 12–18 in.); *A. longissima* (Golden Yellow, long spurs, May–July, 30 in.); *A. Skinneri* (Dark Scarlet and Greenish Yellow, May–July, 24 in.).

Arabis (Rock Cress)—Hardy perennial rock plants which like a sunny position in ordinary well-drained soil or sandy loam. For culture, *see* Rock Plants, p. 283. *Species—A. alpina* (White, May–July, 6 in.); *A. albida fl. pl.* (White [Double], May–June, Trailer); *A. androsacea* (Rose, May, Trailer); *A. muralis* (Rose, July, 6 in.); *A. verna* (Annual, Violet, Apr.–May, 6 in.).

Aralia—Hardy shrubs which like a sunny position and sandy soil, etc. *Culture*—Plant in Nov. No pruning is required. Propagation is by means of root-cuttings in autumn, or suckers in spring. *Species—A. chinensis* and *vars.* (Angelica Tree); *A. spinosa* (Hercules' Club).

Araucaria (Chili Pine or Monkey Puzzle)—Coniferous trees which like a sunny position and well-drained, deep loam. *Culture*—Plant in Apr. or Sept. No pruning is necessary. Propagate by seeds under glass. These trees are unsuitable for town gardens. *Species—A. araucana. Pot Culture—A. excelsa* (Norfolk Island Pine) is only suitable for the cool greenhouse. Pot-up in Mar., using two parts of sandy loam to one part of leaf-mould. Propagate by means of cuttings in heat in Oct., or by "ringing".

Arbutus (Strawberry Tree)—Evergreen shrubs which thrive in a warm, sunny sheltered position in moist, well-drained peat and loam. Trim back the long straggling shoots in Apr. and cut out dead wood. To propagate sow seed in a frame when ripe. Grow in pots till ready to plant out and do not transplant more than necessary. Cuttings of young shoots may also be taken in July and struck in a frame. *Species—A. Andrachne* (White, tinted Green, Mar. and Apr., 10–30 ft.); *A. andrachnoides* (White, Winter, 15–30 ft.); *A. Menziesii* [Madrona] (White, May, 20–100 ft.); *A. Unedo* (Cream-pink, Sept.–Oct., 10–20 ft.).

Arctotis stœchadifolia—Half-hardy annual for sunny, sheltered beds and borders. It grows about 24 in. high and carries pearl-grey, daisy-like flowers in summer. For culture, *see* Annuals, p. 123.

Arenaria (Sandwort)—Dwarf hardy perennial creeping plants, useful for carpeting, for the paved garden and for the rock garden. They like a moist, sandy, gritty loam. For culture, *see* Rock Plants, p. 283. *A. balearica* likes a shady spot and ample leaf-mould in the compost, but *A. montana* loves to tumble over the sides of a rock in full sun. *Species—A. balearica* (White, May and June, 3 in.); *A. montana* (White, May–July, 3 in.); *A. purpurascens* (Reddish-purple, June and July, 3 in.); *A. tetraquetra* (White, June, 3 in.).

Aristolochia—Some species, such as *A. macrophylla (Sipho)*, the Dutchman's Pipe (Brown and Yellow, June–July, 20 ft.), are hardy herbaceous perennial climbers in sheltered positions, but others are only suitable for the greenhouse. *Culture*—Sow under glass in Mar., or take cuttings under glass in Apr. Plant out in the following Mar. (hardy species) or in the greenhouse in a mixture of light, sandy loam and leaf-mould. Thin-out during the spring.

Armeria (Thrift, Sea Pink, Cushion Pink, etc.)—Dwarf hardy perennials mainly seen in the rock garden. They like a sunny, open position in dry, deep loam. For culture, *see* Perennials, p. 281. *Species—A. caespitosa* (Pinky-lilac, June, 4 in.); *A. maritima* (Rose, Red, Lilac, White, June–July, 6–12 in.); *A. plantaginea* (Rose, May–July, 18 in.).

Arnebia (Prophet Flower)—Hardy annuals which thrive in the sun in sandy loam and are excellent for border or rock garden. For culture, *see* Annuals, p. 123. *Species—A. cornuta* (Yellow, Black Dot, June–Aug., 15 in.).

Artemisia (Old Man, Lad's Love, etc.)—Hardy herbaceous perennials and evergreen and deciduous shrubs thriving in ordinary soil. Several of the dwarf-growing kinds make excellent rock plants. *Culture*—Propagate by means of division in Oct., or by cuttings in July. *Species—A. Abrotanum* (Yellow, Aug.–Oct., 3 ft.), well known for its fragrance (Southernwood); *A. argentea* (Yellow or White, June–Sept., 20 in.); *A. lactiflora* (Cream-white, Aug.–Oct., 60 in.); *A. lanata* (Yellow [Silver Foliage], July–Aug., 6 in.).

Arum Lily—*See* Zantedeschia.

Arundinaria—Genus of bamboo, the species of which thrive in a moist climate in a deep, rich loam holding ample leaf-mould, and given protection from north and east winds. Of the hardy kinds, *A. japonica (syn. Bambusa Metake)*, 10 to 15 ft., is the most generally grown. There are also many half-hardy species for the warm greenhouse. *Culture*—Propagate by means of division in May and plant in sheltered positions. Cut out all dead wood in Apr. *See also* Bambusa. *Other Species (Hardy)—A. Falconeri* (25 ft.); *A. nitida* (10 ft.); *A. Simoni* (15 ft.); *A. Veitchii* (15 in.); *A Fortunei*, dwarf (20 in.). The genus is now divided up under numerous headings.

Arundo (Great Reed)—Perennial which thrives in semi-shade on slightly swampy banks in light, rich loam, and grows to a height of 10 ft. *Culture*—Propagate by means of division in May. *Species—A. Donax* (Glaucous Foliage, 10 ft.); *A. Donax variegata* (Leaves Striped White, 10 ft.).

Ash (Fraxinus)—These well-known trees like a sunny position and ordinary soil. *Culture*—Plant in Nov. Thin-out branches when overcrowded. To propagate sow in a frame in autumn.

Asparagus Fern (Sparrow Grass)—Hardy and greenhouse evergreen and deciduous climbing and trailing plants which thrive in a compost of two parts loam to one part of leaf-mould, peat and sand. *Culture*—Pot-up in Mar. using 6 to 10-in pots. Syringe and water well in summer. Propagate by means of seed in Mar. in heat, by cuttings in a propagating case at the same period, or by division in Mar. The hardy species do well in a warm, sunny position in rich, sandy soil. *See also* Smilax. *Species—A. plumosus* and *vars. nanus* and *tenuissimus; A. retrofractus; A. Sprengeri;* and *A. verticillatus.*

Asperula (Woodruff)—Hardy annuals and dwarf-growing perennials useful for beds, borders, edgings, rock garden, etc. The annuals like semi-shade; the perennials a sunny site, and soil with ample grit in it. For culture, *see* Annuals, p. 123, *and* Perennials, p. 281. *Species and Varieties—A. azurea* (Light Blue, June–Sept., 4 in.); *A. Gussonei* (Rose, May–Aug., 4 in.); *A. odorata* (White, May–June, 9 in.); *A. arcadiensis* (Pink [Silver Foliage], June and July, 3 in.).

Asphodelus (Asphodel)—Mostly hardy perennials that thrive in the sun in any soil, though rich, sandy loam is most suitable. For culture, *see* Perennials, p. 281. *Species—A. acaulis* (Pink, May–July, 12–24 in.); *A. albus* (White, May–July, 24–36 in.); *A. ramosus [King's Spear]* (White, May–July, 24–36 in.).

Aster. The China Aster (Callistephus)—Half-hardy, autumn-flowering annual particularly adapted for small beds, edgings, the rock garden, or for pot culture. All varieties thrive best in a deep rich light soil and in hot dry weather should be mulched with well-rotted manure, and frequently supplied with manure water. For culture, *see* Annuals, p. 123. *Pot Culture*—Sow in the open in May. Pot-up three plants in a 6-in. pot in a compost of two-thirds fibrous loam and one-third well-decayed manure. Stand in the open on a hard bed of ashes or on slates and cover to the rims with fibre. Transfer under glass as soon as the buds begin to colour. *Species and Varieties—Callistephus chinensis* [single] (18 in.); *Chrysanthemum-flowered* (12 in.); *Comet* [Broad Florets] (24 in.); *Dwarf Bouquet* (6–9 in.); *Giant Ray* [Stiff and Prominent Florets] (18 in.); *Mignon* (10 in.); *Ostrich Plume* [Branching with Double flowers] (18 in.); *Quilled* (Tubular Florets); *Pæony-flowered* [Incurving Florets] (18 in.); *Victoria* [Double] (15 in.). *See also* Michaelmas Daisy.

Astragalus (Milk Vetch)—Hardy dwarf-growing plants of the broom genus, some of which make excellent subjects for the rock garden. They thrive in the sun in deep loam, sand and mortar. *Culture*—Sow in the spring or summer, or propagate by division in autumn. *Species*—*A. alpinus* (Purple, June–Aug., Trailing); *A. danicus var. albus* (White, May–July, 5 in.); *A. massiliensis* (Violet-purple, May–July, 24 in.).

Astrantia (Masterwort)—Hardy perennials, which like a shady position with cool, moist loam and leaf-mould. The dwarf-growing kinds are excellent for the rock garden. Propagate by means of root division in spring or autumn. *Species*—*A. major* (White, tinged Pink, May–July, 18 in.); *A. minor* (Pale Rose, May–July, 6 in.).

Aubrieta (Rock Cress)—Pretty evergreen perennial trailing plants, which are useful for edgings, or the rock garden. They thrive in the sun in dry, rich, sandy loam and leaf-mould. For culture, *see* Perennials, p. 281. *Varieties*—*Barker's Double* (Rosy-lilac); *Bridesmaid* (Blush-pink); *Crimson King; Godstone* (Violet-blue); *Lavender; Lilac Queen* (Rose Lilac); *Magician* (Purple). All Apr.–June, 4 in.

Aucuba (Spotted or Variegated Laurel)—Hardy evergreen shrub, well suited for shady places and well-drained ordinary soil. It may also be grown in large pots. *Culture*—Plant in Mar. or Oct. Cut back long weak shoots in May. To propagate, take cuttings and strike in the open in autumn, or sow seed in frame when ripe.

Auricula (Primula auricula)—Auriculas are divided into two classes, namely, Show Auriculas and Alpine Auriculas. The best compost is a good fibrous rather heavy loam, adding a little decayed manure and leaf-mould, with a liberal addition of silver sand, and a sprinkling of charcoal or wood ashes. *Culture*—(*Show Auriculas.*) Sow in pans in a warm house on the surface of a compost of half loam and half leaf-mould and gritty sand, when ripe, or from Jan. to Mar. Moist moss should be kept over the surface of the soil until the seedlings are up. When these have three or four leaves, transplant into 3-in. pots. Four to 5-in. pots are large enough for full-sized plants. Where it is essential that the flowers shall come true to type and in the case of choice specimens, it is better to propagate by means of off-sets or root division in Feb. or Mar., or in Aug. after re-potting. Offsets may be placed singly in 3-in. pots, or three in a larger pot. Keep the pots in the open in a cool, sheltered site and remove to the cool greenhouse at the end of Sept. The auricula blossoms, and is in full growth from Feb. to June, when the plants should be removed from the glazed shelter under which they have been flowering, being placed in the open air on a shelf or stage having a north or north-east aspect, and if possible with some glass lights rigged up overhead. In Aug., when the fresh growth commences, the plants should be re-potted, the tap-roots being shortened with a sharp knife. In Nov. place the plants under glass. Keep the plants within 18 in. of the glass, but shade from direct sun. Never allow water to fall on the foliage or to settle on the leaves at the base. Very little artificial heat is required and a close atmosphere is fatal. (*Alpine Auriculas.*) Sow seed in a light sandy soil in a little heat in Mar. Prick-off into boxes as soon as four leaves have formed. Harden-off in a shady cold frame at the end of May. Plant out 6 in. apart in Sept. or Oct. in a partially-shaded position facing north, in well-drained rather heavy loam and cow-manure. Lift, divide and re-plant triennially after flowering. *A few good varieties* (*Show*)—White Edged: *Acme* and *Heather Bell.* Green Edged: *Dr. Horner* and *Prince Charming.* Grey Edged: *George Rudd* and *George Lightbody.* Self: *Gordon Douglas* and *Harrison Weir.* (*Alpines*)— *Admiration, Day Dream, Firefly, Majestic, Roxborough, Silver Wood.*

Azalea—This group of plants are now classified under the Rhododendrons, but for the purpose required here is treated separately under its old and still used head. A compost of sandy peat and loam or two-thirds fibrous loam and one-third leaf-mould is suitable for all species, but they will grow quite well in almost any soil which does not contain lime or chalk. *Culture*—For outdoor culture, *see* Rhododendrons. *Pot Culture* (*A. indica and hybrids*)—Pot-up firmly from Oct. to Nov., using 6 to 10-in. pots and the compost mentioned above. Keep in a cold frame until late Nov., then move in succession into the house and gradually acclimatize to moist, warm conditions. After flowering prune straggling shoots and remove all dead blooms. Re-pot if necessary (usually every second or third year), place the pots in the warmest corner and syringe overhead. Stand in the open in a cool, sheltered position on a bed of ashes or shingle from June to Sept., and water liberally and syringe overhead morning and evening in dry warm weather. In Sept. return to the house. *A mollis*, although hardy, is also useful for the warm greenhouse. To propagate, take cuttings of half-matured wood early in summer and strike in a frame (50° to 60° F.); sow in moist heat and fine sandy peat in spring; or layer. *Species*—(*Hardy*) —*R. japonicum* (*A. mollis*) (Red, Yellow, etc.); *R. nudiflorum* (*A. nudiflora*) (Pink or White); *R. ponticum* (*A. pontica*) (Yellow). All May–June, 3–6 ft. (*Greenhouse*)—*R. indicum* (*A. indica*) (many shades of colour). They flower from Dec. to May, according to the temperature of the house, and grow from 1 to 3 ft. high. Named varieties are almost innumerable and growers' catalogues should be consulted.

Azara—Evergreen shrubs and climbers that are almost hardy, and which like a warm, sheltered position and well-drained sandy-loam. *Culture*—Plant in Mar. or Oct. Thin out the branches when necessary, but otherwise do not prune. Propagate by means of cuttings under glass in summer or by layering in spring. *A. microphylla* is a beautiful shrub with pale yellow flowers in early spring.

Balsam (Impatiens)—Pretty half-hardy annual for sunny beds or borders with rich soil or for the greenhouse. *Culture*—See Annuals, p. 123. Support with neat stakes. *Pot Culture*—Pot-up as required, using 5 to 6-in. pots and a compost of half loam and half-rotten cow-dung and leaf-mould with a little sand, and stand near the glass in a cool greenhouse. Syringe overhead, ventilate, and water liberally. As soon as the buds begin to form water twice a week with a weak liquid manure. Do not "stop" back. When large specimens are desired, shift into 8 to 10-in. pots, using the richest compost available, and plunge the pots into spent hops or tan and feed with manure water. *Species and Varieties*—*Impatiens Balsamina* (many vars.); *I. Holstii* (Vermilion); *I. Oliveri* (Mauve); *I. Sultanii* (Rose).

Bambusa (Bamboo)—There are three great classes of bamboos, namely, *Arundinaria, Bambusa* and *Phyllostachys.* Most species do well in the open, especially if the soil is of a moist, deep, light loamy nature, and has some peat or leaf-mould in it, but in exposed situations they require some protection. The dwarfer kinds are suitable as pot plants. *Culture*—Propagate by means of division in May. Cut out dead canes in Apr. *Pot Culture*—Pot-up in Mar. in a well-drained compost of two-thirds loam and one-third leaf-mould and sharp sand. Water liberally, syringe well overhead in summer, and give weak liquid manure twice a week during the growing period. A moist and moderately-warm atmosphere is essential. *Species—(Hardy)—B. disticha* (2 ft.); and *B. angulata* (4–8 ft.). *(Greenhouse)—Arundinaria Fortunei* (Striped Silver, 2 ft.); *A. pumila* (1–2 ft.); and *Phyllostachys ruscifolia* (1–2 ft.).

Bartonia—*See* Mentzelia Lindleyi.

Begonia—These plants thrive in sunny beds and borders with rich loam, and are also extremely useful in the greenhouse.

Culture—(Tuberous-rooted Species)—For bedding out or for greenhouse decoration June to Oct. Sow in Feb. under glass (Temp. 65° F.) in a finely-sifted and just moist compost of two-thirds loam and one-third leaf-mould and sand. Water before and after sowing and keep the seed-pan moist. Prick off the seedlings into shallow boxes. Pot-off singly into pots and plant out in May or June, or pot-up into 5-in. pots for the greenhouse, keep near the glass, and shade when the sun is hot. Particular varieties may be propagated in spring by means of leaf-cuttings. Ordinary stem cuttings may also be taken in summer. When starting tubers, they should be planted flat or hollow side uppermost in Feb. or Mar., and just covered in shallow trays in heat (60° F.) with moist sandy loam and well-rotted manure for soil. Water in moderation until growth commences. If for summer bedding, harden-off in May in a cold frame and plant-out in June, or, if for the greenhouse, pot-up in 4-in. pots in a compost of two-thirds loam and one-third leaf-mould, well-rotted manure and sand, re-potting when pot-bound into 7 to 8-in. pots. Water well in summer, shade from hot sun, and once the roots have filled the pots, feed with weak manure-water twice a week. Stake any shoots that need support and pick off all dead blooms. Greenhouse temperature 55° F. winter to 70° F. summer. The tubers should be lifted in Oct. when the frost has turned the foliage black. If they must be removed from the beds before this, lift them with a good " ball " of soil, pack in boxes, and place in a sheltered spot to finish ripening. Then shake the soil and foliage away from the roots, allow them to dry for a day or so and store in dry soil in boxes in a cool but frost-proof place. Tuberous begonias in pots must be gradually dried-off and stood in a frost-proof shed or frame for the winter.

Culture—(Fibrous-rooted Species)—This is a large and varied class, including as it does a large number of species and varieties of a sub-shrubby habit, which require an intermediate or greenhouse temperature. Some of them flower more or less all the year round, and a few of them may be used for summer bedding. The most important for this purpose are the many beautiful varieties of *B. semperflorens*, which may be raised from seed sown during Jan. in a temperature of 60° F., or by means of basal cuttings from plants lifted and potted up and kept in a warm house over the winter. The sub-shrubby and perennial species, generally, are propagated by means of ordinary cuttings, or by means of leaf-cuttings, in a temperature of from 60° to 70° F. The winter-flowering section, which is represented by *Gloire de Lorraine* and its varieties, may be increased by means of leaf-cuttings, or by young basal shoots. They are usually secured from plants that have flowered and that have been rested for a few weeks. These are then partly cut back and started in a temperature of from 65° to 70° F., cuttings being secured during Mar.

The other winter-flowering section, which is represented by varieties raised from crossing the species *B. socotrana* with the tuberous-rooted varieties, are by no means easy to grow successfully, and require very careful management during their resting period. After flowering, they should be stood in a house with a temperature of from 55° to 60° F. They should have very little water at the root, on the other hand, they must not suffer from dryness. In May give more water, and when the young shoots are about three inches in length, they should be secured as cuttings, and inserted singly in small pots of sandy compost. They root readily in a close case with a bottom heat of 70° F. During the summer months they should be grown in an average temperature of from 55° to 65° F.

Culture of Ornamental and Variegated-leaved Species—Pot up in Mar. or Apr. in a compost as recommended above, keep in a moist atmosphere, never letting the temperature fall below 50° F., and shading from the strong sun. At that time, water liberally and give a little weak liquid manure. Decrease the water supply in winter, but do not dry off entirely. Propagate by means of seed, leaf-cuttings, or by cuttings of unflowered shoots (Heat 60° to 65° F.). For species and varieties see growers' catalogues.

Bellis (Daisy)—Dwarf-growing hardy perennials, which thrive in the sun in moderately rich soil. For culture, *see* Perennials, p. 281. They grow from 6 to 12 in. high and flower in May.

Benthamia (Bentham's Strawberry Tree)—See *Cornus capitata.*

Berberidopsis corallina (Coral Barberry)—Half-hardy evergreen climbing shrub which thrives in a cool greenhouse, or in a border in the south in well-drained, light loam against walls facing south or west and partially shaded. It carries coral-red flowers in June, and grows to a height of 20 ft. *Culture*—Take cuttings early in summer, or propagate by means of layering in Oct. Plant-out in Apr. and Oct. and thin-out straggly branches when overcrowded.

Berberis (Barberry)—Beautiful hardy flowering shrubs, evergreen and deciduous. *Culture*—Plant evergreens from Mar. to Apr. or from Oct. to Nov.; deciduous, Nov. to Mar., in ordinary soil or sandy loam. Thin-out shoots after flowering when overcrowded and trim to shape. Trimming should be delayed until the spring in the case of shrubs grown for autumn foliage. Most species are propagated by means of seeds in the open in Oct., by half-matured cuttings in a frame in July or Aug., or by layering in Aug. *B. stenophylla* must be propagated by cuttings or layering. *B. Darwinii* is useful for pot culture in the cold or unheated greenhouse. Pot-up in Nov. using 8 to 10-in. pots and a compost of two parts of sandy loam to one part of leaf-mould and rotten manure. *Species and Varieties*—(*Evergreens*)—*B. candidula* (Yellow, Apr.–May, 2 ft.); *B. Darwinii* (Orange, Apr.–May, 8–10 ft.); *B. stenophylla* (Yellow, Apr.–June, 8–10 ft.). (*Deciduous*)—*B. polyantha* (Yellow, May, 6–8 ft.); *B. Thunbergii* (Yellow, Apr.–May, 3 ft.); *B. vulgaris* (Yellow, Apr.–May, 4–15 ft.); *B. Wilsonæ* (Yellow, May, 2–4 ft.) and *B. yunnanensis* (Yellow, May, 4–6 ft.).

Betula (Birch Tree)—Plant in Nov. in a sunny, open, moist position. All species will thrive in a poor, gravelly soil. No pruning is necessary. Propagate by means of seeds, layering, or grafting. *Species*—*B. verrucosa* (Silver Birch); *B. v. var. dalecarlica* (Cut-leaved); *B. v. var. Youngii* (Weeping); and *B. v. var. purpurea* (Purple Birch).

Bignonia (Trumpet Flower)—Some of these are fine half-hardy perennial climbers, closely allied to the Tecoma, *q.v.* They thrive best planted out in borders of the greenhouse.

Boltonia (False Starwort)—Hardy perennial for border or wild garden, thriving in any moist and moderately good loam. For culture, *see* Perennials, p. 281. *Species*—*B. asteroides* (White, July–Sept., 48–60 in.); *B. v. decurrens* (Whitish-pink, Aug.–Sept., 48 in.).

Boronia—Evergreen shrubs which do best in the cool greenhouse in equal parts of sandy loam, peat, and leaf-mould. *Culture*—Pot-up from Apr. to May in 5 to 7-in. pots. Stop-back young plants, give ample air and liquid manure while growing. Prune after flowering, and stand outdoors from June to Sept. To propagate, take cuttings of young shoots in May and strike in sand, peat and charcoal under glass (60° F.) *Species*—*B. elatior* (Carmine); *B. heterophylla* (Cerise); *B. megastigma* (Brownish-purple and Yellow); *B. serrulata* (Scarlet). All Feb. to Apr., 22 to 24 in.

Bouvardia (Jasmine Plant)—Winter-flowering evergreen shrub which likes a mixture of fibrous loam, leaf-mould, sand, and a little well-rotted cow-manure. *Culture*—Pot-up in Mar. in 5 to 8-in. pots. Keep in a frame from June to Sept., water liberally and syringe. In Sept. return to the greenhouse and give liquid manure once the buds begin to form. Cut hard back after flowering, and stop-back young shoots until Aug. (*Temp.* 50° to 60° F. in winter to 60° to 65° F. summer.) Propagate by cuttings of young shoots or root cuttings in Feb. and Mar. in heat (70° F.). *Varieties*—*Bridal Wreath* (White); *King of Scarlets; Mrs. R. Green* (Single, Salmon); *President Garfield* (Double Pink); *Priory Beauty* (Pink).

Box (Buxus)—Plant in Apr. or Sept., in light, well-drained soil. Clip in May and Aug. Propagate by means of cuttings in Aug. or Sept. under bell-glasses, division in Sept. or by layering in Oct. *Species*—*B. sempervirens* (Common Box); and *vars. aurea pendula* (Golden); *argentea* (Silver); *myrtifolia*; and *suffruticosa* (Dwarf-growing).

Brachycome (Swan River Daisy)—Beautiful summer-flowering, dwarf-growing, half-hardy annual. For culture, *see* Annuals, p. 123. *Varieties*— *Azure Fairy; Blue Star; Red Star.* All June and Sept., 9 in.

Bravoa (Twinflower)—Half-hardy bulbous plant which likes a sunny, sheltered position in rich, light soil mixed with old leaf-mould. It grows about 15 in. high and flowers in July and Aug. *Culture*—Plant in a warm border or in the greenhouse in Sept., 4 in. deep and 6 in. apart, and protect with fibre during winter.

Brevoortia (Crimson Satin Flower)—Half-hardy bulbous summer-flowering plants, growing to a height of 30 in. *B. Ida-Maia* (Dark Crimson and Green, Summer, 20 in.). For culture, *see* Brodiæa.

Brodiæa (Californian or Missouri Hyacinth)—Hardy and half-hardy bulbous plants, that thrive in well-drained, deep, sandy soil mixed with leaf-mould, in sunny borders, in the cool greenhouse, or in the rock garden. *Culture*—Plant in Oct., 3 in. deep and 5 in. apart. Protect with ashes during winter, and lift the bulbs from the soil every fourth year only. Propagate by means of offsets in Oct. *Species*—*B. grandiflora* (Violet-blue, June and July, 15 in.); *B. ixioides* (Yellow, Summer, 6 in.); *B. (Ipheion) uniflora* (White or Blue, Apr.–May, 6 in.).

Buckthorn (Rhamnus)—These small trees will do well almost anywhere, provided they have shelter from the wind. *Culture*—Plant in the late autumn or early spring and prune in Feb. Propagate by means of cuttings in the open in Sept., by layering in Oct. or Mar., or sow seed outdoors in Sept. *Rhamnus Alaternus* (Evergreen, 12 ft.) is a good kind.

Buddleia—Beautiful flowering shrubs. Most species are not quite hardy enough to endure severe weather out of doors, but flourish in well-drained, deep, ordinary soil or good loam in warm, sunny, sheltered positions, or in the greenhouse. *Culture*—Plant *B. globosa* in Mar. or Oct. Others Nov. to

Mar. Do not prune *B. alternifolia* or *B. globosa*, merely cut out old wood after flowering. In the case of *B. Davidi* cut last year's shoots back to within 10 in. of old wood in Feb. Propagation is by means of cuttings in a frame in late summer or autumn, or by means of seed when ripe. *Hardy Species—B. alternifolia* (Pale Purple, June, 4–6 ft.); *B. Colvilei* (Rose, July, 20 ft.); *B. Davidi* and *vars.* (Lilac, Aug., 15 ft.); *B. globosa* [Orange Ball Tree] Orange, June, 10 ft.).

Bulbocodium (Spring Meadow Saffron)—Pretty little hardy bulb with crocus-like blooms which likes a well-drained sandy soil and a sunny position. *Culture*—Plant in Aug., 3 in. deep and 4 in. apart, or pot-up if for indoors. Lift from the soil every fourth year, and propagate by means of offsets in Aug. *B. vernum* (Purple-red, Jan.–Mar., 5 in.) is the best species.

Buphthalmum (Ox-eye)—Tall hardy perennial, which thrives in the sun in well-drained loam. For culture, *see* Perennials, p. 281. *Species—B. salicifolium* (Yellow, July–Sept., 24 in.); *B. speciosum* (Golden Orange, July, 60–70 in.).

Butomus umbellatus (Flowering Rush)—Hardy aquatic perennial, which likes a warm, sunny position in a bog or on a muddy bank, or in sheltered still water, with from 1 to 12 in. of water above the crowns. It grows some 30 in. high and carries pink flowers from June to Aug. Propagate by means of division in Mar.

Cacalia coccinea [*syn. Emilia flammea*] (Tassel Flower)—Hardy annual which likes a light soil, with plenty of leaf-mould in it. In summer and autumn it bears orange-red, daisy-like flowers on stems 18 in. high. For culture, *see* Annuals, p. 123.

Cacti—Nearly all species may be grown in a moderately-heated greenhouse. They like a compost of one-half fibrous loam and one-half a mixture of sand, broken bricks, and lime rubble, and a sunny position, except *Epiphyllums*, *Rhipsalis* and *Zygocactus*, which prefer shade and a compost of two-thirds fibrous loam and one-third sand, peat and brick rubble. Pot-up firmly in Feb. or Mar. and re-pot every three or four years, keeping pots as small as possible. A few pieces of charcoal in the compost are beneficial. Give ample ventilation and syringe with tepid water twice a week from Apr. to Sept. Decrease water supply from Oct. to Apr. Propagate by means of cuttings (partially dried) in summer, by grafting in Mar., or by offsets. *Hardy cacti* should be planted in spring in a well-drained, sunny, sheltered site in the rock garden or on a wall or bank in light loam with a mixture of brick rubble, sand and gravel. *Aporocactus, Notocactus* and *Mammillaria*, and those with stems likely to hold moisture, should be covered with glass in winter. *Species —(Hardy)—Cereus Engelmannii* (Purple, June, 18 in.); *Mammillaria setispina* (Pink, Summer, 9 in.); *Opuntia pulchella* (Purple, Summer, 10 in.). *(Half-hardy)—Aporocactus flagelliformis,* Whip Cactus (Pink, June, 12–30 in.); *Pediocactus Simpsonii,* Hedgehog Cactus (Red, June, 5 in.); *Echinopsis cristata purpurea* (Rose, July, 10 in.); *Epiphyllum Aurora boreale* (Orange, June, 18–24 in.); *Mammillaria sulphurea* (Yellow, Summer, 3 in.); *Melocactus communis,* Turk's Cap Cactus (Red, June, 12–30 in.); *Opuntia Ficus-indica,* Prickly Pear (Yellow, June, 30 in.); *Rhipsalis cassutha,* Mistletoe Cactus (White, Apr., 15 in.); *Schlumbergera Russelliana,* Leaf-flowering Cactus (Pink, Nov., 10–24 in.).

Calamintha alpina (Calamint)—Hardy aromatic plant forming a thick carpet of foliage, and carrying sprays of violet flowers all through the summer. Grow in a sunny site in gritty loam. Propagate by seeds in Mar., or by division in Mar. or Sept.

Calandrinia (Rock Purslane or Portulaca)—Dwarf-growing, annual and perennial plants that thrive in the sun in sandy loam. For culture, *see* Annuals, p. 123, *and* Perennials, p. 281. *Species*—*(Annual)*—*C. discolor* (Lilac, 12–18 in.); *C. grandiflora* (Rose, 18 in.); *C. Menziesii* (Purple, 9 in.). *(Perennial)*—*C. umbellata* (Crimson, 9 in.). All July–Sept.

Calceolaria (Slipper Flower)—There are three distinct kinds of calceolaria, the *herbaceous*, raised and reared under glass; the *shrubby*, grown for bedding out; these thrive in fibrous loam mixed with leaf-mould and sand. The third type, being hardy perennials and annuals, make excellent subjects for the rock garden. *Culture*—*(Herbaceous Calceolarias)*—Sow lightly and thinly in a propagating case in June. Pot-up singly in July and keep in a frost-proof frame; re-pot into 3 or 4-in. pots in Sept. and take into the greenhouse. Keep warm and moist at night and give a steady even temperature. Pot-up finally in Feb. or Mar. (before the flower buds being to move), using 7 to 8-in. pots and a compost of two parts loam to one part of leaf-mould and sand, and keep near the glass in a cool greenhouse. Stake securely, shade from the strong sun, and do not over-water. Weak liquid manure should be given at fortnightly intervals, as soon as the buds appear. Seeds should be sown afresh each year to attain the best results. *Culture*—*(Shrubby Calceolarias)*—Take cuttings of vigorous young basal shoots in Sept. and strike under glass, or in a warm north border, and cover with a hand-glass. If the weather turns frosty, throw some covering over the hand-glass. About the middle of Feb., the cuttings must have their growing points pinched back. A fortnight later they may either be potted or kept as cool as possible 3 to 4 in. apart in the pit, and finally transferred to the flower garden about 9 in. apart towards the end of May or early in June. Seed may also be sown under glass in Mar. (Temp. 50°–60° F.). Transplant the seedlings into boxes as soon as they can be handled and next pot-up singly into 3 or 4-in. pots. Transfer to a cold frame in May, and before the plants become pot-bound re-pot into 5 to 6-in. pots, if for greenhouse use, or if for summer bedding, harden-off and plant out early in June. *Culture*—(third type) Annuals, *see* p. 123, Perennials, p. 281. All May to Sept., 9 to 24 in.

Calendula (Pot Marigold)—Hardy annuals which thrive in beds or borders in almost any soil. For culture, *see* Annuals, p. 123. *Named Varieties*— *Favourite* (Sulphur Yellow); *Lemon Queen* (Lemon Yellow); *Orange King* (Bright Orange); *Prince of Orange* (Orange, striped Pale Yellow); and *Yellow Queen* (Golden Yellow). All double, flowering from June to Oct., and about 18 in. in height.

Calla palustris (Bog Arum)—Hardy aquatic plants which spread over the surface of shallow still water. They like a sunny position in firm soil at the margin of ponds. Propagate by means of division in Mar. The White flowers are borne from June to Aug.

Callistemon (Bottle Brush Plant)—Greenhouse evergreens which thrive in full sun, in a cool house, in equal parts of sandy peat and loam. They carry crimson and golden flowers in May and June on stems from 3 to 6 ft. in height. *Culture*—Pot-up in 6 to 10-in. pots, stand out of doors from June to Sept., and trim after flowering. To propagate take cuttings of matured wood in the late spring and strike in a frame.

Calluna vulgaris (Ling-Heather)—Hardy evergreen shrub thriving in full sun in peaty non-calcareous soil. *Culture*—Plant in Oct. or Apr., trim-off dead flower-heads in Apr. To propagate, take cuttings in summer and strike in peaty soil in a frame, or layer. *See also* Erica. *Varieties*—*C. v. var. alba plena* (White Scotch Heather); *C. v. var. Alportii* (Crimson-pink, July–Sept.,

15 in.); *C. v. var. aurea* (Golden Foliage, July–Sept., 12 in.); *C. v. var. alba Serlei* (White [Double], July–Sept., 12 in.).

Calochortus (Butterfly Tulip, Star Tulip, and Mariposa Lily)—Half-hardy bulbous plants that thrive in full sun in sandy leaf-mould. *Culture*—Plant in late Oct., 3 in. deep and 3 in. apart. Cover with straw or fibre in winter, and lift the bulbs when the leaves die down. *Pot Culture*—Pot-up ten bulbs in a 4 to 5-in. pot in Nov. in a compost of two-thirds sandy loam and one-sixth part each of peat and leaf-mould. Keep covered with fibre in a cold frame until late Dec., when transfer to the greenhouse; dry-off after flowering. Propagate by offsets in Nov. *Species*—*C. Howellii* (White, July–Aug., 18 in.); *C. pulchellus* (Yellow-orange, July–Aug., 12 in.); *C. venustus* and *vars.* (Yellow and Red, July and Aug., 15 in.).

Caltha (Marsh Marigold)—Useful hardy perennial for the water-side or moist border. *Culture*—Propagate by means of division of roots in Mar. or July and plant out in moist, rich soil and in full sun or partial shade. *Species*—*C. palustris var. fl. pl.* (Rich Yellow [Double], May–July, 12 in.); *C. leptosepala* (Deep Yellow, Flushed Maroon, May–July, 15 in.); and *C. polypetala* (Golden, May–July, 20 in.).

Calycanthus floridus (Carolina All-spice)—Hardy deciduous shrub which likes a partially-shaded moist position and carries purple-red flowers in May and June, growing to a height of 5 ft. or more. *Culture*—Plant in Nov., and cut out dead wood after flowering. Propagate by means of cuttings or layering in summer.

Camassia (Quamash)—Hardy bulbous plants which thrive in moist, but sunny, borders in a mixture of loam, leaf-mould and rotten manure. *Culture*—Plant in Oct., 4 to 5 in. deep and 10 in. apart; and lift from the soil every fourth year. Propagate by means of offsets in Oct., or by seed under glass in Mar. *Species*—*C. esculenta vars.* (Purple-blue and Silver-white, May and June, 20–30 in.); *C. Leichtlinii* (Cream-white, May and June, 40–60 in.).

Camellia—Hardy evergreen shrubs which thrive in sheltered and semi-shaded positions and in practically any soil, provided it is lime-free. They are also useful for greenhouse culture. *Culture*—Pot-up firmly in May, using 8 to 12-in. pots. They do best when under-potted. Use a compost of one-half part turfy loam and a quarter part each of sand and peat or leaf-mould. As soon as re-established, gradually harden-off, stand out of doors in partial shade on a firm base of ashes or bricks, and keep the roots moist, but not too wet. Move the plants into cold frames or the cold house in Sept. Trim-back all straggling shoots after flowering, syringe daily, sponge the leaves occasionally, and disturb the roots as little as possible. Propagate by grafting in a close propagating frame in early spring, using seedling *C. japonica* as a stock, or cuttings of half-matured shoots in a frame in July or Aug. Seeds may be raised in a moist heat. *Named Varieties*—*C. alba plena* (White, Double); *C. Chandleri* (Double Pink); *C. Donckelaarii* (Rose); *C. Henri Favre* (Rose-salmon); *C. Jupiter* (Rosy-red, Single); *C. Lady Clare* (Pink); and *Mathiotiana* (Rose-red, Double). All bloom between Feb. and May.

Campanula (Bellflower)—Genus, including annuals, biennials and perennials and providing plants for the greenhouse, border and rock garden. Almost all species thrive in an open position in sun or semi-shade in well-drained, light, sandy loam with ample grit and leaf-mould. For culture, *see* Annuals, p. 123, Biennials, p. 125, *and* Perennials, p. 281. *Pot Culture*—(*C. pyramidalis*). Sow in small pots and place in a well-ventilated frame: move into 5 to 6-in. pots in Oct. and keep in a frost-proof frame for the winter. Pot-up again in Mar., using 7 to 8-in. pots and a compost of two-thirds sandy loam and one-third leaf-mould, rotted cow manure, and a little old mortar rubble, harden-off, and stand in the open. Stake as the flower spikes form, move into the house about July, and give liquid manure when the buds form. *C. pyramidalis* and other tall species for the greenhouse may also be increased by means of cuttings in a frame in Mar. or Aug. *Greenhouse Trailing Species*—Propagate by means of seed in heat in Mar., by cuttings in a frame in Aug., or by division in Mar. *Species*—*C. dahurica* (Pale Purple, June–Sept., 18 in.); *C. lactiflora* (Pale Blue or White, June–Aug., 36–48 in.); *C. latifolia* (Pale Blue, June–Sept., 24–48 in.); *C. Medium* (Canterbury Bells) (Various, June–Aug., 10–50 in.); *C. persicifolia* (Blue and White, June–Aug., 24–30 in.); *C. pyramidalis* (Chimney Bellflower) (Blue or White, July—Sept., 40–70 in.); *C. sarmentosa* (Pale Blue, Summer, 12–18 in.). NAMED BORDER VARIETIES OF C. PERSICIFOLIA—*Faerie Queen* (Pale Blue); *Fleur-de-Neige* (White, Double); *Newry Giant* (White, Semi-double); *Shirley* (Blue, Semi-double). ALPINES—*C. Allionii* (Blue, June, 2–3 in.); *C. alpina* (Violet, June–Sept., 4 in.); *C. cæspitosa* (Blue, June–July, 5 in.); *C. carpatica vars.* (Purple, Blue or White, May–Sept., 6–12 in.); *C. garganica* (Mauve, White or Pale Blue, June–Sept., 4 in.); *C. kewensis* (Violet-purple, June–July, 4 in.); *C. muralis* (Purple-blue, June–Aug., 4 in.); *C. Poscharskyana* (Powder Blue, June, 12 in.).

Canary Creeper (*Tropæolum aduncum*)—This well-known creeper flowers best in a rather poor, dry soil, and in a sunny position. *T. aduncum* (Yellow) is half-hardy. *Culture*—Sow late in Apr. very thinly in the open, or under glass in Mar. in a cool greenhouse. If planted indoors, pot-off singly, harden-off and plant out 12 in. apart in May, otherwise thin out when fit to handle.

Canna (Indian Shot)—Half-hardy perennials for the cool greenhouse, or for summer bedding in warm sunny beds and borders with well-manured rich loam. *Culture*—Sow seed ½ in. deep in sandy loam and leaf-mould in a propagating case (Temp. 75° F.), in Feb. or Mar. (the seed having previously been soaked for a day in warm water). Pot-up singly as soon as possible, or propagate by means of division of roots in spring, dividing them so that each section of root contains an eye. Pot-up early in Mar. or Apr. in single pots and, if for outdoor culture, plant out in June about 24 in. apart. If for greenhouse culture, pot-up into 6 to 12-in. pots, using a rich and porous compost of one-half loam and one-quarter part each of rotten cow manure and sandy leaf-mould. At the end of Sept. pot-up those grown out of doors and winter under glass. Keep moderately dry and allow the leaves and stems to die off gradually. *Named Varieties*—*Assaut* (Scarlet); *Beethoven* (Orange); *Italia* (Orange and Yellow); *President* (Scarlet); and *J. B. Van der Schoot* (Yellow Spotted). All Aug. to Oct., 3 to 6 ft.

Caragana arborescens (Pea Tree)—Hardy deciduous trees and shrubs of the cytisus family, which thrive in sunny positions on dry banks in light sandy or ordinary soil. *Culture*—Plant in Oct.; cut out dead wood after flowering. Propagate by means of seed in the open in May, or by layering in July.

Carnation (Dianthus Caryophyllus)—Carnations, picotees and pinks, which are closely allied, are all propagated by seeds, layers and cuttings.

Carnations in the Border—Three weeks before planting time the bed (well-drained medium loam) should be double-dug and a little well-rotted stable manure should be dug in to at least 6 in. below the surface, but manuring must not be overdone. Plant in Sept. or early in Oct., but in heavy and cold soils it is often wise to keep the young plants in a frame until May and then plant out. In Apr. the flowering stems should be supported, and as soon as it is apparent that the principal bud is a healthy one, the less important ones should be pulled off. A small dose of weak liquid manure or soot-water twice a week after watering should be given from the time the buds begin to form until the colour shows. Carnations are perennials, and the beds should only be replanted every third year.

Carnations under Glass—In Sept. or early in Oct. pot-up the young layers singly into 3-in. pots in a compost of two-thirds turfy loam and one-third well-rotted leaf-mould and coarse sand, well sifted and sterilized by baking. Then stand the pots in a cold frame for the winter. Keep slightly moist but no water must settle on the leaves. In Mar., re-pot into 6-in pots, adding a little well-decayed manure and old mortar rubble to the compost. Keep close after potting until established, then give more air and finally remove the lights. In May, re-pot into 8-in. pots and return to the frame for a fortnight. Then stand in the open in a sheltered position, on a firm bed of ashes or on slates. Water liberally, syringe in dry weather, and stake, manure and disbud as advised for those in the open border. When the young plants are some 6 in. high, the heads should be pinched off, and as soon as the side shoots are from 6 to 8 in. in length they will in turn require pinching-back; not later than mid-June, however, for ordinary July-flowering carnations, or mid-Aug. for perpetual-flowering species. Transfer to a light position in the cool greenhouse as soon as the flowers show colour (about July).

Propagation—Choice varieties should be raised from cuttings or layers. *Seed*—Sow 1 in. apart in Apr. or May in seed pans, in a compost of two-thirds loam from decayed turf, one-third well-decomposed cow dung and a little old mortar rubble and bonemeal, and place in a sheltered part of the garden. When the plants show five or six leaves plant out from 10 to 15 in. apart in sunny, well-drained beds. Protect during winter with a cold frame. In cold and heavy soil, some gardeners prefer to sow in Aug., winter in a cold frame and plant out in spring. *Layering*—The season for this is in July or Aug., and the process is fully dealt with on p. 70. *Cuttings*—Cuttings may be struck in a frame with a bottom heat of 60° F. at any time from Nov. to Feb. (the best time is Jan.). Early in Mar. these cuttings, if struck in Jan., will need potting on into larger pots.

Perpetual or Tree Carnations are invaluable for winter blooms. The cultivation and soil are much the same as for the ordinary carnation. The cuttings, which will be furnished by the side shoots, may be struck in silver sand in Feb., Aug. or Sept. in gentle heat (55° F.), or the non-flowering shoots of the old plant may be laid down in a cold shaded frame in Sept. When rooted (in about a month), pot-up in 2½-in. pots and winter in a cool greenhouse near the glass and give ample air. The following summer pot-on into 6-in. pots and then into 8-in. pots, potting being more firm at each move. Pinch back, stand outdoors, and stake as advised above. About the beginning of Sept. the plants may again be taken into the house and watered occasionally with weak liquid manure or soot-water as soon as the roots have filled the pots. Seed may be sown in gentle heat (55° F.) in Feb.

Malmaison Carnations require treatment as detailed for border carnations, but only require one "stopping", and a cooler atmosphere; the winter temperature should rarely rise above 45° F. They should not be placed in the open in summer. Propagate by layers in a frame in July and Aug., or by cuttings in a propagating frame with bottom heat in May or June.

Clove Carnations are a hardy border type, best planted out in Apr.

A few good Varieties—BORDER. SELFS—*Bookham Apricot; Blush Clove* (Blush-white); *Bookham Clove* (Crimson); *Bookham Rose; Bookham Scarlet; Border Yellow; Coral Clove* (Coral-pink); *Crystal Clove* (White); *Fiery Cross*

(Scarlet); *Glamour* (Yellow); *Margaret Keep* (Blush-pink); *Purple Clove; Royal Scot* (Scarlet); *Salmon Clove; The Grey Douglas* (Heliotrope); *Trumpeter* (Rose-madder); *White Clove.*

FANCIES—*Centurion* (Yellow and Scarlet); *Endymion* (Canary-yellow, streaked Blood-red); *Highland Mary* (Primrose-yellow and Rose-pink); *Kelso* (Golden-apricot and Blue-grey); *Linkman* (Yellow and Scarlet); *Mona* (Buff and Rose); *Mrs. Hawksbee* (White and Rose-crimson); *Ravenswood* (White and Maroon-crimson); *Saracen* (Slate-grey, striped Crimson and Rose); *Steerforth Clove* (White and Crimson-maroon); *The Cadi* (Rose-madder, striped Blue and Scarlet); *Viceroy* (Yellow and Carmine-crimson).

PERPETUAL BORDER—*Sussex Avondale* (Salmon-pink); *Sussex Beauty* (Heliotrope); *Sussex Bizarre* (Peach, flaked Heliotrope); *Sussex Crimson; Sussex Maid* (White flaked Rose-pink); *Sussex Pink.*

PICOTEES—(*Yellow ground*). *Exquisite* (Scarlet Edge); *Her Majesty* (Purple Edge); *Margaret Glitters* (Rosy-scarlet Edge); *Mrs. J. J. Kean* (Rose-pink Edge); *Neil Kenyon* (Rose Edge); *Togo* (Crimson Edge).

TREE OR PERPETUALS—*Baroness de Brienen* (Salmon-pink); *Edward Allwood* (Scarlet); *Eileen Low* (Salmon-pink); *Laddie* (Salmon-pink); *Lady Northcliffe* (Salmon-pink); *Mikado* (Heliotrope); *Mary Allwood* (Reddish-salmon); *Mrs. A. J. Cobb* (Crimson); *Saffron* (Yellow); *Tarzan* (Scarlet); *Topsy* (Scarlet); *White Enchantress.*

MALMAISONS—*Baldwin* (Pink); *Calypso* (Soft-flesh); *Duchess of Westminster* (Rose-pink); *Maggie Hodgson* (Crimson); *Nell Gwynne* (White); *Princess of Wales* (Pink).

Carnations, Marguerite—Half-hardy annuals which thrive in open beds in rich, gritty loam. They grow about 18 in. high and flower from Aug. to Oct. If lifted before damaged by the frost they will furnish flowers in the greenhouse through the winter and spring. For culture, *see* Annuals, p. 123.

Carpenteria californica (Californian Mock Orange)—Half-hardy climbing shrubs which like a warm sheltered position and well-drained loam. They grow from 5 to 10 ft. high and flower about mid-summer. *Culture*—Propagate by means of cuttings of young wood in Apr. in a frame, by layering in Sept., or by suckers in autumn. Plant in autumn and prune-out weak wood and dead flowers after flowering.

Carpinus Betulus (Hornbeam)—Hardy deciduous tree which thrives in sunny, open positions in almost any soil and makes a good hedge plant. *Culture*—Plant from Nov. to Feb.; no pruning is necessary. Propagate by seeds, graft in Mar. on the common hornbeam, or layer.

Cassinia—Beautiful evergreen flowering shrubs which like a sunny position in ordinary soil. They grow from 3 to 6 ft. high and flower from July to Sept. *C. fulvida*, 4 ft., with creamy-white flowers, is a good species. *Culture*—Plant from Oct. to Nov., and thin-out branches when overcrowded. To propagate strike cuttings in a frame in Aug.

Castanea (Sweet Chestnut)—Hardy deciduous trees which thrive in full sun in light gravelly loam. *Culture*—Plant in Nov. and thin-out branches when overcrowded. To propagate sow in the open.

Catalpa (Indian Bean Tree)—Hardy deciduous trees which thrive in full sun and in moist, but well-drained rather light loam. They grow 25 to 50 ft. high and flower in July and Aug. *Culture*—Plant from Nov. to Feb. When seeds are not available, take cuttings of leafy shoots in July and insert them in gentle bottom heat, or layer in July.

Catananche (Cupidone)—Hardy perennial or annual plants, which like a sunny spot in a warm dry border and ordinary soil. For culture, *see* Annuals,

p. 123, *and* Perennials, p. 281. *Species—C. lutea* (Yellow, July, 9 in.); *C. cærulea* (Blue, July–Aug., ?? in.); and *C. cærulea, var. alba* (White, July–Aug., 20–30 in.).

Ceanothus (Californian Lilac)—Half-hardy shrubs which like a warm sunny position and well-drained ordinary soil and leaf-mould. There are two distinct classes, one flowering in spring, the other from July to Sept. The latter are hardy deciduous shrubs and the others evergreens, suitable for sheltered walls and mild localities. *Culture*—Plant in Mar. or Oct. Cut spring-flowering species back in May; late-flowering plants must be pruned in early spring. Evergreens grown as bushes will not need severe pruning. To propagate, take cuttings in July or Aug. and strike in a frame, or layer during the same months. *Species and hybrids*—EVERGREEN, SPRING-FLOWERING: *C. Burkwoodii*, hybrid (Rich Blue); *C. dentatus* (Blue); *C. rigidus* (Purplish-Blue); and *C. Veitchianus* (Bright Blue). HYBRID (DECIDUOUS), LATE-FLOWERING: *Ceres* (Rose-pink); *Gloire de Versailles* (Lavender); *Henri Defosse* (Dark Blue); *Indigo* (Indigo Blue); *Marie Simon* (Rose); and *Perle Rose* (Rose-carmine).

Cedar (Cedrus)—Hardy evergreen trees suitable only for large gardens. *Culture*—Plant in Sept. or Oct. when from 1 to 4 ft. high, in a sunny position in well-drained, gravelly, chalky, or sandy soil. No pruning is necessary. To propagate, sow in Mar. or Apr. *Species and Varieties*—*C. atlantica* (Mt. Atlas Cedar, 80–100 ft.); *C. Deodara* (Deodar, 150 ft.); and *C. Libani* (The Cedar of Lebanon, 100 ft.).

Cedronella cana—This plant bears crimson-purple flowers in June on stems 3 ft. high. It is not altogether hardy and should be grown only in warm and sheltered situations. For culture, *see* Perennials, p. 281.

Celastrus (Bitter Sweet, Staff Tree, etc.)—Hardy perennial climbing plants which thrive in most soils and positions. They carry hundreds of brilliant golden-yellow fruits exposing scarlet-coated seeds in autumn. *Culture*—Cut out weak wood and tip stray shoots in Feb., and propagate by means of layering young shoots in Oct. *Species—C. orbiculatus* and *C. scandens.*

Celosia (Prince of Wales' Feathers, or Cockscomb)—Half-hardy annuals which thrive if planted out in June in a warm, sheltered situation in southern districts. Grown in pots in the greenhouse, they may, with a little management, be had in flower the whole winter. For culture, *see* Annuals, p. 123. *Species and Varieties—C. argentea* (Silvery); *C. cristata* (Cockscomb) (Crimson, July–Aug., 18 in.); *C. c. var. coccinea* (Scarlet); *C. c. var. pyramidalis* (Scarlet, Crimson, or Gold, July–Sept., 30 in.).

Celsia (Cretan Mullein)—Half-hardy biennials and perennials which thrive in the cool greenhouse, in a compost of sandy loam and a little leaf-mould. For culture, *see* Biennials, p. 125, *and* Perennials, p. 281. *Species—C Arcturus* (Deep Yellow, spotted Purple, June–Nov., 20 in.); *C. cretica* (Golden-yellow, spotted Brown, June–July, 60 in.).

Centaurea—Large genus of hardy annuals, biennials, and perennials, all of which thrive in a sunny position in any good garden soil. The perennials (Knapweed) make good border plants; *C. Cyanus* (Cornflower) and *C. suaveolens* (Sweet Sultan) are annuals. For culture, *see* Annuals, p. 123, Biennials, p. 125, *and* Perennials, p. 281. *Pot Culture—C. gymnocarpa* (Dusty Miller) and *C. ragusina* are useful in the cold greenhouse. Sow in heat in Jan. and Aug., or take cuttings in Sept. *Species and Varieties*—HARDY ANNUALS—*C. Cyanus* (Cornflower) (White, Pink, Blue, July–Oct., 6–36 in.); *C. depressa* (Blue, Crimson Centre, July–Oct., 12 in.); *C. moschata* (Sweet Sultan) (White to Yellow, Rose and Purple, July–Oct., 20 in.). HARDY PERENNIALS—*C. baby-*

lonica (Yellow, July–Sept., 6–8 ft.); *C. dealbata* (Rose, Silver Foliage, July–Sept., 24 in.); *C. hypoleuca* (Large Mauve, July–Aug., 12–18 in.); *C. macrocephala* (Deep Yellow, July and Aug., 50–60 in.); *C. montana* (Blue, White, Pink and Yellow, July and Aug., 24–30 in.); *C. ruthenica* (Sulphur Yellow, Aug., 50–60 in.).

Cerastium (Mouse-ear, Chickweed, Jerusalem Star)—Genus of dwarf-growing hardy perennials that are useful for carpeting or for the rock and paved gardens. For culture, *see* Rock Plants, p. 283. *Species—C. Bierbersteinii* (White, Silver Foliage, May–June, 6 in.); *C. tomentosum* (White, Silver Foliage, June–Aug., 6 in.).

Ceratostigma (Leadwort)—Low-growing rock plants which thrive in the sun in gritty loam. For culture, *see* Rock Plants, p. 283. *C. plumbaginoides* (Cobalt-blue, July–Sept., 9 in.) is a well-known species.

Cercis (Judas Tree)—Tall deciduous shrubs or small trees which thrive in full sun in moist, sandy, and well-drained loam. In May they carry rose-purple pea-shaped flowers. *Culture*—Plant in Oct. or Nov. To propagate, sow in a frame, or layer in Sept.

Chænomeles—Hardy deciduous flowering trees and shrubs, which thrive in sunny positions in ordinary soil. *Culture*—Plant in Oct. or Nov. Cut-out old wood and shorten side shoots in June. Propagate by means of seeds, layering, suckers, or cuttings in Oct. *Pot Culture*—Pot-up in Nov., in 8 to 10-in. pots, and take into the cold greenhouse. Sink the pots in ashes outdoors from May to Nov. *Species and Varieties—C. lagenaria* (Orange-red), vars. *aurora* (Rose, shaded Yellow); *cardinalis* (Rich Red); *nivalis* (White); and *rubra grandiflora* (Crimson); *C. japonica* (Orange-flame) hybrids. All Jan. to June, 3 to 9 ft.

Charieis heterophylla (Cape Aster)—Pretty little hardy annual, very effective in beds or rock gardens. It grows some 6 in. high and flowers from June to Sept. For culture, *see* Annuals, p. 123.

Chelone (Shellflower)—Hardy perennials, many species of which are now classed with penstemons, which like a sunny or semi-shaded site in moist sandy loam with humus in it. For culture, *see* Perennials, p. 281. *Species and Varieties—C. coccinea* (Red); *C. Lyonii* (Rosy Purple); *C. obliqua* (Pink). All June to Sept., 24 to 36 in.

Chimonanthus præcox (Winter Sweet)—Winter-blooming hardy deciduous shrub, which likes a sunny, sheltered position in deep, moist, sandy loam. It bears pale yellow flowers stained purple, and reaches a height of 7 ft. on walls. *Culture*—Plant in Oct. or Mar., and when grown as a climber cut back side shoots to within five to six " eyes " of the main stems after flowering. Propagate by means of layering in Aug., or by suckers or seed in Mar.

Chionanthus (Fringe Tree)—Hardy deciduous shrubs or small trees, which like a sheltered position in well-drained, moist loam, and bear white flowers in June and July. *Culture*—Plant from Oct. to Nov., and trim to shape after flowering if required. Propagate by means of layering in Sept., or strike cuttings of half-ripe shoots in a close frame during July and Aug.

Chionodoxa (Glory of the Snow)—This bulbous plant requires similar treatment to that accorded to bulbs generally, and thrives in sun or shade and sandy loam in the border, rock garden or greenhouse. *Culture*—Plant in Oct. 2½ in. deep and from 3 to 4 in. apart. Propagate by offsets in Oct. or raise from seed. *See also* Bulbs, p. 141. *Species—C. Luciliæ* and *C. gigantea* (Soft Mauve, Blue and White, Mar., 9 in.); *C. L. grandiflora* (Lavender-blue, White Centre, Mar.–Apr., 9 in.); *C. sardensis* (Deep Blue, Mar.–Apr., 7 in.).

Choisya ternata (Mexican Orange Blossom)—Half-hardy evergreen shrub which likes a sunny sheltered position in sandy loam. It grows from 6 to 10 ft. high and from May to Sept. bears small white flowers. *Culture*—Plant in April or Sept., and in April cut out old wood or trim if required. Propagate by means of layering in Aug., or by cuttings in a frame in Aug. *Pot Culture* —Pot-up in spring in a 6 to 8-in. pot and a compost of peaty loam, leaf-mould and sand. Prune straggly shoots after flowering and put out in the open, with pots sunk in ashes, from July to Oct.

Christmas Rose (Helleborus niger)—Hardy perennial which thrives in well-dug, light and moist soil in a border facing preferably east or west or in a cool house. For culture, *see* Perennials, p. 281. If for the greenhouse, pot-up in Oct. in 6 to 8-in. pots in 2 parts fibrous loam and 1 part rotten manure; select fresh plants annually, planting the old ones out in Apr. or May. This and *Helleborus orientalis* [Lenten Rose] (Jan.–Apr., 18–24 in.) are the most popular species, there being many colour varieties of the latter.

Chrysanthemum—The chrysanthemum is one of the hardiest plants, but owing to the fact that it flowers somewhat late its beautiful blooms are subject to injury from the weather when grown out of doors unless the protection of glass is provided. Chrysanthemums may be classified according to the time of their blooming, as early-flowering, blooming from July to Oct.; semi-early, blooming in Sept. and Oct. in the open; and ordinary or late-flowering, blooming in Nov. and Dec.

Culture of Indoor Chrysanthemums—If seed is used it should be sown as soon as ripe (Feb.) in a pan of sandy soil in a temp. of 60° F.: transplant and pot-on as necessary. *Propagation by Cuttings*—After the plants have finished blooming the stems and all weak shoots from the base should be cut down to within a few inches of the ground and the pots given a position in the cold greenhouse or a frost-proof frame. A half-inch mulch of fine loam and leaf-mould, and a little water, will help the old roots to throw up sturdy young shoots for cuttings. *See* Cuttings, p. 67. Grow in pots in a mixture of well-rotted leaf-mould, grit or silver sand and fibrous loam, in about equal parts, and a dusting of wood ashes, all well sieved. Once the cuttings are rooted (in from three to five weeks), stand the pots near the glass in a frost-proof frame, and give ample ventilation in fine weather. Cuttings of Japanese types must be taken in Dec. or Jan. Nearly all growers differ as to the best time for striking cuttings of the " Decorative " types. Some recommend Nov.; some succeed admirably by inserting them in May; the latter date only when propagating plants to flower in small pots in Dec. Perhaps it is better to make a compromise by striking in Feb. or Mar. *Potting-on*—December-struck cuttings should be well rooted by the middle of Feb. and should then be potted-up into 3 or 3½-in. pots, adding to the compost one-third part well-rotted manure. They should receive their next shift into 5 or 6-in. pots about the first week in Apr. Disturb the roots as little as possible, and add a little more manure and a dusting of bonemeal and powdered charcoal to the compost, which do not sieve. The cultivation should be continued in a frame or on a shelf near the glass. Shade from the sun, then in about a fortnight's time harden-off, stand out of doors by the middle of May, and give a final shift a month or six weeks later. *Summer Treatment*—The pots should be stood in the open on slates in a sheltered position, facing south or west. As soon as the pots are full of roots the plants should be placed in 8 to 9-in. pots; about the middle of June is a good time to complete the final potting-up. No soil is better for them than a compost of two-thirds lumpy fibrous loam, one-sixth well-rotted cow-dung, and one-sixth leaf-mould and a little old mortar rubble and sharp sand liberally coloured with bonemeal and soot. There need not be much drainage. *Staking and Tying*—The plants must be properly supported. *See* Staking and Tying, p. 22. *"Stopping" and Disbudding*—If bushy plants are to be grown, pinch out the tip of the central shoot, when the plants are some 5 or 6 in. high. A second "stopping" will be necessary in early summer. If you grow blooms for exhibition only, no stopping will be needed until the "break-bud" appears in early summer. Pinch-out this bud and all the young shoots just below it, save the three strongest and best placed, and concentrate the whole strength of the plant into these stems and the strength of these stems into a single bud at the top. *Feeding and Autumn Treatment*—From early in Aug. the plants should be fed two or three times a week alternately with sulphate of potash and with weak manure-water. Feeding must cease as soon as the blooms are three parts open, and early in Oct. the plants should be moved under glass. This is a critical change for them, and the leaves should be kept well syringed, *except in dull, damp weather*.

Outdoor Culture of Border Chrysanthemums—Plant out in Mar., or in the case of less hardy sorts, towards the end of May. They should receive the same general treatment in training and watering as those grown indoors, except that the majority should not be "stopped". The soil should be well drained and well dug in winter, but it must not be too rich. A mulch of well-rotted short stable manure in June is beneficial. In planting, 24 to 36 in. should be allowed between each plant, and an open, sunny, sheltered position is essential. Most varieties naturally form bushy plants, but with others it is necessary, from time to time, to pinch-back the tips of the shoots: this pinching-back must not be continued after the end of July. If large blooms are desired the plants should be disbudded. As soon as the flowers are over cut the plants down to the ground, lift them, shake the soil from the roots and place them close together in shallow boxes of light, sandy soil and store in a frost-proof place. In Mar. divide the crowns, retaining the younger and more vigorous portions only, and plant out again in the border, or take cuttings as advised for the indoor kinds. In light and warm soil it is not always necessary to lift the crowns in autumn.

Varieties—GREENHOUSE. *Japanese Exhibition*—*Alice Burgess* (Salmon); *Birmingham* (Crimson); *Duchess of Kent* (Pink); *Duke of Kent* (White); *Edna Green* (Golden Yellow); *F. E. Luxford* (Apricot); *James Bryant* (Chestnut); *John Pockett* (Rosy Crimson); *Majestic* (Golden Amber); *Mrs. John Woolman* (Rose); *Mrs. R. C. Pulling* (Lemon Yellow).

Japanese Decorative—Mid-season flowering—*Ada Stevens* (Yellow); *Adonis* (Salmon Pink); *Crensa* (Gold); *In Memoriam* (Crimson); *Primrose Beauty; Oldland Bronze; Sussex White*. Late-flowering—*Bronze Favourite; Imperial Pink; Sussex Gold;* etc.

Incurved Varieties—*Golden Pride* (Yellow); *Monument* (White); *Ondine* (White, Green tipped); *Progress* (Silver Mauve).

Single Varieties—*Artist* (Red); *Chesswood Beauty* (Crimson); *Mason's Bronze; Molly Godfrey* (Pink); *Phyllis Cooper* (Orange and Yellow); *Rowena* (Yellow); *Susan* (Rose and Bronze).

Anemone-centred Singles—*Elspeth* (Mauve); *Golden Nymph* (Yellow and Gold); *Mary Godfrey* (Pink), *Thora* (Rose); *Winsome* (Crimson).

Pompons—*Bubbles* (Chestnut Bronze); *Mosquito* (Yellow); *Salmon Bouquet; Shell Bouquet; White Bouquet*.

HARDY BORDER VARIETIES—*Arnheim* (Bronze); *August Pink; Carefree* (Chestnut); *Corona* (Orange); *Golden Harvest; Hurricane* (Crimson); *Imperial Yellow; Mary Mona* (Salmon); *New Countess* (Rose Pink); *Royal Pink; Serenus* (White); *Sweetheart* (Salmon Pink); *Zenith* (Maroon).

Hardy Singles—Carrie Luxford (Crimson); *Doreen Woolman* (Golden Flame); *Maidenhood* (Primrose); *Mrs. H. Woolman* (White); *Shirley Crimson; The Dome* (Salmon and Gold).

Chrysanthemum, Annual (Corn Marigold, Crown Daisy)—These showy plants thrive in sunny beds or borders. For culture, *see* Annuals, p. 123. *Named Varieties—Eastern Star* (Yellow Brown Eye); *Evening Star* (Golden Yellow); *Morning Star* (Primrose); *The Sultan* (Maroon); and *White Pearl* (Double). All flower from June to Sept., 20 in.

Chrysanthemum, Perennial (Ox-Eye Daisy)—These, like the annual species, make a good show in sunny borders and ordinary soil. For culture, *see* Perennials, p. 281. *Species—C. alpinum* (White, June–Sept., 5 in.); *C. arcticum* (White, tinged Pink, Oct., 18 in.); *C. coccineum* (Scarlet, June–Sept., 36 in.); *C. maximum* (White, July–Sept., 36 in.); *C. uliginosum* (White, Sept.–Oct., 3–5 ft.).

Cimicifuga (Bugwort, Bugbane or Snake-root)—Hardy perennial which thrives in a deep, moist loam and fairly sunny position. For culture, *see* Perennials, p. 281. *Species—C. cordifolia* (Creamy-white, July–Aug., 36 in.); *C. racemosa* (Cream-white, July–Aug., 36–48 in.); *C. simplex* (White, Aug.–Oct., 36 in.).

Cineraria—Beautiful greenhouse perennials which, by careful management, may be had in flower from Nov. to May. They thrive in a compost of 2 parts fibrous loam to 1 part of leaf-mould, well-decayed cow-manure and a little sand and old mortar rubble, and are best grown from seed. *Culture*—The first sowing should be made in Apr. in pans filled with equal parts of loam and leaf-mould and one-sixth part of sand, and placed in slight bottom heat. Cover with glass and paper and keep slightly moist. Stand the seedlings in partial shade, move into 3-in. pots as soon as possible, gradually harden-off and remove the lights of the frame entirely by day from July to the end of Sept. Shift the young plants into 4½ to 5-in. pots as required, and give them their final shift in Sept. into 6 to 8-in. pots. Keep moist and syringe every afternoon in hot weather, then towards the end of Sept. the plants should be placed in a cool greenhouse, and weak liquid manure or soot-water given alternately with water. Another sowing may be made in a cold frame in May, and a third in June. Pot-on as above, but at proportionately later dates. *Cineraria maritima* (*Senecio Cineraria*) is a beautiful foliage plant for summer bedding, or cold greenhouse. Sow under glass in Mar.

Species and Varieties—C. maritima (Silver Foliage, Summer, 18 in.); and *Senecio cruentus* (Cineraria), of which there are many varieties. (Various colours, winter and spring, 18–30 in.).

Cistus (Rock Rose)—Evergreen perennial shrubs mostly hardy in warm sheltered sites. They love the sun and do well in dry, well-drained sandy loam or ordinary soil to which ample lime-rubble has been added. *Culture*—Do not prune, merely keep the shrubs in shape by means of "stopping" in Mar. and by removing dead blooms. Propagate by means of layering in Aug., sow seed in Apr., or take cuttings of half-matured wood in Aug. and strike in a shaded frame. Grow in pots till ready for planting out. *Species—C. cyprius* (White, Spotted Red, June–July, 40–60 in.); *C. ladaniferus* (White [Spotted Red], June–July, 48–60 in.); *C. purpureus* (Purple-red [Blotched Crimson], June–July, 36–48 in.), etc.

Clarkia—Hardy annuals which thrive in fairly moist rich soil in the border or cold greenhouse. For culture, *see* Annuals, p. 123. For the greenhouse sow in a frame in Aug., and pot-up as required, using 6 to 7-in. pots for three plants. *Varieties—Brilliant Rose* (Rose); *Firefly* (Crimson); *Marginata*

(Pink, margined White); *Orange King* (Orange); *Scarlet Beauty* (Scarlet); *Purple Queen* (Purple); *Salmon Queen* (Salmon); and *Snowball* (White). All July to Oct., 24 in.

Claytonia (Spring Beauty)—Dwarf-growing hardy perennials which thrive in sun or shade and in any soil. *Culture*—Sow in Mar., where the plants are to flower. *Species*—*C. sibirica* (Rose) and *C. virginica* (White). Both spring, 6 in.

Clematis—Beautiful hardy climbers which do well against walls and on trellises, facing north, east or west, or in the greenhouse. A sunny position is most suitable, but the lower part of the stems require shade. Although not particular as to soil, they prefer light to heavy land if it has been well manured; a mixture of well-drained loam, well-rotted manure and old mortar rubble is most satisfactory. *Culture*—Propagate by means of layering in summer and plant out in Mar. Cut away dead and weak wood, giving ample light and air to the growths retained, and fasten the shoots up securely. Propagation may also be carried out by means of grafting, by cuttings or seed. Most varieties require pruning after flowering, but *C. vitalba* is best pruned in Mar., while *C. Jackmannii* and *C. Viticella vars.* should be cut down to 6 in. in Nov. or to 1 ft. in spring. *Pot Culture*—Pot-up in Mar. using 5 to 10-in. pots and a compost of 2 parts peaty loam to 1 part of leaf-mould, well-rotted manure and sand. *Varieties*—EARLY-FLOWERING—(Florida Group) *Countess of Lovelace* (Lavender-blue); *Duchess of Edinburgh* (Double, White). LATE-FLOWERING—(Jackmannii Group) *Gipsy Queen* (Purple) and *Snow White* (White). (Lanuginosa Group) *Henryi* (Greenish-white); *Beauty of Worcester* (Blue-violet); *Fairy Queen* (Flesh Pink); and *Mrs. Pope* (Lavender). (Patens Group) *Duke of Edinburgh* (Purple-violet); *Miss Bateman* (White); and *The Queen* (Lavender); *C. montana* (White); and *var. rubens* (Rose); *C. tangutica* (Golden Yellow), and *C. Flammula* (White). (Viticella Group) *C. Ascotiensis* (Azure Blue), and *Viticella alba* (White, Semi-double).

Clerodendron—Beautiful deciduous shrubs or small trees, which thrive in a sunny sheltered position in well-drained, rich loam. *Culture*—Plant in Oct. or Nov. Propagate by means of seed, cuttings of half-ripened shoots in a frame, or by root cuttings. *C. fœtidum* is a good plant for the cold greenhouse. *Hardy Species*—*C. Fargesii* (White, Red Calyx, 10–12 ft.); *C. fœtidum* (Purple, 3–6 ft.); *C. trichotomum* (White, Red Calyx, 10–12 ft.). All July to Sept.

Clianthus—Evergreen climbing shrubs which succeed best in the warm sunny border of a cool greenhouse in sandy peat and fibrous loam. *C. puniceus* (Crimson), *vars. magnificus* (Red) and *carneus* (Flesh), Parrot's Bill and Lobster's Claw, blossom freely out of doors against a trellis or south wall. *Culture*—Sow in Feb. singly in pots, and when 3 to 4 in. high move into 4½-in. pots and keep in these until ready for planting out in Apr., or in the case of *C. Dampieri* (Glory Pea), into a border in the house. Syringe house plants daily in hot dry weather, and trim back straggling shoots after flowering. They may also be raised by means of cuttings in a frame. (Temp. 70° F.) in May or June.

Clivia (Imantophyllum)—Beautiful evergreen plants with lily-like blooms, for the cool greenhouse. *Culture*—Plant in Feb. in 9-in. pots in a mixture of rich sandy loam, leaf-mould and old manure, keep in a cool place, and let the roots fill the pots, as the plants flourish best when root-bound. Water well in summer, keep cool and on the dry side during winter, and sponge the leaves occasionally with tepid water. Weak manure-water should be given twice a week while the buds are forming. Propagate by means of division of suckers in Feb., or by seed sown when ripe. *Species*—*C. citrina* (Yellow); *C. miniata* and *vars.* (Orange-scarlet); *C. nobilis* (Red and Yellow). All Mar. to Apr., 20 in. Clivias make very useful room plants.

Cobæa (Cup and Saucer Plant)—Beautiful evergreen climbers that thrive in the cool greenhouse. They grow to a height of 20 ft. and flower from July to Sept. *C. scandens* (Purple and Greenish-white) will also thrive in the open in warm sheltered positions in the south and west of England; in more exposed positions it must be treated as an annual and be raised afresh each year. *Culture*—Sow thinly under glass (Temp. 45° F.) in light rich soil in Feb., or propagate by cuttings of young shoots in Jan. or Feb., and raise in a propagating case. Pot-up into 3 or 4-in. pots, harden-off, and if growing in the open, plant out 24 in. apart in June in equal parts of loam, leaf-mould and sand, or grow on in pots and keep in the cool greenhouse. In Feb. prune laterals back to two buds and cut out all weak growth.

Colchicum (Meadow Saffron or Autumn Crocus)—Hardy bulbous poisonous plants usually grown in the rock garden. *Culture*—Plant in July or Aug. in full sun, 5 in. deep and 6 in. apart, in moist, cool loam. Lift from the ground (triennially) in Aug. to increase. *Species*—*C. autumnale* (Lilac-rose, Sept.–Oct., 6 in.); *C. montanum* (Lilac or White, Sept.–Oct., 4 in.); *C. speciosum* (Crimson, Purple or White Eye, Sept.–Oct., 10 in.).

Coleus Blumei—Half-hardy annual and perennial foliage plants, useful for bedding-out or the cool greenhouse. *Culture*—Sow thinly in heat (70° F.) in Mar. Named varieties must be propagated by means of cuttings at any time from spring to autumn, struck singly in pots sunk to their rims in fibre in a frame with good bottom heat (70° F.), and in a moist atmosphere; the best time is Mar. These plants like a light, rich soil; 2 parts of loam to 1 part of leaf-mould and sand being recommended. Place near the glass, but shade from strong sun. When rooted, re-pot into 3-in. pots, pinch-back, and pot-on till they are finally in 5 to 6-in. pots. *Varieties*—*Beckwith's Gem; Countess of Dudley; Decorator; Pride of the Market; Sunset;* and *Verschaffeltii* (largely used for bedding). All these flower in summer and grow from 6 to 24 in. in height.

Collinsia (Collin's Flower)—Hardy annuals for sunny beds, borders or the greenhouse. For culture, *see* Annuals, p. 123. *Species*—*C. bicolor* (Reddish-purple and White, July–Oct., 12 in.); *C. grandiflora* (Purple-blue and White, July–Oct., 12 in.).

Colutea (Bladder Senna)—Deciduous broom-like shrub, thriving in almost any position or soil. *Culture*—Plant in Oct. or Nov., and in Mar. cut the previous year's growth well back. To propagate, take cuttings in Sept., or sow in the open in spring. *Species*—*C. arborescens* (Yellow, June–Aug., 10 ft.); *C. cruenta* (Red and Yellow, June–Aug., 6–8 ft.); *C. media* (Reddish-brown, June–Aug., 10 ft.).

Commelina (Day Flower)—Annual and perennial plants, which thrive in a sunny position in warm, well-drained borders and rich light soil. For culture, *see* Annuals, p. 123, *and* Perennials, p. 281. *Species*—*C. cœlestis* (Rich Blue, Aug. and Sept., 18 in.).

Convolvulus (Bindweed)—Large family of hardy annual and perennial climbing and trailing plants, most of which like a sunny position and rather poor soil. For culture, *see* Annuals, p. 123, *and* Perennials, p. 281. *Species* —Annuals—*C. tricolor* (White to Purple and Blue, June–Oct., 8–9 ft.); *C. tricolor alba* (White, July–Oct., 12 in.). Perennials—*C. Cneorum* (Soft Pink with Silver Foliage, June–Sept., 18 in.); *C. mauritanicus* (Blue, June–Sept., 12 in.).

Coreopsis (Tickseed)—Hardy annuals, biennials and perennials, most of which are best treated as biennials. The tall varieties are effective in mixed borders, and the dwarf kinds make fine bedding plants. A moist, sandy loam and a sunny position are most suitable, and ample water is needed in summer. For culture, *see* Annuals, p. 123, Biennials, p. 125, *and* Perennials, p. 281. *Species*—ANNUALS—*C. coronata* (Orange and Brown, July–Oct., 18 in.); *C. Drummondii* (Golden Yellow, July–Oct., 24 in.); *C. tinctoria* (Yellow and Bronze, July–Oct., 18 in.). PERENNIALS—*C. grandiflora* (Golden Yellow, July–Oct., 24–30 in.); *C. lanceolata* (Yellow, July–Oct., 24–30 in.); *C. rosea* (Reddish-pink, July–Sept., 18 in.); *C. verticillata* (Golden Yellow, July–Sept., 24 in.).

Cornus (Cornel, Dogwood, Cornelian Cherry)—Deciduous shrubs and trees and hardy herbaceous perennials. *Culture*—Sow under glass, or propagate by means of layering in Oct., or by suckers in Nov. Plant out in spring or early autumn in the shade, in a mixture of moist leaf-mould and peat, or ordinary soil. *C. Mas*, the Cornelian Cherry (10 to 25 ft.), thrives quite well in a dry soil. Thin-out after flowering when the branches are overcrowded. *Species and Varieties*—*C. alba sibirica variegata* (Silvery Variegation); *C. alba var. Spæthii* (Golden Foliage); *C. capitata* (syn. Benthamia fragifera) (Cream and Pink flowers, Spring, Scarlet fruits, 12 ft.). A half-hardy evergreen shrub which may be grown in the open in warm sheltered situations in the south; *C. florida rubra* (Rosy-pink Floral Bracts); *C. Kousa* (White Floral Bracts), etc. All May, 7 to 12 ft.

Corokia—Half-hardy evergreen flowering shrubs which thrive in a warm sunny position, and in ordinary soil. *Culture*—Plant in Apr. or Oct., and prune only to keep in shape. To propagate, strike half-matured cuttings in a frame in Aug. *Species*—*C. buddleioides* (White, Apr.–May, 3–4 ft.); *C. Cotoneaster* (Yellow, May, 6 ft.); *C. macrocarpa* (Orange, May–June, 6 ft.).

Coronilla (Crown Vetch or Scorpion Senna)—Half-hardy evergreen or deciduous shrubs, and herbaceous perennials, which succeed well against a south wall with a little winter protection, also in the rock garden, or cold greenhouse. *Culture*—Plant in Mar. or Oct. in well-drained ordinary soil, or in sandy loam (rock garden species). *Pot Culture*—Pot-up in Mar., using 6 to 8-in. pots and a compost of 2 parts sandy loam to 1 part of peat. Prune into shape and cut out old and dead wood in Feb., and stand in the open after flowering until Sept. To propagate, sow in a frame in Mar., or take cuttings of young wood in Apr. or Aug. (greenhouse plants) and strike in a frame (Temp. 60° F.). The rock garden species are propagated by seed as above, or by division of roots in Oct. *Species*—*C. cappadocica* (*syn. C. iberica*) (Cream-yellow, July–Aug., 4 in.)· *C. minima* (Yellow, June–July, 3 in.); *C. varia* (Lilac-pink, Aug.–Sept., 12–18 in.); SHRUBS—*C. Emerus* (Yellow, June–Aug.), and *C. glauca* (Yellow, Apr. to May).

Cortaderia (Pampas Grass)—Perennial grasses which thrive in sunny, sheltered positions, and well-drained soil. They grow 6 to 8 ft. high and flower in autumn. For culture, *see* Perennials, p. 281.

Cortusa Matthiolii (Bear's Ear)—Dwarf-growing rock plants, closely allied to the Primula, which thrive in partial shade in rich sandy loam and leaf-mould, and flower in July. See Rock Plants, p. 283.

Corydalis (Fumitory)—Hardy annual and perennial rock garden or border plants, which require shade and comparatively poor soil. For culture, *see* Annuals, p. 123, *and* Perennials, p. 281. *Species*—*(Perennials)*—*C. Capnoides* (Cream, May–Sept., 12 in.); *C. cava* (Purple and Rose, May, 12 in.); *C. lutea* (Yellow, June–Sept., 6–12 in.).

Corylopsis—Hardy deciduous shrubs which like a sunny, sheltered position, and well-drained, ordinary soil. *Culture*—Plant in Oct. or Nov. Little pruning is required. Propagate by means of layering in the summer. *Pot Culture* —Pot-up from Oct. to Feb., using 6 to 8-in. pots and turfy loam. Sink the pots in ashes in the open, from May to Dec., then take into the cold greenhouse. After flowering prune out weak wood and dead flower shoots. *Species*—*C. glabrescens; C. pauciflora; C. spicata;* and *C. Willmottiæ.* All Yellow, Mar. to Apr., 4 to 8 ft.

Cosmos (Mexican Aster)—Half-hardy annuals and perennials which thrive in warm, dry borders and in ordinary soil. The early-flowering annuals should be chosen. For culture, *see* Annuals, p. 123, *and* Perennials, p. 281. *Species*—ANNUALS—*C. bipinnatus* (Pink, White, and Crimson, June–Oct., 30–70 in.); *C. sulphureus* (Yellow, June–Oct., 20 in.); *C. diversifolius* (Lilac to Rose, June–Oct., 24 in.). *Named Varieties*—*Early Dawn* (Pink and White); *Klondyke* (Yellow); *Rose Queen* (Rosy Red); and *White Queen* (White).

Cotoneaster (Rockspray)—Hardy shrubs or small trees, most of which grow best in poor or chalky soil. *Culture*—Plant from Oct. to Mar. No pruning is necessary, though some species require thinning-out after flowering. To propagate, take cuttings of hard wood in a frame in July or Aug., or layer in Sept. or Oct. Seed may be sown in the open in Mar. or Sept. *Species*—*C. buxifolia* (E) (White, Apr., 8–12 ft.); *C. Dammeri* (E) (White, Apr.–May, prostrate); *C. Franchettii* (E) (White, May, 7–10 ft.); *C. horizontalis* (E) (Pale Pink, Apr., 2–4 ft.); *C. microphylla* (E) (Rosy White, May, 2–3 ft.); *C. microphylla var. thymifolia* (E) (Pinkish, Apr., 9–12 in.); *C. salicifolia* (E) (White, May, 6 ft.). (E)=Evergreen.

Cotyledon (Pennywort)—Dwarf-growing rock plants which thrive in sun or shade in dry, gritty loam and sand, and which flower in June. For culture, *see* Rock Plants, p. 283. *See also* Echeveria.

Cratægus (Thorn)—Hardy deciduous trees or shrubs, useful for hedges, etc *Culture*—Plant in Oct. or Nov. in a sunny position and ordinary soil. Thin-out the branches when overcrowded. To propagate, sow seed when ripe, bud or graft. *See also* Pyracantha. *Species*—*C. crus-galli* (White); *C. Oxyacantha fl. albo plena* (White, Double); *C. O. fl. roseo pl.* (Pink, Double); *C. O. punicea* (Scarlet, Single). All May, 15 ft.

Crinum (Cape Lily)—Half-hardy bulbous plant for the cool greenhouse. *C. Powellii* and *var. album* will grow outdoors in a sunny, sheltered, moist border, in well-drained, deep and rich sandy loam and peat. *Culture*—Plant 6 in. deep in Mar., surrounded with coarse sand, and protect with fibre in winter. Do not disturb unless overcrowded. *Pot Culture*—Pot-up in the spring (triennially) one bulb in each 9 to 10-in. pot in a compost of two parts fibrous loam to one part sandy peat. Propagate by means of offsets in Mar. *Species and Varieties*—*C. longifolium* (Pink or White); *C. Powellii* (Rose-red or White). All June to Aug., 24 to 36 in.

Crocus—Besides those which bloom in the early spring there are species and hybrids that flower in the autumn and winter. *Culture*—They like a good light soil to which a little bonemeal has been added, and thrive in sun or shade in a warm rock garden, border, or in pots, and are also useful for naturalizing in grass or for the wild garden. Crocuses are increased by offsets or by seed, the former being the usual method. Offsets are treated the same as old bulbs and will bloom the second year. Seed should be sown in pans of light sandy loam as soon as ripe, and placed in a sheltered situation out of doors until late autumn. During heavy rain and cold weather protect with a cold frame. They may remain in the same pans during summer, but lift in autumn and plant in beds of mellow loam in the reserve garden, 2 in. apart and 3 in. deep; here they will form strong bulbs and flower the third or fourth spring. Plant mature bulbs from 2 to 3 in. deep and 4 in. apart, autumn-flowering species from July to Aug.; spring-flowering species in Sept. or Oct. Divide and replant every third year. *Pot Culture*—Plant about seven corms half an inch deep in a 5 to 6-in. pot in autumn, using a compost of good, fairly light, sandy loam and leaf-mould, and keep covered with ashes or fibre in a frame until growth commences, then water and transfer to the cool house. Stand out in the open and keep dry in summer, and re-pot in Sept. *Species*—EARLY SPRING—*C. biflorus* (White, veined Violet); *C. chrysanthus* (Orange-yellow and Red); *C. Imperati* (Lilac or Buff and Black); *C. mœsiacus* (Golden-Yellow); *C. Sieberi* (Lilac-blue and Gold); *C. Tommasinianus* (Lavender and Orange); *C. versicolor* (White, feathered Purple); *C. vernus* and *vars.* (Various). AUTUMN—*C. asturicus* (Purple); *C. byzantinus* (Lavender); *C. ochroleucus* (Yellow); *C. pulchellus* (Lavender-blue and Orange Throat); *C. sativus* (Violet, Mauve and Orange); *C. speciosus* (Violet-blue and Orange); *C. zonatus* (Lilac-pink with Orange Throat). NAMED VARIETIES— *Grandeur Triomphante* (White and Blue); *King of the Whites* (White); *Large Yellow* (Yellow); *L'Unique* (Lilac-pink); *Van Speyk* (Purple, veined White); and *Yellow Hammer* (Yellow). All 3 to 4 in.

Cryptomeria japonica (Japanese Cedar)—Handsome evergreen trees which thrive in deep sandy loam in a sheltered, sunny situation. *Culture*—Plant from Sept. to Nov. No pruning is required. To propagate, sow in Mar. or Apr. or strike cuttings under hand-lights in Aug. The variety *elegans* is an attractive small tree.

Cucurbita (Ornamental Gourds)—Half-hardy climbing plants, many of which are very ornamental. Treated in a similar way to ordinary marrows, most will thrive in the open. Any good seedman's catalogue will give several good varieties.

Cuphea (Cigar Flower)—Hardy and half-hardy annuals, perennials and shrubs, are better treated as half-hardy. For culture, *see* Annuals, p. 123, *and* Perennials, p. 281. (*Shrubby Species*)—Propagate by cuttings of young wood in bottom heat (70° F.) in spring. Trim the following Jan., and re-pot if necessary in Feb.

Cupressus (Cypress)—Quick-growing conifers which thrive in sunny, sheltered positions in almost any soil. *Culture*—Plant in Apr. or Sept. No pruning is required, except in the case of hedge plants. They may be propagated by means of cuttings in a frame in Aug. or Sept.; some, however, are best raised from seed in Mar. *C. macrocarpa* (the Monterey Cypress), which thrives by the sea, makes a good hedge plant.

Cyclamen (Sowbread)—Tuberous-rooted plants, useful alike for rock garden, border, naturalizing in grass and for greenhouse culture. Of the hardy cyclamen there are two types, the spring-blooming and autumn-blooming. *Culture*—*Hardy Species*—Plant in Aug. 2 in. deep and 2½ in. apart in a shady position in light sandy loam mixed with peat or leaf-mould and mortar. Protect with fibre in winter and top-dress annually with leaf-mould and rotten manure. Propagate by means of seed in gentle heat in spring, and do not plant the young corms in their permanent positions until of moderate size. *Pot Culture*—(*C. persicum*)—Soak the pot and corm that have been dried-off in water and stand on a shelf in the greenhouse. Pot-up in Aug., placing one corm in a 5-in. pot in a fresh compost of rich sandy loam and leaf-mould, and keep close for a few days, then give ample air and not too much heat (60° F.). Moist, steady heat, and shade from strong sun, are essential. After flowering, decrease water supply, dry-off, and keep the roots cool and almost dry until next potting-up. Keep the plants indoors from Sept. to May, and in a cold frame with the pots on their sides from June to Aug. Only use the same corms for pot culture for two years in succession. One-year-old plants give the finest flowers; cyclamen are, therefore, best raised annually from seed. To propagate, sow thinly in pans in a finely-sieved compost of two-thirds loam and one-third leaf-mould and sand from Aug. to Nov., and place in a cold frame or on a shelf near the light in the cool greenhouse. Prick-off into pans, then pot-up singly into thumb pots and subsequently into larger pots until, in July, they are in 5 to 6-in. pots in which they may be flowered. *Species*—*C. coum* (Purple, Red and White, Jan.-Mar., 3 in.);, *C. europæum* (Red and White, July-Nov., 3 in.); *C. neapolitanum* (Rose, White and Purple Throat, Aug.-Sept., 6 in.); *C. persicum* (White to Crimson, Nov.-Mar., 6-10 in.).

Cydonia (Quince)—Hardy deciduous tree which thrives in sunny position in ordinary soil. Plant in Oct. or Nov. Propagate by seed, layers, suckers or cuttings in Oct.

Cynoglossum (Hound's Tongue)—Annuals, biennials and perennials which thrive in rather poor, ordinary soil, and bear deep blue forget-me-not-like flowers from June to Aug. For culture, *see* Annuals, p. 123, Biennials, p. 125, *and* Perennials, p. 281.

Cytisus (Broom)—Genus of shrubs, mostly hardy and deciduous, which thrive in light ordinary soil, in a dry, sunny position. The species and hybrids *C. Ardoinii* (Deep Yellow), *C. Beanii* (Golden Yellow), *C. kewensis* (Cream), and *C. purpureus* (Rose-purple), flowering in May and June, are all prostrate or trailing, and suitable for the rock garden. *C. præcox* (Sulphur-yellow, Apr.-May, 6 ft.) and the purple-flowered hybrids *C. Dallimorei, Donard Seedling*, and *Dorothy Walpole* (May, 5-6 ft.) are the best border species, while for pot culture, *C. canariensis* and *C. racemosus* (both Yellow, 3 ft.) will flower in the house from Jan. to Mar. *Culture*—Cut back all branches by at least a third and plant in Oct. Small plants give little trouble. Except when quite young only trim to keep in shape; pruning must be systematic and regular so that it is not necessary to cut into old wood. Spring-blooming species should be trimmed and pruned directly after flowering; late-flowering kinds must not be pruned until the following Feb. or Mar. *Pot Culture*—Pot-up in May, after flowering, using a compost of two parts turfy loam to one part lumpy leaf-mould and coarse sand. Prune hard back after flowering, then keep in the warm and syringe in fine weather. Harden-off and sink the pots in ashes outdoors from May to Oct., then move into the cool greenhouse. To propagate, sow in the open in Sept., take cuttings in Mar. or Aug. and strike in a frame and grow in pots near the glass until ready for planting out. Young plants need occasional "stopping back". The Genista is closely allied to the Cytisus.

Dabœcia (Irish Heath)—Hardy evergreen shrubs which thrive in sandy peat and loam with no lime in it. *Culture*—Plant out in Mar. or Oct., and cut off dead blooms in Oct. To propagate, strike cuttings in a frame in July or Aug., layer in Sept. or sow seed. *Species and Varieties*—*D. cantabrica* (Rosy-purple); *D. c. alba* (White); *D. c. bicolor* (Purple and White). All June to Sept., 1 ft.

Daffodils—The word *daffodil* is popularly applied to those types of narcissi with long, trumpet-like coronas. For culture, *see* Narcissus.

Dahlia—The dahlia is easily grown in ordinary garden soil, and in warm

PLATE 13 DISBUDDING CHRYSANTHEMUMS To obtain large blooms all buds except the top one should be nipped out. Before disbudding, *above left*, and after, *above right*. *Below*, a plant showing the four main shoots left for flowering.

Chaenomeles lagenaria   *Cornus Nuttallii*

PLATE 14 FLOWERING SHRUBS

Rhododendron Falconeri   *Jasminum nudiflorum*

districts can be left in the ground all winter if a heap of ashes or sand is placed over the tubers. It is somewhat tender, however, and it is better to lift it as soon as the plants have died down, and to store the tubers for the winter. The ideal soil is a rich, sandy loam containing sufficient humus to make it retentive of moisture.

Culture—Dahlias may be multiplied by seeds or by dividing the base of the old stem in Apr., taking care that an "eye" and a tuber or two are attached to each portion. Another way is to cut off the young shoots at their base and strike them in small pots. *Seed*—Sow about 1 in. apart in shallow pans or boxes in Mar. The soil should be light and sandy with a mixture of leaf-mould. Place the pans on a warm shelf, and in Apr. pot-off either singly or round the edge of 6-in. pots. Place in a cold frame, gradually harden-off, and plant out 2 to 3 ft. apart, early in June. After flowering, the young tubers are taken up and treated as old tubers. *Cuttings*—In Feb., Mar. or even the first week in Apr., tubers which have been wintered in a dry place are placed in shallow boxes containing a slightly moist compost of two-thirds finely sieved loam and one-third leaf-mould and sand, which does not quite cover them, and are set over a hotbed close up to the glass (Temp. 65° F.). A number of strong shoots soon appear; when these are 3 to 4 in. long they are taken off and struck round the edges of 4-in. pots, filled with equal parts of sandy loam and leaf-mould. They should be watered, and again placed in the same hotbed, and shaded from the sun. Pot-up singly as soon as the cuttings have struck (about three weeks) and transfer to a cold frame. Pot-on as required, harden-off, and plant out early in June.

Preparing the Ground and Planting—In autumn the beds should be prepared; they should be in an open, but sheltered, position and should catch the morning sun, but must have a little shade in the afternoon. Damp, low-lying situations should be avoided. Dahlias will be best displayed in beds 3 ft. wide with alleys between. The beds should be marked by stakes placed at each corner, 4 in. of the surface soil being removed and 4 in. of thoroughly rotted manure and bonemeal at the rate of 3 oz. to the square yard being put in its place. The whole is then dug to a depth of 18 in. or 2 feet, and the manure thoroughly mixed with the soil. Towards the end of May the soil should be top-dressed with wood ashes which should then be thoroughly raked in. The three-foot beds will each receive a row of plants and the four to five-foot stakes are firmly fixed at planting time 3, 4 and 5 ft. apart, according to the size of the plants, which are planted 4 in. deep so that the crown is just above the surface. After planting a good watering should be given, and soot sprinkled around. Syringe every evening in dry weather, and search for slugs, earwigs and other pests. During June and July water as often as twice a week in hot dry weather, and assist the roots by stirring the soil with a fork every two or three weeks. Remove all dead or straggling shoots and keep the plant trim and well staked. A surface mulch of rotted manure, 3 in. deep, will help to keep the roots cool and moist; if this is not applied, weak liquid manure should be given every third or fourth day throughout Aug. and Sept. When dahlias are intended either for exhibition or for highly developed flowers, early in July, when the plants are 18 in. high, pinch-out the top and thin-out the stems that form after this, to six at the most and leave only one bud on a shoot. Where a show of colour, or flowers for picking, is required, eight or nine main stems may be left; constant thinning-out of stems is necessary. Flowers for exhibition should be protected both from the sun and rain. As the autumn approaches examine the shoots tied-up and slacken the raffia or bass where necessary. When the frost turns their foliage brown or black, take up the plants, leaving 6 in. or so of stem attached. Hang the tubers up to dry with the stem downwards for a few days, then plunge them with a little old soil still left on them into a box of ashes, fibre, chaff or sand in order to preserve them from damp, frost and heat.

Varieties—LARGE AND MEDIUM DECORATIVE TYPES—*Ballago's Glory* (Red, tipped Gold); *Blaze* (Orange-scarlet); *Chas. L. Mastick* (Orange-salmon); *Clara Carder* (Rich Pink); *Daily Mail* (Yellow and Orange); *D'Arcy Sainsbury* (White); *Earl Baldwin* (Lilac-rose); *Jersey Beauty* (Salmon-pink); *Liberator* (Crimson); *Pink Daily Mail; Pius XI* (Yellow and White); *Queen Elizabeth* (Yellow); *Thos A. Edison* (Purple).

SMALL DECORATIVE TYPES—*Baby Fonteneux* (Rose); *Bloodstone* (Crimson); *Catalina* (White and Lavender); *Graig Park Gem* (Scarlet); *Verity Wadsworth* (Yellow); *Willy den Ouden* (Red and Orange).

LARGE AND MEDIUM CACTUS TYPES—*Boldness* (Crimson-Scarlet); *Brother Justinus* (Apricot and Yellow); *Miss Belgium* (Orange); *New Vision* (Pink); *Nagel's Bijou* (Salmon-orange); *Pink Spiral* (Pink and Yellow); *Royal Velvet* (Crimson); *Skua* (Rose-pink); *Trent* (Scarlet); *Yellow Miss Belgium*.

SMALL CACTUS TYPES—*Andries' Orange; Baby Royal* (Salmon-pink); *Barrie* (Red); *Kennet* (Crimson); *Little Fawn* (Fawn and Pink); *Market Glory* (Lilac and Rose); *Mia* (Mulberry Red); *Peaceful* (Pink); *Snow Queen* (White); *Tip* (Yellow); *Spencer's Darling* (Pink and Yellow).

CHARM AND PAEONY-FLOWERED TYPES—*Bishop of Llandaff* (Scarlet); *Dorothy Russell* (Scarlet); *Lemon Beauty; Morning Glow* (Orange-scarlet); *Mabel Smith* (Fawn); *Norah Bell* (Pink and Yellow).

BEDDING TYPES (Not over 2 ft.)—*Coltness Gem* (Scarlet); *Maureen Creighton* (Red); *Park Beauty* (Orange); *Mrs. M. Hoyle* (Crimson); *Mrs. W. Clarke* (Rose and Gold); *Princess Marie-Jose* (Pale Pink); *Shirley Yellow; Windermere* (Rose and Yellow). * Single.

SMALL POMPON TYPES—*Little Beeswing* (Scarlet and Gold); *Raider* (Yellow); *Apiary* (Crimson); *Doria* (Ruby); *Johnnie* (Maroon); *Jill* (Orange); *Mrs. J. Telfer* (White); *Tunis* (Scarlet); *Muriel Ann* (Pink).

LARGE POMPON TYPES—*Pride of Berlin* (Violet); *Jean Lister* (White); *J. van Citters* (Crimson and Gold); *Yellow Prince*.

DOUBLE SHOW AND FANCY TYPES—*Bonney Blue* (Violet); *W. H. Williams* (Scarlet); *David Johnson* (Salmon); *Duke of Fife* (Cardinal Red); *Gloire de Lyon* (White); *Marjorie* (Fawn and Yellow).

SINGLE COLLARETTE TYPES—*Admiral* (Crimson and White Collar); *Bonfire* (Scarlet with White Collar); *Canopus* (Yellow self); *Glenmore* (Carmine, tipped Straw); *Meg Nichol* (Lavender self); *Ooty* (Scarlet, tipped Gold); *Radiance* (Scarlet self); *Swallow* (White self).

All flower from July to Oct., 18 to 72 in.

Daphne—Dwarf-growing deciduous and evergreen shrubs, which thrive in a sunny sheltered position in well-drained, deep, sandy loam and peat. *Culture*—Plant in Mar. or Oct. No pruning is necessary. Propagate by layering in Aug., grafting in May, or seeds. *D. Mezereum* (Purple, Rose and White, 2–4 ft.), which is usually propagated by means of seed, is the best known of the hardy deciduous species. It thrives in ordinary garden loam, but needs shade from the hot sun. If trimming is necessary, it should be done in Apr. For the rock garden none are better than *D. alpina* (White, May, 1½ ft.), *D. Blagayana* (Ivory, May, ½ ft.), and *D. Cneorum* (Purple-pink, May–Aug., 1 ft.). They thrive in partial shade in sandy loam and peat or leaf-mould. *Greenhouse Culture*—*D. odora* (Pink, 2 ft.), and *D. o. alba* (White), often but wrongly named *D. indica* in gardens, are too tender for the open air, except in S.W. Pot-up in Apr., using 5 to 7-in. pots and a compost of peaty loam and sand. Plunge the pots in a cool, shady position out of doors from May to Sept., syringe daily in fine weather, and keep just moist. Move into the house in Sept. and gradually give more heat. Treatment as advised for *Forcing*, p. 118, will bring the blooms out by Dec. Propagate by means of cuttings under glass from Apr. to July.

Delphinium (Larkspur)—Large genus of hardy annuals, biennials and perennials, which like a sunny site in deep, highly enriched and well-drained friable loam, and need ample water in hot dry weather. If flower stalks are cut down as soon as they have bloomed a second crop of bloom will be obtained in early autumn. For culture, *see* Annuals, p. 123, Biennials, p. 125, *and* Perennials, p. 281. *Pot Culture*—Pot-up in Oct. or Nov. in 5 to 6-in. pots, and winter well up near the glass in a cool house. *Species*—(PERENNIALS)— *D. cardinale* (Scarlet); *D. cashmerianum* (Purple-blue); *D. nudicaule* (Orange-scarlet); *D. tanguticum* (Blue and White); *D. sulphureum* (Sulphur-yellow). All June to Aug., 24 to 60 in. For named varieties growers' catalogues should be consulted.

Desfontainea spinosa—Evergreen shrubs which are almost hardy in England. They thrive in warm, sheltered borders or in pots in the greenhouse, in a well-drained compost of equal parts of loam and peat with a little sand added. They grow to a height of 10 ft. and flower from July to Sept. *Culture*—Plant in spring or autumn. Propagate by means of cuttings in slight heat in spring.

Desmodium (Tick Trefoil and Telegraph Plant)—Hardy perennials and shrubs, also greenhouse deciduous shrubs. The former thrive in sunny sheltered borders in ordinary soil, the latter in the cool greenhouse. For culture, *see* Perennials, p. 281. *Greenhouse Shrubs*—Pot-up in Mar. in a compost of sandy loam and peat. Propagate by means of cuttings in frame or from seed. *Species*—*D. gyrans* (greenhouse) (White, July, 2 ft.); and *D. tiliifolium* (Lilac, July–Oct., 3–4 ft.).

Deutzia—Hardy deciduous flowering shrubs, which thrive in a sheltered, partly shaded position in rich, well-drained ordinary soil in the shrubbery, or in the greenhouse. *Culture*—Plant in Oct. or Nov., mulch annually after flowering, also thin-out well and cut away weak and old wood. To propagate, strike cuttings of soft wood in June in a frame with bottom heat. *Pot Culture* —Pot-up from Sept. to Nov., in rich, sandy loam, using as small a pot as convenient. Keep cool, but frost-proof, then in Dec. or Jan. move into the greenhouse and gradually raise the temperature to 65° F. As soon as the buds form, water with weak manure-water, or dress with artificial manure once a week until the colour of the flowers is visible. Deutzias are well adapted for forcing, but should be exempted from this process every alternate year. *Species and Varieties*—*D. discolor grandiflora* (Pink); *D. d. major* (White); *D. gracilis* (White); *D. longifolia Veitchii* (Rose-purple); *D. magnifica* (Double White); *D. scabra* (syn. *crenata*) *fl. pl.* (Double Pink); *D. Vilmorinæ* (White). All May to June, 3 to 6 ft.

Dianthus—Beautiful and extensive genus which embraces the Carnation, Picotee, Pink and Sweet William (*see* separately).

Dicentra (Dielytra or Bleeding Heart)—Hardy perennials which thrive in a sheltered, sunny site and a light dry soil with ample leaf-mould in it. Although hardy it is safer to winter them in a cold frame. They are often forced in the greenhouse in late winter. *Pot Culture*—Pot-up in Sept. in well-manured sandy loam, stand in the cold frame, plunged in ashes, and keep just moist until Nov., then move into the greenhouse (55° F.). After flowering, continue to water until the leaves die down, and stand in the open

from May to Sept. Dicentras require ample water and, when making full
growth, the pots may be stood in saucers of water. Propagate by division in
Apr. or Sept., and plant out during those months. In the open the flowers are
borne from May to July. *Species—D. Cucullaria* (White, 5 in.); *D. eximia*
(Purple, 15 in.); *D. formosa* (Red, 9 in.); *D. spectabilis* (Red or White,
24 in.).

Dictamnus (Burning Bush, Dittany or Fraxinella)—Hardy perennials, suit-
able for sunny or semi-shaded borders and dry, light soil. For culture, *see*
Perennials, p. 281. *Species—D. albus* (White); and *D. a. var. purpureus*
(Purple-red). Both June to Aug., 30 in.

Diervilla (Bush Honeysuckle or Weigela)—Hardy deciduous shrubs which
thrive in sun or shade in almost any soil, though moist fibrous loam and leaf-
mould suits them best. *Culture*—Plant in Oct. or Nov., and after flowering
cut out old and straggly wood. To propagate strike cuttings of soft wood in
June in a frame, or matured cuttings in the open in Oct. *D. rosea* will flower
in Mar. in the cool greenhouse. Pot-up annually in Oct., using 8 to 12-in.
pots, and a compost of two parts sandy loam to one part of leaf-mould and
rotten manure. Plant out in June after flowering, and don't re-pot for at least
two seasons. Prune as above. *Species and Varieties—D. amabilis* (Pale Rose,
Apr.–May, 6 ft.); *D. Abel Carrière* (Carmine-red, Apr.–May, 5 ft.); *D. Eva
Rathke* (Crimson-purple, May–Sept., 3–4 ft.); *D. florida* (Deep Rose, 5–6 ft.);
and *D. f. alba* (White), etc.

Digitalis (Foxglove)—Handsome biennials and hardy perennials, that thrive
in the shade in almost any fairly rich soil. For culture, *see* Biennials, p. 125,
and Perennials, p. 281. *Species—D. ambigua* (Yellow, spotted, 2 ft.); *D.
ferruginea* (Wine coloured, 3–4 ft.); *D. lutea* (Pale Yellow, 2 ft.); *D. purpurea*
(White and Purple). All June to Sept.

Dimorphotheca (Cape Daisy or Star of the Veldt)—Half-hardy annual
which likes a sunny position in light soil and is useful for inclusion in the
rock garden. It flowers from July to Oct. and grows 12 in. high. For
culture, *see* Annuals, p. 123.

Dodecatheon—The American Cowslip, which thrives well in cool shady
borders, or the rock or marsh garden in rich, deep loam. For culture, *see*
Rock Plants, p. 283. *Varieties—D. Hendersonii* (Rose, May, 9 in.); *D.
Jeffreyi* (Purple-rose, June–July, 18 in.); *D. Meadia* (Lilac, Rose and White,
May–June, 12–18 in.).

Dog's Tooth Violet (*Erythronium Dens-canis*)—Little bulbous plant which
does well in light soil, and is useful as an edging to borders or in the rock
garden. *Culture*—Plant 4 to 6 in. deep and 4 inches apart in partial shade
in Sept. in moist, well-drained sandy loam and ample leaf-mould. Surround
the tubers with about an inch of silver sand and do not lift more than necessary, but mulch annually with well-rotted manure and leaf-mould. Propagate
by means of seed in a frame in Aug. Thin-out, but do not plant the seedlings
out until the third Sept. after sowing. The plants are also increased by offsets. *Pot Culture*—Plant in Aug. in 5 to 6-in. pots, using a compost of loam,
peat and leaf-mould, and keep in a cold frame during the winter, giving but
little water until Feb. Then increase the supply and take into the cold
greenhouse. *Species and Varieties—Erythronium citrinum* (Yellow); *revolutum* (Pink); *Hartwegii* (Creamy-white). All Apr. to May, 10 in.

Doronicum (Leopard's Bane)—Hardy perennials which thrive in sunny
borders and ordinary soil, or under almost any conditions. Cut down the
shoots that have flowered and dress with well-rotted manure to encourage a
second crop of bloom. For culture, *see* Perennials, p. 281. *Species—D.*

austriacum (Golden-yellow, Apr.–May, 18 in.); *D. plantagineum excelsum* (Yellow, Mar.–June, 24–36 in.).

Draba—Dwarf-growing rock plants which thrive in a moderately sunny spot, in well-drained gritty loam. For culture, *see* Rock Plants, p. 283. *Species*—*D. Aizoon* (Bright Yellow); *D. Dedeana* (White); *D. pyrenaica* (Pale Mauve-pink). All Mar. to May, 3 in.

Dracocephalum (Dragon's Head)—Hardy perennials useful for cool shady borders, or rock gardens with light soil. For culture, *see* Perennials, p. 281. *Species*—*D. grandiflorum* (Blue, 15 in.); *D. Ruyschianum* (Purple, 15 in.). All flower from July to Aug.

Drosera (Sundew or Youthwort)—Curious dwarf-growing plants which thrive in a warm, sheltered position in the bog or wild garden. They grow some 3 in. high and flower about midsummer. Propagate by means of seed or root cuttings in Mar.

Dryas (Mountain Avens)—Evergreen trailing hardy perennials which like sun or partial shade and a cool gritty loam with lime and leaf-mould in it. They are excellent in the rock garden. For culture, *see* Rock Plants, p. 283. *Species*—*D. Drummondii* (Golden-yellow); *D. octopetala* (White). Both June–July, 3 in.

Eccremocarpus scaber—Half-hardy climber which thrives in any well-drained light loam against south walls, trellises and pillars, and is also useful as a greenhouse climber. *Culture*—Propagate by means of cuttings in a frame in autumn, or sow in heat in Jan.; plant out in Apr. After flowering cut away dead wood and protect the roots in winter. *Species*—*E. scaber* (Orange-red) and *E. s. var. ruber* (Red). Both flowering from July to Sept., 10 to 20 ft.

Echeveria—Half-hardy dwarf-growing rosette-shaped plants which thrive in warm, sunny sheltered positions, but which must be brought indoors in Oct. The red and yellow flowers are borne on short stems. *Culture*—Pot-up in Mar. in 4 to 5-in. pots in a compost of loam and mortar rubble. Propagate by means of offsets or leaf-cuttings in summer. *See also* Cotyledon.

Echinacea—Hardy perennials which thrive in sunny borders and well-drained light loam. They reach a height of about 3 ft. and flower in Aug. and Sept. *E. purpurea* (Reddish-purple) is the best species. For culture, *see* Perennials, p. 281.

Echinops (Globe Thistle)—Hardy perennials that thrive in the sun in light loam, but do not like being disturbed. For culture, *see* Perennials, p. 281. *Species*—*E. bannaticus* (Blue, July–Sept., 36–60 in.); *E. exaltatus* (White, July–Aug., 60–70 in.); and *E. Ritro* (Blue, Summer, 36–60 in.).

Edelweiss (Leontopodium)—Hardy alpine plant which requires a sunny position, in sandy loam and old mortar rubble. The cream-white, star-shaped flowers are borne from June to Sept. on stems 6 in. high. For culture, *see* Rock Plants, p. 283.

Elæagnus (Oleaster or Wild Olive)—Hardy evergreen and deciduous shrubs which grow freely in full sun in almost any soil. *Culture*—Plant in Mar. or from Sept. to Nov., and cut out dead wood when required. To propagate, strike cuttings of matured wood in Oct. in a frame, or layer. *Species and Varieties*—*E. argentea* (6–12 ft.); **E. glabra* (15–20 ft.); *E. multiflora* (6–10 ft.); **E. pungens* (10–15 ft.). * denotes evergreen.

Enkianthus—Beautiful flowering shrubs which like a sunny sheltered position and moist peat or non-calcareous sandy loam and leaf-mould. *Culture*—Plant in Oct. or Nov.; no pruning is necessary. To propagate, sow seeds or strike cuttings of mature shoots in a frame in Oct. *Species*—*E. campanulatus* (Cream, Yellow and Red, May, 4–8 ft.); *E. japonicus* (White, Apr., 3–6 ft.).

Epacris (Australian Heath)—Heath-like winter-flowering evergreen shrubs that thrive in the cool greenhouse. *Culture*—Pot-up when growth recommences (about May), using 5-in. pots and a compost of sandy peat. Keep close until established and then stand in a cool greenhouse during the summer months. Water moderately, and give liquid manure while growing, but do not syringe. Cut long shoots well back and thin-out after flowering. Propagate by cuttings of young wood with a little bottom heat in spring, or sow seed in pots in Mar.

Epilobium (The Willow Herb)—Hardy perennials, the dwarf-growing species of which are useful for the rock garden, and the marsh or water-garden. They do well in sun or shade in moist ordinary soil, but prefer a gritty loam with some peat in it. For culture, *see* Perennials, p. 281. *Species* —*E. angustifolium* (Crimson, July–Aug., 36–40 in.); *E. Dodonæi* (Rose-pink, June–Aug., 24–36 in.); *E. obcordatum* (Rosy-purple, Aug–Oct., 3–6 in.).

Epimedium (Barrenwort)—Dwarf-growing perennials which thrive in sun or shade in the rock garden in sandy loam with a little peat. For culture, *see* Rock Plants, p. 283. *Species*—*E. alpinum* (Yellow and Crimson, Apr.–June, 9 in.); *E. grandiflorum var. violaceum* (Large Violet, Apr.–May, 8–12 in.); *E. rubrum* (Rose, Apr.–May, 10 in.); etc.

Eranthis—*See* Aconite.

Eremurus (Fox-tail Lily, Giant Asphodel, or King's Spear)—Tall hardy perennials which thrive in sunny sheltered borders in rich loam. For culture, *see* Perennials, p. 281. *Species*—*E. Bungei* (Golden Yellow, June–July, 20–40 in.); *E. Elwesii* (Soft Rose, June, 50 in.).

Erica—Important genus of hardy and greenhouse evergreen flowering shrubs, often known as Heath or Heather. *Culture*—(*Hardy Species*)—Plant in Oct. in a sunny position in well-drained sand and peat, or in any light garden loam without lime in it (except *E. carnea*, which likes lime). Do not prune, but merely keep in shape by removing dead blooms from the spring-flowering species in June, from the summer and autumn bloomers in Mar.; and from winter-flowerers in Apr. To propagate, strike cuttings of half-matured wood in July in a frame, sow seed in Mar., divide the roots, or layer in autumn. *Culture*—(*Greenhouse Species*)—Propagate by means of cuttings of tender tops of young shoots in Mar. or Apr. or in Sept. (Temp. 50° F.) in well-drained pots or pans of sandy peat. Pot-up into 2-in. pots as soon as rooted. "Stop-back" to make "bushy" plants. Re-pot in Sept. into 5-in. pots and transfer to a light, airy position; re-pot into 6-in. pots, if need be, in Mar., and summer on a hard bed of ashes in a cold frame in full sun. Mature plants should be potted-up in Sept. in 6 to 7-in. pots in a compost of sandy loam and peat in equal proportions and should be stood in the cold greenhouse. Trim after flowering. The winter-flowering kinds should be turned out into the frames after hardening-off in Apr.; the summer-flowering species in July, when they have finished blooming. In the cool house *E. gracilis* (Red-purple) flowers in Nov. and Dec., and *E. hyemalis* (Purple-pink) from Dec. to Feb. *See also* Calluna. *Hardy Species*—*E. arborea* (White, Feb.–May, 15 ft.); *E. carnea* (Carmine-crimson and White, Nov.–Apr., ½–1 ft.); *E. cinerea* (Purple, Sept., ¾ ft.); *E. c. alba* (White); *E. darleyensis* (Rosy-red, Nov.–Apr., 1–1½ ft.); *E. lusitanica* (White, Jan.–Apr., 6–10 ft.); *E. mediterranea* (Lilac-rose, Mar.–May, 3–4 ft.); *E. m. alba* (White); etc.

Erigeron (Fleabane)—The species grown are hardy perennials which thrive in sunny borders or in the rock garden in ordinary soil. For culture, *see* Perennials, p. 281. *Species and Varieties*—*E. B. Ladhams* (Orange-rose, May–Sept., 30 in.); *E. Pink Pearl* (June–Aug., 18–30 in.); *E. Quakeress* (Pale

Lilac, July–Sept., 30 in.); *E. alpinus* (Purple, July, 10 in.); *E. aurantiacus* (Orange, July–Aug., 6–12 in.).

Erinus (Summer Starwort)—Hardy evergreen rock garden or wall plant thriving in sun or shade in sandy loam and old mortar rubble. For culture, *see* Rock Plants, p. 283. *Species—E. alpinus* (Lilac-rose and White); *E. a. carmineus* (Carmine). All May to July, 4 in.

Eritrichium—Beautiful hardy alpines that grow best in sheltered, semi-shaded positions in a cool compost of gritty loam, leaf-mould, peat, and sand mixed with broken limestone and sandstone. Propagation is by division in Apr., or by seed. They need protection from frost and moisture in winter.

Erodium (Heron's Bill)—Partly hardy and partly half-hardy perennials which do well in sandy loam in dry, warm, sheltered situations in the rock garden. For culture, *see* Rock Plants, p. 283. *Species—E. chamædryoides* (White, veined Pink, May–Sept., 3 in.); *E. hybridum* (Pale Crimson-purple, May–Sept., 10–20 in.); *E. macradenum* (White, tinged Rose, blotched Violet, June–July, 6 in.), etc.

Eryngium (Sea Holly)—Tall hardy perennials, which like a dry, sandy soil and a sunny position in a warm border. For culture, *see* Perennials, p. 281. *Species—E. amethystinum* (Metallic Blue, June–Aug., 24 in.); *E. giganteum* (Bluish, July–Sept., 30–40 in.), etc.

Erysimum (Fairy Wallflower, Hedge Mustard)—Hardy annuals, biennials and perennials, excellent for sunny borders and rock gardens when grown in gritty and sandy loam. For culture, *see* Annuals, p. 123, Biennials, p. 125, *and* Perennials, p. 281. *Species—E. Perofskianum* (Yellow and Orange, July–Oct., 12–18 in.); *E. linifolium* (Lavender, May–Sept., 6 in.); *E. rupestre* (Sulphur, June, 9 in.).

Escallonia (Chilian Gum Box)—Half-hardy evergreen (except *E. Philippiana*, which is deciduous and hardy) shrubs, which succeed in sheltered situations in well-drained soil. *Culture*—Plant in Oct. or Nov., or in Mar. or Apr. Cut out old wood, shorten laterals after flowering (Aug.), and trim to shape. Autumn-flowering species should not be pruned until the following Mar. To propagate, strike cuttings of half-matured shoots in July or Aug. in a frame. *Species—E. floribunda* (White, July–Sept., 5–10 ft.); *E. langleyensis* (Rose-carmine, June, 10–15 ft.); *E. Philippiana* (White, June–July, 6–8 ft.); *E. rubra* (Deep Red, Sept.–Oct., 6–12 ft.), etc.

Eschscholzia (Californian Poppy)—Hardy annuals which thrive in sunny beds or rock garden (dwarfs) in poor, light soil. For culture, *see* Annuals, p. 123. *Species—E. cæspitosa* (Yellow, May–Oct., 9 in.); *E. californica* (Orange and Yellow, Red, etc., May–Oct., 18 in.).

Eucalyptus (Gum Tree)—Half-hardy evergreen trees, which thrive in the cool greenhouse in a compost of 2 parts of fibrous loam to 1 part of leaf-mould and charcoal. *Culture*—Pot-up in Mar., using 6 to 8-in. pots; plant outdoors in a sunny position from June to Sept. To propagate, sow in gentle heat (60° F.) in early spring, or strike cuttings of mature shoots under glass in June.

Eulalia (Zebra-striped Grass)—Hardy perennial grass, suitable for borders and cool greenhouses. It thrives in ordinary soil and is propagated by means of division in Mar. or Apr.

Euonymus (Spindle Tree)—Deciduous and evergreen shrubs and small trees, which like a sunny position and good loam. *Culture*—Plant evergreens in Apr. or Sept. and Oct., deciduous from Nov. to Mar. No pruning is necessary. Propagate in autumn by means of cuttings from the previous year's growth, or by seeds. *Species and Varieties—E. alatus (syn. amurensis)* (D)

(Scarlet Leaves, Autumn, 6–9 ft.); *E. europæus* (D) (Pink Fruit, Autumn, 10–25 ft.); *E. atropurpureus* (D) (Purple Foliage, 6 ft.); *E. japonicus* (E), (Deep Glossy Foliage, 6–10 ft.), etc. (D)=Deciduous, (E)=Evergreen.

Eupatorium (Hemp Agrimony)—Evergreen greenhouse shrubs and hardy perennials. *Culture*—*(Shrubs)*—Propagate by means of cutting in heat in spring. Keep the cuttings warm and near the glass, harden-off and plant outdoors in the sun in June. Stop-back occasionally until July, and cut old plants well back after flowering. Pot-up in Sept., using 6 to 8-in. pots and a compost of rich loam with some peat in it, and place in a cool house. *(Perennials)*—Propagate by division of roots in Mar. *Species*—*E. cannabinum* (Pink, June Sept., 48 in.); *E. perfoliatum* (White, June–Sept., 40 in.); *E. purpureum* (Purple, June–Sept., 48–60 in.); *E. ianthinum* (Lilac, Jan.–Feb., 15 in.); *E. petiolare* (White, Apr.–May, 30–40 in.).

Euphorbia (Spurge)—The hardy perennials are the only ones worth growing; *E. epithymoides* (Yellow, 15 in.), and *E. Myrsinites* (Yellow, 6 in.), both like a gritty loam and full sun. *See* Perennials, p. 281.

Eustoma Russellianum—Handsome biennial with purple flowers in July and Aug. For culture, *see* Biennials, p. 125.

Everlasting Pea (*Lathyrus latifolius*)—Beautiful hardy climber. Moist, good soil and a sunny position suit it best. For culture, *see* Perennials, p. 281. *Named Varieties*—*White Pearl* (White), and *Pink Beauty* (Carmine-rose). Both June to Sept., 6 ft.

Exochorda (Pearl Bush)—Hardy deciduous shrubs, closely allied to the Spiræas. They thrive in sunny, sheltered positions in rich loam. *E. grandiflora* (White, May–June, 5–10 ft.) is the best species. *Culture*—Plant in Oct. or Nov. and cut back straggling shoots after flowering. To propagate, strike cuttings of half-ripe shoots in late summer in a frame.

Fabiana (False Heath)—Half-hardy evergreen summer-flowering shrubs, suitable for outdoor culture in sandy loam with some peat in it in warm, sheltered situations. In northern counties they should only be grown in the cool greenhouse. *Pot Culture*—After flowering, cut back weak and straggling stems, pot-up, and summer in the open on a bed of hard ashes. Return to the house in Sept. Water liberally in spring and summer. Propagate in Apr. or May by means of cuttings of young shoots in a warm frame, or sow in heat in Mar. *F. imbricata* (3–6 ft.), has white flowers.

Fagus (Beech)—This well-known tree thrives in chalk soils and is a good tree for woodland planting. *Culture*—Plant in Oct. or Nov. No pruning is necessary. Propagation of varieties is usually carried out in Mar. by means of grafting on the common beech. *Species and Varieties*—*F. sylvatica* (Common Beech); *F. s. variegata* (Golden Beech); *F. s. cuprea* (Copper Beech); *F. s. pendula* (Weeping Beech).

Fatsia japonica (Japanese Aralia)—Semi-hardy evergreen shrub which thrives well in the cool house; in good loam in warm, sheltered positions it will grow out of doors. It grows some 12 ft. high and carries cream-white flowers in Oct. and Nov. *Culture*—Plant in Mar. or Apr., or pot-up in Mar., using a compost of two parts of loam to one part of leaf-mould and sand. Water well, syringing in spring and summer, and shade from the sun. To propagate, sow seed when ripe in heat (70° F.), insert 2-in. pieces of stem in sandy soil in a propagator in spring or Sept., or increase by "ringing".

Ferns—Hardy ferns thrive in sheltered and shady positions in moist but well-drained deep loam with plenty of leaf-mould, peat and coarse sand in it. Dead fronds should be left to act as a protection in winter. Half-hardy kinds require slight artificial heat in winter and tender ferns a temperature of 60° F. Pot-up in spring when growth commences in a compost of 2 parts fibrous loam and 1 part well-sieved manure, leaf-mould and coarse sand, keep moist and syringe. Propagate, preferably in Mar. or July, by means of " spores " sown in the same manner as seed, in equal parts of loam, peat, leaf-mould, and sand (sterilized with boiling water, *see* p. 16), by division in Mar. or Apr., or, in some cases, remove and pot-up the minute plants growing on the fronds. *Species—(Hardy)—Adiantum pedatum* (Maidenhair Fern); *Asplenium officinarum* (Spleenwort); *Athyrium Filix-fœmina* (Lady Fern); *Blechnum Spicant* (*syn. Lomaria*) (Hard Fern); *Dryopteris spinulosa* (Broad Buckler Fern); *Osmunda regalis* (Royal Fern); *Polypodium vulgare* (Polypody); *Polystichum aculeatum* (Hard Shield Fern); and *Polystichum aculeatum cristatum* (Soft Shield Fern).

Forget-Me-Not (Myosotis)—There are annual and perennial species, some of the latter being grown as biennials. All thrive in the sun in ordinary soil, and are useful for bedding, for the rock garden and for the cool greenhouse. *Culture—See* Annuals, p. 123, Biennials, p. 125, *and* Perennials, p. 281. *Pot Culture*—Pot-up in Oct., using 4 to 5-in. pots and sandy soil, and keep in a cold frame through the winter; move into the cool house in early spring. *Species—M. cæspitosa* (*M. Rehsteineri*) (Blue, Apr.–May, 2 in.); *M. dissiti-flora* (Light Blue, Apr.–June, 6–9 in.); *M. scorpioides var. semperflorens* (Sky-blue and Yellow, May–Sept., 6–9 in.); *M. pyrenaica* (Blue, Pink and White, June–Aug., 6 in.).

Forsythia (Golden Bell Tree)—Hardy deciduous shrubs, thriving in ordinary soil and in sunny positions. *Culture*—Plant from Oct. to Nov., and cut well back after flowering. To propagate, strike cuttings of soft wood in a frame in June, or July, and layer. *F. spectabilis* is useful for the cold greenhouse. Pot-up from Oct. to Dec., using an 8 to 10-in. pot and a compost of 2 parts of loam to 1 part of leaf-mould and sand; sink the pot in ashes outdoors from May to Oct. *Species and Varieties—F. intermedia vars. densiflora* and *spectabilis* and *F. suspensa* and *viridissima* (Golden Yellow, Mar., 6–10 ft.).

Fothergilla—Hardy deciduous shrubs which like a moist, sandy loam and peat. They grow some 3 to 6 ft. high and flower from Apr. to June. *Culture* —Plant from Oct. to Mar. Propagate by means of cuttings in late summer, by layering in autumn, or sow in heat in spring.

Francoa ramosa (Bridal Wreath)—Graceful cool greenhouse plant with small white or rosy-red flowers in late summer. *Culture*—Sow in Mar. with slight bottom heat (55° F.), or propagate by means of cuttings under glass in June. Pot-up from Feb. to Mar., using 6 to 8-in. pots and a compost of sandy loam and leaf-mould. Discard the old plants, and raise a fresh batch annually.

Freesia—Species of almost hardy bulbous plants for the warm, sunny border or cold greenhouse. *Culture*—Plant in Aug., 2 in. apart, in light, well-drained soil, protect with fibre in winter, and lift after flowering. *Indoors*— Pot-up in succession from July to Dec., 1 in. deep and 2 in. apart, in equal parts of sandy loam, leaf-mould and rotten manure. Place the pots under a south wall, or in a frame in the case of coloured varieties, until the bulbs begin to grow (about six weeks). Then, if standing in the open, transfer to a cold frame, and in a fortnight place on a shelf near the glass. Thin stakes are necessary for support, and freesias require bi-weekly doses of liquid manure as soon as the buds form. The bulbs will bloom from Jan. to Apr. Keep dry in a sunny frame from May to July, and shake clear of soil and pot-up each year. They can be increased easily from seed. Sow the seed when ripe, in Aug. or Sept., in 5-in. pots in well-sieved sandy loam and leaf-mould, and place in a cool frame exposed to the sun's rays; thin-out to leave five or six plants in each pot. Soak the seed for twenty-four hours before sowing. Freesias do not like transplanting. They may also be propagated by means of offsets in July or Aug. *Named Varieties—Purity* (White): *Excelsior* (Cream): *Lemon King; Orange King; Rose Beauty,* etc.

Fritillaria—Hardy bulbous plants, which succeed in any garden soil, although a dry, deep, rich (*F. Meleagris* moist), sandy loam gives the most satisfactory results. They are excellent for shady borders, the rock garden, for naturalizing in grass, and (some species) for pots. *Culture*—Plant in Oct. 4 in. deep and 7 in. apart (except *F. imperialis,* which should be 10 in. apart), and do not lift from the ground, unless overcrowded; when necessary lift and re-plant immediately. *Pot Culture*—Plant in the autumn in 4 to 5-in. pots in a mixture of loam, peat, leaf-mould, rotten manure, and sand, and give occasional doses of liquid manure when the buds form. Propagate by means of bulbous offsets in Oct. *Species—F. aurea* (Golden Yellow, 8 in.): *F. citrina* (Yellow-green, 8–12 in.): *F. imperialis* (Red or Orange and Yellow, 30 in.): *F. libanotica* (Lilac and Yellow, 15 in.): *F. Meleagris* (Purple or White, 10 in.): *F. persica* (Persian Lily) (Violet, 24 in.). All Apr. to May flowering.

Fuchsia—Fuchsias grow in almost any soil and are excellent for the cold greenhouse or the open border in summer. Feeding them with weak manure water of any kind is preferable to mixing manure with the soil, and after they are well rooted they should never be watered with clear water, but should always have a stimulant. A carefully-shaded house, guarded against the ingress of bees, is the best place for them when in blossom. *Culture*—Sow in heat (70° F.) in the spring, but the more satisfactory way is to take cuttings in spring or autumn. Plants that have been at rest during the winter should be started in Feb. or Mar. and large early-flowering specimens will be produced by cutting down the old plants and re-potting them in good rich compost. When re-potted, keep them in a temperature of 55° F., and syringe overhead daily in fine weather. Insert cuttings taken from these plants in pots filled with two-thirds fibrous loam and one-third leaf-mould, well-rotted manure, and old mortar rubble, and plunge the pots in a bottom heat of 60° F. In three weeks they may be potted into 3-in. pots, and re-plunged in the same bed, keeping the temperature from 50° to 60° F. As soon as necessary shift into fresh pots, until they receive their final shift into 6, 9, or 12-in. pots towards the end of June: or into the open about the end of May. Cuttings can also be taken of semi-matured wood in Aug. The plants should be kept close up to the glass and will require " stopping " at least six times, and careful training. Never " stop " a plant within two months of the time it is required to bloom. A regular, moist temperature must be maintained, and the foliage should be sprayed in warm weather. During bright sunshine the glass should be slightly shaded. In July or Aug. the plants should be stood in a sunny position in the open. *Species*—(HARDY)—*F. corallina* (Purple and Red): *F. magellanica* (Scarlet): *F. m. globosa* (Violet and Purple): *F. m. riccartonii* (Bright Red). (HALF-HARDY)—*F. cordifolia* (Red and Green): *F. corymbiflora* (Scarlet): *F. excorticata* (Purple). All July to Sept., 5 to 6 ft. There are numerous named varieties.

Funkia—*See* Hosta.

Gaillardia (Blanket Flower)—Annuals and perennials, both kinds being usually treated as half-hardy. They thrive in any light, rich soil in sunny beds. For culture, *see* Annuals, p. 123, *and* Perennials, p. 281. *Named Annual Varieties—The Bride* (White): *Crimson Glow* (Crimson); *Lorenziana* and *Picta* (Red and Yellow). *Named Perennial Varieties—Grandiflora; Masterpiece* (Red); *The King* and *Sunset* (Red and Yellow). All June to Oct., 12 to 30 in.

Galega (Goat's Rue)—Hardy border perennial which thrives almost anywhere and in any soil. For culture, *see* Perennials, p. 281. *Species—G. officinalis* (Lilac-Blue, White and Pink, June–Oct., 48 in.); *G. officinalis var. Hartlandii* (Pale Lilac-blue and White, June–Oct., 50 in.).

Galtonia candicans (Cape Hyacinth)—Tall, hardy, bulbous plants, flowering in Aug. and Sept., and loving a sunny border and well-manured, deeply-dug, sandy loam and leaf-mould. *Culture*—Plant in Mar. or Oct. from 4 to 6 in. deep and 15 in. apart, letting the bulbs rest on sand. If the soil is cold and heavy, the bulbs must be lifted annually. *Pot Culture*—Place one bulb ½ in. deep in a 6-in. pot and set in a cold greenhouse. Only grow in a pot for one year, after which plant out. Propagate by means of seed in the open as soon as ripe, or by offsets in autumn.

Gardenia—Evergreen flowering shrubs suitable for hothouse or warm greenhouse, and which require much heat and plenty of water when growing. They thrive in equal parts of peat, loam and rotten manure with a little charcoal added. *Culture*—Prune into shape and pot-up in Feb. or Mar., putting year-old plants into 5 to 6-in. pots; 8-in. pots should be large enough for old specimens. Syringe daily, and give liquid manure when the buds form. Propagate in Feb. or Mar. by means of shoots with a " heel ", in pots in sandy peat, in a propagating frame with a bottom heat of 70° to 80° F. *Named Variety of G. jasminoides Fortuniana* (Cape Jasmine), and *G. Thunbergia.*

Garrya (Californian Garrya)—Hardy evergreen shrubs with yellow or greenish-white flowers from Nov. to Mar. *Culture*—Plant in May in ordinary soil and a sunny, sheltered position. In May trim back long shoots a little and cut out dead wood. To propagate, strike cuttings in Aug. in a frame, or layer. *Species—G. elliptica* (6–12 ft. or more).

Gaultheria (Winter Green, Shallon, etc.)—Genus of evergreen shrubs, some of which are hardy and suitable for the woodland or rock garden. *Culture*—Plant in Apr. or Oct. in cool, moist, ordinary, lime-free soil and leaf-mould in semi-shaded position. Thin-out old shoots when overcrowded. Propagate by means of seed in heat in Mar., division or layering in Oct. *Species—G. procumbens* (White and Pink, July–Aug., creeping); *G. Shallon* (White and Red, May–July, 3–6 ft.).

Gaura—Hardy perennials which are best treated as annuals, and thrive in light, warm, rich soil in sunny borders. They reach a height of 36 in. and flower from June to Oct. *See* Annuals, p. 123.

Gazania (Treasure Flower)—Showy summer bedding-plant with yellow and bronze flowers from June to Oct.; also useful for cool greenhouse. *Culture* —Propagate by means of basal cuttings in summer in a cold frame. Plant out in June in a sunny position. Protect from frost in winter. For indoors, pot-up in Mar. in sandy loam and peat.

Genista (Broom)—The Genistas, which are closely related to the Cytisus, are hardy flowering shrubs, valuable for the greenhouse, border, shrubbery, or rock garden. *Culture*—Plant in Oct. in dry, light soil in a sunny position. The early-flowering types should have the old wood thinned-out and should be trimmed into shape directly after flowering; the later bloomers should be cut hard back in Feb. or Mar. Do not prune *G. aethnensis, G. cinerea* or *G. virgata*, merely keep in shape by "stopping" and removing dead blooms. To propagate, sow in a frame when ripe, or strike cuttings of half-matured wood in a frame during Aug. and grow on in pots until planted out, as they do not transplant readily. *Species*—*G. aethnensis* (Golden-yellow, July–Aug., 10–20 ft.); *G. cinerea* (Golden, June–July, 8–10 ft.); *G. hispanica*, the Spanish Broom (Golden, May–June, 1–3 ft.); *G. pilosa* (Yellow, May–June, trailer); *G. tinctoria fl. pl.* (Golden [Double], July–Aug., 1–2 ft.).

Gentiana—Beautiful little rock plants which need as much approximation to alpine conditions as possible. A moist, but well-drained, gritty, peaty loam and leaf-mould, to which has been added a fair amount of old mortar rubble, suits them well. Ample moisture is essential through the summer and most species do best in partial shade. For culture, *see* Rock Plants, p. 283. The Gentians are impatient of root division, and indeed of transplanting. *Species and Varieties*—*G. acaulis* (Deep Blue, May–June, 2–3 in.); *G. asclepiadea* (Violet, Sept., 12–14 in.); *G. lutea* (Yellow, May–June, 24–36 in.); *G. Freyiana* (Blue, Aug.–Sept., 3–4 in.); *G. Pneumonanthe* (Violet, Aug., 6–9 in.); *G. verna* (Deep Blue, Apr.–May, 2 in.).

Geranium (Crane's Bill)—Ordinary garden soil, provided it is fairly light and well drained, suits the hardy geraniums; a sunny, open site is essential. The dwarf kinds are suitable for the rock garden, and thrive in poor, sandy and gritty soil. An autumnal dressing of granite chips will help them to survive the winter. *Culture*—Sow in Mar. or Aug. (under glass), or in Apr. in the open, or the plants may be increased by division from Oct. to Mar. Cuttings of matured side-shoots can also be struck in Aug. in a frame. For half-hardy greenhouse bedding-plants and show varieties, *see* Pelargonium. *Species*—(HARDY)—*G. armenum* (Red-purple, 18–24 in.); *G. Endressii* (Rose-pink, 15 in.); *G. grandiflorum* (Blue, 18 in.); *G. pratense* (Mauve, Blue or White, 20–30 in.). (*Dwarfs*)—*G. Farreri* (Pink, 6 in.); *G. sanguineum* (Crimson-purple, 9 in.); *G. s. album* (White, 9 in.); *G. s. lancastriense* (Rose and Crimson, 6 in.). All June to Sept.

Geum (Avens)—Hardy perennials which thrive in sunny borders in almost any well-drained, light, rich soil; the rock garden species love a deep, gritty loam, and *G. reptans* and *G. rivale* require plenty of moisture. For culture, *see* Perennials, p. 281. *Species and Varieties*—*G. Borisii* (Orange-scarlet); *G. Lady Stratheden* (Double, Golden-yellow); *G. montanum* (Yellow); *G. Mrs. Bradshaw* (Bright Red); *G. Orangeman* (Orange); *G. reptans* (Golden-yellow); *G. rivale* [Leonard's] (Crimson-pink). All April to Oct., 6 to 24 in.

Gillia—Hardy annuals and half-hardy biennials which thrive in ordinary soil in warm, sunny borders. For culture, *see* Annuals, p. 123, *and* Biennials, p. 125. *Species*—(ANNUALS)—*G. densiflora* (Lilac-pink, 12 in.); *G. micrantha var. aurea* (Yellow, 5 in.); *G. tricolor* (Pale Purple, White and Yellow, 10–20 in.). (BIENNIALS)—*G. aggregata* and *G.* (Ipomopsis) *rubra* (Crimson-scarlet, 24–48 in.). June to Oct.

Ginkgo biloba (Maidenhair Tree)—Hardy deciduous tree thriving in deep loam in a sheltered position. *Culture*—Plant in Oct. No pruning is required. Propagate in Mar. by means of seed in a frame. A good town tree growing 60 ft. or more in height.

Gladiolus (Sword Lily and Corn Flag)—Gladioli are divided into two sections, namely, the early-flowering (blooming from June to July), and the late-flowering (blooming in Aug. and Sept.). They like a deep, well-dug, firm loam and a warm spot well exposed to the sun and sheltered from cutting winds. *Culture*—Line the pocket in which the bulbs are to rest with a little coarse sand. Plant in Mar. or Apr. 4 in. deep and 4 to 6 in. apart, in rows 15 to 20 in. apart. Each flower spike will need staking securely. If seed is no object, the first flower stems should be cut down, when many of the bulbs will throw up a second flower-stem. The bulbs are taken up in Oct. or Nov. and stored. Prepare for planting in the following Mar. or Apr. by rubbing off the old roots and soil adhering at the bottom of the bulbs, and save the débris. *Propagation*—Examine this débris, and thousands of little scaly-looking rubbish will be found, which are young gladioli bulblets. Draw a drill 2 to 3 in. deep on a bit of rich soil in the reserve garden, and sow the bulblets thinly in Mar. Keep moist and some of these will flower late in autumn, many the second year, and all the third year. These young bulblets require exactly the same treatment as the old ones. Gladioli may also be raised from seed in May in a cold frame. If, however, it is desired that all the young plants shall come " true to type ", propagation must be effected by offsets. *Pot Culture*—Place one corm 3 in. deep in a 6-in. pot in a compost of 2 parts sandy loam to 1 part of leaf-mould and rotten manure and ample sharp sand, in Oct. or Nov.; cover with fibre till growth starts, and keep in a frame until Mar. Then put in a light airy position in a cold greenhouse to bloom. Dry-off after flowering, store, and keep dry from May to Oct. *G. Colvillei* is good for pot culture, and makes a good room plant. *Species—* (EARLY)—*G. byzantinus* (Purple-red, 20 in.); *G. cardinalis* (Scarlet, White Spots, 30 in.); *G. Colvillei* (Purple, White Spots, 18 in.); *G. C. albus* (White, 18 in.). All June to July. (LATE)—*G. brenchleyensis* (Scarlet); *G. ganda-vensis* (Various); *G. primulinus* (hybrids) (Various); *G. ramosus* (Purple, Rose and White). All Aug. to Sept., 24 in. Named varieties are innumerable and catalogues should be consulted.

Globularia (Globe Daisy)—Dwarf-growing perennials, which thrive in the sun and in moist light loam. They are useful for the paved or rock garden. For culture, *see* Rock Plants, p. 283. *Species—G. cordifolia; G. trichosantha.* Both Blue, May to July, 8 in.

Gloxinia—Tender tuberous-rooted perennials, which thrive in a fibrous peaty loam mixed with leaf-mould, cow-dung, sharp sand and charcoal. *Culture*—Start the tubers in succession from Jan. to Apr. by placing them in a box in a 2-in. layer of the above compost (Temp. 60° F.). Keep just moist, and as soon as from 2 to 3 in. growth has been made, plant one tuber in each 4-in. pot. Maintain the same heat and moisture, shade from the sun, and water liberally when well rooted. Pot-up into 5-in. pots as soon as pot-bound, and again into 6-in. pots when the buds are forming. After flowering, dry-off and store the tubers in peat or coconut fibre. Propagate at the end of Jan. by means of seed in a compost of peat, sand, and fine rich loam, thinly covered with coarse sand only, and exposed to a bottom heat of about 70° F. Prick-off 1 in. apart as soon as possible, and gradually reduce the temperature to 60° F.; pot-up singly into 4-in. pots, and place near the glass. Maintain the temperature, and keep moist, but do not let moisture touch the leaves. Pot-up by stages, until the flowering pots (5 to 7 in.) are reached. Seed may also be sown in a cold house in June. Old tubers, when started in heat in Feb. in boxes of damp fibre, supply shoots from which cuttings may be made; these should be placed in a close propagating frame and subjected to moist and gentle heat. Another method of propagation is by means of leaf-cuttings taken at any time. *Varieties—Mauve Queen* (Mauve); *Beacon* (Crimson); *Cyclops* (Rose-scarlet and White); *Pink Beauty* (Pink). All June to Oct., 12 in.

Godetia—Hardy annuals, useful for summer bedding. (*See* Œnothera). For culture, *see* Annuals, p. 123. *Named Varieties—Duchess of Albany* (White); *Apple Blossom* (Pink); *Lady Albemarle* (Crimson); *Duke of York* (Red and White); *New Lavender* (Mauve); and *Azalea-flowered* (Various). All June to Oct., 6 to 24 in.

Golden Rod (Solidago)—Hardy perennials which thrive in sun or shade in almost any soil. For culture, *see* Perennials, p. 281. *Species—S. canadensis, S. elliptica, S. rigida, S. Vigaurea.* All Golden Yellow, Aug. to Oct., 2 to 4 ft.

Gunnera—Hardy perennial foliage plants, which thrive in rich soil and sheltered, shady positions. They are valuable for margins of lakes, and for shrubberies. The crowns require slight winter protection. *See* Perennials, p. 281. *G. chilensis* (Crimson fruit, Aug., 5 ft.); *G. manicate.*

Gypsophila (Chalk plant, or Gauze Flower)—Hardy annuals and perennials which thrive in dry, well-limed loam, in sunny borders or the rock garden. For culture, *see* Annuals, p. 123, *and* Rock Plants, p. 283. *Species—(Annuals) —G. elegans* (White [Large], 18 in.); *G. muralis* (Pink, 6 in.). *(Perennials)— G. cerastioides* (White, veined Red, 3 in.); *G. paniculata* (White [Single and Double], 30 in.); *G. repens* (White and Pink, 4–6 in.). All May to Sept.

Haberlea—Hardy perennials suitable for a shady spot in the rock garden in moist peat, leaf-mould and sand. For culture, *see* Rock Plants, p. 283. *H. rhodopensis* (Lilac, May–July, 6 in.) is a favourite.

Habranthus pratensis—*See Hippeastrum pratense.*

Halesia (Silver Bell or Snowdrop Tree)—Hardy deciduous summer-flowering trees or shrubs (8–30 ft.) which thrive in well-drained, moist sandy loam in a sunny, sheltered position. *Culture*—Plant in Oct. or Nov.; thin-out the branches when overcrowded. To propagate sow in a frame in Mar., or take cuttings in Oct.

Hamamelis (Witch Hazel)—Small deciduous flowering trees or shrubs which thrive in sunny positions in moist but well-drained loam with peat and leaf-mould in it. *Culture*—Plant Oct. to Nov. Just thin-out and trim the branches in Apr. when overcrowded. To propagate, sow seed when ripe in a frame, layer in late summer, or graft. *Species—H. japonica* and *H. j. arborea* (Yellow, Jan.–Feb., 8–15 ft.); *H. j. Zuccariniana* (Pale Yellow, Dec.–Feb., 3–6 ft.); *H. mollis* (Golden Yellow, Dec.–Feb., 8–10 ft.).

Hebe (Veronica)—Shrubs from New Zealand, formerly united with Veronica, which can be grown outdoors in mild districts. The dwarf species are suitable for the rock garden. *Species—Veronica Andersonii* (Purple or Blue, July, 2 ft.); *H. Autumn Glory* (Violet, Sept., 1½ ft.); *V. buxifolia* (White, June–Aug., 2 ft.); *V. cupressoides* (Pale Purple, July, 2 ft.); *V. Hectori* (Lilac, July, 1 ft.); *V. speciosa* and *vars.* (Rose Purple, Blue, July–Sept., 3–4 ft.); *V. Traversii* (White, 5–6 ft.). For culture, *see* Veronica.

Hebenstretia comosa—Half-hardy perennial, growing about 18 in. high, with fragrant semi-double orange-red and white flowers, from July to Sept. For culture, *see* Perennials, p. 281.

Hedysarum—Genus of hardy biennials, perennials and shrubs, useful for borders and the rock garden. They thrive in the sun and in ordinary soil. For culture, *see* Biennials, p. 125, *and* Perennials, p. 281. *Species—(Biennials) H. coronarium* (Scarlet, June–Sept., 36 in.). *(Perennials)—H. capitatum* (Rose, Summer, 24 in.); *H. microcalyx* (Purple, June–July, 20 in.); *H. obscurum* (Purple-red, June–Aug., 6 in.). *(Shrub)—H. multijugum* (Purple-red, June–Sept., 36–72 in.).

Helenium (Sneezeweed)—Hardy perennials which thrive in sunny borders in rich, ordinary, well-drained soil. For culture, *see* Perennials, p. 281. *Species—H. autumnale* (Yellow, July–Oct., 48 in.); *H. a. var. pumilum; H. Hoopesii* (Orange, July–Oct., 30 in.). *Named varieties of H. autumnale— Riverton Beauty* (Yellow [Chocolate Centre], Aug.–Oct., 36–60 in.); *Riverton Gem* (Red [Shot Gold], Aug.–Oct., 36–60 in.).

Helianthemum (Sun Rose)—Shrubbery evergreens which love the sun and do best on dry banks, or in the rock garden in sandy soil. For culture, *see* Cistus. *Species*—*H. glaucum, var. croceum* (Yellow, May–Sept., 6 in.); *H. nummularium varieties*—*Fireball* (Red); *Rose Queen; Rubens* (Orange); *The Bride* (White); *tigrinum* (Salmon) and *venustum plenum* (Double, Scarlet), and many others.

Helianthus (Sunflower)—Hardy annuals and perennials which grow freely in a sunny site in any rich, well-dug soil. For culture, *see* Annuals, p. 123, *and* Perennials, p. 281. *Varieties*—(ANNUALS). *Named Varieties of H. annuus Golden Nigger* (Deep Yellow); *Langley Gem* (Primrose, flushed Pink, Double); *Primrose Dame* (Pale Yellow). All July to Oct. *Named Varieties of H. debiles*—*Apollo* (Gold and Maroon); *Mars* (Golden Red); and *Venus* (Cream, tinged Yellow). (PERENNIALS)—*H. decapetalus.* (Yellow [single or double], Aug.–Oct., 60–100 in.); *H. orgyalis* (Yellow [Black Centre], Sept.–Oct., 100 in.); *H. rigidus var. Miss Mellish* (Yellow, Sept–Oct., 100 in.).

Helichrysum ("Everlasting Flowers")—These are mostly half-hardy or hardy perennials or annuals, which thrive in sunny positions and gritty loam and are mostly suitable for borders, or as pot plants indoors, while the dwarf species make excellent rock plants. For culture, *see* Annuals, p. 123, *and* Perennials, p. 281. *Species* (*Half-hardy Annuals*)—*H. bracteatum* and *vars.* (White, Brown, Red, Pink, and Yellow, July–Oct., 36 in.); *H. orientale* (Yellow, July–Oct., 24 in.). (*Hardy Perennial*)—*H. bellidioides* (White, July–Oct., 5 in.).

Heliotropium peruvianum (Cherry Pie)—Soft-wooded shrubs, for summer bedding, and pot culture, and succeeding best in light, rich loam and leafmould. *Culture*—Seed sown thinly in spring in moderate heat makes good plants for summer and autumn decoration. Pot-off in Apr. into 4-in. pots, pinch-back when 3 to 4 in. high, harden-off and plant out, about 12 in. apart, in June. The finest plants are obtained from cuttings taken in the same way as for verbenas and bedding calceolarias. Take the cuttings in spring or autumn (preferably late Aug.) and strike in boxes in a frame in moderate heat; syringe in hot weather, and in five or six weeks pot-up into 3 or 4-in. pots and move into the cool house. *Pot Culture*—Pot-up annually in Mar., using 6 to 8-in. pots and a compost of two parts loam to one part of leafmould and sand. "Stop" back to make bushy, and prune well back in February. *Named Varieties*—*Lord Roberts; Mrs. J. W. Lowther; President Garfield; Swanley Giant; The Speaker;* and *White Lady.* All May to Sept., 12 to 36 in.

Helipterum—These half-hardy annuals, which now include the acroclinums and the rhodanthes, are everlastings, valuable alike for greenhouse (rhodanthes) and flower garden. They succeed best in a light, rich soil and warm sheltered positions. For culture, *see* Annuals, p. 123. *Pot Culture*—(*Rhodanthes*). Sow ¼ in. apart in Aug. (50° F.). Place the seedlings near the glass and keep fairly dry at first. Pot as soon as possible into the flowering pots. *Species*—*H. Manglesii* (Rose and Silver); *H. M. var. maculatum* (Pink, Yellow or White); *H. roseum* (Rose). All June to Oct., 12 to 18 in.

Helonias (Stud Flower)—Hardy herbaceous plants which thrive in moist, sandy and peaty loam in semi-shade, and which grow about 15 in. high and flower in Apr. and May. *Culture*—Sow in a frame in Apr., or propagate by means of division in Apr. or Oct.

Hemerocallis (Day Lily)—Hardy perennials which do well in moist, light, and deep soil in a shady border or marsh garden. Propagate by division in Apr. or Nov. *Species and Varieties*—*H. aurantiaca* (Apricot-orange); *H. Dumortieri* (Yellow and Red-brown); *H. Gold Dust* (Golden); *H. Sovereign*

(Orange-yellow); *H. fulva var. Kwanso fl. pl.* (Bronze-yellow), etc. All May to Aug., 12 to 36 in. Individual flowers only last a day.

Heracleum (Cow Parsnip)—Tall hardy biennials and perennials most suited to the wild or woodland garden or to the shrub border. For culture, *see* Biennials, p. 125, *and* Perennials, p. 281. *Species—(Biennial)—H. asperum* (3 ft.). *(Perennial)—H. Leichtlinii* (6 ft.); *H. persicum* (10 ft.). All carry white flowers; the biennials blooming from May to July, the perennials from June to Oct.

Herniaria glabra and others of this species are useful little creeping plants for the paved or rock garden. They like a sunny position and gritty loam, and are propagated by means of division in the spring.

Heuchera (Alum Root)—Hardy perennials which do well in warm, rich and light soil, in a sunny border. The dwarf species are useful for the rock garden. For culture, *see* Perennials, p. 281. *Species and Varieties—H. brizoides* (Rosy-red); *H. hybrida* (Red to White); *H. sanguinea var. gracillima* (Coral Scarlet). All May to Sept., 20 to 30 in.

Hibiscus (Rose, Shrubby, or Syrian Mallow)—Beautiful hardy and half-hardy plants, suitable for borders and indoor decoration. *Culture*—Plant the hardy sorts in sandy loam in Mar. in a sheltered position in sun or shade; do not prune, merely keep in shape by " stopping " and removing dead blooms after flowering. Propagate by sowing seeds about Apr., by cuttings in a frame in Sept., or by grafting. Those intended for indoor culture require a compost of fibrous peat and rich fine loam with a large proportion of sand; a little charcoal added is often beneficial. Propagate these from seeds sown over gentle heat, or by cuttings struck early in spring in a close frame. *Species —(Hardy Annual)—H. Trionum* (Purple, July–Sept., 2–4 ft.). *(Shrubs)—H. coccineus* (Bright Scarlet, Aug.–Oct., 4–5 ft.); *H. syriacus* and *vars.* (White, Blue, Pink, or Crimson, Single or Double, Aug.–Oct., 7 ft.), etc. *(Greenhouse Shrubs)—H. Rosa-sinensis* (Red, 10 ft.).

Hieracium (Hawkweed)—Hardy perennials, some of the dwarf-growing species of which thrive in ordinary soil in a sunny rock garden or border. For culture, *see* Perennials, p. 281. *Species—H. alpinum* (Yellow, July, 6 in.); *H. aurantiacum* (Orange, June–Aug., 20 in.).

Hippeastrum (Equestrian Star)—Large genus of bulbous plants, including Amaryllis, Habranthus, etc. Jacobea Lily, now *Sprekelia formosissima*, is usually grown in pots in the warm greenhouse in rich and heavy loam, to which bone dust and charcoal have been freely added, but it succeeds at the foot of a south wall. *H. pratense (Habranthus pratensis)* is suitable for a sunny border, rock garden, or pot culture. Plant in Oct. and protect with fibre in winter. *Culture*—Other Hippeastrums should be planted in Feb. Water well and give liquid manure when the buds appear. Keep dry after flowering. Re-pot every 3 or 4 years and propagate by offsets treated as old bulbs.

Hippophæ rhamnoides (Sea Buckthorn)—Hardy deciduous shrubs or trees (10–40 ft.) which thrive in moist ordinary soil in open positions (preferably near the sea). *Culture*—Plant in Oct. or Feb. and cut back weak shoots in Feb. Propagate by means of seed in the open, by suckers or layers in autumn, and by root-cuttings in spring.

Holly (Ilex)—Hardy trees and shrubs which thrive in sun or shade in almost any well-drained soil. Plant in May or Sept.; prune with secateurs in Apr. (hedges in May or Aug.). To propagate, sow in Mar. in shallow drills in the open. The seeds usually take two years to germinate, and many people prefer to strike cuttings of half-matured wood in Aug. in a cold frame, or to layer in summer.

PLATE 15 Carnation, Helena Allwood

PLATE 16 PLANTING A RHODODENDRON Dig a fair sized hole, *left*, so that it may be lined with peat or well rotted leaf mould, *above*. Place the rhododendron in the hole and spread the peat around the roots, *left*, before filling in the soil, *below left*. The soil should be well firmed down, *below*, and in dry weather the plant should be well watered in. Never plant rhododendrons too deep, this is fatal.

Hollyhock (Althæa rosea)—Though really perennials these are best treated as biennials. They like a sunny position in well-drained and deeply-worked rich loam. In summer give a liberal supply of water, and a good mulch of well-rotted manure. A dose of weak liquid manure every ten days should be given as soon as the plants reach a height of 3½ to 4 ft. *Propagation*—Sow seed thinly in drills 1 in. deep early in May in the open. When about 4 in. high transplant 8 in. apart in a nursery bed, and plant out 3 ft. apart in Oct. On cold heavy soils it is better to sow in boxes in May or June, pot-up in winter, place in a frame, and plant out in Apr. For Staking and Tying, see p. 22. Cuttings may be struck in sandy soil under a hand-glass in spring or the plants can be increased by division just as the new growth is starting. *Species and Varieties*—*A. alba superba* (White); *A. delicata* (Cream); *A. Queen of the Yellows* (Yellow); *A. Constance* (Pink); *A. James Vert* (Salmon); *A. Britannia* (Scarlet); *A. Palling Belle* (Silvery-pink); *A. King Albert* (Purple); *A. Black Knight* (Black); *American Fringed* (Various, Semi-double); *A. ficifolia, the Fig-leaved Hollyhock* (Red, Orange or Yellow, Single or Double). All flower from July to Sept. and grow 6 to 10 ft. in height.

Holodiscus discolor (*syn. Spiræa discolor*)—Shrub, 8 to 12 ft. For culture, *see* Spiræa (Shrub).

Honesty (Lunaria annua)—Hardy biennials 24 to 30 in. high carrying purple, mauve or white flowers. They thrive in semi-shaded borders or wild garden in moderately rich soil. *See* Biennials, p. 125.

Honeysuckle—*See* Lonicera.

Horminum pyrenaicum (Pyrenean Clary)—Hardy perennial which grows about 10 in. high and bears purple-blue flowers from June to Aug. It does well in dry ordinary soil in sunny borders or in the rock garden. For culture, *see* Perennials, p. 281.

Hosta (Plantain Lily)—Hardy herbaceous plants, suitable for the border, rock garden, shrubbery or cold greenhouse. They require rich, well-dug soil and thrive in sun or shade. *Culture*—Propagate by means of division in spring or autumn or pot-up in Mar. *Species*—*H. plantaginea* (White, July–Sept., 18 in.); *H. Sieboldiana* (Pale Lilac, July–Aug., 12–18 in.); *H. ventricosa* (Lilac-blue, July–Aug., 12–18 in.).

Humea (Incense Plant)—Handsome foliage plant which thrives in rich sandy loam and leaf-mould in sunny beds or borders and which may be grown in the cold greenhouse in an 8-in pot. The best-known species is *H. elegans*, a half-hardy, biennial. *See* Biennials, p. 125.

Humulus (Hop)—Hardy annual and perennial climbers, delighting in rich, deep, sandy loam. *H. Lupulus aureus* (Golden Hop) and *H. japonicus variegatus* (Silver Variegated Hop), both annuals, must have poor soil. For culture, *see* Annuals. p. 123, *and* Perennials, p. 281. Cut the latter down to the ground in late autumn.

Hyacinth (Hyacınthus)—Hyacinths can be divided into two classes: the *early-flowering Roman Hyacinths*, so useful for pot work and for forcing, and the *Dutch Hyacinths*, also good for pot work, but specially suitable for spring-bedding. The best soil for hyacinths is a well-manured, deeply-dug, sandy loam with leaf-mould in it, but they will grow in almost any soil or in coconut fibre, water or sand. *Culture*—Plant in a sunny position from Sept. to Nov. about 4 in. deep, and from 5 to 10 in. apart, according to variety. *Pot Culture*—To obtain bloom from Dec. to Apr., plant in succession from Aug. to Nov. A free, porous soil, composed of 2 parts of turfy loam to 1 part of well-rotted manure, leaf-mould and sand, thoroughly incorporated and sieved, is necessary. For three bulbs a 5½-in pot will be sufficient. *See also* general cultural details in the chapter on Bulbs, p. 141. *Named Varieties*—(White) *L'Innocence;* (Yellow) *City of Haarlem;* (Pink) *Pink Pearl;* (Red) *La Victoire;* (Blue) *King of the Blues* (dark); (Deep Blue) *Ostara;* (Light Blue) *Myosotis.*

Hydrangea—The common hydrangea—*H. macrophylla*—is a half-hardy summer-flowering deciduous shrub, which thrives in a sheltered position in well-drained and richly-manured sandy loam. *H. paniculata* and var. *grandiflora* (Creamy-white) are quite hardy. *Culture*—The same treatment, both indoors and out, will suit these species, bearing in mind that although *H. paniculata* is quite hardy, *H. macrophylla* is not. The two species also require different treatment as to pruning. *H. macrophylla* should be pruned in the summer; *H. paniculata* in Mar. Plant in Mar. *Pot Culture*—Pot-up from Feb. to Mar., using from 5 to 12-in. pots and a compost of 2 parts rich loam and 1 part of rotten manure and sand. When grown in small pots one stem only is encouraged. After flowering, stand in the open until Sept. *H. macrophylla* is also suitable for forcing in the warm greenhouse. Blue flowers may be procured by planting in a lime-free soil and by watering freely with a weak solution of alum: one teaspoonful in one gallon of rain-water, or with 3 oz. of aluminium sulphate in one gallon of water. Both these solutions should stand for at least twelve hours before use. To propagate, strike cuttings of young wood in May, or of strong matured shoots that have not flowered in Aug.; both in a frame. Autumn-struck cuttings should be wintered in a frame with an even temperature of 40° F. *Named Varieties of H. macrophylla—Etincelant* (Carmine); *Helge* (Dark Rose); *Le Cygne* (White); *La Marne* (Mauve); *Mme. Moullière* (White); *Triumph* (Rose-pink). For bluing, *Blue Prince,* etc.

Hymenocallis—Hardy and half-hardy bulbous plants from 12 to 24 in. high with white or yellow flowers from Feb. to Oct. They require a light, rich loam. *Culture*—Plant about 4 in. deep in Sept. and protect with ashes or fibre in winter. Lift about every fourth year. Propagate by means of bulbils, or seed.

Hypericum (St. John's Wort, Aaron's Beard or Rose of Sharon)—This genus includes a number of hardy shrubs, evergreens and deciduous, as well as hardy annuals and perennials. The annuals are hardly worth growing, but some of the dwarf-growing perennials and evergreen shrubs make excellent rock or edging plants. Sandy loam and a sunny site suit them best. For culture, *see* Perennials, p. 281. (*Shrubs*)—Plant in Nov.; cut well back in Mar. Propagate by means of cuttings in July or sow seed when ripe. *Species* —(*Perennial*)—*H. fragile* (8 in.); *H. gracile* (5 in.); *H. tomentosum* (6–9 in.). (*Shrub*)—*H. calycinum* (12–18 in.); *H. elatum* (48–60 in.); *H. Hookerianum* (*syn. oblongifolium*) (3–5 ft.); *H. Moserianum* (12–18 in.); *H. patulum Henryi* (18–36 in.);. All carry yellow flowers from July to Aug., except *H. tomentosum*, which blooms from Aug. to Oct.

Iberis (Candytuft)—Hardy annuals and perennials, both of which succeed in any soil with lime in it, but prefer dry, sandy loam and a sunny position. For culture, *see* Annuals, p. 123, *and* Perennials, p. 281. *Species*—(*Annual*) —*I. umbellata* (Purple, Crimson and Pink, July–Oct., 12 in.). (*Perennials*)— *I. gibraltarica* (Lilac-pink, May–July, 12 in.) [this needs a warm, sheltered position]; *I. sempervirens* (White, May–June, 6–12 in.).

Ice Plant [Mesembryanthemum] (Cryophytum crystallinum)—Useful half-hardy annuals and perennials for rock-work, thriving in fairly good soil, in a dry sunny situation. For culture, *see* Annuals, p. 123, Perennials, p. 281.

Incarvillea—Hardy annuals and tuberous-rooted perennials growing from

6 to 36 in. high and flowering from May to Aug. They thrive in well-drained rich loam in sunny borders. *Culture*—Sow in pans in a frame in Apr., thin, and plant out in spring and autumn. Seed can be sown in the open early in May; increase also by division in Mar. or Oct. *I. Delavayi* (Crimson-pink or Purple, 15 in.) is the most popular.

Inula (Fleabane)—Hardy perennials useful for sunny borders or for the wild garden. For culture, *see* Perennials, p. 281. *Species*—*I. grandiflora* (Orange-yellow); *I. Hookeri* (Yellow); *I. Oculis-Christi* (Golden-yellow). All June to Aug., 24 to 36 in.

Ipomœa (Moon Flower, Morning Glory, etc.)—Large genus of half-hardy climbing plants, closely allied to the convolvulus, all requiring a rich, light soil. *Culture*—*(Annuals)*—Sow seed singly in Apr. in small pots under glass, and plant out 24 in. apart in May or June against a trellis or sunny wall. *(Perennials)*—These are best propagated by means of cuttings of side shoots struck in a frame between Mar. and Aug. *Species and Varieties*—*I. Learii* (Blue Dawn Flower, sub-tropical climber). (ANNUALS)—*I. purpurea* (Various [Single and Double]); *I. tricolor* [*rubro-cœrulea*] (Sky-blue). All June to Sept., 8 to 10 ft.

Iresine—Half-hardy ornamental foliage plants suitable for warm, sunny, and sheltered beds or for pot culture indoors. They grow about 18 in. high and thrive in ordinary soil. *Culture*—Strike cuttings of young shoots in a frame in late summer or in spring. Plant out in June 8 in. apart, or pot-up in Mar., using 5 to 8-in. pots and a mixture of peat, loam, leaf-mould and sand.

Iris—Genus of hardy plants usually divided into two sections—namely the bulbous and the non-bulbous or rhizomatous-rooted. To the latter class belong the Flags or Bearded Irises, the Kæmpferi or Japanese group and the Sibirica Irises; to the bulbous class belong the English, Dutch and Spanish Irises. The cultivation of irises is simple, the plants succeeding in a sunny position in any light, rich garden soil, though sandy loam with 50 per cent peat or leaf-mould is most suitable for the bulbous species. The English Iris needs a heavier and cooler soil than the Dutch and Spanish species, and it is necessary to lift bulbs of the last two triennially, rest them for a few months, and then re-plant. For the tall Bearded Iris the soil should be deeply dug, well-manured and should have some old mortar rubble incorporated; it will, however, grow in almost any well-drained soil. The Japanese Irises love marshy land, require a position in full sun, and should occasionally be transplanted and divided in Aug. after blooming. The three following types also belong to the rhizomatous group: the *Evansia* section, the *Oncocyclus* or Cushion Irises and the *Regelia* Irises.

Culture—*(Bulbous-rooted)*—Plant 3 to 4 in. deep in Sept. or Oct., with a little sand round the bulbs (Spanish, 4 in.; Dutch, 5 in.; and English, 6 in. apart). Most spring and autumn-flowering species require to be lifted from the ground in Aug., summer-flowering kinds should be lifted every third year, in Oct., after the plants have died down. English irises should be left undisturbed; the Dutch irises need just the same treatment as the Spanish. *Pot Culture*—Many of the bulbous irises make good pot plants; among these are *I. alata*, *I. persica*, *I. reticulata*, and the English and Spanish kinds. They need a compost of two-thirds fibrous loam, one-third leaf-mould and sand; plant five bulbs in a 6-in. pot in Sept. or Oct. They may be propagated by offsets in Oct.

Non-bulbous or Rhizomatous Species—Sow seed in Apr. in a cold frame, or propagate by division in Aug. Plant out in Aug. or Sept.; Bearded Irises (tall) 20 in. apart; (medium) 15 in. apart; (dwarf) 5 in. apart. The upper part of the rhizomes should lie on the surface of the soil, so as to be exposed to the air and sun. The dwarf Bearded Rock species may be propagated by seed sown in Sept. under glass, by offshoots in Oct., or by division in the spring after flowering. Lift and re-plant the rhizomes triennially.

Species and Varieties—BULBOUS-ROOTED. *Spring-flowering*—*I. Histrio* (Lilac-blue and Yellow, Jan.–Feb., 6 in.); *I. orchioides* (Yellow, Lilac Spots, Mar.–May, 20 in.); *I. persica Heldreichii* (Purple, Yellow and Green, Mar. 4 in.); *I. reticulata Krelagei* (Purple, Red and Orange, Jan.–Feb., 8 in.). *Summer-flowering*—*I. xiphioides* (*English Iris*) (Purple, Mauve, Pink and Blue, July, 10–25 in.; *I. Xiphium* (*Spanish Iris*) (Blue, Yellow and White, June 20 in.). *Autumn-flowering*—*I. alata* (Sky-blue and Yellow, Nov.–Jan., 4 in.). NON-BULBOUS OR RHIZOMATOUS—*I. fulva* (*syn. cuprea*) (Red-bronze, June–July, 20 in.); *I. fœtidissima* (Bluish-lilac or Yellow, June, 30 in.); *I. Kœmpferi* (Various, July–Sept., 18–30 in.); *I. Monnieri* (Yellow and White, June–July, 36–48 in.); *I. Monspur* (Light Blue, Lavender or Violet, July–Aug., 50 in.); *I. ochroleuca* (White and Yellow, June–July, 48 in.); *I. sibirica* (Blue, White and Yellow, May–June, 36 in.); *I. spuria* (Deep Blue, June, 40 in.); *I. unguicularis* [*syn. stylosa*] (Various, Nov.–Mar., 6–12 in.).

Itea virginica—Hardy deciduous summer-flowering shrubs (3–5 ft.) which like a moist, peaty soil and partial shade; plant in Oct., and thin-out the branches when overcrowded. Propagate by means of seed in the open in Apr. or by suckers in Oct.

Ivy (Hedera)—There are many kinds of this well-known climber. The common sorts thrive against walls in ordinary rich soil; the variegated kinds prefer walls facing south or west, and like ample lime in the soil. *Culture*—Strike cuttings in autumn in sandy soil in a shady border, or layer; plant out in showery weather between the following Oct. and Apr. When established, old leaves and untidy shoots need clipping hard back in Apr. *Species and Varieties*—*H. Cænwoodiana* (Small Green Leaf); *H. colichica, var. dentata* (Large Green Leaves); *H. Helix* (Common Ivy); *H. H. vars. angularis, aurea* (Yellow); *hibernica* (Irish Ivy); *purpurea* (Bronze), etc.

Ixia (African Corn Lily)—Half-hardy bulbs which thrive in warm, dry, sunny borders or in the rock garden in rich, sandy loam and leaf-mould or peat, or in pots in the cold greenhouse. *Culture*—Plant in Sept., 4 in. deep and 3 in. apart. Do not lift, but in winter cover the bulbs with ashes or fibre. *Pot Culture*—Pot-up from Aug. to Sept., placing six bulbs in a 6-in. pot in a compost of 2 parts turfy loam to 1 part each of leaf-mould, rotten cow-dung and sand. Dry-off after the foliage dies. Propagate by means of seed in a frame in Sept. or by offsets in Oct. Seedlings take three years to flower. *Named Varieties*—*Bridesmaid* (White); *King of the Yellows* (Yellow); *Queen of the Roses* (Rose); *Excelsior* (Red); *Azurea* (Blue, Purple Centre). All May and June, 15 in.

Ixiolirion (Ixia Lily)—Half-hardy bulbous plants which grow about 15 in. high, flower in June, and do well in well-drained sandy loam in a warm, sunny border or rock garden. *Culture*—Plant in Sept., 5 in. deep and 3 in. apart; do not lift the bulbs, but protect them with fibre during the winter. If grown in pots, treat as Ixia.

Jacobæa Lily (*Sprekelia formosissima*)—Grow in pots in the warm greenhouse in well-drained, rich and heavy loam, to which bone dust and charcoal have been freely added. *Culture*—Plant in Feb.; water well and give liquid manure when the buds appear; and keep dry after flowering. Re-pot every three or four years, and propagate by offsets treated as old bulbs.

Jamesia americana—Hardy deciduous flowering shrub which likes a damp rich soil and a sunny position. *Culture*—Plant from Oct. to Nov.; thin-out branches when overcrowded. To propagate, sow seed when ripe, or in autumn strike cuttings.

Jasmine (Jasminum)—*J. officinale,* the common white jasmine which blooms in June and July, is the best known; *J. revolutum,* with yellow flowers in May, is better grown in bush form; *J. nudiflorum* has yellow flowers in winter and is useful outdoors or in the cold greenhouse; there are also beautiful hothouse species. Hardy. kinds like rich loam and most do well against walls and pergolas facing north or west. *Culture*—Strike cuttings of ripe wood in summer in a frame, or layer. Plant out from Oct. to Mar., and after flowering prune shoots that have bloomed. *Pot Culture—(Cold House)*—Pot-up in Feb. or Mar., using 6 to 8-in. pots and a compost of two-thirds loam and one-third leaf-mould and well-rotted manure with a little sand; give weak liquid manure twice a week as soon as the buds form. (*Warm House*)—Pot-up in Mar.; keep moist and syringe frequently until the plants have bloomed; then keep moderately dry.

Juglans (Walnut)—Hardy deciduous nut-bearing trees which thrive in well-drained loam in a sunny, open position. *Culture*—Plant in Oct. when three to four years old. Thin-out branches when overcrowded. To propagate, plant nuts 4 in. deep in the open. *J. regia* (Common walnut).

Juniper (Juniperus)—Handsome evergreen shrubs which thrive in the sun in moist, well-drained and deep loam with mortar rubble. *Culture*—Plant in May or Sept.; no pruning is required. To propagate, strike cuttings in a frame in Sept., or raise from seed.

Kalmia (American Laurel)—Hardy evergreen shrubs which should be treated as the rhododendron (*which see*); they are also suitable for gentle forcing. To propagate, sow in a frame in spring, strike cuttings in a frame in Oct., or layer in Oct. *Species*—the best known are *K. latifolia,* the Calico Bush, or Mountain Laurel (Rose and White, June, 8-15 ft.); *K. angustifolia,* the Sheep Laurel (Purple-red, June, 3 ft.).

Kentranthus (Valerian)—Hardy perennial, which likes a sunny position and dry, limy soil, and is useful for border, rock garden, or walls. For culture, *see* Perennials, p. 281. *Species*—*K. angustifolius* (Crimson, May–July, 24 in.); *K. ruber* (Crimson, Rose, June–Aug., 24-36 in.); *K. r. var. albus.*

Kerria (Jew's Mallow)—Hardy deciduous shrubs, bearing orange flowers in Mar. and Apr. *K japonica* (4 ft., Single) and *vars. fl. pl.* (8-9 ft., Double) and *aurea variegata* are usually grown; as climbers they run up to double the heights mentioned. They do well in sandy soil in sunny positions against walls facing south or west. *Culture*—Strike cuttings of young shoots in a frame in autumn, or propagate by division of roots in late autumn. Plant out from Oct. to Mar. About June or early July cut out the oldest wood. *Pot Culture*—In the cool greenhouse *K. j. fl. pl.* may be had in flower in Feb. Pot-up annually in Oct., using 8 to 10-in. pots and a compost of 2 parts of sandy loam to 1 part of leaf-mould and rotten manure. Prune after flowering and plant outdoors.

Kniphofia (Tritoma, Red-hot Poker, Flame Flower, Torch Lily)—Tall hardy perennials which thrive in well-drained and deep sandy soil in sunny or partially-shaded borders; they may also be potted-up in Apr. or Nov. in 8 to 10-in. pots and grown in the cold greenhouse. For culture, *see* Perennials, p. 281. *Species and Varieties*—*K. caulescens* (Red and Yellow, May, 40 in.); *K. modesta* (White, May–Sept., 30 in.); *K. uvaria grandiflora* (Orange-red, July–Sept., 70 in.). *Named—Golden Spur; Harkness Hybrid; Mount Etna; Royal Standard.*

Kochia (Summer Cypress)—Half-hardy annuals useful for summer bedding, for borders and the cold greenhouse. *See* Annuals, p. 123.

Laburnum (Golden Rain or Golden Chain)—Hardy deciduous trees with yellow flowers in May; almost any soil and a sunny position suit them well. *Culture*—Plant in Nov.; trim back weak shoots after flowering and cut out dead wood in winter. In the cool greenhouse *L. anagyroides* will flower from Feb. to Apr. *Pot Culture*—Pot-up in Oct., using 8 to 10-in. pots and a compost of 2 parts sandy loam to 1 part of leaf-mould and rotten manure. Prune as above after flowering and plant out in the open. Do not re-pot for forcing for two seasons. To propagate, sow in a frame in spring; budding and grafting are sometimes resorted to. The seeds are *poisonous*.

Lachenalia (Cape Cowslip)—Beautiful bulbous-rooted flowering plants suitable for greenhouse culture. *Culture*—Pot-up in Aug., ½ in. deep in a compost of peaty loam with decayed cow manure and sand. Put one bulb in a 4-in. pot, or five bulbs in a 6 to 7-in. pot. Keep in a cold, frost-proof frame until early Dec., watering only when dry, then transfer to a shelf near the glass in the greenhouse (50° F.), and water as growth commences. Keep quite dry in pots from May to Aug. Propagate by offsets in Aug. *Named Species and Varieties*—*L. pendula* (Red and Yellow); *L. tricolor var. Nelsonii* (Golden Yellow); *L. t. var. luteola* (Yellow-green, tipped Red).

Lantana (Surinum Tea Plant)—Bushy evergreen half-hardy shrubs, 6 to 8 in. high, flowering from June to Sept. Useful for the greenhouse and flower garden. *Culture*—Pot-up as soon as the young shoots break after pruning, using 6 to 7-in. pots and a compost of 2 parts of loam to 1 part of leaf-mould, well-rotted manure and sand. Syringe in spring and summer. If planted out during the summer, they must be wintered indoors. Seeds sown in heat (75° F.) in Mar. make the summer and autumn-blooming plants. They are also propagated in spring or autumn by cuttings of half-matured wood in heat. *Varieties*—*Drap d'Or* (Yellow); *Favorita* (Yellow and Red); *La Neige* (White); and *Magenta King* (Purple-red).

Lapageria—Beautiful evergreen climbers for the cool greenhouse, which require a well-drained turfy loam plentifully mixed with sand, an equal portion of peat and a little charcoal. They grow to a height of 10 ft. and flower in Oct. and Nov. *Culture*—Propagate by seed sown as soon as ripe in gentle heat or by layers after flowering, the latter being the best way. Pot firmly, or plant in border in Mar., shade and water well. Cut out weak shoots only after flowering. *Species and Varieties*—*L. rosea* (Rose); and *vars. albiflora* (White), and *Nash Park* (Rosy-red).

Larix (Larch)—One of the few deciduous conifers. It grows from 30 to 100 ft. in height and thrives in a sunny position and in ordinary soil. *Culture* —Plant in Oct. Remove dead wood when necessary. Propagate by means of seed in the open in Nov. *Species*—*L. decidua [europæa]* (Common Larch); *L. pendula* (Weeping Larch).

Larkspur (Annual Delphinium)—Showy hardy annuals; the dwarfs (12 in.) are excellent for edging; and taller sorts in mixed borders. For culture, *see* Annuals, p. 123. *Species*—*D. cardiopetalum* (Blue); *D. Consolida* (Purple); *D. Ajacis* (Blue).

Lathyrus (Everlasting Pea, Sweet Pea)—Annual and perennial climbing plants, the most popular of which are the Sweet Pea and the Everlasting Pea, *which see* under those headings.

Laurel (Prunus Laurocerasus)—Evergreen shrubs which thrive in almost any soil and are useful for hedges. Prune carefully in May and Sept. with a knife—shears must not be used—and when some years old, cut out old wood.

Plant young bushes 2 ft. apart in Mar. or Sept., and cut the vigorous young shoots back below the level of the others. Propagate by means of cuttings and layering.

Laurus—This genus includes two species only, viz. *Laurus canariensis* and *L. nobilis* (evergreen), the true Bay Laurel or Sweet Bay. The latter thrives in well-drained fibrous loam, leaf-mould and peat in a sheltered position in sun or shade. Strike cuttings in a frame in Aug.

Lavandula (Lavender)—The best-known species, *L. Spica* (Mauve to White), the common lavender, thrives in light and well-drained soil in sunny positions, grows about 3 ft. high, and flowers in July and Aug. *Culture*—Plant in Mar. or Sept., and clip after flowering. To propagate, strike cuttings in Oct.

Lavatera (Mallow)—Hardy annuals, biennials and perennials, which thrive in the sun in any soil. For culture, *see* Annuals, p. 123, Biennials, p. 125, *and* Perennials, p. 281. *Species*—ANNUAL—*L. trimestris* (Rose or White). BIENNIAL—*L. arborea* (Violet). PERENNIAL—*L. thuringiaca* (Blue). All July to Sept., 30 to 60 in.

Layia (Tidy Tips)—Hardy annuals suitable for sunny beds, borders or rock gardens. For culture, *see* Annuals, p. 123. *Species*—*L. densiflora* (Mauve and White); *L. elegans* (Yellow, margined White); *L. glandulosa* (White). All July to Sept., 10 in.

Ledum (Labrador Tea)—Hardy evergreen shrubs which thrive in cool, moist loam deficient in lime, in sun or semi-shade. *Culture*—Plant in May or Sept. No pruning is necessary. Propagate in Sept. by means of layering, or cuttings, or by seed in spring. *Species*—*L. groenlandicum* [*latifolium*] (White, tinged Pink); *L. palustre* (Pink). Apr. to May, 10 to 40 in.

Leiophyllum (Sand Myrtle)—Hardy dwarf evergreen shrubs for the rock garden, that thrive in fibrous loam in the sun, and flower in summer. *Culture* —Plant in Apr. or Sept. Propagation is by means of seed in a frame in spring, or by layering in Sept.

Leptospermum—Evergreen shrubs which thrive in the cool greenhouse in a compost of 2 parts peat to 1 of loam and a little sand. *L. scoparium* (White) may be grown outdoors in a warm, sheltered situation. Propagate by cuttings (with bottom heat) in May, or by seed in slight heat in Mar. *Species and Varieties*—*L. Donard Beauty* (Red, margined Rose, 50 in.); *L. grandiflorum* (White, 80 in.); *L. scoparium Chapmanii* (Rose Scarlet, 50 in.). June to Aug. flowering.

Leptosyne—Annuals and perennials which thrive in the sun in ordinary soil. For culture, *see* Annuals, p. 123, *and* Perennials, p. 281. *Species and Varieties*—ANNUAL—*L. Douglasii* (12 in.); *L. Stillmanii* (20 in.). PERENNIAL —*L. maritima* (30 in.). All Yellow, Summer.

Leucojum (Snowflake)—Hardy bulbs which thrive in any garden soil in semi-shade, and are useful for borders or the rock garden. *Culture*—Plant in Sept. 3 to 4 in. deep and 5 in. apart; lift every seven years. Propagate by offsets or by seed. *Species*—*L. æstivum* (White, spotted Green, May, 15 in.); *L. autumnale* (White, tinged Red, Oct., 10 in.); *L. vernum* (White, Mar. 9 in.).

Lewisia (Bitter-root)—Useful little rock plants for a dry sunny crevice and in gritty loam. Protect from wet in winter. For culture, *see* Rock Plants, p. 283. *Species*—*L. Cotyledon* (Pink, striped Buff or White, May–June, 4 in.); *L. rediviva* (Pink and White, May–Aug.); *L. Tweedyi* (Salmor-Pink, 8 in.).

Liatris (Blazing Star, or Kansas Feather)—Hardy perennials, better grown as biennials. They thrive in almost any soil in a warm, sunny border. For culture, *see* Biennials, p. 125. *Species*—*L. graminifolia* (Pink, 36 in.); *L. spicata* (Mauve-purple, 40 in.). All Aug. to Oct.

Libertia—Herbaceous perennials for the border or rock garden. They need a light soil. For culture, *see* Perennials, p. 281. *Species*—*L. formosa* (White, 20 in.); *L. ixioides* (White, 40 in.). All Mar. to May.

Libocedrus (Incense Cedar)—Hardy and half-hardy evergreen coniferous trees, the most popular species of which is *L. decurrens*. It likes a well-drained loam and a warm, sheltered position. *Culture*—Sow seed Oct. to Apr., or strike cuttings in frame in Sept.

Ligustrum (Privet)—Hardy evergreen and deciduous shrubs, usually grown as hedge-plants, but poisonous to cattle. They thrive in ordinary soil and in full sun. *Culture*—Plant from Nov. to Mar.; clip in summer and cut out dead wood. To propagate, strike cuttings in the open in autumn. *Species*—*L. ovalifolium* (Common Privet) and *L. o. aureum* (Golden Privet) are those most used. *L. lucidum* is a tall evergreen privet.

Lilac—*See* Syringa.

Lilium (Lily)—There are many different species and varieties of lilies, but they are for the most part hardy bulbous perennials requiring practically the same management. Lilies thrive in deep, well-dug garden soil, or in a moist, well-drained fibrous loam with well-decayed leaf-mould and gritty sand in it. A few, such as *L. auratum*, *L. giganteum* and *L. pardalinum*, love a peaty soil, but with the majority the presence of peat will cause failure.

Culture—Plant in Oct. in groups of five or seven, 4 to 5 in. deep (about three times their own depth), and from 6 to 12 in. apart. according to species; the bulbs should, as a rule, when planted, rest on sand, and they should not be disturbed oftener than every three years. A yearly top-dressing of well-decayed manure each spring will be beneficial. Lilies which form roots from the base of the stem should be planted among low-growing shrubs; these particular lilies may be planted at any time, and somewhat deeper than the non-stem-rooting kinds. When in bloom, all lilies must be carefully staked, and all dead flowers should at once be removed, but the stems must not be cut down until they have died off. The Madonna Lily (*L. candidum*) requires different treatment. Transplant this lily in Aug., only lift when necessary and top-dress with well-rotted manure each spring.

Pot Culture—Plant in late autumn; a 12-in. pot will take six bulbs, a large bulb of *L. auratum* would require a 10-in. pot to itself. The bulbs should be covered by 1 in. of soil which should be made firm, and care must be taken that the bulbs do not touch the sides of the pots. They should be treated in their first stage of growth exactly as hyacinths grown in pots, except that the pots must be only partly filled with soil. The pots should remain buried in ashes or fibre, in a frame till the plants begin to grow, when, as the stems grow, the pots are gradually filled up to within about an inch of the rim. Those intended to flower early should be placed under glass, while late bloomers should remain out of doors in a sheltered situation. Propagation is carried out by means of offsets in October, by planting scales from bulbs in sandy soil in a cold frame, or seed in pans in cold frames in Aug. Seedlings of most species do not flower until they are 2 to 5 years old.

Species and Varieties—*L. auratum* [Japanese Lily] (White, Yellow and Crimson, Aug.-Sept., 40 in.); *L. candidum* [White Madonna Lily] (White, June–July, 50 in.); *L. chalcedonicum* [Turk's Cap] (Bright Scarlet, July–Aug., 40 in.); *L. croceum* (Orange, July–Aug., 36–60 in.); *L. formosanum* [Trumpet Lily] (White, July–Aug., 30 in.); *L. Martagon* (Rosy-violet, Wine-red and white, July, 40 in.); *L. pardalinum* [Panther Lily] Scarlet, Orange and Yellow, July, 60 in.); *L. regale* (White and Yellow, July, 24–40 in.); *L. testaceum* (syn. *excelsum*) [Nankeen Lily] (Nankeen Yellow, Anthers Scarlet,

June–July, 60 in.); *L. tigrinum splendens* [Tiger Lily] (Scarlet-orange, dark Purple Spots, Aug.–Sept., 50 in.). There are many others.

Lily of the Valley (Convallaria majalis)—To grow Lilies of the Valley well the roots should be set in bunches a foot apart in a mixture of sandy loam, leaf-mould and old manure in a partially-shaded position; they can hardly be treated too liberally. *Culture*—Plant in Oct., only just covering with soil, and mulch with a 2-in. layer of leaf-mould, which should be removed in the spring. Dress annually in summer with leaf-mould and rotten manure, lift from the soil every fourth year, and propagate by means of division in Oct. *Pot Culture*—Plump crowns should be potted-up 1 in. apart in Nov., using 5 to 6-in. pots and a compost of sandy loam and leaf-mould, and so that only the tops obtrude. Water well and keep in a cool frame for a few days, then take into the house in batches as bloom is required. The pots must be kept in the dark until the shoots are 5 to 6 in. in height, after this gradually admit light, raise the temperature to between 60° and 70° F., and give warm water in increasing amounts as growth goes on. After flowering, plant the crowns in the border.

Limnanthes—Dwarf hardy annuals, which flower in summer, and are useful for edging or rock garden. For culture, *see* Annuals, p. 123.

Limonium (Statice, Sea Lavender)—These beautiful "Everlasting" flowers thrive in sunny borders or in the rock garden in well-drained sandy loam and leaf-mould. For culture, *see* Annuals, p. 123. Nearly all the annuals are better treated as half-hardy; for Perennials, *see* p. 281. *Pot Culture*—Pot-up half-hardy species in a compost of two-thirds fibrous loam and one-third peat to which has been added a little leaf-mould and sand and some well-decayed cow-manure. Pot-on as the roots fill the pots, until 8 to 9-in. pots are reached. *Species*—(HALF-HARDY ANNUAL)—*L. sinuatum hybridum* (Mauve, White and Rose, June–Oct., 15–30 in.); *L. Suworowii* (Rosy-purple or White, June–Oct., 12–18 in). (HARDY PERENNIAL)—*L. Gmelinii* (Purple-blue, July–Sept., 18–24 in.); *L. incanum* (Red or Pinky-white, July–Aug., 15 in.); *L. tataricum* (Red, July–Sept., 20 in.).

Linaria (Toad Flax)—These are mostly hardy annuals and perennials. All species like a light sandy soil and a sunny, dry position; the rock garden species need a gritty soil. For culture, *see* Annuals, p. 123, *and* Perennials, p. 281. *Species*—(ANNUAL)—*L. bipartita* (Red, White or Purple, 12 in.); *L. reticulata* (Yellow and Purple, 12–18 in.). (PERENNIAL)—*L. alpina* (Violet, blotched Orange, 3 in.); *L. Cymbalaria* (Mauve and Orange, Trailer); *L. dalmatica* (Orange and Yellow, 40 in.). All June to Sept. Many others.

Linnæa borealis (Twin-flower)—Hardy evergreen trailing shrub which thrives in a mixture of sand and peat in the shade on moist banks, and flowers in June and July. *Culture*—Propagate by means of division in Mar. or Oct. or increase by layering.

Linum (Flax or Linseed-oil Plant)—Hardy annuals and perennials which thrive in dry, light soil in a sunny position. The rock garden species need the addition of ample grit. For culture, *see* Annuals, p. 123, *and* Perennials, p. 281. *Pot Culture*—Pot-up in Mar. or Apr., using 5 to 6-in. pots and a compost of loam and peat with a little sand mixed. In Feb. or Mar. prune back the previous year's growth to within an inch from the base. *Species*—(ANNUAL)—*L. grandiflorum* (Crimson-scarlet, Black Centre, Oct., 12 in.); *L. usitatissimum* (Blue, July–Oct., 24 in.). (PERENNIAL)—*L. alpinum* (Blue, May–June, 6–9 in.); *L. flavum* (Golden, June–Sept., 10 in.); *L. hirsutum* (Blue and White, May–Sept., 9 in.); *L. narbonense* (Deep Blue, May–Sept., 12–24 in.); *L. perenne* (Pale Blue, May–Sept., 12–24 in.).

Lippia (Sweet Verbena)—Only one kind of this sweet-smelling deciduous shrub is grown to any extent. *L. citriodora*, with purple blooms in Aug. It can be grown in the open or against a wall in the South and West of England and in other parts it is suitable for the cold greenhouse, but requires protection from the frost in winter, even under shelter. *Culture*—Re-pot into a smaller pot in the spring, in rich mould, loam and sandy peat or leaf-mould for preference; when well rooted transfer to a larger pot. It succeeds also in the warm greenhouse. Cut young shoots hard back to the old wood in Feb. and pinch back the young shoots from time to time, but not later than June. Propagate by means of cuttings of young wood in gentle heat in spring. *L. citriodora* (syn. *Aloysia citriodora*) has lemon-scented foliage.

Liquidambar styraciflua (Sweet Gum)—Hardy deciduous trees, growing 40 to 80 ft. high, and which like a cool, moist ordinary soil and a sunny position. Propagate by seed or by cuttings.

Liriodendron (Tulip Tree)—Tall deciduous trees, flowering in July and Aug., and which thrive in well-drained soil in a sunny position. *Culture*—Plant in Nov.; in autumn cut out dead wood. To propagate, sow seed in a frame in Mar.

Lithospermum (Gromwell)—Hardy trailing evergreen shrubs and perennials, which do well in a mixture of gritty loam and peat in moderately sunny positions, and are excellent for dry walls, rock gardens and for edging. For culture, *see* Rock Plants, p. 283. *Species*—*L. diffusum* (Blue); *L. graminifolium* (Sky Blue); *L. intermedium* (Deep Blue); *L. oleifolium* (Blue). All June to Sept.

Lobelia—Genus of half-hardy annuals and perennials, of which the low-growing kinds are suitable for edging, thriving in deep, well-manured and moist soil in sunny positions. *L. gracilis* is equally beautiful in pots or beds; all varieties of the greenhouse perennial *L. Erinus* are valuable for edging and for hanging baskets or vases. Treat all these as half-hardy annuals. The tall perennial species are valuable in the mixed border. *Culture*—(*Annuals*)—*See* p. 123. If required for greenhouse use pot-up singly into 3 or 4-in. pots in the compost mentioned below. (*Perennials*)—*See* p. 281. As soon as the foliage is dead in autumn, the stems are cut down and the roots lifted and stored in boxes of dry soil in a frost-proof frame; water is given in Mar. to re-start growth and late in Apr. the roots are divided and planted out. *Pot Culture*—(*L. cardinalis* and *vars.*)—Pot-up in Mar., using 6 to 8-in. pots and a compost of fibrous loam, leaf-mould, rotten manure and sand; keep in a frame on ashes until about to bloom, then transfer to the cool greenhouse. After blooming, cut down the flower stems, return to the frame in Oct., and cover with ashes for the winter; give a good watering in Feb., and a month later divide and re-pot if necessary. *Species and Varieties*—(ANNUAL)—*L. Erinus*—*Kathleen Mallard* (Double, Dark Blue); *Celestial* (Cobalt Blue); and *Imperial Blue* (Dark). All July to Oct., 6 in. *L. gracilis* (Celestial Blue, 12 in.); *L. tenuior* (Blue, White Eye, 12 in.). (PERENNIAL)—*L. cardinalis* (Crimson-scarlet, 24–36 in.); *L. fulgens* (Scarlet, 30 in.); *L. syphilitica* (Blue and White, 24–30 in.). All June to Sept. *Named Varieties*—*Kimbridge* (Magenta); *B. Ladhams* (Scarlet); *Queen Victoria* (Red); *Purple Emperor, Salmon Queen*.

Lonicera (Honeysuckle)—Genus comprising all the trailing and climbing hardy and half-hardy deciduous or evergreen plants known as Honeysuckles. These thrive in any good, moderately dry garden soil and frequently in shaded positions. *Culture*—Strike cuttings of ripe shoots in the open in late summer; let the cuttings stand in the bed for a year, then plant out from Oct. to Apr. If preferred, propagate by layering or from seed. After flowering cut away old wood and trim back shoots. For garden use *L. Periclymenum var. belgica* and *L. P. var, serotina*, the early and late Dutch honeysuckles, are excellent. *L. sempervirens* forms a beautiful greenhouse climber, and *L. Standishii* and *L. fragrantissima* (Bush Honeysuckles) flower outside early in Feb. *Pot Culture*—Pot-up in late autumn in a compost of sandy loam, leaf-mould and rotten manure, and keep in a cold house until Feb., then move to a sunny position in the cool house; the plants may be stood out from June to Oct.

Lophospermum—Half-hardy annual climbers which thrive in ordinary rich soil in warm sheltered positions outdoors, or in the cool greenhouse. For culture, *see* Maurandia.

Lotus (Bird's Foot Trefoil)—Hardy perennial species that grow well in ordinary soil and are well suited for sunny borders or for the rock garden. For culture, *see* Perennials, p. 281. *Species*—*L. corniculatus* (Yellow, July–Aug., 6 in.); *L. Bertholetti, syn. peliorhynchus* (Scarlet. June, 10 in.); *Tetragonolobus purpureus* (Purple, July–Sept., 6–12 in.).

Lupinus (Lupins)—Hardy annuals and perennials valuable for borders and wild garden; the dwarf species are excellent for bedding. They thrive in light, rich and well-drained soil deficient in lime and in sunny positions. For culture, *see* Annuals, p. 123, *and* Perennials, p. 281. Stake the plants early, cut the stems to the ground after blooming, and mulch with well-decayed manure. *Species and Varieties*—(ANNUALS)—*L. Hartwegii* (Pale Blue); *L. nanus* (Lilac Blue and White). (PERENNIALS)—*L. arboreus* (Yellow, White and Blue); *L. leucophyllus* (Rose-pink); *L. polyphyllus* (Blue, White and Rose). All May to Oct., 12 to 60 in. *Named Varieties*—(White) *Snowbird;* (Cream) *Mrs. Morris;* (Yellow) *Canary Bird;* (Coral Pink) *George Russell;* (Salmon) *Nellie Allen;* (Crimson) *Downer's Delight;* (Blue) *Lady Diana Abdy;* (Blue and White) *Admiration;* (Purple) *Ruth Phillips;* (Violet and White) *Jane Ayr.*

Lychnis (Catchfly, Campion, Ragged-Robin, Rose of Heaven)—Hardy annuals, biennials and perennials which thrive in any good soil, especially in rich light loam, and like a sunny position; the rock garden species need a gritty loam. For culture, *see* Annuals, p. 123, Biennials, p. 125, *and* Perennials, p. 281. *Species and Varieties*—*L. alpina* (Rose, Apr.–June, 6 in.); *L. chalcedonica* (Scarlet and White, June–Sept., 30 in.); *L. fulgens* (Salmon, June–Sept., 12 in.); *L. Haageana* (Crimson, July–Aug., 12 in.); *L. Viscaria splendens fl. pl.* (Rose, June–July, 12–18 in.).

Lycium chinense (Box Thorn)—Hardy deciduous climbing shrubs which thrive in shrub borders and against sunny walls. *Culture*—Strike cuttings of ripe shoots, or layer in the open in Oct. Let the cuttings stand in the beds for a year, then plant out from Oct. to Mar. In winter cut out weak shoots and top strong shoots.

Lysimachia (Creeping Jenny, Moneywort, or Loosestrife)—These herbaceous perennials do best in moist, rich, ordinary soil in semi-shade. The low-growing species make excellent subjects for carpeting in the rock garden; the taller kinds for border or wild garden. *Culture*—Propagate by means of division in Apr. or Oct., no protection is required during winter. *Species*—(TALL)—*L. clethroides* (White, 30 in.); *L. punctata* (Yellow, 30 in.). (DWARF) *L. Nummularia aurea* (Creeping Jenny) (Yellow, Trailer). All June to Sept.

Lythrum (Purple Loosestrife)—Hardy perennials thriving in rich, sandy soil in shady, moist borders, or in the wild garden. For culture, *see* Perennials, p. 281. *Species*—*L. Salicaria* (Purple and Rose, 50 in.); *L. virgatum* (Rose Queen) (Rose, 40 in.). All June to Sept.

Macleaya [*Bocconia*] (Plume Poppy)—Hardy perennial which thrives in sunny borders and light, rich soil. For culture, *see* Perennials, p. 281. *Species*—*M. cordata* (Whitish-cream, June–Oct., 70 in.); *M. microcarpa* (Creamy-bronze, June–Oct., 90 in.).

Magnolia—Hardy and half-hardy deciduous and evergreen shrubs to which a good, deep, well-drained loam with ample leaf-mould and a sunny position are essential. Transplant as little as possible, and prune when required (which is but rarely) in summer. *Culture (Hardy Species)*—*M. denudata, M. Soulangiana* and *M. stellata,* etc. Plant in Apr. or Oct. Propagate by means of grafting under glass in spring, layering, cuttings and seeds. *M. grandiflora:* Plant in Apr. or Sept. To propagate, sow seed in a frame, strike cuttings of matured wood of the current year in heat in July, or layer during that period. *Pot Culture* (generally *M. stellata*)—Pot-up in Oct. or Nov., using 8 to 12-in. pots and a compost of sandy loam, leaf-mould and rotten manure. After flowering prune out weak wood and dead flower shoots, and sink the pots to their rims in ashes outdoors from May to Dec., when the pots should be moved into the house.

Maianthemum (Twin-leaved Lily of the Valley)—Beautiful little hardy perennials, useful for carpeting in the rock garden, and which like a mixture of loam and leaf-mould and a shady position. *Culture*—Propagate by means of division in Apr. or Sept. (*M. bifolium,* 5 in., White flowers.)

Malope (Mallow-wort)—Tall hardy annuals useful for sunny beds or borders. For culture, *see* Annuals, p. 123. *Species*—*M. trifida* (Crimson, Red and White).

Malus (Crabs)—Genus of hardy deciduous trees at one time included in Pyrus. Most species bear delicate blossom and ornamental fruit. *Culture*—Plant in Nov. in sunny position, sheltered from cold winds. *Pot Culture*—Pot-up annually (when small) in Oct., using 8 to 12-in. pots and a compost of 2 parts of sandy loam to 1 of leaf-mould and rotted manure. In Dec. propagate by means of seed, budding or grafting. There are numerous species and varieties.

Malva (Marsh Mallow)—Hardy and half-hardy annuals and perennials which like a well-drained border of ordinary soil and a sunny position. For culture, *see* Annuals, p. 123, *and* Perennials, p. 281. *Species*—(HARDY ANNUALS)—*M. crispa* (White, 60 in.). (HARDY PERENNIALS)—*M. Alcea* (Purplish-red, 50 in.); *M. moschata* (Rose and White, 30 in.). All June to Sept.

Marguerite (Chrysanthemum frutescens)—These popular half-hardy plants like a soil that is not too rich. *Culture*—Sow under glass in Apr., or strike cuttings of young shoots in a cold frame in Sept.; protect in severe weather. Pot-up into 4-in. pots in Mar., harden-off and plant out towards the end of May, or re-pot into 6-in. pots, harden-off, and stand on ashes in the open until Sept., then move into 7-in. pots and transfer to a cool, but frost-proof, house for the winter. Young plants grown on for pot culture should be "stopped" during the spring and summer. *Varieties*—*Broussonetii* (White, Single); *Etoile d'Or* (Yellow); and *Queen Alexandra* (White, Double).

Marvel of Peru (Mirabilis)—Genus of greenhouse and hardy perennials which grow best in sunny positions and in a light, rich loam, but do well in any good garden soil. They are best treated in the same manner as dahlias, and can be grown from seeds sown in gentle heat from Mar. to Apr., hardened-off and planted out in May. (*Mirabilis Jalapa,* Red, Pink and White.)

Maurandia—Beautiful, but somewhat tender, deciduous climbers which will grow in the open in rich, ordinary soil in a warm, sheltered position. *Culture*—Sow in heat in Mar., or strike cuttings of young shoots under glass in summer. Plant out in June. *Pot Culture*—Pot-up in Mar., using 6 to 7-in. pots and a compost of 2 parts of loam to 1 part of leaf-mould and sand. Trim straggly shoots in autumn. *Species*—*M. Barclaiana* (Violet-purple); *M. erubescens* (Rose); and *M. scandens* (Purple). All July to Sept., 10 ft.

Mazus—Hardy creeping perennials that are excellent for the paved or rock garden, and which thrive in a mixture of well-drained loam and leaf-mould and in sunny positions. For culture, *see* Rock Plants, p. 283. *Species*—*M. Pumilio* (Purple-mauve); *M. reptans* (Mauve).

Meconopsis—The best of this genus are hardy herbaceous perennials or biennials. They thrive in gritty loam and peat, and in partial shade in borders or rock garden. For culture, *see* Rock Plants, p. 125 *and* Perennials, p. 281. *Species*—(BIENNIAL)—*M. integrifolia* (Yellow, 15–20 in.); *M. Prattii* (Blue-purple, 20–36 in.); *M. regia* (Yellow, 4–5 ft.); *M. Wallichii* (Pale Blue, 4–6 ft.). (PERENNIAL)—*M. betonicifolia* (Blue, 3–4 ft.); *M. cambrica fl. pl.* (Yellow, Orange, Double, 12–18 in.). All May to Aug.

Mentzelia Lindleyi (Bartonia)—Pretty little hardy annual for the border or rock garden. It grows to a height of 15 in. and bears yellow flowers from June to Oct. For culture, *see* Annuals, p. 123.

Menyanthes trifoliata (Bog Bean)—Hardy perennial which thrives in ordinary soil and a sunny position in bog or in still, shallow water. It bears rosy lilac flowers from Mar. to June. *Culture*—Strike cuttings in mud in summer; plant out in Mar.

Mertensia (Lungwort and Oyster Plant)—Hardy perennials which thrive in almost any moist, cool soil with a little peat in it in shady borders or in the rock garden. For culture, *see* Perennials, p. 281. *Species*—*M. echioides* (Blue); *M. maritima* (Pink, later Blue); *M. primuloides* (Deep-blue, Yellow Centre); *M. virginica* (Purple and Blue, 24 in.). All May to Aug., 4 to 24 in.

Michaelmas Daisy (Starwort)—Hardy perennial asters which thrive in the sun in ordinary well-drained soil and are excellent for borders and wild gardens; while the dwarf kinds make excellent subjects for the rock garden. They flower from July to Nov., and grow from 6 in. to 6 ft. in height according to species. For culture, *see* Perennials, p. 281. NAMED VARIETIES OF A. AMELLUS—*Beauté Parfait* (Dark Blue); *Beauty of Ronsdorf* (Mauve); *King George* (Purple-blue); and *Perry's Favourite* (Pale Pink). NAMED VARIETIES OF A. CORDIFOLIUS—*Diana* (Lilac) and *Silver Spray* (Pale Lilac). NAMED VARIETIES OF A. ERICOIDES—*Enchantress* (Pink); *Ophir* (Mauve); *Perfection* (White); and *Simplicity* (Blue). NAMED VARIETIES OF A. NOVÆ ANGLIÆ—*Barr's Pink* (Pink); *Mrs. F. J. Rayner* (Crimson); and *Purple Prince* (Purple). NAMED VARIETIES OF A. NOVI BELGII—*Aldenham Pink* (Pink); *Beauty of Colwall* (Blue); *Beechwood Rival* (Red Shade); *The Bishop* (Purple); *Climax* (Heliotrope-blue); *The Sexton* (Rich Blue); *King of the Belgians* (Pale Mauve).

Michauxia—Tall hardy biennials which thrive in moist, sandy loam in sunny borders. *See* Biennials, p. 125. *Species*—*M. campanuloides* (Pink, July–Aug., 50 in.).

Mignonette (Reseda odorata)—Sweet-scented perennial that is commonly grown as an annual; it likes a fairly rich soil with lime in it and a sunny position. For culture, *see* Annuals, p. 123. Seedlings grown in the open should not be transplanted. *Pot Culture*—Sow in pots under glass in Mar., June, Aug. and Sept., using a compost of 2 parts of loam to 1 part of rotted cow-manure and a little crushed lime-rubble and sand, and placing several seeds in each 6-in. pot. Thin to four plants in each pot and stand near the glass or grow in a frame. Cut off all dead flowers, and prune back straggly shoots. *Named Varieties—Crimson Giant; Golden Gem; Pearl* (Cream); *Machet* (Buff); *Salmon Queen* (Salmon-pink); *Giant Red* (Red). All July to Sept., 9 to 18 in.

Mimulus (Musk or Monkey Flower)—Hardy and half-hardy annuals and hardy perennials. Seed of the annuals sown in spring makes good bedding plants, and seed sown in autumn produces early-flowering plants for the greenhouse. They like a shady site with moist, rich soil. The smaller species are useful for edging and for the rock garden. For culture, *see* Annuals, p. 123, *and* Perennials, p. 281. *Pot Culture*—Pot-up in May, using 5 to 6-in. pots and a compost of 2 parts of loam and 1 part of leaf-mould, peat and sand. Pinch back to make bushy, and keep cool in winter. *Species and Varieties*—HALF-HARDY ANNUAL—*M. tigrinus* (Yellow, Spotted, June, 9 in.). HARDY PERENNIALS—*M. Burnetii* (Pale Brown, 10 in.); *M. cardinalis* (Scarlet, 20 in.); *M. cupreus* (Orange, 12 in.); *M. luteus* (Yellow Spotted, 9 in.); *M. moschatus* (Yellow, 6 in.); *M. ringens* (Pale-blue, 10 in.). All flower from June to Aug.

Mistletoe (Viscum album)—This parasite is easy to cultivate; an incision should be made in the bark on the underside of a three-year-old branch of an apple tree—many other trees, such as the pear, plum, ash, birch, etc., answer equally well—and in Feb. into this incision insert some ripe mistletoe berries, and carefully tie the bark over with a piece of bass, or woollen yarn. Growth is exceedingly slow at first.

Mitraria coccinea (Mitre Flower)—Half-hardy evergreen shrub that will grow outdoors during summer in warm, semi-shaded and sheltered situations. Plant in Apr. in moist, peaty soil. *Pot Culture*—Pot-up in Mar. in a compost of two-thirds turfy peat and one-third sand. To propagate, strike cuttings of young shoots in a frame in summer.

Monarda (Bee's Balm, Horse Mint, Oswego Tea, Red Sage or Bergamot)—Useful perennials thriving in deep, moist loam in sunny borders. They will, however, grow anywhere. For culture, *see* Perennials, p. 281. *Species*—*M. didyma* (Red, July–Sept., 24 in.); *M. fistulosa* (Pink, July–Sept., 24 in.). *Varieties*—*Rose Queen, Sunset* (Purple).

Montbretia—*See* Tritonia.

Morina (Whorl-flower)—Half-hardy and hardy perennials, excellent for the border or rock garden. They like a warm, sunny position and a rich gritty loam. In exposed districts winter in a frame. Sow in Mar., or propagate by offsets. *Species*—*M. longifolia* (Rose and White); *M. persica* (Pink). Both July to Aug., 30 in.

Morisia monantha [*syn. hypogæa*] (Mediterranean Cress)—Hardy little summer-flowering rock plants which thrive in well-drained, deep, gritty loam in an open, fairly sunny spot. *See* Rock Plants, p. 283.

Morus (Mulberry)—Hardy deciduous trees which thrive in the sun in deep, moist but well-drained ordinary soil. They grow 25 to 30 ft. high and flower in May and June. *Culture*—Plant in Oct., and do not shorten the long tap roots; little pruning is necessary. Propagate by means of cuttings or layers in Oct.

Muscari (Grape Hyacinth)—Hardy bulbous plants which thrive in good loam in warm, sunny borders or in the rock garden, or in pots. *Culture*—Plant in Oct. from 2 to 3 in. deep and 3 in. apart; lift from the ground only when overcrowded. Propagate by means of offsets in Oct. *Pot Culture*—Pot-up annually in Oct., 1½ in. deep in 5-in. pots; dry-off in a cold frame after flowering. *Species*—(EARLY)—*M. botryoides* (Blue and White varieties, Feb.-

Mar., 6 in.). (LATE)—*M. conicum var. Heavenly Blue* (Sky-blue, Apr.–May, 8 in.). *M. racemosum* (Deep Blue, Apr.–May, 6 in.).

Mutisia—Hardy climbing plant usually grown in the cold greenhouse. *Culture*—Pot-up in a large pot in a compost of two-thirds loam and one-third leaf-mould and ample sand. Water liberally and syringe from May to July, but keep only just moist during the autumn and winter. *Species—M. decurrens* (Orange-Yellow, July, 12 ft.); *M. Clematis* (Red, July, 20 ft.).

Myosotidium—Half-hardy perennial which needs a warm, sunny position and a fairly rich and moist soil. Propagation is by seed sown in May and June, or by root-cuttings in Oct. *Variety—M. nobile* (Blue and Cream, May, 20 in.).

Myrtle (Myrtus)—Beautiful evergreen greenhouse shrubs which will grow out of doors in warm, sunny and sheltered situations. *Culture*—Plant in May or Sept. in loam and leaf-mould; the addition of a little peat is beneficial. Trim in Apr., not in autumn. *Pot Culture*—Pot-up in Mar. (triennially), using 5 to 12-in. pots and a compost of 2 parts of sandy loam to 1 part of leaf-mould; stand outdoors from July to Oct., and prune in Feb. To propagate strike cuttings in a frame in July, or layer in Sept.

Narcissus—Beautiful hardy bulbs which are excellent for beds, borders, the rock garden (most species), for naturalizing in grass, and for pots. Most species thrive in well-dug and well-drained ordinary soil, though some few, notably the *Hooped Petticoat,* the *Cyclamen-flowered* and the *Angel's Tears,* prefer warm, deep and moist sandy loam; the *Polyanthus Narcissi* like a rather stiff soil. Partial shade is desirable, but they will grow well in full sun. *Culture*—Plant from Aug. to Oct., the sooner the better, 4 in. deep in heavy soil and 7 in. deep in light soil, and about 4 in. apart, making exception of small species which should be 2 to 3 in. deep, and the May-flowering double white narcissus, which must be not less than 9 in. deep in well-worked moist loam. If used for naturalizing, the bulbs should be left in the ground, but in beds or borders they should be raised triennially in July. *Greenhouse Culture*—Pot-up from Aug. to Nov., using a compost of half fibrous loam to a quarter part each of sand and leaf-mould or rotten manure, and place from three large to twelve small bulbs in a 4 to 5-in. pot and keep in the open in a cool, shady site under a 3-in. layer of coconut fibre until growth commences, then move into the cool house in batches. Dry-off when the foliage dies and plant out in the open the following year. The bulbs of the Polyanthus Narcissus being large, a 5-in. pot will be needed for a single specimen. Daffodils will not stand forcing, and only gentle heat should be used. Propagate by means of offsets at lifting time, re-planting the offsets immediately in a reserve garden; seed may also be sown in pans or boxes in Aug., but they take four to six years to flower. *See also chapter on* Bulb Growing. *Named Varieties*—TRUMPET (Trumpet as long or longer than the perianth segments)—(White) *Beersheba;* (Yellow) *Golden Spur;* (Bi-color; White or cream perianth with yellow trumpet) *Queen of the Bicolors.* SHORT CUP OR INCOMPARABILIS (Cup not less than one-third, but less than equal to the length of the perianth segments, outer petals yellow or white, cup yellow or red)—*Criterion, Damson* and *Sir Watkin.* BARRI (Cup not less than one-third the length of the perianth segments; bright-coloured cups, perianths yellow or white)—*Chinese White, La Riante,* and *Firetail.* LEEDSII OR EUCHARIS-FLOWERED (Outer petals white, with white or pale yellow or cream cups, sometimes tinged pink)—*Bridesmaid, Duchess of Westminster* and *White Lady.* TRIANDRUS OR " ANGEL'S TEARS " (Short cup and reflexed outer petals)—*Agnes Harvey, Queen of Spain* and *Venetia.* CYCLAMEN-FLOWERED

(Pale yellow with darker and very narrow trumpet)—*N. cyclamineus.*
JONQUIL-FLOWERED—*Buttercup, Jonquilla* and *N. odorus rugulosus.* TAZETTA
OR POLYANTHUS (These are all bunch-flowered and white with yellow cups)—
Cheerfulness, St. Agnes and *Paper White.* POETICUS OR POET'S (Petals white
or yellow with red eye)—*Actæa, Sarchedon, White Standard* and *Pheasant's
Eye.* DOUBLE—*Butter and Eggs, Inglescombe* and *Telemonius plenus.* See
also catalogues.

Nasturtium (Tropæolum majus and nanum)—Many varieties are well
known as climbers; the dwarf varieties are useful for bedding or edging, and
for the rock garden. *Culture*—Sow thinly from Mar. to June ½ in. deep in
light, poor soil, and thin-out to from 12 to 18 in. apart when fit to handle.
The double varieties do not seed, and cuttings must be struck in a cold
frame in Aug. or Sept.

Nemesia—Half-hardy annuals which make excellent bedding, rock garden
or pot plants. For culture, *see* Annuals, p. 123. *Species*—*N. floribunda*
(White and Yellow); *N. strumosa* (Red, Pink, Orange, Yellow, Blue and
White); *N. versicolor* (White and Mauve). *Named Varieties*—*Aurora* (Red
and White); *Blue Gem; Cherry Red; Orange Prince;* and *Twilight* (Mauve
and White). All June to Sept., 12 in.

Nemophila (Californian Bluebell)—Dwarf-growing hardy annuals for
edgings to sunny beds, or for the rock garden. For culture, *see* Annuals,
p. 123. *Species*—*N. insignis* (Sky-blue, White Centre); *N. Menziesii* (Purple,
Blue, White, blotched Black); *N. M. discoidalis* (Maroon and White). All
July to Sept., 3 to 9 in.

Nepeta (Catmint)—Hardy perennials which thrive in sunny positions and
in ordinary soil, and are useful for edgings to large borders, or for the rock
garden. For culture, *see* Perennials, p. 281. *Species*—*N. hederacea* and
N. Faassenii. Both Blue, May to Sept., 18 in.

Nerine—Beautiful bulbous plants which thrive in the cool greenhouse in rich
loam, mixed with leaf-mould, cow-manure and sand. *Culture*—Plant singly in
Aug. in 4 to 5-in. pots, water well when the flower buds appear and feed with
liquid manure. Keep dry from June to Aug., with the pots exposed to the sun,
and when the flower shoots again rise soak the pots and top-dress with fresh
soil. Re-pot every fourth year, and propagate by offsets in Aug., or sow seed
when ripe. *Species and Varieties*—*N. Bowdenii* (Pink); *N. curvifolia, var.
Fothergillii major* (Scarlet); *N. pudica* (White); *N. sarniensis* (Pale Salmon);
N. s. var. corusca (Orange-scarlet); many hybrids. All Sept. to Dec.. 20 in.

Nerium—The best known of this genus of evergreen shrubs is *N. Oleander,*
the Common Oleander. The blossoms and wood are *poisonous. Culture*—
Pot when required in Feb., using 6 to 12-in. pots and a compost of 2 parts
loam to 1 of leaf-mould, peat and a little sand. Keep in a sunny position in
the cool greenhouse, and sponge the leaves frequently. Remove the shoots
at the base of the flower buds, and prune to within three buds of the old
wood. Keep fairly dry during winter. To propagate, place cuttings of well-
ripened shoots in bottles of water, in a sunny frame in summer; when well
rooted, pot-up in light soil and "stop" from time to time.

Nertera depressa (Coral-berried Duckweed)—Dwarf-growing creeping
plant, for the rock garden, or for edging. It thrives in the shade in warm,
moist, sandy loam and leaf-mould, but must be protected from frost. For
culture, *see* Rock Plants, p. 283.

Nicotiana (Tobacco Plant)—Although treated as annuals, tobacco plants
are perennials, and if the roots are protected from frost they will come up
again year after year. Among the sorts usually grown are *N. alata* and *N.*

Sanderæ. The first has white flowers, fragrant in the evening; the second bears red or white flowers, but these are not so fragrant. They thrive in rich soil in sunny beds and borders. For culture, *see* Annuals, p. 123. For greenhouse use, seed sown in a frame in Aug. will furnish bloom from Jan. to Mar.

Nierembergia (Cup Flower)—Half-hardy perennials which thrive in moist loam in a sunny position. *N. repens, syn. rivularis,* with creamy-white flowers streaked with purple, from June to Aug., is a useful little rock plant. For culture, *see* Rock Plants, p. 283.

Nigella (Devil-in-a-Bush, Love-in-a-Mist, Jack-in-Prison)—Hardy annuals useful for sunny beds and borders. For culture, *see* Annuals, p. 123. *Species and Varieties—N. damascena* (Pale Blue or White); *N. hispanica* (Deep Purple); *N. Miss Jekyll* (Deep Blue, double); *N. orientalis* (Yellow and Red). All June to Sept., 18 in.

Nuphar—Genus numbering but a few species, among which is *N. luteum,* the Yellow Water Lily. This is hardy and, like all of its kind, may be grown in a pond or slow stream, and managed in the same way as Nymphæa, *which see. Species—N. advena* and *N. lutea.* Both Yellow, June to Aug., 12 to 18 in.

Nymphæa—Genus of water-lilies including the common White Water Lily. The hardy species have white, rose, orange, or yellow flowers. Most species like a sunny, sheltered position in slow-moving water; those from hot countries require a hothouse. *Culture*—Sow seed in spring in rich loam in a basket under water, or propagate by means of division from Apr. to June and plant in rich loam, leaf-mould and cow-dung in weighted openwork baskets sunk so that there is from 12 to 60 in. of water above the crowns, according to species. Many good species and hybrids.

Nymphoides peltatum (Limnanthemum nymphoides) (Fringed Golden Buck Bean)—Hardy aquatic plants, flowering in July and Aug., and enjoying a sunny position in slow-moving water. Sow seed, or propagate by division in Mar., and plant with not more than 12 in. of water above the crowns.

Nyssa sylvatica (Tupelo Tree)—Hardy deciduous tree thriving in moist deep loam, or any good soil in sunny positions. *Culture*—Plant in Nov. (as young as possible). No pruning is necessary. Propagate by means of seed or layering. It does not transplant well.

Œnothera (Evening Primrose, Godetia)—Annuals, biennials and perennials, for bedding, borders, or for the rock garden, and also grown in the greenhouse. All the species thrive in rich, sandy loam, or any good soil, and in sunny positions. For annuals, *see* Godetia, and for culture of the Evening Primrose, *see* Biennials, p. 125, *and* Perennials, p. 281. The genus is sometimes split up. *Species*—(BIENNIAL)—*O.* (*Lavauxia*) *acaulis* (White, tinted Rose, 10 in.); *O. biennis grandiflora* (Pale Yellow, 30 in.); (PERENNIAL)—*O.* (*Pachylophus*) *cæspitosa* (Pale Yellow or White, 4–6 in.); *O.* (*Kneiffia*) *grauca Fraseri* (Golden Yellow, 20 in.); *O.* (*Megapterium*) *missourensis* (Yellow, Trailer); *O.* (*Hartmannia*) *speciosa* (White to Rose, 30 in.). All June to Oct. flowering.

Olearia Haastii (New Zealand Daisy Bush)—Hardy evergreen shrubs from 4 to 9 ft. high and bearing white flowers in late summer. They like a sheltered position and well-drained soil. *Culture*—Plant in May or Oct. Trim to shape when necessary in Mar., and every four or five years, cut hard back. *Pot Culture of Greenhouse Species*—In the cool greenhouse they may be had in flower in Mar. Pot-up when required in Oct., using 6 to 7-in. pots and a compost of 2 parts of sandy loam to 1 part of leaf-mould and rotten manure. Sink the pots in ashes in a sunny spot outdoors from May to Dec., then take indoors and keep fairly dry until growth starts. To propagate, sow in a frame in Mar., or strike cuttings in a frame in Sept.

Omphalodes (Creeping or Rock Forget-Me-Not, Navelwort)—Annual and perennial creeping plants for semi-shade in the border or rock garden and loving a moist, sandy or gritty loam. For culture, *see* Annuals, p. 123, *and* Perennials, p. 281. *Species*—(ANNUAL)—*O. linifolia* (White, July, 9 in.). (PERENNIAL)—*O. cornifolia* [*O. cappadocica*] (Porcelain Blue, May–June, 9 in.); *O. Luciliæ* (Lilac Blue, June–Sept., 6 in.); *O. verna* (Porcelain Blue, Apr.–May, 4 in.).

Ononis (Rest Harrow)—Hardy perennials which thrive in sunny rock gardens and in almost any soil. For culture, *see* Rock Plants, p. 283. *Species* —*O. fruticosa* (Purple-pink, May–Aug., 24–36 in.); *O. spinosa* (Rose-purple, July–Sept., 10 in.).

Onosma (Alpine Comfrey)—Hardy perennial and biennial rock plants which thrive in well-drained, gritty loam, peat and sand on hot, sunny ledges. Sow under glass in Mar., or strike cuttings in summer. *Species*—*O. alboroseum* (White, tinged Rose); *O. stellulatum* (Yellow); *O. tauricum* (Lemon-yellow). All June to July.

Orange (Citrus—Dwarf)—The dwarf fruiting species which are usually grown in the cool greenhouse are grafted plants. They thrive in a compost of three-quarters turfy loam and one-quarter leaf-mould, rotten manure and sand. In winter they need full sun, but in summer should be shaded from direct sun. Thin to shape only. The trees may be propagated by seed in gentle heat (65° F.), by budding in July, or by grafting in Mar.; but cuttings struck in spring produce bushes which fruit earlier. The culture of the lemon (*Citrus Limonum*) and the lime (*Citrus aurantiifolia*) is identical with that of the orange.

Orchids—Besides the numerous beautiful orchids which may be grown in the greenhouse, there are many hardy species which thrive outdoors in sheltered borders, in the rock garden or bog garden, notably the *Calopogon, Calypso, Cypripedium* (*Lady's Slipper*), *Epipactis, Goodyera* (*Adder's Violet*), *Habenaria* (*Butterfly Orchid*), *Listera, Ophrys* (*Bee and Fly Orchis*), *Orchis Serapias and Spiranthes* (*Ladies' Tresses*). Most of these thrive in moist, sandy loam and leaf-mould or peat and in semi-shaded positions; the *Ophrys, Orchis* and *Spiranthes* like a sunny position. Propagate most species by division in spring or autumn; in some cases by offsets. Greenhouse orchids vary considerably in their requirements and need careful attention. Space does not permit of these being dealt with thoroughly, and the reader is referred to a work devoted to orchid-growing.

Ornithogalum (Star of Bethlehem)—Hardy and half-hardy bulbous-rooted plants, for warm borders, for the rock garden and naturalizing in grass, and (chiefly *O. arabicum*) for pots. They 'hrive in ordinary soil in sun or semi-shade. *Culture*—Plant from Sept. to Oct., $3\frac{1}{2}$ in. deep and 3 in. apart, and protect from frost in winter. *Pot Culture*—Pot-up from Aug. to Nov., placing three bulbs in a 6-in. pot, or singly in a smaller pot, and using a compost of 2 parts of turfy loam to 1 part of leaf-mould and sand; grow near the glass in a cold greenhouse. Propagate by means of offsets. *Species*—*O. arabicum* (White with Black Centre, May and June, 30 in.); *O. nutans* [Wild Hyacinth] (Greenish-white, May, 15 in.); *O. umbellatum* (White, Green Streaks, May, 10–15 in.).

Orontium aquaticum (Golden Club)—Hardy aquatic plants which thrive in slow-moving water. Propagate by means of root division in Mar., and plant with from 6 to 12 in. of water above the crowns.

Osmanthus—Hardy evergreen shrubs, some of which resemble hollies. *Culture*—Plant in May or Sept. in sandy loam in sun or partial shade. No pruning is necessary, but long straggling shoots should be cut back in June. To propagate, strike cuttings of ripened shoots in a frame in Sept., or layer in summer. *O. Delavayi* (White, Mar. and Apr., 4–6 ft.) is the best species. *O. ilicifolius* has small, fragrant, white flowers in late autumn.

Osmaronia (Nuttallia) cerasiformis (Osoberry)—Hardy deciduous shrub growing from 5 to 10 ft. high, and bearing white flowers from Feb. to Mar. *Culture*—Plant in Oct. or Nov. in sun or semi-shade and in ordinary soil; thin-out old wood when overcrowded.

Ourisia—Hardy perennial creeping plants which thrive in moist sandy loam in the shade, and are excellent for moist ledges in the rock garden. For culture, *see* Rock Plants, p. 283. *Species*—*O. coccinea* (Scarlet, May–Sept., 9 in.) is the best.

Oxalis (Cape Shamrock, Wood Sorrel)—Hardy and half-hardy annuals, perennials, and bulbous plants admirably adapted for pots, warm borders, and the rock garden. They succeed in any well-drained, light, sandy soil and leaf-mould; the rock garden species need a gritty loam and a position in semi-shade. For culture of Annuals, *see* p. 123, *and* Perennials, p. 281. (*Bulbous Species*)—Plant from Sept. to Nov. 3 in deep and 10 in. apart. Hardy species should not be lifted from the ground, but half-hardy kinds must. In light warm soils, however, protection from frost by means of ashes or fibre will be sufficient. Propagation is by means of small bulbs removed from the parent and planted in Sept. *Pot Culture*—Pot-up in Mar. ¾ in. deep, in 5 to 6-in. pots in a compost of 2 parts of sandy loam to 1 of leaf-mould. *See* Bulbs, p. 141. *Species and Varieties*—(ANNUAL)—*O. corniculata* (Yellow, Aug.–Oct., 4 in.), *O. rosea* (Rosy, 15 in.). (PERENNIAL)—*O. adenophylla* (Lilac-pink, dark Eye, May–July, 5 in.); *O. enneaphylla* (White, May–Sept., 6 in.); *O. floribunda* (Red, Rose, Mauve or White, Mar., 6 in.); *O. lobata* (Yellow, Sept.–Oct., 4 in.); *O. purpurata* (Carmine, Aug.–Sept., 8 in.); *O. tuberosa* (Rose, Oct.–Nov., 6 in.).

Oxydendrum arboreum (Sorrel Tree)—Hardy deciduous trees, which thrive in a loamy or peaty soil and in a sheltered position. They grow some 20 ft. high and bear white flowers in July and Aug. Plant in May or Oct. To propagate, sow in a frame in Mar.

Ozothamnus rosmarinifolius (Snow in Summer)—Dark evergreen half-hardy shrub (8–10 ft.), bearing white flowers in May and June. It needs the protection of a wall. Plant in rich loam or peat in a sunny site, and propagate by cuttings of young wood in a frame.

Pæonia—Pæonies are divided into two classes, the *herbaceous*, and the *tree or shrubby*. They are mostly hardy and thrive in sun or partial shade in sheltered beds, in well-dug loam enriched with rotten cow-dung, but they will grow in almost any soil. *Culture*—(*Herbaceous*)—Propagate by means of division in Apr. or Oct. and plant out 3 ft. apart, with the crowns 3 in. deep. Transplant as little as possible, never oftener than every five years, and if root divisions are required, they should be cut out with the plant *in situ*. Mulch with well-decayed manure each spring. (*P. Moutan, the Tree or Shrubby Species*)—Plant in Sept. or early Oct., and protect from frost. If given gentle forcing in pots, they will furnish early blooms, but force only in alternate years. Increase by layering or by grafting on *P. officinalis* and *Moutan* stock. *Varieties*—(HERBACEOUS). (Single)—(White) *Bridesmaid;* (White and Pink) *Eastern Brocade;* (Rose-pink) *Avant Garde;* (Deep Pink) *Eva;* (Salmon) *Kelway's Gorgeous;* (Yellow) *Lemon Queen;* (Cherry Red) *Lord Kitchener;* and (Crimson) *Victor Hugo.* (Double) (Large White) *Duchess de Nemours;* (Blush-white) *Lady Alexander Duff;* (Coral-pink) *Kel-*

way's David; (Bright Pink) *Natalie;* (Crimson) *President Poincaré;* (Crimson) *Richard Carvell;* and (Purple) *Louis Van Houtte.* All May to July flowering. P. MOUTAN (TREE PÆONY)—(Single)—(White) *Queen Alexandra;* (Salmon-pink) *Countess of Crewe;* and (Crimson) *Eastern Queen.* (Double)—(White) *Aphrodite;* (Flesh-pink) *Duchess of Marlborough;* (Rose) *Reine Elizabeth;* and (Scarlet) *Eastern Prince.* All flower in June.

Palms—Some species require a considerable amount of heat, but such species as the *Areca* (Betel-nut Palm), *Chamærops* (Fan Palm), *Corypha* (Cabbage Palm), *Howea* (Curly Palm), and *Phœnix* (Date Palm), may be grown easily in a house merely protected from frost. Palms are usually bought by the amateur as small plants, and should be re-potted in a compost of fibrous loam and silver sand, or fibrous peat and grit. Spring or early summer is the best time for potting. The roots must not be injured and they must be planted firmly the same depth as before. Water well both summer and winter, sponge the leaves with warm soft water, and syringe morning and evening in spring and summer. Partial shade is required in hot weather, and a little liquid manure made from cow-manure and soot is beneficial, and should the foliage turn yellowish, a small lump of sulphate of iron on the surface of the soil will remedy this. Propagation is usually by means of division in Apr., by suckers in Sept., or by seed.

Pancratium illyricum and P. maritimum (Mediterranean Lily, or Sea Daffodil)—Semi-hardy bulbous plants which thrive in light rich loam and peat in sunny, sheltered positions in warm and well-drained borders. There are also many stove and greenhouse species. Both plants bear white flowers in May and June on stems 18 in. high. *Culture*—Plant in Oct. or Mar., 5 in. deep and 10 in. apart. Do not lift, but protect with fibre in winter. *Pot Culture*—Re-pot every third or fourth year (in Mar.) in two-thirds loam to one-third well-rotted manure and a little sand. Dry-off gradually after blooming, and stand hardy species in the open from May to Sept. Propagate by means of offsets in Oct. or Mar.

Pansy (Heartsease)—*See* Viola.

Papaver (Poppy)—Hardy annuals, biennials, and perennials which thrive in the sun in almost any soil, though a deep, rich soil is best. They are useful for beds, borders and the wild garden. *P. alpinum* is a useful rock species; it needs a gritty loam and is raised from seed sown in autumn. All dead flowers must be picked off, or the season of blooming will be greatly reduced. For culture, *see* Annuals, p. 123, Biennials, p. 125, *and* Perennials, p. 281. The latter should not be lifted oftener than every three or four years. *Species* —(ANNUAL)—*P. glaucum* (Deep Scarlet, June–Sept., 20 in.); *P. lævigatum* (Red, White and Black, May–Sept., 25 in.); *P. somniferum* [Opium Poppy] (Crimson, Mauve, Rose, Violet and White [Double and Fringed], July–Oct., 30 in.); *P. Rhœas* [Shirley Poppy] (Orange, Pink, Red, Lavender, Blue and White [Single and Double], June–Sept., 24 in.). (BIENNIAL)—*P. alpinum* (Yellow, Salmon, White and Orange, May–Sept., 6–9 in.). (PERENNIAL) —*P. bracteatum* (Scarlet and Black, May–Sept., 36–48 in.); *P. nudicaule* [Iceland Poppy] (Orange, Yellow, Buff, Salmon and White, May–Sept., 6–24 in.); *P. orientale* (Various, May–June, 30–50 in.). *Named Varieties*— (*P. orientale*)—(White) *Perry's White;* (Cerise) *Ethel Swete;* (Scarlet) *Lord Lamborne;* (Vermilion) *Goliath;* (Orange) *Orange King;* (Salmon-pink) *Mrs. Perry.*

Paradisea Liliastrum (St. Bruno's Lily)—Beautiful bulbs which grow about 20 in. high, bear white flowers in May and June, and grow in well-drained light soil in sun or partial shade in the border or wild garden. *Culture*—Plant from 9 to 12 in. apart in Oct. or Mar., and mulch with old manure in Mar. Propagate by means of division in Sept. or Oct.

Parnassia (Grass of Parnassus)—Hardy perennials for the bog, marsh, or water garden, or for the moist shady border. *Culture*—Sow in the open in autumn, or propagate by means of division in Apr. *Species*—*P. fimbriata; P. nubicola; P. palustris.* All white, June to Aug., 5 to 10 in.

Paronychia—Little creeping plants for the paved or rock garden, which thrive in the sun in gritty loam and are propagated by means of division in Mar., by cuttings under glass, or by seed. For culture, *see* Rock Plants, p. 283.

Parrotia persica (Persian Witch Hazel)—Hardy deciduous trees growing from 30 to 40 ft. high, and which flower in Mar. They like a dry ordinary soil, and a sunny, sheltered position. *Culture*—Plant in Nov. No pruning is necessary. Propagate by means of layering in summer.

Passiflora (Passion-flower)—Genus of beautiful climbing shrubs, which grow in almost any well-drained soil, though sandy loam is best, and should be given a position against a sunny wall facing south or west; the root-run should be restricted to encourage flowering. *Culture*—Strike cuttings of young shoots in a frame in summer. Plant out in Oct. or Mar.; cut back shoots to half their length in Feb. or Mar., and cut out weak wood. *Greenhouse Culture*—Plant in Mar. in a compost of 2 parts of fibrous loam to 1 part of peat and sand, and syringe and water well in summer. Prune back to within two buds of the old wood in winter, and cut away all weak shoots in spring. *P. cærulea* (Blue, June–Sept., 25 ft.) is the most hardy; for the cool greenhouse, the white variety, *Constance Elliott* (June–Sept., 25 ft.), is recommended.

Pelargonium—There is frequent confusion over the names *geranium* and *pelargonium*. The former term covers both sections of plants, but is more generally assigned to the hardy perennial sorts (*see* Geranium). The term " pelargonium " includes all half-hardy greenhouse and bedding plants and the show varieties. All pelargoniums need a light airy position, but no draughts, and only sufficient artificial heat to keep out frost is needed. *Propagation*—About six months after cuttings are struck the plants should come into bloom; June and July are the best months for taking cuttings. The pots are prepared in the usual manner, and filled with a compost of five-eighths of loam to one-eighth part each of sand, leaf-mould, and rotted cow-manure; a liberal sprinkling of bonemeal should be added. The cuttings should be taken in dry weather when the parent plant has had no water for some days, and they should be kept dry for twenty-four hours before potting. Place five cuttings round the edge of each 4-in. pot and about an inch or an inch and a half deep. If the cuttings are struck in Aug. or Sept., the protection of a frame is not essential and the pots may be sunk in a sheltered south border, where they will require no shading unless the sun is very hot; if a frame is used, the lights should only be put on as a protection against heavy rain. Gradually harden-off the cuttings for potting-off into 3-in. pots as soon as they are rooted. If they grow too freely before it is time to take them into the house or frames (Sept.), the top shoots should be broken off; these tops may be used to provide another batch of cuttings. Through the winter months, little water and only just sufficient heat (50° F.) to exclude frost, should be given. Pick-off all flower-buds as they appear, and as the weather improves give more air. Late in Mar. or early in Apr. re-pot into 5 or 6-in. pots, so that they may be grown on to be hardened-off and planted out late in May or in early June. From Apr. onwards, plants grown for flowering in pots should receive weekly doses of weak liquid manure or soot water, and should be grown near the glass in a cool greenhouse, being pinched-back to make them bushy. Plants stopped-back not later than Feb. will flower in May; when blooming is to be delayed until July, pinching-back may be continued until towards the end of Apr. After flowering, ripen the growth in the sun in the open, then cut the stems back to from 3 to 4 in. from the base in July and rest the plants with the pots on their sides in a frame for two months. Then pot-up in fresh soil, keep in the frame, and remove all buds until the plants are moved into the house early in Sept.

Plants for Autumn and Winter Flowering—A further batch of cuttings taken from old plants " started " in gentle heat can, if desired, be struck in the spring (Mar.), and potted-up singly into 3-in. pots about May. When these pots are full of roots, move the young plants into 4-in. pots; harden-off in a cold frame ready for setting out in the open on a hard bed of ashes in June, or into the open beds, if for summer bedding. Plants for flowering indoors in autumn and winter should be stopped-back in July, and all flower buds picked off until Sept. Early in August move them into 6-in. pots and transfer to a light and airy shelf in the greenhouse at the beginning of Sept.; as the season advances a little heat (55° F.) will make the plants blossom. Zonal, Ivy-leaved, and Scarlet-leaved pelargoniums, if treated in this way, will flower in autumn and winter; Regals so treated, however, will not come into bloom until Mar., and will continue to flower until the middle of June. Plants may also be raised from seed, but this is rarely attempted by the amateur. *Varieties*—(REGAL AND DECORATIVE)—*Duchess of Kent, Brides-maid, Carisbrooke, Elsie Godfrey's Pride, Market Favourite, Magpie, Mrs. W. J. Godfrey, Pictor, Pearl, Princess Mary, Queen of the West.* (ZONAL)—Single-flowered for Pots—(Amaranth) *Amarantha;* (Scarlet) *Canopus;* (Magenta) *Mrs. Eddowes;* (Rose-pink) *Freyda;* (Salmon) *Harry Wood;* (Orange) *Janet Scott;* (Pink) *Carolina;* (Crimson-lake) *Ryecroft Gem;* (White) *Snowstorm.* Double for Pots—(Purple) *Fantome;* (Rose) *Hornsey Violet;* (Crimson) *Ryecroft Pride;* (White) *Ryecroft White.* Bedding—(Scarlet) *Paul Crampel;* (Salmon) *Salmon Crampel;* (White) *Dr. Nansen;* (Red) *Decorator.* (IVY-LEAVED)—(Rose) *Madame Crousse;* (Scarlet) *Scarlet Crousse,* and *Sir Percy Blakeney;* (Cream) *Alliance;* (White and Purple) *L'Elegant.* (SCENTED-LEAVED)—*P. crispum; P. odoratissimum;* and *P. quercifolium.*

Peltandra (Water Arrow Arum)—Beautiful hardy aquatic plants which thrive in the sun in ordinary soil at the water's edge. They grow from 24 to 36 in. high, and flower in July. Propagate by means of division of roots in Mar. *Species*—*P. virginica.*

Penstemon (Beard Tongue)—Graceful perennials, both dwarf and tall. The dwarf species are excellent for the rock garden, while the taller species make beautiful bed or border plants if treated as half-hardy biennials. All kinds thrive in a warm, sandy loam with a third-part humus in it. For culture, *see* Biennials, p. 125, *and* Perennials, p. 281. *See also* Chelone. *Species and Varieties* (ROCK GARDEN)—*P. barbatus* (Scarlet); *P. Bridgesii* (Reddish); *P. Roezlii* (Magenta, 6 in.); *P. Hartwegii* and *vars.* (Crimson); and *P. Scouleri* and *var. alba.* All June to Oct.-flowering. *Named Varieties* —(BORDER)—(Crimson) *Crimson Gem;* (Pink) *Daydream;* (Scarlet and White) *George Home;* (Mauve) *Mauve Bedder;* (Rose and White) *Mrs. Ed. Matthews;* (Crimson and Violet) *Mrs. John Forbes;* (Salmon-pink) *Montrose;* (Pink) *Pink Beauty;* (Crimson) *Southgate Gem;* (Scarlet and Cinnamon) *Thos. H. Cook;* (White) *White Bedder.* All 20 to 30 in.

Perilla nankinensis—Half-hardy annuals with purple foliage, useful for summer bedding and greenhouse. For culture, *see* Annuals, p. 123.

Pernettya mucronata (Prickly Heath)—Hardy evergreen shrubs which do well in moderate sun in cool and moist, well-drained peaty loam. *Culture*— Plant in Mar. or Oct.; no pruning is necessary. *Pot Culture*—Pot-up in Oct. or Nov., using 6 to 8-in. pots and a compost of 2 parts of peat to 1 part of leaf-mould and sand, and place in the cold greenhouse. Plant outdoors when the berries fall. To propagate, sow in a frame in Mar., take cuttings in summer, or divide roots in autumn. *Varieties*—*P. m. alba* (White berries); *P. m. atrococcinea* (Purple Berries); and *P. m. speciosa* (Crimson). All July, 2 to 5 ft.

Petasites—Hardy herbaceous plants, the most popular species of which is *P. fragrans*, the Winter Heliotrope, which grows some 10 in. high and carries whitish flowers in late winter. Almost any moist soil suits petasites well; it needs partial shade. Propagate by means of division in Feb. or Mar., or seed can be sown in May or June.

Petunia—Half-hardy soft-wooded perennials, best treated as half-hardy annuals. They like a sunny position and a moderately rich, light soil, and may be used for borders, bedding and (double varieties) for pot culture. *Culture*—*See* Annuals, p. 123. If pricked-off into pots for greenhouse use they must be potted-on frequently until in their flowering pots. Double varieties should be propagated by means of cuttings of young wood in a temperature of 60° F. in the spring, or of mature shoots in a cold frame in Aug. *Pot Culture*—Pot-up in May, using 6 to 10-in. pots and a compost of 2 parts loam to 1 part leaf-mould and dry, well-rotted manure, and keep in cool greenhouse. Pinch-back to five joints from the old stem as soon as established in the flowering pots. Early training and staking is essential. Flowering may be retarded by standing the plants in a cold frame or on a bed of ashes in the open any time after the middle of May. *Species and Varieties*—*P. violacea* (*syn. integrifolia*) and *P. axillaris* (*syn. nyctaginiflora*). (Numerous varieties, see catalogues.) June to Oct., 12 in.

Phacelia—Dwarf-growing hardy annuals, suitable for edging, for the border, or the rock garden. They like a sunny or semi-shaded position and ordinary soil. For culture, *see* Annuals, p. 123. *Species*—*P. campanularia* (Deep Blue, 8 in.); *P. tanacetifolia* (Pale Mauve, 20 in.); *P. Whitlavia* (Deep Blue, 8 in.). All June to Aug.

Phædranassa Carmioli (Queen Lily)—Half-hardy bulbous plants, growing about 18 in. high and flowering in spring. They like a well-drained, deep, sandy loam, and thrive in sunny, sheltered positions in warm borders, or in pots in the greenhouse. *Culture*—Plant 6 to 9 in. apart and 5 in. deep in Mar. or Oct., and protect with fibre in winter. Propagate by means of offsets in Mar. or Oct.

Philadelphus (Mock Orange)—Beautiful hardy deciduous flowering shrubs frequently better known under the name of Syringa, a name which rightly belongs to the Lilacs. They thrive in any good garden soil and like a sunny position. *Culture*—Plant in Oct. or Nov. Thin-out the shoots well immediately after flowering and cut back old and weak wood of the previous year to the young lateral growths at the base. If much overgrown, cut hard back in Mar. *Pot Culture*—In the cool greenhouse, *P. Lemoinei* may be had in flower in Mar.; pot-up annually in Oct., using 8 to 10-in. pots and compost of 2 parts of sandy loam to 1 part of leaf-mould and well-rotted manure. Prune as already described, and sink the pots to their rims in ashes outdoors from May to Dec. To propagate, strike cuttings in a frame in July or Aug. *Species and Hybrids*—*P. coronarius* (White); *P. microphyllus* (White); *P. Lemoinei erectus* (White); *P. Norma* (White, single); *P. Virginal* (White, double); *P. purpureo*

215

maculatus (White Petals, stained Purple); and *P. Voie Lactee.* All May to July, 3 to 15 ft.

Phillyrea (Mock Privet)—Hardy evergreen shrubs which thrive almost anywhere and in any soil. *Culture*—Plant in May or Sept. Propagate by means of cuttings in a frame, or by layering in Sept. *Species—P. angustifolia* (White, May–June, 9 ft.); *P. decora* (White, April, 6–8 ft.); *P. media* (White, May, 6–8 ft.).

Phlox—Magnificent genus of annuals and perennials which need a certain amount of sun and enjoy an open position, but one sheltered from strong winds. The *Phlox Drummondii* varieties—half-hardy annuals—make splendid bedding and potting plants. *Phlox paniculata* [*syn. decussata*] and *P. maculata*, perennials, look fine in borders, while the dwarf perennials or *Mossy Phloxes* are excellent for the rock garden. The annual and herbaceous kinds succeed best in deep, rich and moist but well-drained loam. Stake early and thin-out all weak growths. For culture, *see* Annuals, p. 123, *and* Perennials, p. 281. *Pot Culture—(Perennials)*—Pot-up in Oct., using 5 to 6-in. pots and a rich, sandy soil. Stand in a cold greenhouse, and water freely from Apr. to Oct., then decrease the water supply. Give liquid manure from May to Sept. *(Annuals)*—If seed is sown in a frame in Aug. and the seedlings are potted-up and transplanted to the greenhouse, blooms may be had from Jan. to Mar. *Species—*(ANNUAL)*—P. Drummondii* (Various, June–Oct., 6–12 in.). (PERENNIAL)—*P. paniculata* [*syn. decussata*] (Various, July–Oct., 40 in.). *Named Varieties of P. paniculata*—(White) *Flau A. Buchner;* (Soft Pink) *P. D. Williams;* (Salmon Pink) *Daily Sketch;* (Scarlet) *Leo; Schlagster,* and *A. E. Amos;* (Salmon Orange) *Spitfire;* (Purplish-red) *San Antonio;* (Dark Purple) *William Ramsey;* (Pale Lavender) *Antoine Mercier;* (Violet-blue) *Border Gem; P. Arendsii* hybrids; (Lilac) *Amanda;* (Rose) *Hanna.* (*Alpine*) —*P. adsurgens* (Pink, 6 in.); *P. amœna* (Carmine-pink, May–July, 6 in.); *P. divaricata* (Lavender-blue, May–July, 6–12 in.); *P. ovata* (Red, May–July, 10 in.); *P. subulata* and *vars.* (Pink, Mauve, Blue and White, May–June, 4 in.); *P. stolonifera* (Rose-purple, June, 6 in.).

Phormium (New Zealand Flax)—Tall perennials which require a fairly sheltered, sunny position in well-drained loam, and flower from June to Sept. *Culture*—Sow in a frame in Mar., or propagate by means of division of roots in Apr. *P. Cookianum* (Yellow, 60 in.) and *P. tenax* (Crimson, 70 in.) are the best species.

Phyllodoce—Race of dwarf, heath-like, evergreen, shrubby plants, rarely exceeding 7 or 8 in. in height, and excellent subjects for the rock garden. They prefer a well-drained soil of equal parts of peat, leaf-mould and a little loam and sand, and a moist position in sun or semi-shade. *Culture*—Plant in Oct. or Mar. No pruning is required. Propagate by means of cuttings in a frame in Oct., or layer at that time. *Species—P. Breweri* (Yellowish, May, 8–12 in.); *P. cœrulea* (Reddish-purple, June, 6–8 in.); *P. empetriformis* (Pink, June, 8 in.).

Physalis (Winter Cherry, Chinese Lantern or Cape Gooseberry)—Half-hardy and hardy perennials, growing from 20 to 40 in. high, and flowering from June to Oct. They like warm, light and rich soil, and a sunny position in a sheltered border. For culture, *see* Perennials, p. 281. *See also* Solanum capsicastrum.

Physostegia (False Dragon's Head)—Hardy perennials, growing from 20 to 40 in. high, and bearing red flowers in late summer. They like partial shade and a rich sandy soil. *See* Perennials, p. 281.

Phyteuma (Horned Rampion)—Hardy perennials. The smaller species thrive in the rock garden in rich, gritty loam; the taller kinds in a deep, rich soil in the border and in a warm, sunny position. For culture, *see* Perennials, p. 281. *Species*—*P. comosum* (Pale Blue, June–July, 3 in.); *P. Scheuchzeri* (Blue, May–June, 18 in.); *P. Halleri* (Violet, May and June, 6 in.); *P. spicatum* (Lilac, May and June, 2 ft.).

Picea (Spruce)—Hardy evergreen trees which thrive in well-drained loam and in sunny positions. *Culture*—Plant from Oct. to Nov. or in Mar. and Apr.; no pruning is required. Propagate by means of seed. *Species*—*P. Abies (P. excelsa)* (Norway Spruce, 50–100 ft.); *P. orientalis* (Oriental Spruce, 60 ft.); *P. pungens glauca* (Blue Spruce, Grey-blue foliage, 20 ft.); *P. Abies, var. pygmæa* (1½ ft.).

Picotees—These are a kind of carnation, distinguished by a narrow, dark-coloured edging to the petals, or by the petals being covered with tiny dots; the ground colour is usually white or yellow. Only the yellow-ground picotees are grown in the open; cultivation is in every respect the same as for the carnation, *which see*. *Varieties*—[Yellow Ground] *Exquisite* (Scarlet Margined); *Her Majesty* (Purple Edged); *Margaret Glitters* (Rosy-scarlet Edged); *Neil Kenyon* (Rose Edged); *Togo* (Crimson Edged).

Pieris (Lily of the Valley Bush)—Hardy evergreen shrubs, which like a moist peaty loam and sand and a sheltered position in sun or partial shade. *Culture*—Plant from Sept. to Oct. Do not prune, but keep in shape by means of " stopping " and removing dead flowers in May. Propagate by means of layering in autumn. Good kinds are *P. floribunda* (White, Apr.–May, 3–6 ft.) and *P. japonica* (White, March–Apr., 4–10 ft.). *See also* Andromeda.

Pinguicula (Butterwort, or Bog Violet)—Hardy perennial bog plants which thrive in moist peaty loam and in a shady position. *Culture*—Propagate by means of division in Apr. *Species*—*P. alpina* (White); *P. grandiflora* (Blue); *P. vulgaris* [Bog Violet] (Purple-violet). All Apr. and May, 3 to 4 in.

Pinks (Dianthus)—Beautiful hardy perennials closely allied to picotees and carnations, and requiring very similar cultivation. They are excellent border and edging plants. New varieties may be obtained from seed sown in Apr., May and June, and old plants may be increased by cuttings of basal shoots that have not flowered, struck 2 in. apart in a frame in July. When well rooted they should be planted in a bed in rows 6 in. apart and with 3 in. between the plants. If preferred the cuttings can be struck in a sheltered north border. Here they should remain till Sept., when they may be planted in a bed or pots, in a compost of two-thirds loam from decayed turf and one-third well-decomposed cow-dung. After being gently watered, the pots may be placed in a cold frame, the lights being closed for the following four-and-twenty hours. In Mar. re-pot into 24's in which they are to bloom. The best soil for this potting is a mixture of good loam and well-rotted manure from an old hot-bed, with a little white sea-sand and old mortar rubble added if the soil is at all heavy; Mar. is also the best time to plant border pinks out in the open. These resent disturbance and should remain in position for several years; the ground, however, should be limed periodically and an annual dressing with a phosphate manure must be given. Pinks are also easily increased by division if lifted in Sept., or they may be layered in July and the young plants can be moved to their new flowering positions in autumn, seed may also be sown under glass in July. The biennial *Dianthus chinensis*, the Chinese or Indian Pink, is best raised from seed in the autumn, wintered in a frame, and set out in the following May; a sunny position is essential and a well-limed or chalky soil is a great advantage. Its variety *D. c. Heddewigii* and its named sorts are best treated as annuals. Another delightful class includes the Alpine or rock-garden pinks; these are easily grown in a sunny position and in sandy soil. Perpetual-flowering pinks (*D. Allwoodii*), if lifted in autumn and potted-up, will continue to bloom in the greenhouse throughout the winter. They are not particular as to soil, will stand the winter in the open border well, and are easily raised from cuttings or by layering in summer. *See also* Carnation. *Varieties*—(PERENNIAL). (*Border*)—(Pink) *Apple Blossom;* (Carmine, Red Centre) *Bookham Pride;* (Rose-pink) *Dainty Lass;* (Salmon, Laced Red) *Fair Rosamund;* (Salmon, Crimson Centre) *Jean Douglas;* (Shell-pink, Crimson Centre) *May Blossom;* (White) *Mrs. Sinkins;* (White, Margined Deep Maroon) *Peter Pan;* (Salmon-rose and Carmine) *Rosemary;* (Reddish-pink and Crimson) *Sunset;* (Salmon, Laced Crimson) *Vera;* (White) *White Ladies*. Consult the catalogues for numerous varieties. All May to July, 12 in. (Alpine)—*D. alpinus* (Pink or White); *D. cæsius* (Rose); *D. neglectus* (Reddish-pink). All June, 5 in. (BIENNIAL)—*Named Varieties of D. e. Heddewigii and vars.*—*Aurora* (Salmon-red, Double); *The Bride* (White, Ringed with Purple, Single); *Crimson Bell* (Blood Red, Single); *Empress* (Crimson and Rose, Single); *Salmon Queen* (Single, Fringed); *Scarlet Queen* (Single, Fringed); *Snowdrift* (White, Double, Fringed); *Vesuvius* (Orange, Single, Fringed). All July to Oct., 6 to 12 in.

Pinus (Pine)—Large family of hardy evergreen trees growing, according to species, from 4½ to 200 ft. high. They like a sunny position and prefer light loam, but will grow well in most soils. *Culture*—Plant in May or Sept. when from 2 to 3 ft. high. No pruning is required. Never plant pines near a smoky city.

Platanus (Plane)—Hardy deciduous trees, which thrive in sunny positions, in any well-drained soil. *Culture*—Plant in Nov. Prune in winter when the wood is overcrowded. To propagate, sow in Mar., take cuttings in autumn, or layer.

Platycodon (Chinese Bell-flower)—Hardy perennials which thrive in well-drained, deep sandy loam, in open, shady positions, and are excellent for the border or rock garden. They grow from 10 to 25 in. high, and flower in July and Aug. *See* Perennials, p. 281.

Platystemon (Cream Cups)—Hardy annuals which like a sunny position and light ordinary soil, and are useful for beds, borders, or for the rock garden. The yellow flowers are borne in summer on 10-in. stalks. For culture, *see* Annuals, p. 123.

Plumbago (Leadwort)—Genus comprising about ten species of plants, mostly perennials, some suitable only for the greenhouse and others hardy. The most noteworthy for greenhouse culture is *P. capensis*, an admirable pillar plant, with pale lavender-blue flowers in Sept. *Culture*—Pot-up annually in Mar. in 6 to 8-in. pots, or plant in the cool-house border. A compost of 2 parts of loam and 1 part of leaf-mould and coarse sand is best. Water well and syringe in warm weather, but keep dry from Oct. to Mar. Young pot plants (not climbers) should be pinched back once or twice; with bushes, cut back the shoots to within 10 in. of the previous year's growth in Oct. Climbers should be trained in a single stem in much the same manner as a vine. Cut back all laterals of climbers to within 5 in. of their base after flowering, and prune back again to within 2 to 3 in. from their base early in Feb., and if grown in the greenhouse border, mulch annually in spring with well-rotted manure. Propagate by cuttings of semi-matured side shoots in gentle bottom heat in spring or early summer. *See also* Ceratostigma.

Podophyllum (Duckfoot or May Apple)—Hardy perennials which thrive in partial shade in moist peaty loam, and are useful for the bog or rock garden. They grow from 10 to 30 in. high and carry purple or white flowers in May. Propagate by means of division in Apr.

Polemonium (Jacob's Ladder, or Greek Valerian)—Hardy perennials for sunny borders, or the wild garden, and requiring well-drained loam. Rock garden species need partial shade and a compost of gritty loam and leaf-mould. For culture, *see* Perennials, p. 281. *Species—P. cœruleum* and *vars.* (Blue or White, June–Sept., 18 in.); *P. confertum* (Blue or Violet, June–July, 6–8 in.); *P. mellitum* (Bluish-white, June, 6–8 in.); *P. reptans* (Slate-blue, Mar.–June, 12 in.).

Polianthes tuberosa (Tuberose)—Half-hardy bulbous plants growing from 24 to 36 in. high and flowering in Sept. They thrive in sunny positions in sheltered warm borders, in a mixture of sandy loam, leaf-mould, and well-rotted manure, or they may be flowered in pots in the greenhouse. *Culture* —Plant in Mar., 6 in. deep and 6 in. apart, and do not water until they begin to grow. *Pot Culture*—Plant bulbs singly in 4 to 5-in. pots (African kinds) late autumn, (American kinds) early spring, and plunge the pots in fibre in a warm frame (bottom heat 65° F.). When their roots fill the pots, re-pot, and repeat the treatment until the buds appear. The bulbs only flower for one season. Propagation is by means of offsets.

Polyanthus (Primula variabilis)—These are generally classified as *Gold-laced, Fancies, and Selfs,* and make an excellent show, especially during Apr. and May, in partially-shaded beds and borders, mostly as edging plants. They need a moist, deep, good loam. There are innumerable named varieties. The *Munsted* strain is excellent; the colours are numerous and the flowers are borne from Mar. to June on 8-in. stems. *Culture*—Sow under glass in Apr. or May, prick-off into boxes, and place in a cold frame. Harden-off and plant out 9 in. apart in a shady and sheltered reserve border in June, and transfer to their flowering positions in Oct. Seed may also be sown in the open in July, or the polyanthus can be propagated by division immediately after flowering. *Pot Culture*—Pot-up singly in 8-in. pots in Oct. and keep in a cold frame until just before bloom is required, when transfer to the cool house. *See also* Auricula.

Polygala (Milkwort)—Useful little plants, mostly shrubby evergreens or hardy perennials, which thrive in a mixture of cool, moist and gritty loam and peat, or leaf-mould, in partial shade in sheltered positions. They are excellent for the rock garden, border or wild garden. For culture, *see* Perennials, p. 281. *Shrubby Species* are increased by cuttings of young shoots struck in coarse sand in a propagating case in spring. *Pot Culture*—(*Shrubby Species*)—Pot-up in Mar. in a compost of one-half peat, one-quarter fibrous loam and one-quarter sand. Shade from direct sun and syringe. Remove all dead flower heads, and, after flowering, cut the shoots of the current year back to within 6 in. of the old wood; then syringe and stand in the sun to ripen the wood. Remove to the house in Sept. *Species— P. calcarea* (Purple, Blue, Mauve, or Rose, May–Sept., 5 in.); *P. Chamœbuxus* (Purple and Yellow, June–July, 3 in.).

Polygonatum—Hardy perennials of which the best known is *P. multiflorum* (Solomon's Seal or David's Harp), and which thrive in almost any soil and situation. For culture, *see* Perennials, p. 281.

Polygonum (Knotwort)—Large genus including hardy annuals, hardy and half-hardy perennials, shrubs, climbers and trailers. The tall hardy perennials are useful for the wild garden or border, and grow in any ordinary loam, and in partial shade. *P. affine* (Pink, July–Oct., 8 in.) is a rock species. For culture, *see* Annuals, p. 123, *and* Perennials, p. 281. In the case of shrubby species, do not prune, but cut out old wood from the centre and trim away thin straggly shoots. *Species*—(ANNUAL)—*P. orientale* (Purple-rose, June–Sept., 4–5 ft.). (PERENNIAL)—*P. campanulatum* (Pink, July–Sept., 3 ft.).

Poncirus trifoliata (Hardy Orange or Bengal Quince)—Hardy deciduous shrub which likes a sunny position in well-drained fibrous loam and leaf-mould. *Culture*—Sow in Mar. in a frame, or take cuttings of half-ripened shoots. Plant out in Mar. or Oct. After flowering (Apr. or May) cut out dead wood and trim to shape only.

Pontederia cordata (Water Plantain)—Hardy perennial aquatics bearing blue flowers from June to Oct., and which like a sheltered position in good loam and still, shallow water. *Culture*—Propagate by division in Apr.

Poppy—*See* Papaver.

Populus (Poplar)—Large genus of hardy deciduous trees suitable only for large gardens, and which thrive in moist loam in sunny positions. *Culture*—Plant in Nov. No pruning is required. To propagate, strike cuttings of matured wood in the open in Oct. *Species*—*P. nigra, var. italica* is the Lombardy Poplar and *P. tremula* is the Aspen.

Potentilla (Cinquefoil)—Genus of plants, some species of which bear a resemblance to the strawberry in flower, and have a similar manner of propagation. Many species are of a low-growing and shrubby nature, others are hardy perennials. All do well in sun or semi-shade, in the border or rock garden (dwarf kinds), in deep, sandy soil. Sow seed in light loam in spring, increase by division in Mar. or Oct., or strike cuttings of ripened shoots in a frame in autumn. The old and dead wood should be thinned-out in Sept. *Species and Varieties*—(BORDER)—*P. argyrophylla var. atrosanguinea* (Crimson); *P. Gibson's Scarlet; P. grandiflora* (Yellow); *P. Hopwoodiana* (Apricot). All May to Sept., 12 to 18 in. (ALPINES)—*P. alba* (White); *P. nepalensis var. minor* (Crimson); *P. n. var. Miss Willmott* (Rose); *P. nitida* (Pale Pink); *P. Tonguei* (Orange, spotted Crimson). All May to Sept., 6 to 9 in. (SHRUBBY)—*P. fruticosa* (Yellow); *P. f. Veitchii* (White); *P. f. Vilmoriniana* (Sulphur). All July to Sept., 3 to 4 ft.

Poterium (Burnet)—Hardy perennials which thrive in ordinary soil in sunny borders. For culture, *see* Perennials, p. 281. These plants grow from 10 to 30 in. high, and flower from July to Sept. *Species*—*P. canadense* (Rosy-purple), and *P. obtusum* (Rose).

Pratia—Hardy dwarf-growing rock plants, which thrive in sandy peat and leaf-mould in sunny positions on well-drained banks, and from May to Aug. carry white or blue flowers on 3-in. stems. For culture, *see* Rock Plants, p. 283.

Primrose (Primula vulgaris)—*See* Primula.

Primula—Large genus, including some of the most popular flowers, the auricula, the cowslip, the polyanthus, and the primrose. In the greenhouse, in the rock garden or bog garden, in beds and growing wild in the woods, the primula is one of the most useful genera that exist. The majority thrive in rich deep loam and appreciate the admixture of leaf-mould and grit with the soil (except higher alpine species which appreciate the addition of old mortar rubble and full sun). They are all moisture-lovers, but must have a well-drained soil. The majority like partial shade unless unlimited moisture is available in hot weather. *Culture*—Sow seed in pots or pans under glass in May, in a compost of equal parts of loam, leaf-mould and sand, all sieved through a ½-in. mesh, and well mixed. Cover thinly with fine sandy soil and keep in a temperature of 60° F. Prick-off 1 in. apart into pans as soon as possible and, in about three weeks, pot-up singly into 3-in. pots; harden off, and keep on a bed of hard ashes in a shaded frame; transfer to 5 to 6-in.

pots in Sept. Propagate also by means of division in Sept. or in spring. *Pot Culture*—Pot-up firmly in Sept. or Oct., using 5 to 6-in. pots and a compost of half loam and half leaf-mould, rotted manure and coarse sand, and keep in a frame until Nov., pinching-off any flower buds that form, then transfer to the cool greenhouse for flowering. A little soot-water may be given from time to time while the buds are forming. Discard the plants after flowering, except choice varieties. *See also* Auricula, Polyanthus, etc. Alpine primulas are of great value in the rock garden and the bog garden. The first group thrives among the rocks in rich loam; the second class loves a cool, moist, but well-drained soil. Space does not permit us to deal more fully with these, but below the first group is marked with an * and the second †. *Species and Varieties*—*P. vulgaris* (*Primrose*) (Various, Apr., 6 in.); **P. Auricula* (Golden Yellow, Mar.–May, 6 in.); †*P. Beesiana* (Magenta, May–June, 20–30 in.); †*P. Bulleyana* (Orange Scarlet, Apr.–May, 12–18 in.); †*P. denticulata* (Lilac and White, Feb.–Apr., 12–18 in.); †*P. farinosa* (Rose-purple, May, 6 in.); †*P. japonica* (*vars.*) (Various, May–Aug., 12–24 in.); †*P. Juliæ* (Magenta, Apr. and May, 4 in.); *P. kewensis* (Pale Yellow, Apr., 15 in.); *P. malacoides* (Pale Mauve, Pink or White, Sept.–May, 12–24 in.); **P. marginata* (Lavender-blue, margined White, May, 6 in.); †*P. minima* (Rose-pink, May–June, 2 in.); **P. nivalis* (White, Feb.–May, 6 in.); *P. obconica* (*vars.*) (Various, spring, 9–12 in.); †*P. pulverulenta* (Crimson-maroon, Apr.–May, 20 in.); *P. Sieboldii* (*vars.*) (Red, Purple, Lilac, May–June, 12 in.); †*P. sikkimensis* (Sulphur-yellow, May–June, 20 in.); *P. sinensis* (Various, Sept.–Apr., 12 in.); *P. stellata* (Various, Sept.–May, 12–24 in.). Those without distinguishing marks are for the greenhouse.

Prunella (Self-heal)—Dwarf-growing hardy perennials, thriving in moist, light and rich soil, in the sunny border or rock garden. For culture, *see* Perennials, p. 281. *Species*—*P. grandiflora* (Purple, Red, Blue or White, 8 in.); *P. vulgaris laciniata alba* (White, 6 in.). All July to Sept.

Prunus—Large genus of hardy deciduous flowering, fruit-bearing trees, including *P. Amygdalus* [*communis*] (Almond), *P. Armeniaca* (Apricot), *P. avium* (Gean), *P. cerasifera* (Cherry Plum), etc. They do best in a deeply-dug and well-manured soil rich in lime, or in localities with a chalk subsoil. *Culture*—Plant in Oct. in sunny position sheltered from N. and E. winds. To propagate, sow seed, or bud in the open in summer on plum stocks. *Pot Culture*—*P. sinensis* is a useful species for cultivation in the cold greenhouse. Pot-up in Nov., using 6 to 8-in. pots and well-manured ordinary soil. After flowering sink the pots in ashes outdoors from May to Dec. In the main, pruning should be as for ordinary fruiting plum trees (*which see*), but prune out weak wood and dead flower shoots after flowering. The Japanese Cherries, vars. of *P. serrulata*, *var. Lannesiana* and *P. triloba fl. pl.*, may be grown in the cool house. Pot-up in Oct., using 8 to 12-in. pots and a compost of 2 parts of sandy loam to 1 part of leaf-mould and rotten manure.

Puschkinia scilloides (Striped Squill)—Hardy bulbous plant which grows about 6 in. high and flowers in Apr. and May. It thrives in deep, rich, sandy soil, mixed with leaf-mould, in warm sunny borders or in the rock garden. *Culture*—Plant in Oct., 3 in. deep and 3 in. apart. Protect with fibre in winter, and lift triennially.

Pyracantha (Fire Thorn, Evergreen Thorn, or Cratægus Pyracantha)— Beautiful hardy evergreen bushes or climbing shrubs which thrive in good light loam in sunny positions and against walls facing south. All bear white flowers from May to June. *Culture*—Sow seed when ripe, or strike cuttings in summer. Plant in Oct. or Apr., trim to shape in early spring, but clip as little as possible. *See also* Cratægus.

Pyrethrum [*syn. Chrysanthemum coccineum*]—Hardy perennials, now included under the genus Chrysanthemums, and which thrive in cool, light, deep and moderately rich soil in sunny, open borders. For culture, *see* Perennials, p. 281.

Pyrus—Genus of hardy deciduous trees including *P. nivalis* (Snowtree), *P. ussuriensis* (Sand Pear). *Culture*—Plant in Nov. in a sunny position sheltered from cold winds, in deeply-dug and well-manured ordinary soil. Thin-out the branches when overcrowded, and cut out dead wood and weak shoots after flowering. Propagate by means of seed, grafting, or budding in the open. For Pyrus (Crab), *see* Malus.

Quamoclit lobata (Mina)—Half-hardy annual climbers, which thrive in rich, well-drained soil in warm, sunny, sheltered positions. *See* Annuals, p. 123.

Quercus (Oak)—Large genus of hardy deciduous and evergreen trees, the majority of which are too large for the average garden. There are, however, a few species from Japan, which here rarely attain more than bush-form except in mild districts. *Culture*—Plant young trees in Oct. in a sunny position in deep, good loam; thin-out the branches in summer when required. To propagate, sow ripe acorns in the open in Sept. or Oct., or graft in spring. *Quercus Robur* (Common Oak) and other species.

Ramonda (Pyrenean Primrose, Rosette Mullein)—Small hardy perennial rock plant which thrives in the shade, in a mixture of loam, peat and leaf-mould. For culture, *see* Rock Plants, p. 283. *Species*—*R. Myconi* (*pyrenaica*) (Pale Purple-blue, Orange Centre); *R. M. vars. alba* and *rosea; R. Nathaliae* (Deep Purple-blue). All May to Aug., 6 in.

Ranunculus—Large genus of herbaceous perennials and tuberous-rooted plants, including the common buttercup, most species of which thrive in partial shade, in moist, deep, well-dug, rich, sandy soil with ample leaf-mould in it. They are also useful for pot culture, and the dwarf-growing kinds for the rock garden. *Culture*—(*Perennials*)—Propagate by means of division in Nov. or Apr., the plants should remain in position for several years. (*Tuberous*)—Plant the tubers, claws downward, 2 to 3 in deep and 4 to 6 in. apart, early in Mar., surrounding with sand and charcoal. Lift the tubers after flowering. *Species*—(FIBROUS-ROOTED)—*R. aconitifolius fl. pl.* (White [Double], May–July, 24–30 in.); *R. acris fl. pl.* (Yellow [Double], May–June, 24 in.); *R. aquatilis* (White, May and June, 2–12 in.); *R. Lingua major* (Yellow, June–Aug., 30–50 in.). (TUBEROUS-ROOTED)—*R. asiaticus vars.* (Persian, French and Turban) (Various, May–July, 6 in.). (ALPINE)—*R. alpestris* (White, May–Aug., 4 in.); *R. amplexicaulis* (White, May–Aug., 10 in.).

Raphiolepis—Vigorous evergreen flowering shrub which grows well in well-drained, ordinary soil. In cold districts it should be given the protection of a south wall. Pruning is rarely necessary, but may be done in Mar. Propagation is by cuttings under glass. The best species are:—*R. indica* (Rosy-red, 4 ft.), and *R. umbellata* (White, 3 ft.). All species may be forced in the greenhouse in spring.

Rheum (Rhubarb)—The ornamental rhubarbs which thrive on moist, sunny banks or in the water garden in deep, rich loam, are grown chiefly for their foliage. For culture, *see* Perennials, p. 281.

Rhododendron—Among the most handsome and finest of all our flowering shrubs are the hardy rhododendrons. Most hardy species thrive best in a position sheltered from north and east winds and in semi-shade, and prefer well-trenched and well-drained moist peaty loam, but will grow in almost any soil deficient in lime or chalk, providing it contains ample decaying vegetable humus, and is sufficiently porous. Most flower in May and June, but a few early varieties bloom from Christmas onwards. Rhododendrons bear frequent transplanting so long as the ball of earth round their roots is not broken. They are surface-rooters and w̲ill not grow on steep banks, where the roots parch up in summer. Except in the case of such hybrids as *Bagshot Ruby, The Bride,* or *Pink Pearl,* which will grow in full sun, rhododendrons require some sun which should, however, be intermittent. These shade conditions are best supplied by trees and large bushes planted among the rhododendrons. In addition to the hardy and half-hardy species, there are choice greenhouse kinds, which require moist warmth all the year; these are best grown in a cool house during the winter and kept under glass in summer (Temp. 50° F.). When purchasing rhododendrons, care must be taken that the species chosen are suitable for the climate. *Culture*—Plant and "heel-in" very firmly in Oct. or Nov. or at any time in winter and spring, up to May, providing the soil is not water-logged and that there is no frost. When planting add some well-rotted leaf-mould, and mix it well with the other soil. Fresh stable manure must not be used. If the weather is dry, soak the hole well before planting, and in any case, a little leaf-mould should be placed at the bottom for the roots to rest upon. Bushy species should be set 6 ft. apart, and smaller lime-hating subjects, such as azaleas, kalmias, daphnes and heaths, can be used to fill the gaps until the rhododendrons have grown a bit. Do not prune young bushes, merely keep them in shape by means of "stopping" and removing dead blooms immediately after flowering. When it is necessary to cut back old and straggling plants, do so in Apr. Top-dress annually in Mar. with good leaf-mould, and every second or third year give a 4-in. top-dressing of old hot-bed manure in May. *Propagation*—To propagate hybrids, graft (stock *R. ponticum*) under glass from Jan. to May, layer well-matured shoots in late summer, or take cuttings. Species may be increased by means of seed sown thinly in Mar. or Apr. in pans, in a compost of equal parts of well-sieved leaf-mould or peat and coarse sand in a cold frame. Most species may be raised from cuttings of semi-matured shoots, struck in a frame with bottom heat, and practically all species can be layered in summer. For Pot Culture, *see* Azalea. Species and varieties are innumerable (*see* growers' catalogues). A few good hybrids are—*Alice* (Deep Rose-pink); *Ascot Brilliant* (Deep Blood-red); *Bagshot Ruby* (Ruby-red); *Charles Dickens* (Dark Scarlet); *Countess of Derby* (Rose); *Cunningham's White* (White, tinged Pink); *Doncaster* (Bright Scarlet, spotted Dark Brown); *Duchess of Connaught* (White, flecked Lemon); *fastuosum fl. pl.* (Pale Lavender [Semi-double]); *Mother of Pearl* (Bluish-white, Red Stamens); *Pink Pearl* (Flesh-pink); *Sappho* (White, heavily spotted Maroon); and *Unknown Warrior* (Rose-crimson).

Rhus (Lacquer Tree or Stag's Horn, etc.)—Hardy deciduous trees and shrubs which like a sunny position and good loam. *Culture*—Plant in Oct.; cut out all old and dead wood. To propagate, strike cuttings of matured shoots under bell-glasses in Sept., or layer in Sept. *Species*—*R. Toxicodendron* [Poison Ivy] (Shrub, 10 ft.); *R. typhina* [Stag's Horn] (Greenish flowers in June, Orange foliage in autumn, 10–25 ft.).

Ribes—Hardy deciduous shrubs, akin to the currant and gooseberry, which thrive in the shade in ordinary garden soil, and are treated in exactly the same way as gooseberries and currants, *which see*. *Species*—*R. alpinum* (Yellow), *R. sanguineum* (Flowering Currant) with rosy-red flowers in Apr., and *R. speciosum* (Fuchsia-flowered Gooseberry) with red flowers, are best.

Ricinus communis (Castor-oil Plant)—Half-hardy plants which thrive in rich loam in warm beds or in the cold greenhouse. *Culture*—Sow singly in pots in Mar. under glass (Temp. 50° F.); pot-on into 5-in. pots, harden-off, and plant out in June, or pot-on into 6 to 8-in. pots and keep indoors. One of the best varieties is *R. communis var. Gibsonii.*

Robinia (Hardy or Rose Acacia and False Acacia)—Hardy deciduous summer-flowering trees, which like a well-drained light soil, and a sunny, sheltered position. *R. Pseudo-Acacia*, the Locust Tree or False Acacia (White, 50 ft.), is the most common. The most attractive species for the garden, however, is *R. hispida*, the Rose Acacia (Pink, 9 ft.). *Culture*—Plant in Nov. Do not prune, but merely trim to keep in shape. Propagate by means of seed or by grafting.

Rocket (Hesperis, Dame's Violet)—Early spring-flowering hardy annuals, biennials and perennials, which grow freely in any light soil in a sunny position, and are excellent for the mixed border. For culture, *see* Annuals, p. 123, Biennials, p. 125, *and* Perennials, p. 281. *Species*—(BIENNIAL)—*H. tristis* (Cream, Brownish-red, Purple, May–Sept., 12–24 in.). (PERENNIAL)—*H. matronalis* (White, Red, Rose, Purple [Single and Double], June–July, 20 in.); *H. violacea* (Violet, May–July, 18 in.).

Rodgersia—Hardy perennials growing 4 ft. high and bearing pink or white flowers in June or July, and which thrive in partial shade in a moist border or by water's edge in peaty soil. *See* Perennials, p. 281. *R. æsculifolia* (Pink) and *R. pinnata* (Red) are good species.

Romneya (Californian or Bush Poppy)—Deciduous flowering shrubs or shrubby perennials. They are almost hardy and thrive in the sun in well-drained, sandy, enriched loam, in a sheltered position or under a south wall. *Culture*—Plant in Mar.; cut out all dead wood in the spring, and cut back any weak growth. In severe winters protect with straw, bracken, or sacking; in the north, these plants must be grown under glass. *Pot Culture*—Pot-up annually in Apr., in a compost of sandy peat and leaf-mould in 6 to 7-in. pots. To propagate, divide the roots in Mar., or strike root-cuttings in a frame in the autumn. *R. Coulteri* (White, June–Sept., 5 ft.) is the best known.

Rosa (Wild Rose, Briar)—This includes all the wild roses and briars; most species are strong growers. *Culture*—Plant from Nov. to Mar., in a sunny position and in ordinary soil. In Mar., cut away old wood and cut back long shoots. To propagate, strike matured cuttings in the open in Oct. or Nov.

Roses—Roses are divisible roughly into several groups or classes. The largest classes, containing most of the popular roses of to-day, are the Hybrid Perpetuals, the Floribundas and the Teas. These groups include subdivisions; thus the Hybrid Perpetuals are often held to include Hybrid Teas and Perpetual Bourbons, while the Noisettes are classed with the Teas.

Soil—The very best of all soil for roses is a deep stiff loam. The worst soil for roses, after pure sand, or nearly so, is the black soil of the town garden, very porous, and over-full of organic matter. Peaty soils, if rich in character, are quite good for roses, a general rule being that the more gravelly or sandy a soil the less favourable for the rose. An essential for good rose soil is that it should be well drained, and this means a substratum of porous material, chalk or gravel, not many feet below the surface. Gravel has had a bad reputation for roses, but it is not altogether deserved. It is usually considered too dry and hot for roses to thrive in, but really, if a little care is taken to improve it, it will grow very good roses. Tea roses, for example, bloom in perfection on a gravel soil, and many of the briars and the newer hybrids enjoy just such a light dryish medium. Chalk, providing that it is

PLATE 2

Two suitable plants for the rock garden, *Lithospermum diffusum* (blue)
and *Aethionema* '*Warley Rose*' (pink)

deep enough below the surface, and that there is a good depth of soil on top, is not a bad subsoil. It is well drained, and not too dry in hot weather. Where it is very close to the surface it is bad, and needs a lot of work and preparation if it is going to grow good roses. Eighteen inches of decent loam is the minimum for roses on chalk, and where the loam is shallower than this special places must be prepared for the plants and extra soil supplied.

Situation—Roses like shelter, and they like an open situation. They dislike wind, although they like fresh air, and hate to be shut in by big trees. The spot to look for, then, is one sheltered from frosts and violent winds, and not too close to high hedges or trees. Shelter is desirable from north and east winds, and if there is room for choice, the rose garden should be on the highest part of the available land, other conditions of soil and shelter being equal. " Frost falls ", as the country people say, and where the roses are planted on a slope let the more delicate kinds be at the top.

Planting—Early Nov. is the best time of all for this operation, though it mav be done right through the winter—should conditions be favourable—until the end of Mar.

First the soil must be thoroughly broken up to a depth of at least 2 or 3 ft. Next, the soil must be thoroughly well drained. Before the roses arrive the soil should be re-turned to a depth of about 18 in., and a good allowance of manure incorporated with it. The lowest layer of soil in the bed should consist of rich, fairly retentive soil, which will hold a certain amount of water, while the upper layers should be lighter and more friable, to encourage the plants to produce plenty of good fibrous roots. The holes to receive the roots should be dug, from a foot to 18 in. square and deep enough where bush roses or dwarfs are to be planted, for the point of junction of the scion and the stock to be covered when planted to a depth of about an inch. Where standard roses are being planted the holes should be about 6 in. deep. (*See also* Planting Fruit Trees, p. 310.)

Pruning Roses after Planting—When roses are planted during the autumn and winter months their first pruning should be left until the spring, but when spring-planted it should be done at the time of putting in. The trees should be gone over carefully and all dead wood cut clean out, together with weak and sappy, unripened wood, and any shoots which have received injury. Standards should then be cut back to within about 4 in. of their union with the stock bush trees being dealt with a little less severely, having about 6 in. of every shoot left above the ground. This pruning is only meant to be carried out the first time after planting. The subsequent treatment varies with the variety.

Pruning Established Roses—The time of pruning roses differs with the variety. Hybrid Perpetuals, both dwarf and bush, as well as standards and Hybrid Teas, are pruned during Mar., bush and standard Teas and Noisettes during Apr., while the climbing roses, Hybrid Perpetuals, Hybrid Teas, Teas, and Noisettes should be looked over twice in the year, being well thinned as soon as they have flowered in the summer and pruned properly in Mar. (*See also* Pruning, p. 302.) Roses may be roughly divided into classes for purposes of pruning. The first with which we are concerned is that of the Hybrid Perpetuals, Hybrid Teas, Teas, and Noisettes, which require hard pruning. All dead, unripe, and weak shoots should be cut clean out, and the centre of the plant thinned well to allow good room either with a sharp knife or the fingers. The shoots retained should be cut back to from four to six buds. Examples of this type are: *Admiration, Earl Beatty, Glory of Rome, The Doctor, Madame Abel Chatenay* and *Mrs. Sam McGredy.*

AG—P   225

The Hybrid Perpetuals, Hybrid Teas, Teas, and Noisettes which require moderate pruning are the next class. These should have the dead unripe and weak shoots cut clean away. The shoots which cross, or may cross when full grown, should be cut out, the plant never being allowed to get crowded in the middle. The strong, well-ripened, last-year shoots which are left should be cut back to from six to eight eyes. Examples of roses needing this treatment are: *Betty Uprichard, Dainty Bess, Emma Wright, Ena Harkness,* and *Lady Hillingdon.*

There are also varieties of Hybrid Perpetuals, Hybrid Teas, Teas, and Noisetts which require light pruning. They should be treated as the previous classes, but still less wood should be cut away. The centre of the plant should be kept open, but beyond this the strong shoots from the base should be left about 8 in. long, while the other shoots should be cut back till on their laterals or side shoots there are from one to three buds left. The base shoots should be left 12 in. long, while the laterals on the older wood may be reduced to four or five eyes. Roses needing pruning of this kind are such plants as *Caroline Testout, Frau Karl Druschki, La France, Irish Elegance, Lady Waterlow,* and most of the Floribundas.

The next section includes the climbing kinds of Hybrid Perpetuals, Hybrid Teas, and Teas, as well as some of the other climbers. These roses need very little pruning, most of them doing best if left to grow naturally. The necessary thinning-out of dead wood and of the shoots which are likely to overcrowd the plant, together with the worn-out wood of over two years' growth, will keep the plants in full vigour and blossom. The removal of the old wood can be done in the summer, directly after the plants have done blooming, and the young shoots should at once be tied in to take the place of those removed. It is at this time that any necessary re-shaping of the rose should be done, crowded growths being thinned and the branches re-spaced over the wall or trellis so as to keep as much flowering wood as possible. Where the base of the plant becomes bare, as often happens with climbing roses, the space may be filled either by bending down one or more of the lower shoots to cover the bare spaces or by shortening one or two of the base shoots to induce them to throw out laterals. Among these climbing roses are *Climbing Cramoisie, Superieure,* and *Mrs. Herbert Stevens.*

Propagating Roses—The most usual method of propagating the rose is by budding. The operation of budding is fully described on p. 80, but in the case of the rose the selection of the bud is so important a part of the operation that it must be touched on separately. The bud must be taken from a shoot which is mature enough to have borne or to be able to bear a flower—what is called a " ripe " shoot. A ripe shoot may be selected by trying it with the finger, which should be gently rubbed over the prickles. If these latter fall off easily the shoot is in a fit condition for budding. Budding should be done in the summer, between June and Sept., the earlier season being good if enough really ripe shoots can be found. This is an important point, however, and if there is any doubt the budding should be put off. The stock is chosen with reference to the soil or situation in which it is to be grown. Certain kinds do best in light soils, others in heavy, some in dry, and some in moist ground. Some varieties of rose, again, do better on one stock than another; very few of the choicer kinds are grown on their own roots. Roses are often propagated from cuttings, and certainly where the roses do as well on their own roots they are easier to deal with than when budded. There is always a risk that the stock may shoot out vigorously and choke the more delicate scion. Climbers and ramblers, as a rule, do well grown in this way, as do a good number of the Hybrid Perpetuals. When making cuttings it is simplest and best to take cuttings from well-ripened wood, which carries a good number of strong healthy leaves, in the summer, after the roses have done flowering. These cuttings will root well in the open air. A shoot should be selected which has borne a flower, and should be cut off with about three or four leaves attached. The leaf nearest the flower should be removed, the shoot being cut off short above the second leaf and just below the lowest. If the cuttings are to be rooted absolutely in the open a bed should be prepared in a shaded situation, the soil being worked up a little with decayed manure, sand and leaf-mould. A frame is more satisfactory than the open ground, but is not essential. The cuttings should be set 3 to 4 in. apart, and should be well watered in, water being again given with a sprinkler morning and evening. The cuttings do as well or better planted in pots, as they seem to root more quickly. A hand light or a cold frame placed over them will help rooting. (*See also* Cuttings, p. 303).

Where roses are grown from seed, a method only employed where new varieties are being raised, the essential point is that the seed should be allowed to ripen thoroughly and should never become dry. The pods should be left on the plant until they are almost dropping, and should then be picked, stalk and all, and the latter set in damp sand until the following Nov. or Dec., when the seed is to be sown. The seeds often take a complete year to germinate, so that hope need not be given up if the seedlings show no signs of life for many months. Where seedlings are being raised for the sake of new varieties the tiny plants are budded on to briars even during their first year; as soon, in fact, as it is possible to take a bud from them. The seedlings will usually flower in their first year, but a bud should in all cases be secured if possible, as the little plants often die after flowering, the effort seeming to exhaust them completely.

For varieties the reader is referred to growers' catalogues.

Rosmarinus officinalis (Rosemary)—Hardy evergreen shrubby perennials, which like a sunny position and a light, dry soil, but which will grow almost anywhere; they grow 3 to 6 ft. high and flower in Apr. and May. *R. o. prostrata* is a trailing rock plant. *Culture*—Plant in Mar. or Sept., trim to shape after flowering. To propagate, sow in a frame in Apr., or strike cuttings under bell-glasses in July.

Rubus (Bramble, Raspberry, etc.)—Large genus of hardy deciduous flowering shrubs and climbers, including the ordinary blackberry, loganberry, and raspberry. These like a shady position and rich loam. A few, such as *R. deliciosus*, are grown in bush form; many, as in the case of *R. candicans*, are selected for the beauty of their flowers; some, such as *R. flagelliflorus*, for the decorative value of their foliage; and others again for their white stems in winter. *Culture*—Plant in Oct.; cut out old and dead wood after flowering. Propagate by means of suckers in the autumn.

Rudbeckia (Cone-flower)—Hardy annuals and perennials which like a well-drained ordinary soil and a sunny position. Stake early. For culture, *see* Annuals, p. 123, *and* Perennials, p. 281. *Species*—(ANNUALS)—*R. bicolor* (Yellow and Purple, 2 ft.); *R. hirta* (Yellow and Purple, 2½ ft.). (PERENNIALS) —*R. grandiflora* (Yellow and Purple, July–Sept., 40 in.); *R. laciniata fl. pl.* (Golden-yellow [Double], Aug.–Sept., 60 in.); *R. purpurea* (*Echinacea purpurea*) (Purple, July–Sept., 70 in.); *R. speciosa* (syn. *R. Newmanii*) (Orange, Purple-black Centre, July–Sept., 24 in.).

Sagittaria (Arrow Head)—Hardy aquatic plants which thrive in a mixture of clay, sandy loam, and rotted manure, grow from 10 to 30 in. high and flower from June to Oct. *Culture*—Sow seed ¼ in. deep in Apr., or propagate by means of division in Mar. Plant in Mar. in weighted baskets in shallow still water. *Species—S. sagittifolia* (White).

Salix (Willow)—Genus of hardy deciduous trees and shrubs, excellent for growing near a pond or stream. *S. babylonica* is the common Weeping Willow. There are a few species with brightly-coloured stems; these are usually cut hard back annually in spring. *Culture*—Plant in Nov. in a sunny position and in moist soil at the water's margin or in deep, heavy loam. Pruning, except when the trees are cut hard back annually as mentioned above is not necessary, but dead wood should be cut out. To propagate, strike cuttings of matured wood in the open in Nov. or Mar.

Salpiglossis—Half-hardy annuals suitable for a rich soil in sunny beds, or for pot culture. For culture, *see* Annuals, p. 123. *Species—S. sinuata* (Purple, etc.). July to Sept., 18 in.

Salvia—There are many species belonging to this genus; annuals, biennials and perennials, which are grown in the greenhouse or in the garden as ornamental bedding-plants; all thrive in the sun in rich, ordinary soil. For culture, *see* Annuals, p. 123, Biennials, p. 125, *and* Perennials, p. 281. *Pot Culture*—Sow in moderate heat in Feb., prick-off early, and pot-on as required, never allowing the plants to become pot-bound, and using eventually 6 to 8-in. pots and a compost of two-thirds turfy loam, and one-third coarse sand, leaf-mould and well-rotted manure. Grow on in an average temperature of 60° F., harden-off in a cold frame, summer with the pots plunged in ashes in the open, and take into the cool house early in Oct. Pinch-back occasionally till Aug., and syringe daily. After blooming, keep the roots fairly dry and cool till Mar., then give more moisture and slight heat. Rather than raise from seed, however, strike cuttings of young wood in Apr. *Species*—(HALF-HARDY ANNUAL)—*S. carduacea* (Lilac-blue); *S. coccinea* (Scarlet); *S. Horminum* (Various). All June to Sept., 12 to 18 in. (HARDY PERENNIAL) —*S. argentea* (Pale-rose); *S. glutinosa* (Yellow); *S. superba* [*syn. virgata nemorosa*] (Purple-blue); *S. uliginosa* (Deep Blue). All June to Sept., 24 to 60 in. (HALF-HARDY PERENNIAL)—*S. patens* (Deep Blue); *S. splendens var. Pride of Zurich* (Scarlet). Both June to Dec., 18 to 70 in.

Sambucus (Elder)—Deciduous shrubs or small trees bearing white flowers in summer. *S. nigra* is the Common Elder; its two varieties, *S. n. albovariegata* (silver-leaved) and *S. n. foliis aureis* (golden-leaved), are very attractive. *S. racemosus*, the Berried Elder, flowers a month earlier. The flowers are followed by large clusters of red berries. *Culture*—Plant in Oct. in partial shade, and in moist loam, or if need be in almost any soil and situation; cut well back in spring. To propagate, strike cuttings in the open in Oct.

Sanguinaria (Bloodroot)—Hardy perennials which like sandy loam and a sunny position in the border or rock garden. They grow 6 in. high and flower in spring. For culture, *see* Perennials, p. 281.

Sanvitalia procumbens—Pretty trailing hardy annual carrying yellow flowers with purple centres from June to Sept., and useful for edgings and the rock garden. For culture, *see* Annuals, p. 123.

Saponaria (Soapwort)—Hardy annuals of tufted habit and perennials, the creeping species of which are excellent for edgings or for the rock garden, and bear cutting back if necessary for a late autumn display. The taller kinds are useful in the wild garden. All like a sunny position and dry, light, gritty loam. For culture, *see* Annuals, p. 123, *and* Perennials, p. 281. *Species*— (ANNUAL)—*S. calabrica* (Rosy-red, June–Oct., 6 in.); *S. Vaccaria* (Rose and White, June–Aug., 20 in.). (PERENNIAL).—*S. cæspitosa* (Rosy-pink, June–Sept.,

4 in.); *S. ocymoides and alba* (Rose and White, May–July, 6 in.); *S. officinalis* [Single and Double] (Rose or White, July and Aug., 20 in.).

Saxifraga (Saxifrage, Rockfoil)—Large genus, including numerous species of which there are many varieties, and the group is swelled by a seemingly endless number of hybrids.

Euaizoonia (Encrusted or Silvery Saxifrages) are happiest among limestone rocks or in the moraine, but will grow almost anywhere if given a rather gritty soil and a warm, sunny site. Seed can be sown when ripe in pans of light compost in a frame, or the roots can be divided in summer. *Species and Varieties*—*S. Aizoon* and *vars.* (Creamy-white, Yellow or Rose, 6–10 in.); *S. Cotyledon* and *vars.* (White, 18 in.); *S. Hostii* [*syn. elatior*] (White, Spotted Pink, 15 in.); *S. mutata* (Orange, 18 in.). All May to July.

Dactyloides (Mossy Saxifrages)—These plants will grow in almost any well-drained soil, but prefer a compost of gritty loam, leaf-mould and sand, and should be given a cool position in semi-shade. Increase by division of roots in summer, or sow seed in spring in gentle heat. *Species and Varieties*—*S. Clibranii* (Crimson, 5 in.); *S. decipiens* [*syn. cæspitosa*] (Red to White, 6 in.); *S. hypnoides* (White, 5 in.); *S. Miss Willmott* (Cream, blotched Chocolate, 6–9 in.); *S. moschata* and *vars.* (Creamy-white, Rose, and Red, 2–6 in.); and *S. muscoides* (White or Red, 4 in.). All flower from May to June.

Kabschias ("Cushion" or Tufted Saxifrages)—These plants need an open and cool, but fairly sunny site, facing preferably east or west, in the rock garden. The most suitable compost consists of one-third stone chippings and two-thirds calcareous loam, leaf-mould and sand. Above all, the soil must be well drained, and ample moisture should be available in summer. Plants in the open may, in winter, be given the protection of a frame-light, or a sheet of glass. Increase by division of roots after flowering, by cuttings in the spring or autumn, or raise from seed in gentle heat in spring. *Species and Hybrids*—*S. Boydii* (Yellow, Mar.–May, 3 in.); *S. Burseriana* and *vars.* (White or Yellow, Feb.–April, 4 in.); *S. cæsia* (White, May–June, 3 in.); *S. corymbosa var. luteoviridis* (Yellow, Apr.–May, 5 in.); *S. Elizabethæ* (Citron-yellow, Mar.–May, 4 in.); *S. Grisebachii* (Crimson, Apr.–May, 5 in.); *S. lilacina* (Lavender-rose, Apr.–May, 2 in.); *S. marginata* and *vars.* (White or Yellow, Mar.–May, 5 in.); *S. media* (Purple, Apr.–May, 4 in.), and others.

Porphyrions—Give these plants a cool position in partial shade and a well-drained compost of moist, gritty loam and leaf-mould. Increase by division. *Species*—*S. Hirculus major* (Golden, July–Sept., 5 in.); *S. oppositifolia* and *vars.* (Crimson-purple, Mar.–May, 2 in.); *S. retusa* (Rose, May–July, 4 in.).

Megasea (*Bergenia*)—These thrive in sun or semi-shade in ordinary garden loam. Propagate by seed (gentle heat) in the spring; or by division in the autumn. *Species*—*B. cordifolia* (Rose, 12–18 in.); *B. ligulata speciosa* (Purple-rose, 12–24 in.); *B. Stracheyi* (Pink and White, 10 in.). All April to May-flowering.

Diptera—This section likes a position in the alpine house in light gritty loam, or a sheltered situation in the rock garden. Propagate by means of seed, by division or layering. *Species*—*S. cuscutiformis* (White, June, trailing); *S. Fortunei* (White, July–Sept., 10 in.); *S. sarmentosa* (Mother of Thousands) (Yellow or White, June–Sept., 10 in.).

Robertsonia—These like a shady position in light, gritty loam. Propagate by means of seed (gentle heat) in the spring, or by division in the summer. *Species*—*S. cuneifolia* (White, 5 in.); *S. umbrosa var. primuloides* (Rose, 5 in.); *S. umbrosa* and *vars.* (*London Pride*) (Rose and White, 10 in.). All May to June-flowering.

Trachyphyllum—These thrive in semi-shade in moist, gritty loam. Propagate by means of seed (gentle heat) in the spring, or by division in summer. *Species*—*S. aspera; S. flagellaris.* All Yellow, flowering from May to June, 3 to 5 in.

Scabious (Scabiosa or Pincushion Flower)—Annuals, biennials and perennials, which thrive in sunny, open borders and in well-drained rich and light soil. They also make good pot plants for bearing winter blooms if lifted and taken into the greenhouse in Sept. For culture, *see* Annuals, p. 123, Biennials, p. 125, *and* Perennials, p. 281. *Species*—(ANNUAL)—*S. atropurpurea. Named Varieties*—*Black Prince* (Maroon); *Coral Pink* (Pink); *Fairy* (Pale Lavender); *Fire King* (Crimson); *Scarlet King* (Scarlet); and *Yellow Prince* (Yellow). All June to Oct., 24 to 36 in. (PERENNIAL)—*S. arvensis* (Lilac, June–Oct., 18 in.); *S. caucasica* and *vars.* NAMED VARS. OF *S. caucasica*—*Clive Greaves* (Mauve); *Collarette* (Violet); *Diamond* (Violet-blue); *Edith* (Silver-lavender); *Elsie* (Pale Blue); *Isaac House* (Deep Blue); *Miss Willmott* (White) and *Princess* (Deep Lavender). All May to Sept.-flowering and growing to a height of from 24 to 36 in.

Schizanthus (Butterfly Flower, Fringe Flower, Poor Man's Orchid)—Half-hardy annual which thrives in a compost of 2 parts of fibrous loam to 1 part of leaf-mould and a little pounded mortar rubble. The species chiefly grown in the open ground is *S. pinnatus. Culture*—Sow thinly in the open in Apr. or under glass with moderate heat in late Feb. for summer bloom; in Aug. for spring flowers. Prick-off 3 in. apart, harden-off, and plant out 9 to 12 in. apart in Apr. *Pot Culture*—Sow several seeds in a 5-in. pot in Sept., keep in a temperature of 60° F., and moderately moist; thin-out to five seedlings in each pot, and top the young plants occasionally. Winter on a sunny shelf near the glass in a cold greenhouse, and in Feb. pot-up with three plants in 6 to 7-in. pots and stake carefully. In three weeks' time nip-out the heads; only slight heat is needed to bring the plants into bloom. *Species*—*S. Grahami* (Scarlet); *S. pinnatus* (Purple and White); *S. p. grandiflora* (Orange markings); *S. retusus* and *vars.* (Salmon-rose and Orange); *S. wisetoniensis* (Various). All Mar. to Oct., 18 to 48 in., except *S. pinnatus,* which flowers from June to Sept.

Schizopetalon—Fragrant little half-hardy annual bearing white flowers on stems a foot high in summer. A succession of sowings should be made in the open in a warm, rich soil from May onwards. *S. Walkeri.*

Schizostylis coccinea (Kaffir Lily, Crimson Flag or Winter Gladiolus)—Half-hardy rhizomatous-rooted plant which grows from 20 to 30 in. high and flowers in Oct. and Nov. It thrives in sunny, sheltered borders with a south aspect, and moist but well-drained, light, rich soil, and is also useful for pot culture in the cool greenhouse. *Culture*—Plant in Mar. or Oct.; protect with fibre in winter. Lift and divide the roots every few years in Mar., and propagate by means of offsets during that month. *Pot Culture*—Plant in Nov. in a compost of two-thirds loam and one-third leaf-mould, well-rotted manure and coarse sand and stand in a cold frame, giving no water until growth commences. Sink pots outdoors in a sunny position in summer, and late in Sept., when the buds show, transfer to the cold house.

Scilla (Squill)—Hardy spring-flowering bulbous plants, which do well in warm, sunny borders, in the rock garden, or in pots. *Culture*—Plant in Sept. or Oct., 2½ in. deep and 4 in. apart, in good garden or sandy soil. Propagate by means of offsets in Sept. *Pot Culture*—Pot-up from Aug. to Nov., placing about eight bulbs in a 5 to 6-in. pot, and using a compost of 2 parts of light, rich loam to 1 part of leaf-mould. Keep the pots in a frame and covered with fibre until growth starts, then transfer to the cold greenhouse. Plant out in the open after flowering. *Species—S. bifolia* (White, Pink, Blue, Feb. and Mar., 6 in.); *S. hispanica* and *vars.* (*Spanish Squill*) (White, Pink, Blue, Apr. and May, 15–20 in.); *S. nonscripta* (*nutans*) (*Bluebell*) (Blue, Rose or White, May, 15 in.); *S. peruviana* (Blue and White, May and June, 12 in.); *S. sibirica* (Blue, Mar., 6 in.).

Scirpus (Club Rush)—Hardy perennial marsh or aquatic plants of which *S. lacustris*, the Common Bulrush, is the best known. *Culture—*Propagate by means of division in Mar., and plant out in shallow water at the edge of a pond or stream. *Pot Culture—S. nodosus* is a greenhouse species, thriving in a compost of 2 parts of loam to 1 part of leaf-mould and sand; pot-up in Mar. in a 6-in. pot.

Scutellaria (Skull-caps)—These pretty little rock plants grow in poor, shallow and dry soil, and carry pink or purple flowers on 6 to 10-in. stems from Aug. to Oct. *Culture—*Sow in the open in May or June, or increase by division in Mar. or Oct. *S. alpina* (Purple).

Sedum (Stonecrop)—Large family of hardy plants, mostly perennials, the low-growing species being chiefly suitable for the rock, paved or wall garden; the taller kinds are useful in the border. Sedums do well in a dry, light soil with lime in it; the summer-flowering kinds like a sunny position; autumn-flowering species do equally well in sun or shade. The smaller kinds require the protection of glass in winter. For culture, *see* Perennials, p. 281. *Species —(Perennial)—S. acre var. aureum* (Yellow, May and June, 3 in.); *S. dasyphyllum* (Pink and White, June–Aug., 3 in.); *S. Ewersii* (Rose-purple, June–Aug., 6 in.); *S. spectabile* (Rosy-flesh, July–Sept., 12–18 in.).

Sempervivum (Houseleek)—Large genus of curious succulent plants, mostly hardy perennials, although some require the protection and warmth of a greenhouse. They are well suited to sunny chinks or bare ledges in the rock garden, and thrive in sandy loam. For culture, *see* Rock Plants, p. 283. Except for *S. arachnoideum*, the Cob-web Houseleek, the hardy kinds need no protection in winter. *Species—S. arachnoideum* (Reddish-pink, June–Aug., 5 in.); *S. arenarium* (Yellow, June, 8 in.); *S. tectorum* (Common Houseleek) (Red, July, 10 in.).

Senecio (Groundsel or Ragwort)—Large genus of annual and perennial plants, some hardy and others only suitable for the greenhouse. Those in cultivation like a moist, deep and moderately light loam and a sunny position. For culture, *see* Annuals, p. 123, *and* Perennials, p. 281. *Greenhouse Culture* —Pot-up in Mar. in a compost of two-thirds fibrous loam and one-third sand, leaf-mould and a little well-rotted manure. Propagate by cuttings struck in spring in a frame with slight bottom heat. *Species—*(HARDY ANNUAL)—*S. elegans* and *vars.* (Purple, Rose or White, June–Oct., 12–20 in.). (HARDY PERENNIAL)—*S. Doria* (Yellow, Aug., 4 ft.); *S. pulcher* (Purple, Aug.–Oct., 20 in.); *S. tanguticus* (Yellow, Aug.–Oct., 3–6 ft.).

Sequoia—Hardy ornamental evergreen coniferous trees which thrive in a sunny position and in well-drained deep loam. *Culture—*Plant in May or Sept., no pruning is required. *S. sempervirens* (Redwood).

Shortia (Crimson Leaf)—Hardy dwarf-growing perennials which thrive in a moist but well-drained compost of two-thirds sandy peat and one-third loam together with some rough grit and charcoal. A sheltered, shady position in the rock garden suits them. In spring they carry white or rose flowers on stems 4 to 6 in. high. For culture, *see* Rock Plants, 283.

Sidalcea—Hardy perennial plants which do well in sunny borders and in a moist loam. For culture, *see* Perennials, p. 281. *Species and Varieties—S.*

candida (White); *S. malvæflora rosea* (Pink); *S. Rosy Gem* (Bright Pink). All July to Sept., 36 in.

Silene—Genus containing a considerable number of species, including the plants known as the Campion and Catchfly. They are for the most part hardy annuals, biennials and perennials, excellent for borders or the rock garden, and like a sunny, open position and a well-drained sandy loam. Most of the alpine species need a moist gritty loam. For culture, *see* Annuals, p. 123, Biennials, p. 125, *and* Perennials, p. 281. *Species*—(ANNUAL) —*S. Armeria* (Pink, July–Aug., 24 in.); *S. pendula compacta* (Blue, White, Rose, spring–summer, 4–6 in.). (PERENNIAL)—*S. acaulis* (Pink, June–Aug., 2 in.); *S. alpestris* (White, May–June, 5 in.); *S. Elizabethæ* (Rose, June–Aug., 6 in.); *S. laciniata* (Scarlet, July–Aug., 20 in.); *S. virginica* (Crimson, June–Aug., 6 in.).

Sisyrinchium (Satin Flower)—Hardy perennials useful in the border, the rock garden, or the alpine house. A cool and fairly moist loam with one-third peat leaf-mould and sand, or sandy peat, suits them best. *Pot Culture* —Pot-up annually in Sept., and place in a sunny position in the cold house. After blooming, keep in a cold frame until re-potting. For culture, *see* Perennials, p. 281. *Species*—*S. angustifolium* (Light Blue, May–July, 5–10 in.); *S. Bermudiana* (Deep Blue, May–June, 10 in.); *S. grandiflorum* (Purple, Mar.–May, 10 in.).

Skimmia—Hardy evergreen shrubs which like a sunny, sheltered position and a deep rich loam. They grow about 3 ft. high, flower in Apr. and carry scarlet berries in autumn. *Culture*—Plant in Mar. or Oct., grouping one male plant with six females. No pruning is necessary. To propagate take cuttings, or layer in the summer.

Smilax (Greenbriar)—Beautiful evergreen climbing plants which thrive in the cool greenhouse in a mixture of 2 parts of loam to 1 part of leaf-mould and sand. There are also a few hardy species which may be grown in the open. *Culture*—Pot-up in Mar., using 5 to 6-in. pots, stand in semi-shade, syringe and water well in hot weather. Cut old plants right back each Mar. Propagate by means of seed in slight heat (65° F.) in spring, or by means of division in Mar. *S. herbacea* is an herbaceous species.

Snowdrop (Galanthus)—Snowdrops thrive in the shade in well-drained moist, gritty loam, and are excellent for beds, for the rock garden, for growing in pots or for naturalizing in grass. *Culture*—Plant in Aug. or Sept., 3 in. deep and 3 in. apart; lift every fourth year only, and propagate by means of offsets. *Pot Culture*—Plant 1 in. deep in Sept. or Oct., using 4 to 5-in. pots and a compost of 2 parts of ordinary soil to 1 part of leaf-mould and sand, and keep in a cold frame covered with ashes or fibre until growth commences. Dry-off after flowering. *Species and Varieties*—(EARLY) —*G. Elwesii* (White, marked Green, Jan., 8 in.); *G. nivalis* (White, Jan., 6 in.); *G. plicatus* (White, Jan. 12 in.). (LATE)—*G. Ikariæ* (White, Mar.–Apr., 8 in.). (WINTER)—*G. Fosteri* (White, 8 in.).

Solanum Capsicastrum (Berried Solanum or Winter Cherry)—Beautiful evergreen greenhouse shrubs which do well in a compost of rich loam, peat and sand, and in winter bear red cherry-like berries. *Culture*—Sow in Mar. (Temp. 60° F.), or strike cuttings of young growths after blooming (Feb.) in moderate heat. Pinch-back when 4 in. high, pot-up in June in 5-in. pots and stand outdoors in a sunny, sheltered position for the summer. Pinch-back again two or three times before July, and early in Oct. move into the house, place near the glass. Cut back shoots of old plants in Feb.

Soldanella (Moonwort)—Pretty hardy perennial rock plant thriving in the shade, in moist, gritty loam and peat, and which in winter must be protected with a pane of glass. For culture, *see* Rock Plants, p. 283. *Species—S. alpina* (Violet-blue, May–June, 4 in.); *S. a. var. pyrolæfolia* (Lilac, Mar., 6 in.); *S. pusilla* (Violet, June–July, 3 in.).

Sparaxis—Half-hardy bulbous plants which may be grown in the open in sunny positions in warm sheltered borders and in well-drained sandy soil, or in pots in the greenhouse. *Culture*—Plant in Sept. or Oct., 2½ in. deep and 3 in. apart, and cover with fibre in winter. *Pot Culture*—Pot-up in Sept., placing six bulbs in a 5-in. pot, and stand in a cold frame covered with fibre until growth commences. The culture of these plants is very similar to that required for Ixias *(which see)*. *Species—S. grandiflora* and *vars.* (Violet, White or Crimson, Apr.–May, 18 in.); *S. tricolor* (Orange-red and Purple, May, 20 in.).

Spartium junceum (Spanish Broom)—Beautiful evergreen shrubs which thrive in a sunny position in poor, dry or sandy soil. They grow some 8 to 12 ft. high and carry yellow flowers from July to Sept. *Culture*—Plant in Oct. Cut back long shoots in Mar. To propagate, strike cuttings of young wood in a frame in July, or sow seeds; grow the young plants in pots until ready to be planted out.

Specularia (Legousia, Corn Violet, Venus' Looking Glass)—Hardy little annuals which thrive in sandy loam and peat in the rock garden. Sow in autumn and thin-out to at least 6 in. apart. *Species—L. falcata* (Blue); *L. hybrida fl. pl.* (Lilac or Blue); *L. perfoliata* (Purple and Blue); *L. Speculum Veneris* (Purple or White). All June to Sept.-flowering.

Spiræa—Genus of plants, both herbaceous and woody and mostly hardy perennials, which thrive in moist, rich loam and in a semi-shaded position. They are excellent in the border, for forcing indoors, and as room plants. *Culture*—Propagate by means of division in Mar. or Oct.; cuttings of young wood may also be struck in a frame in autumn. Thin-out the older wood of spring-flowering shrubs after flowering, if the bushes have become unshapely. Shrubs that flower between July and Sept. should have all weak wood cut right away in Feb., and all other shoots that have flowered must be cut back by at least one half. *Pot Culture*—Pot-up in Oct., using 8 to 10-in. pots and a compost of two-thirds sandy loam and one-third leaf-mould and a little well-rotted manure. Keep almost dry in a frost-proof frame till growth starts, then take into the cool house in succession as bloom is required. In a fort-night's time raise the temperature by five degrees or so, and give bi-weekly doses of weak liquid manure. Stand in a saucer of water in hot weather. Prune as advised above, harden-off in a frame, and sink the pots in ashes outdoors from May to Oct., then re-pot, if necessary, and place in a cold frame. *Species* (SHRUBS)—WHITE FLOWERS—*S. arguta* (6–8 ft.); *S. bracteata* (4–8 ft.); *S. canescens* (6–10 ft.); *S. prunifolia fl. pl.* (6–8 ft.); *S. Thunbergii* (3–5 ft.). PINK—*S. Douglasii* (4–6 ft.); *S. japonica Anthony Waterer* (1–2 ft.); *S. Margaritæ* (4–5 ft.); *S. Menziesii triumphans* (4–6 ft.).

Sternbergia (Yellow Star Flower, Winter Daffodil)—Half-hardy bulbous plants, which thrive in sunny positions in warm borders, in the rock garden or greenhouse, in sandy soil mixed with a little leaf-mould and mortar rubble. *Culture*—Plant in Apr., 4 in. deep and 5 in. apart; *S. Fischeriana*, which flowers in Feb., should be planted in July or Aug. Protect from frost with fibre and lift from the ground triennially; or pot-up in July and grow in the greenhouse. Propagate by means of offsets in Apr. *Species—S. colchiciflora* (Yellow, Aug.); *S. lutea* (Yellow, Aug.–Sept.); *S. Fischeriana* (Yellow, Feb.–Mar.). All grow about 10 in. high.

Stewartia (Stuartia)—Hardy deciduous shrubs requiring a sunny, sheltered site and rich, sandy loam and leaf-mould. Cut away all dead and weak wood every two or three years. Propagate by means of cuttings of ripened wood struck under glass in late summer, or by layering. *Species—S. Malacho-dendron* (Virginica); *S. pentagyna;* and *S. Pseudo-Camellia.* (All Creamy-white, June to July, 6 to 10 ft.).

Stock—Beautiful half-hardy annuals and biennials, which thrive in the sun in a rich and not too dry soil with lime in it.

Before being set out in their flowering positions, seedlings should be examined to see that they are double, the single-flowered being discarded; seedlings that will produce double-flowered plants generally have long, pale green, concave leaves, while the foliage of the single-flowered is, as a rule, deeper in colour, somewhat convex and more rigid.

The Ten-weeks' Stock (Matthiola annua) is a favourite for bedding. This half-hardy annual grows 6 to 24 in. high, and usually blooms ten or twelve weeks after being sown. For culture, *see* Annuals, p. 123.

Intermediate Stocks—These furnish flowers in the borders from June to Oct. and are excellent in a cold greenhouse for flowering in late winter and early spring. For spring-flowering, sow thinly in light soil in boxes or pots in a cold frame in Aug. Thin or transplant singly into small pots when fit to handle, using a compost of 2 parts of turfy loam to 1 part of well-rotted manure. Stand the pots in the open until frost is imminent, then transfer to a frost-proof frame. Pot-up from Oct. to Feb., using 6 to 7-in. pots, transfer to the cold greenhouse in Jan. and keep near the glass, or if for summer-flowering in the open, keep them in a frame until Apr., when harden-off and plant out in May. If preferred, treat as Ten-weeks' Stocks.

East Lothian Stocks—These are half-hardy biennials which bloom from June to Sept., and are popular for bedding. For early-flowering, sow during July in a compost of two-thirds loam to one-third leaf-mould and sand, in a cold frame. Winter in cold frames, or pits, and plant out the following spring. *See* Biennials, p. 125. If preferred these stocks may be treated as half-hardy annuals.

Brompton or Giant Stocks—These are half-hardy biennials flowering in May, June and July. The seed should be sown in July thinly in drills about 6 in. apart in a light, sandy bed with an east aspect. When about 3 in. high, thin-out the seedlings to 6 in. apart, winter in a cold frame and plant out in Mar.

Nice or Winter-flowering Stocks—For winter-flowering in the cool green-house sow in a cold frame in June, pot-up three seedlings in a 5-in. pot, grow on in a frame and transfer to the cool house early in Dec. For spring-flowering, sow in a frame in Aug., grow as above and take into the house when winter-flowering plants are over.

Varieties—BROMPTON—(White) *Cottager's White;* (Rose) *Sunrise;* (Scarlet) *Old English Scarlet;* (Purple) *Cottager's Purple;* (Green) *Improved Green.* EAST LOTHIAN—(White) *White Wallflower-leaved;* (Crimson) *Crimson Wall-flower-leaved.* INTERMEDIATE—(White) *Crystal White;* (Lilac) *Queen Alex-andra;* (Scarlet) *Covent Garden.* NICE OR WINTER-FLOWERING—(White) *Mont Blanc;* (White and Rose) *Riviera Market;* (White, Rose, Salmon, Mauve, or Crimson) *Beauty of Nice;* (Pale Yellow) *Yellow Prince;* (Pink) *Empress Elizabeth;* (Lilac) *Queen of the Belgians.* TEN-WEEK—(White) *Snowdrift;* (Primrose) *Princess Mary;* (Salmon) *Salmon Beauty;* (Pale Red) *Almond Blossom;* (Crimson) *Crimson King;* (Scarlet) *Fireball;* (Mauve) *Mauve Beauty;* (Violet) *Violet Queen;* (Blue) *Celestial;* (Various) *Giant Perfection, Perfection Ten-week,* and *Superb Bedding.*

Stock, Night-scented (Matthiola bicornis)—This most fragrant of hardy annuals likes a fairly rich soil, with lime or old mortar rubble in it. For culture, *see* Annuals, p. 123.

Stokesia (Stoke's Aster)—Hardy perennials which thrive in sunny borders and in light, well-drained soil, grow some 1 to 2 ft. in height, and bear blue or white flowers in early autumn. *Species—S. laevis.* See Perennials, p. 281.

Streptocarpus (Cape Primrose)—Lovely perennial suitable for culture in the warm greenhouse. *Culture*—Pot-up annually in Feb. or Mar., using 6-in. pots and a compost of equal parts of sandy loam and leaf-mould. Propagate by means of seed in gentle heat (60° F.) in Feb., by leaf-cuttings or by division in Mar. If seed is sown, the small plants should be pricked-off singly into small pots and gradually re-potted until in 6-in. pots. They must be kept moist and shaded from strong sun. *Species, etc.—S. caulescens* (Pale Blue); *S. Dunnii* (Rose); *S. Galpinii* (Mauve and White); *S. Rexii* (Blue); *S. Wendlandii* (Rose or Blue). All May to Oct., 10 to 20 in.

Styrax (Storax)—Hardy deciduous shrubs or small trees, that like a sunny, sheltered position and a moist, rich, sandy loam. *Culture*—Plant in Oct. In autumn thin-out any weak shoots. Propagate by means of layering in autumn. *Species—S. Hemsleyana* (10–20 ft.); *S. japonica* (8 ft.); *S. Obassia* (8 ft.). All White, June to July.

Sweet Pea (Lathyrus)—Sweet Peas enjoy a rich soil properly prepared prior to sowing. A trench 2 ft. wide should be dug out to a depth of from 2 to 3 ft., while a plentiful supply of well-rotted horse-manure should be worked into the lower strata some 10 in. below the surface. With the top spit may be incorporated a little leaf-mould, bonemeal, soot and lime, but no stable manure. Sweet Peas can be sown in the open on a dry day, generally early in Mar., but rather earlier in a warm sheltered situation. It is often beneficial to soak the seeds in warm water overnight, especially if the weather is very dry. The seed should be sown 1½ in. deep and 3 in. apart and the surface dusted with soot. When about 4 in. high, thin-out to 6 in. apart and support by means of twigs. As the plants grow taller, stakes 7 to 8 ft. in height should be placed in position. Wire peaguards or strands of black cotton should be used to keep the birds from the seeds. To secure the finest blooms, however, the seeds should be sown in late autumn or early in Feb. in 5-in. pots, placing six seeds in each, or a single seed in a small pot. The seeds may also be sown some 2 in. apart in boxes about 4 in. deep, but the seedlings must be potted-off singly as soon as possible. A compost of two-thirds fibrous loam and one-third leaf-mould, to which a sprinkling of bonemeal, wood-ashes and coarse sand have been added, will be found most suitable. Raise the young plants on a shelf near the glass in a cool greenhouse or in a frost-proof frame. Before being planted out into the open, early in Mar., when the plants are about 4 in. high, the plants should be hardened-off in a cold frame. Not more than three growths should be allowed to spring from each root, and when the plants have grown to 3 or 4 ft. high, they should be given, after rain or a soaking with clear water, a little soot-water or weak liquid manure (the colour of weak tea) once a week. The application of the latter must not be overdone. Water applied to sweet peas must have been exposed to the air for at least twenty-four hours; stone-cold water may cause the buds to drop. Plants so raised should flower from early June to late Sept.; if desired, early in May blooms may be had by growing the peas throughout in the greenhouse. The after-attention is very simple, but it is of prime importance to keep the plants free from seeds. If seeds are required, a portion of the row or one clump may be set apart for the purpose. The tips should be pinched-out when they reach 6 to 8 in. above the top of the stakes, and the soil between the plants should be kept continually stirred. Named varieties are innumerable and catalogues should be consulted.

Sweet William (Dianthus barbatus)—Beautiful hardy perennial, best treated as a biennial. For culture, *see* Biennials, p. 125. Sweet Williams can also be propagated by cuttings, by division of roots, or by layering. *Varieties—Auricula-eyed* (Rich Colours and White Eyes); *Giant White* (Self); *Harlequin* (Multi-coloured); *Nigricans* (Deep Purple); *Pheasant's Eye* (Double Strain, Crimson and White Eye); and *Scarlet Beauty* (Self). All June to Sept., 9 to 18 in.

Symphoricarpos (Snowberry)—Hardy deciduous shrubs which thrive in sun or shade and in ordinary soil. They grow some 5 ft. high and flower in July and Aug. *Culture*—Plant in Oct. or Nov.; cut out dead wood and weak shoots annually in Mar., and every few years lift the shrubs in autumn, divide the roots and replant the younger and more vigorous parts.

Syringa (Lilac)—Hardy deciduous shrubs which thrive in the sun in moist, well-manured, well-drained, and rather heavy loam. They grow from 5 to 15 ft. high and flower in Apr. and May. *Culture*—Plant in Oct. or Nov. Periodically cut away all suckers from the roots of grafted plants, disbud surplus buds in spring, and cut out old and weak wood after flowering, but never trim away the young or half-matured shoots. Propagate by means of layering in June, by matured cuttings in the open in Oct., or by suckers in Oct. *Forcing*—For decoration in the greenhouse, pot-up in Oct. or Nov., using 6 to 10-in. pots and a compost of 2 parts sandy loam to 1 part of leaf-mould and a little sand and bonemeal, stand in a sheltered, frost-proof position, and move into the house in succession as bloom is desired. After flowering, remove all dead blooms, syringe and keep up the heat for three weeks or so, then harden-off and sink the pots in ashes outdoors from May until the Oct. of the following year; never force two years running. Prune as above. Named varieties are kept true to type by crown or cleft-grafting in Mar.

For Mock Orange or *Philadelphus coronarius*, commonly called Syringa, *see* Philadelphus. *Named Varieties*—(SINGLE) (White) *F. C. Van Tol* and *Marie Legraye;* (Rich Red) *Congo;* (Crimson Purple) *Massena;* (Purple) *Souvenir de Louis Spath;* (Rich Mauve) *Charles X;* and (Slate Blue) *Hugo Koster.* (DOUBLE) (White) *Madame Lemoine;* (Rosy Pink) *Belle de Nancy;* (Violet) *Alphonse Lavallée;* (Soft Mauve) *Kathleen Hovermeyer;* (Red-purple) *Charles Joly;* (Lilac Blue) *President Grevy.*

Tagetes (African and French Marigolds)—Half-hardy annuals for warm, sunny beds and borders. *T. erecta* requires rich soil; *T. patula* thrives in poor soil. For culture, *see* Annuals, p. 123. *See also* Calendula.

Species—*T. erecta* (African Marigold). *Named Varieties*—*Giant Orange* (Double); *Lemon Queen* (Single). Both June to Sept., 20 to 40 inches. *T. patula* (French Marigold). *Named Varieties*—*Cloth of Gold; Yellow Bedder; Star of India* (Crimson-red, Striped Yellow); and *Silver King.* All June to Sept., 9 to 18 in.; *T. tenuifolia* (*T. signata*) (Yellow flowers and finely-cut foliage, 12–18 in.).

Tamarix or Tamarisk—Hardy deciduous or evergreen shrubs which do well anywhere in light ordinary soil, growing from 5 to 10 ft. high and flowering from May to Sept. *Culture*—Plant in Oct. or Nov. Prune summer-flowering species in Mar., spring-flowering kinds after flowering. Strike cuttings in the open in Oct. *Species*—*T. tetrandra* and *T. pentandra.*

Taxus (Yew)—Hardy evergreen trees or shrubs which thrive in sun or shade and in ordinary soil. *T. baccata* is the Common Yew, usually used for hedges. *Culture*—Plant in May or Sept. When necessary trim in May or Aug. Propagate by means of seed in the open in Mar., or by cuttings of young wood in a frame in Sept.

Tecoma (Trumpet Flower)—Evergreen climbing shrubs which thrive in well-drained, light soil on warm sunny walls or in the greenhouse. *Culture* —Strike cuttings of ripe wood in a frame with bottom heat in autumn. Plant in dry, open weather between Oct. and Apr. *Species*—*T. Garrocha*, shrub for the cool greenhouse (Flowers Yellow, Salmon and Scarlet, leaves pinnate, 5–6 ft.); *T. Smithii*, shrub (Flowers Yellow and Orange, winter).

Tecomaria capensis (*Tecoma capensis*) (Cape Honeysuckle)—Partial climber with Orange-red flowers, at one time included under Tecoma and needing similar treatment. Suitable for the cool greenhouse.

Teucrium (Germander)—This genus includes some useful little herbaceous plants and a few evergreen shrubs. The herbaceous perennials thrive in the sun in gritty loam in the border or rock garden. For culture, *see* Perennials. p. 281. The shrubs need a warm, sunny and sheltered position; a sandy loam suits them best. They are increased by cuttings of young shoots. *Species*— (PERENNIAL)—*T. Chamædrys* (Bluish-red. July–Aug., 10 in.); *T. Marum* (Deep Pink, Aug.–Sept., 10 in.). (SHRUBBY)—*T. flavum* (Yellow, Aug.–Sept., 30 in.); *T. fruticans* (Pale Lavender-blue, Mar.–Sept., 4–6 ft.).

Thalictrum (Meadow Rue)—Hardy perennials which thrive in well-drained, rich, sandy loam, in sunny or shady borders, or by the side of a stream. Dwarf kinds are useful rock plants. *T. minus var. adiantifolium* and *T. dipterocarpum* are excellent for cold greenhouse. For culture, *see* Perennials, p. 281. *Pot Culture*—Lift from the open and pot-up in Nov., using 5 to 6-in. pots and a compost of equal parts of rich loam and leaf-mould. *Species*— *T. minus var. adiantifolium* (Yellow, June–Sept., 20 in.); *T. alpinum* (Greenish, May–June, 5 in.); *T. dipterocarpum* (Rose, Purple, or White, June–Sept., 36–50 in.); *T. glaucum* (Yellow, July–Aug., 48–72 in.).

Thermopsis (False Lupin)—Hardy perennials which grow from 12 to 30 in. high and flower in summer. They do well in sheltered, sunny borders and in rich, sandy soil. *See* Perennials, p. 281. (*Several species.*)

Thunbergia alata—Evergreen climbers carrying pretty flowers from June to Sept., and much used for hanging baskets and for greenhouse staging. They like a rich, fibrous loam mixed with leaf-mould and sand, and are raised from seed in Mar. in sandy soil, in a temperature of 60° F., or from cuttings subjected to gentle bottom heat. Pot-on for flowering into 4 to 5-in. pots, or harden-off and set out in the open in June in a warm, sheltered bed.

Thuja (Arbor-vitæ)—Hardy evergreen trees often used instead of yew as hedge plants. Thev succeed in sunny positions in any moist garden soil. *Culture*—Plant in May or Sept. No pruning is necessary. Trim hedge plants in Apr. and Sept. Propagate by means of seeds in a frame, or by cuttings in a frame in Sept.

Thymus (Thyme)—Hardy trailing plants that are useful for the rock or paved garden, and which thrive in the sun in well-drained, sandy loam. For culture, *see* Rock Plants, p. 283. *Species*—*T. Serpyllum* and *vars.*

Tiarella cordifolia (Foam Flower)—Hardy perennials which like a shadv position in the border or rock garden and a moist, ordinary soil. They grow some 9 in. high and carry creamy-white flowers from Apr. to June. For culture, *see* Perennials, p. 281.

Tigridia (Tiger Iris)—Half-hardy bulbous plants which do best in a light,

rich, sandy loam and leaf-mould, in a warm, sunny position in a dry border
or rock garden, or in the greenhouse. *Culture*—Plant about the middle of
Apr., 4 in. deep and 6 in. apart, letting the bulbs rest on sand. Lift from
the ground in Nov. For Pot Culture, six bulbs may be placed in a 6-in. pot,
the latter being kept in a frame or cool house until growth has started.
Propagate by means of offsets in Apr. *Species*—*T. Pavonia* (Scarlet, Marked
Yellow and Purple); *T. P. var. conchiflora* (Yellow, Purple Spots); *T. P. var.
grandiflora rubra* (Crimson, Scarlet). All flower from May to July, 12 to
18 in.

Tilia (Lime)—Hardy deciduous trees, which thrive in sunny, sheltered positions and in moist, rich soil. They bear fragrant yellowish-green flowers from
June to Aug. *Culture*—Plant in Oct. or Nov. Thin-out the branches when
overcrowded.

Torenia—Half-hardy annuals of trailing nature, which flower in Aug. and
are suitable for hanging baskets. They need a compost of sandy loam and
leaf-mould. For culture, *see* Annuals, p. 123.

Trachelium cæruleum (Throatwort)—Half-hardy biennial which thrives in
leaf-mould and sandy loam in sunny beds or borders. It grows about 18 in.
high and flowers in July and Aug. For culture, *see* Biennials, p. 125. *T.
cæruleum* is a good pot plant for the cool house.

Tradescantia (Spiderwort)—Hardy and half-hardy perennial plants suitable
for beds and cool greenhouse. They thrive in sun or shade in any good well-
drained soil. For culture, *see* Perennials, p. 281. *T. canaliculata (reflexa)*
(Blue, June–Sept., 20 in.) and *T. virginiana* (Purple, Red, Blue or White, June–
Sept., 20 in.), the Common Spiderwort, and its varieties, are good repre-
sentatives of the hardy species.

Trientalis (Starflower and Chickweed-Wintergreen)—Small hardy perennials, suitable for a light, rich, peaty soil, in a shady and moist position in the
rock garden. They may also be used as a border edging. *T. americana* (Starflower) bears white flowers on 6-in. stems in June or July, and *T. europæa*
in Apr. or May. Propagate by means of seed in summer, or by division in
spring.

Trifolium (Clover, Shamrock, Trefoil)—Hardy annuals and perennials
which thrive in any light soil, and are easily raised from seed or propagated
by means of division of roots.

Trillium (Wood Lily or Trinity Flower)—Hardy tuberous-rooted perennials,
which thrive in well-drained, moist, peaty soil, in partial shade in border or
rock garden, or in pots in cold greenhouse. *Culture*—Plant in Oct. Lift
from the soil when overcrowded. Propagate by means of seed sown in a
frame in Mar., or in the open in June, or increase by division of roots in Oct.
Species—*T. grandiflorum* (Rose or White, June–July, 6–12 in.); *T. erectum*
(Deep Purple, May–June, 5–10 in.).

Tritonia (Montbretia)—Hardy bulbous plants, which thrive in rich, sandy
loam and leaf-mould in warm, sunny beds or borders, or in pots. *Culture*—
Plant in Apr., 4 in. deep and 4 to 6 in. apart. Cover with fibre in winter, and
lift every four years only; half-hardy varieties must be lifted each Oct. *Pot
Culture*—Pot-up in Apr., placing five bulbs in a 7 to 8-in. pot, and using a
compost of 2 parts of peaty loam to 1 part of leaf-mould and sand. Sink the
pots in ashes in a frost-proof frame, and transfer to the greenhouse early in
June. Re-pot the plants every year; propagate by means of offsets. *Named
Varieties*—*Drap d'Or* (Yellow); *Etoile de Feu* (Orange); *Fire King* (Fiery
Red); *Lord Nelson* (Scarlet); *Phare* (Crimson); *rosea* (Rosy-pink); *Salmon
King* (Salmon). All July to Sept., 2 to 4 ft.

Trollius (Globe Flower)—Hardy herbaceous perennials, which thrive in rich, moist loam, in shady borders or in the marsh garden. For culture, *see* Perennials, p. 281. *Species—T. asiaticus* (Yellow or Orange, May and June, 24 in.); *T. europæus* (Orange, May–June, 30 in.); *T. Ledebourii* (Golden Yellow, Apr.–May, 30–40 in.).

Tropæolum—Beautiful climbers, mostly half-hardy annuals, invaluable for covering trellises out of doors and for training up pillars and rafters in the cool greenhouse. The best known are *T. aduncum* (*peregrinum*) (Canary Creeper), *T. majus* and *T. nanum* (Nasturtium); for cultural details, *see* Canary Creeper and Nasturtium. For outdoor use, *T. aduncum* and *T. majus* are especially good, also the perennial species, *T. polyphyllum* and *T. speciosum* (Flame Nasturtium). *T. peltophorum* (*Lobbianum*) blooms beautifully through the winter in the greenhouse, and likes a light, but not too rich a soil. Pot-up from Mar. to Apr. in 6 to 10-in. pots and grow near the glass. Propagate by means of seed, or by cuttings in heat in Mar. or Apr.

Tulips—Tulips look best massed in beds or borders, carpeted with other spring flowers. The best tulip for all-round purposes is probably the *Keizer Kroon*. For planting permanently, the *Cottage* and *Darwin* tulips are best. *Culture*—Tulips require a fair amount of sand in a well-drained, deeply-dug, rich loam with a cool, moist subsoil, and a sunny, sheltered position, not subject to draughts and cold winds. Plant early in Nov., from 4 to 5 in. deep and from 8 to 10 in. apart. It is best to lift the bulbs and plant them in a different bed each year. If this cannot be done, the soil should be well dug and improved by the use of bonemeal or well-rotted cow-manure. *Pot Culture*—The early single and double dwarf *Duc Van Thol* tulips are excellent for this purpose. The former may be planted six or eight bulbs in a good-sized pot; but of the latter, three bulbs are sufficient. All tulips require a good supply of water when in flower and should be shaded from the sun; hard forcing will prevent flowering. The soil and treatment necessary for tulips grown in pots are the same as recommended for hyacinths. Propagation is carried out by means of offsets, separated from the bulbs when lifted in summer, and planted in Sept. or Oct. *See also chapter on* Bulb Culture. Named varieties are innumerable and catalogues should be consulted.

Tunica—Dwarf-growing hardy perennials for the rock garden and for edgings to borders. A sandy loam suits them best, in sun or shade. For culture, *see* Perennials, p. 281. *Species—T. Saxifraga* (Pale Rose or White, June–Aug., Trailing).

Typha (Reed Mace, Bulrush, or Cat-o'-nine-tails)—Genus of aquatic plants, which thrive on a swampy bank, in the marsh garden, or at the edge of a sheltered pond with from 1 to 12 in. of water above the crowns. They grow some 6 ft. high and flower in late summer. *Species—T. latifolia.*

Ulex (Furze, or Gorse)—Free-flowering evergreen shrubs bearing yellow flowers, and which like a sunny position and a poor, dry soil. *U. europæus fl. pl.* (5 ft.) flowering from Mar. to June and *U. nanus* (18 in.) flowering from Sept. to Dec., are both useful for hedges. *Culture*—Plant out from pots at any time between Mar. and Oct.; cut back when overgrown, and propagate by means of cuttings in a frame in Aug., or sow seed in a frame in Mar.

Ulmus (Elm)—Hardy deciduous trees which thrive in almost any soil and in practically any position. *Culture*—Plant in Oct. or Nov. Thin-out the branches in the summer when required. Propagate by means of seeds, grafting, or from sucker growths. *Several species and vars.*

Ursinia—Half-hardy annuals which can be grown in the open during summer in well-drained soil and sunny position. Propagated by means of seed sown thinly *in situ*. Thin in seedling stage.

Vaccinium—Large genus of shrubby plants which includes the Whortleberry or Bilberry (*V. Myrtillus*). There are several species grown for the beauty of their flowers, fruit and tinted foliage in autumn; these require a moist, sandy and peaty loam. Propagate by means of cuttings struck under glass in spring and summer, by root-suckers, or by seed sown in autumn when ripe. Plant out in Mar. *Species*—*V. Arctostaphylos* [Bear Berry] (Greenish-white, 6 ft.); *V. corymbosum* [Blueberry] (Pale Pink or White, 5 ft.); *V. Myrtillus* [Whortleberry] (Pale Pink, 1½ ft.). All May-flowering.

Valeriana—Hardy perennials of which the smaller species are useful for the rock garden. The best known are *V. officinalis* (All Heal), and *V. Phu*. They thrive in sunny borders and in any ordinary soil. For culture, *see* Perennials, p. 281. Both flower from June to Oct.

Vallota speciosa (Scarborough Lily)—Half-hardy bulbous plants, which thrive in a compost of 2 parts of sandy loam to 1 part of leaf-mould. They require the protection of the cool greenhouse or sunny window, and flower on stems from 1 to 2 ft. high in Aug. and Sept. *Culture*—Plant in July or Aug. singly in 5 to 8-in. pots, with the crowns 6 in. below the surface. Winter near the glass and give liquid manure when the buds form. Water moderately till the leaves die in spring, and keep fairly dry and exposed to the sun from May to Sept. Leave in the same pot for three or four years. Propagate by means of seed in spring, or by offsets in Aug.

Venidium fastuosum—Half-hardy annuals which thrive in sunny, dry, well-drained situations outdoors. Sow in flowering position towards the end of Apr.

Verbascum (Mullein)—Hardy biennials and perennials which may be grown in sunny borders or in the wild garden in light, ordinary soil. For culture, *see* Biennials, p. 125, *and* Perennials, p. 281. *Species*—(BIENNIAL)—*V. olympicum* (Golden Yellow, Grey Foliage, June–Sept., 70 in.). (PERENNIAL)—*V. Chaixii* (Yellow, Mauve Centre, June–Sept., 50–90 in.); *V. phœniceum* (Purple, White or Rose, June–Sept., 20–30 in.). Good hybrids, *Cotswold Beauty, Pink Domino.*

Verbena—Half-hardy annuals, biennials and perennials, which do well in rich sandy loam, in sunny beds. For culture, *see* Annuals, p. 123, *and* Biennials, p. 125. (*Perennials*)—Sow in heat (Temp. 60° F.) in Feb. and treat as biennials. With named varieties, at any rate, strike cuttings of sturdy shoots that have no flower buds in a frame in spring or early autumn. Autumn-struck verbenas are best left in the cutting pots until Feb.; and, unlike calceolarias, if sufficient old plants are kept over the winter for stock, spring-struck cuttings are best. Plant out 10 in. apart in June. *Pot Culture*—Pot-up in Mar., using 5 to 6-in. pots and a compost of sandy loam and leaf-mould, and a little well-rotted manure. Stop-back the young shoots to make bushy plants. *Named Varieties*—(HALF-HARDY PERENNIALS)—(White, Scented) *Boule de Neige;* (Pink) *Miss Willmott; Crimson King; King of the Scarlets; Purple Emperor.*

Veronica (Speedwell)—SHRUBBY SPECIES—Now included in the genus Hebe are amongst the most valuable of summer and autumn-blooming plants, both for greenhouse culture and for out of doors, where, with a dry subsoil and somewhat sheltered, sunny situation, the plants will generally stand uninjured through the winter. *Culture*—Plant in Apr. or Sept. Trim annually to keep in shape only, but it is usually necessary to prune hard back every few years. To propagate, strike cuttings of matured wood in a frame in Aug., the young shoots should occasionally be pinched-back, but no "stopping" must be done after June. *Pot Culture*—Pot-up in the early summer, using 6 to 8-in. pots and a compost of 2 parts of loam to 1 part of leaf-mould. Harden-off and stand in the open from May to Sept., then take into the cold house. After flowering, prune severely in Mar., and place the pots near the glass. ANNUAL SPECIES—The miniature species, such as *V. glauca*, *V. syriaca* and *V. s. var. alba*, make very pretty plants for small beds and edgings. *Culture* —Sow in the open in Sept., and thin-out to 5 in. apart as soon as fit to handle. HERBACEOUS PERENNIAL SPECIES—These thrive in sunny positions and in any fairly good garden soil, especially if it is rather gritty. Every fourth year the plants should be lifted and divided, the younger outer crowns only being replanted. Propagate by means of division in Mar. and (some species) in Oct. Some of the dwarf-growing species make excellent rock plants. For culture, *see* Rock Plants, p. 283. *Species and Varieties—*(ANNUAL)*—V. syriaca var. alba* (White, summer, 6 in.); *V. glauca* (Blue, summer, 6 in.). (PERENNIAL)*—V. Allionii* (Deep Blue, May–July, 5 in.); *V. austriaca alba* (White, June–July, 12 in.); *V. caucasica* (Pale Red, June–Aug., 10 in.); *V. incana* (Violet-blue, Silver Foliage, June–Sept., 6–9 in.); *V. prostrata* (Dark Blue, June–July, 2–3 in.); *V. longifolia, var. subsessilis* (Deep Blue, July–Sept., 20–30 in.); *V. virginica* (*Leptandra*) (White, July–Sept., 30–36 in.).

Viburnum—Hardy deciduous trees and shrubs which thrive in any soil, but prefer a moist, well-drained deep loam, and are most useful for shrubberies. The best-known shrubby species is *V. Opulus sterile*, the Guelder Rose or Snowball Tree. *V. tomentosum plicatum*, a splendid border shrub, is also a useful sort for the greenhouse. Pot-up in Oct., using 7 to 10-in. pots and ordinary loam. Prune after flowering, and plant out for two years in the open. *V. Tinus* (Laurustinus) is an evergreen species making a bush 8 ft. in height, and best planted in sun or shade under trees and facing north. It flowers in autumn and all through the winter months. It is also useful for pot culture indoors. In the latter case pot-up in the early autumn, using 6 to 10-in. pots and well-drained sandy loam. Cut well back after flowering, and put out in the open in semi-shade from May to Oct. Other good species are *V. Carlesii*, with pinkish-white flowers in Apr. and May; *V. fragrans*, pink or white, Jan. to Mar.; and *V. tomentosum*, creamy-white, May and June. *General Culture in the Open*—Plant in a sunny position, deciduous species in Oct., Nov., or Mar.; evergreens in May or Sept. Trim into shape annually and, when necessary, cut out old wood in July (deciduous) and May (evergreen species). Propagate by means of cuttings in a frame in June, or layer in Oct.

Vinca (Periwinkle)—Hardy periwinkles are evergreen shrubs, which grow in any well-drained ordinary soil, and look well in borders or on rock-work. *V. major* (20 in.) and *V. minor* (9 in.) have purple-blue flowers from June to Sept. There are also mauve and white varieties. *Culture*—Plant from Mar. to Oct. Cut back straggling shoots in Apr. Propagate by means of division in Mar. or Oct.

Viola—The viola and pansy are so similar in their cultural requirements that we treat them under the one heading. Violas, sometimes called Tufted Pansies, are much used for bedding or as edging plants, where they will flower from May until well into Nov. Any ordinary, deeply-dug, moderately rich loam will suit them. A sprinkling of good compost and a dressing of soot or bonemeal should be scattered on the top. Heavy clay is not good for violas. A cool, but not damp, position in partial shade is best. *Culture*— Violas may be propagated from seed, by cuttings, or by division of the roots.

Seed intended for spring flowers should be sown in boxes in June, using a good light soil, and the box should be covered with a sheet of glass until the seeds are up. When fit to handle transplant 2 in. apart into other boxes; water liberally and shade from sun. As frosty weather approaches, the boxes should be placed in a cold frame for the winter. At the beginning of Apr., transplant about 9 to 12 in. apart into partially-shaded beds, keeping the " balls " as far as possible intact. Cuttings of new, but vigorous growths from the centre of the plant may be struck in Sept. in a shady frame and planted out in Mar. for blooming the following year. Propagation by cuttings may take place any time from Apr. to the end of Oct., although Aug. and Sept. are the best months. For early flowering, it is best to propagate by division of old roots in Sept. The hardier kinds can be wintered successfully in the open in any shady nook in the garden, but not under trees. The less hardy kinds should be wintered in cold frames. Pansies bear larger and brighter flowers if raised from seed; violas, however, are more vigorous when propagated by cuttings. All dead blooms should be periodically picked off. *Pot Culture*—Strike cuttings in July or Aug., and when rooted, plant in 4-in. pots, and plunge in ashes or coconut fibre in a cold frame, where they should remain until the end of Mar. Then shift them into 8-in. pots, keep close for a few days, then admit air gradually. *Alpine Species*—There are also many delightful alpine species which need similar treatment to that described for the bedding viola, but the soil should be somewhat more loose, gritty and moist. Named varieties are innumerable and catalogues should be consulted.

Violet (Viola odorata)—Violets may be grown in pots, by placing two or three runners or offsets in a pot in Apr. or May, and keeping them in a frame, slightly shaded from the hot sun in summer; loam, leaf-mould and sand suit them admirably, but the violet is not particular as to soil. Russian violets, and sometimes the Neapolitan, will flower from Sept. to Apr., if given the protection of glass; true violets flower in Mar. and Apr. There are many varieties, but their culture is so similar that they may all be considered together. The grower should start with good stock from a reliable source, and, although the violet is a perennial, it is best to renew the stock each year.

Cultivation—The violet should be propagated annually in June; when the plants have flowered, remove them from the soil, divide them into single crowns, cutting off all runners and dead foliage and selecting the finest outside crowns only; then plant out the single varieties 15 in. apart each way, and the double kinds 10 to 12 in. apart and press the soil firmly round the roots, but do not bury the crowns. A rich, well-dug and well-drained bed with an east aspect, where they can receive the morning sun, should be chosen. When the plants show signs of growth, stir the soil about their roots with a small hoe, water liberally, and syringe them in the evenings of dry, hot days. Pinch-off all runners as they appear, and give a little shade from the sun in hot weather. Nothing more, save fortnightly doses of weak liquid manure or dustings with an artificial fertilizer and soot is required for their culture during the summer months. The double varieties should be wintered in pots under glass or in a frame. Violets may also be propagated by cuttings struck in a cold frame in Sept. or Oct.

Pot Culture—To obtain bloom during the winter months, the best compost is 4 parts of turfy loam to 1 part each of rotted manure, leaf-mould and sand, and a sprinkling of soot, well mixed together. In Sept. raise the violets carefully from the bed in which they have been growing with as much earth on their roots as possible, and remove all side-shoots and runners. One strong plant should be put in each 6 to 7-in. pot with the crowns just above the soil. The pots should be well drained with broken bones instead of pot-sherds and after planting the pots should be well watered to settle the soil about the roots. A sufficient number of frames should be arranged in a sunny, sheltered southern aspect, placing them in such a manner that the lights will throw off rain quickly. Put in a layer of old tan about 4 in. thick, and in this the pots should be plunged in rows up to their rims. The bed of tan should be 6 to 9 in. higher at the back than at the front, and should be raised so that the plants are from 6 to 9 in. from the lights. Keep the frame almost closed for three or four days after planting, and shade if the sun is strong. After the first fortnight, and when the tempera-ture is above 50° F., the lights may be removed during the day, and at night they should be tilted up at the back for the admission of air. When the temperature is below 50° F., the lights should be left on, but even then air should be admitted from behind during the daytime. If the temperature is below 40° F., the admission of air should be very partial, if it is admitted at all. At no time after the plants begin to bloom should the lights be entirely removed, except for the purpose of watering or gathering the flowers. When the weather is cold, a covering of mats should be applied at nights. In hard frosts, two mats should be put on as well as litter round the sides of the frame. Care must be taken to wet the leaves as little as possible.

Varieties—(DOUBLE)—(White) *Comte de Brazza;* (Lavender, Blue and White) *Marie Louise;* (Violet Pink) *Madame Millet;* (Pale Blue) *Duchess de Parme;* (Dark Blue, White Throat) *Mrs. Arthur.* (SINGLE)—(White) *White Czar;* (Rose-pink) *Cœur d'Alsace;* (Rose, Pink and White) *Rosea Delicat-issima;* (Rose and Lavender) *Mrs. Lloyd George* (Semi-double); (Purple) *Admiral Avellan;* (Violet) *Prince of Wales.*

Virginian Stock (Malcomia)—Hardy annual which thrives in sunny beds and in fairly light soil and which is useful for edgings. For culture, *see* Annuals, p. 123. *Varieties*—(Crimson) *Fairy Queen;* (Purple and Crimson) *Crimson King.* Both June to Oct., 6 in.

Vitis (Vine)—Hardy deciduous climbers, including the popular Virginian Creeper. They grow well in deeply-dug, moist soil with a little lime in it, and should be planted only in sheltered positions. *Culture*—Strike cuttings in a frame in Sept. Plant in dry and open weather from Nov. to Mar.; trim in winter. *Species*—*V. Coignetiæ* is known as the Crimson Glory Vine; other good species are *V. Thunbergii* and *V. vinifera purpurea,* the Teinturier Grape.

Wahlenbergia (Edraianthus, Tufted Harebell)—Dwarf-growing, hardy perennial rock plants, which like a sunny position and gritty loam, with a little lime-rubble. For culture, *see* Rock Plants, p. 283. *Species*—*W. Pumilio (Edraianthus Pumilio)* (Violet-blue, 2 in.); *E. serpyllifolius major* (Violet, 2–3 in.). All May to June.

Waitzia (Everlasting Flowers)—Half-hardy annuals, which can be grown in warm, sunny borders or in the greenhouse. For culture, *see* Annuals, p. 123. *W. grandiflora* (Golden-yellow, July–Sept., 20 in.).

Wallflower (Cheiranthus)—Hardy biennials and perennials which may be grown in sunny, open beds or borders, in the rock garden or in the cold greenhouse, in dry, sandy loam with some lime in it. Double wallflowers, except German varieties, must be raised from cuttings. The perennial species are usually grown as biennials. For culture, *see* Biennials, p. 125. *Pot Culture*—Pot-up in Sept., using 5 to 6-in. pots and ordinary soil, and keep in a cold frame until the buds appear. *Species and Varieties*—*C. Allionii* (Bright Orange, 10 in.); *C. alpinus* (Pale Yellow, 6 in.); *C. kewensis* (Chestnut, 12 in.); *C. Marshallii* (Orange-yellow, 6 in.). All Apr. to June. *Named Varieties*—

(C. Cheiri)—(Pale Yellow) *Primrose Dame;* (Bright Yellow) *Cloth of Gold;* (Golden) *Harpur Crewe* (Double); *Ivory White; Orange Bedder;* (Apricot) *Eastern Queen; Blood Red;* (Crimson) *Vulcan;* (Brown) *Harbinger; Purple Queen.*

Watsonia (Bugle Lily)—Half-hardy bulbous plants which should be grown in sunny positions in warm, sheltered borders and in sandy loam, peat, and leaf-mould, or in the cold greenhouse. *Culture*—Plant in Oct. or Mar., 3 in. deep and 4 in. apart. Pot plants should be kept dry in winter. Propagate by means of offsets in Oct. *Species*—*W. coccinea* (Scarlet, 20 in.); *W. densiflora* (Pink, 15 in.). All June to Aug.

Wisteria—Hardy May-flowering deciduous climbers that do well in any good garden soil, but prefer moist, deep and well-drained sandy loam. *W. sinensis (chinensis)*, of which there are three or four varieties, is the best known; *W. floribunda, var. multijuga* is a newer form with mauve, rose or white flowers, and longer racemes. *Culture*—Propagate by means of layering young wood in the summer, and plant out in permanent position in dry, open weather from Oct. to Apr. Both winter and summer pruning are essential to promote flower buds, and straggling shoots should be cut away, but sturdy laterals should be encouraged to grow out some 3 ft. from the main stems; once the climbers are trained in this way, the young shoots should, in winter, be cut hard back to within a couple of inches of the old wood. *Pot Culture*—In the cool greenhouse *W. sinensis* will flower from Feb. to Apr.; pot-up in Oct., using 8 to 12-in. pots and a compost of rich, sandy loam. Prune in Jan. or Feb., cutting back straggly shoots to within an inch of the base; sink the pots to their rims in ashes outdoors in a sunny spot from May to Dec.

Wulfenia carinthiaca—Hardy perennial which likes a shady position in the rock garden in loam and peat. It carries purple-blue flowers in July and Aug. on 9-in. stems. *See* Rock Plants, p. 283.

Xeranthemum (Immortelles)—Showy class of everlasting flowers, all of which are hardy and thrive in sunny beds or borders and in rich soil. The best known are: *X. annuum* (Purple, Rose, or White) and *X. inapertum* (Purple or White flowers); both grow 12 in. high and flower from July to Sept. For culture, *see* Annuals, p. 123.

Xerophyllum asphodeloides (Turkey's Beard)—Hardy perennials for the border, marsh, or wild garden. They love partial shade, and a moist gritty loam and leaf-mould. They carry spikes of white flowers 2 ft. high in May. For culture, *see* Perennials, p. 281.

Yucca—These are all practically hardy evergreen plants of quaint appearance, forming striking objects when planted on lawns, banks, or in the rock garden; they are also useful for winter bedding. Yuccas do best in sheltered, sunny positions in well-drained ordinary soil. *Culture*—Plant in Mar. or Apr.; cut away dead leaves in Mar. and dead flowers in Oct. *Pot Culture*—Pot-up in a compost of two-thirds fibrous loam and one-sixth coarse sand, and one-sixth finely-crushed brick rubble. Propagate by means of tops, with the leaves trimmed off, planted in pots of very sandy and porous soil, by rhizomes in spring, or by seed. *Y. gloriosa* is known as Adam's Needle.

Zantedeschia (Arum Lily)—The Arum Lily is easy to cultivate either in the greenhouse or in a room. Re-pot every Oct. in rich, light mould, preferably loam with equal parts of sand and cow-dung, the offsets having been removed, and the old soil well shaken out. A 6-in. pot may be used for each plant, or three may be placed in a 9 to 10-in. pot. From this time till June, or earlier if the plants have flowered, they should have abundance of water and occasional doses of liquid manure; it is best to keep the pot always standing in a deep saucer full of water. After this, however, they must be planted out in rich soil, or stood in the open in the semi-shade, kept moist, and be given occasional doses of manure-water till Oct., when the same treatment should be repeated. Propagate by means of offsets. The yellow species are less hardy and thrive best in the warm greenhouse. Pot-up in Feb. Withhold water gradually after flowering and keep the pot in a frost-proof frame through the winter. *Species and Varieties—Zantedeschia aethiopica; Z. a. Childsiana* (White, 24 in.); *Z. a. Little Gem* (White, dwarf); *Z. Rehmannii* (Rose); *Z. melanoleuca* (Purple and Yellow); and *Z. Elliottiana* (Yellow, Aug., 24 in.). The arum (except the yellow varieties) usually flowers in Apr. In catalogues the Arum Lily is still listed as Richardia.

Zauschneria (Californian Fuchsia)—Handsome perennials which thrive in gritty loam in the rock garden. For culture, *see* Rock Plants, p. 283. *Z. californica* (Scarlet, July–Sept., 12–18 in.) is the best known.

Zea (Indian Corn or Maize)—Half-hardy annuals which thrive in ordinary soil in warm, sunny situations. For culture, *see* Annuals, p. 123. *Z. Mays* (3 ft.) is also useful for greenhouse purposes.

Zephyranthes (Zephyr Flower)—Bulbous-rooted plants, some species of which are sufficiently hardy to thrive in warm, sunny borders and in rich and well-drained peaty loam; the more tender kinds should be grown in pots in the greenhouse. *Culture*—Plant in Oct., 4 in. deep and 3 in. apart, with the bulbs resting in sand, and protect with fibre in winter. Lift when over-crowded, and propagate by means of offsets in Oct. *Pot Culture*—Pot-up from Aug. to Nov., placing four to five bulbs in a 5-in. pot in a compost of 2 parts of loam to 1 part each of leaf-mould and peat with a little silver sand. Dry-off gradually after flowering. *Species—Z. candida* (White); *Z. grandiflora* (*carinata*) (Pale Pink); and *Z. rosea* (Rose). All May to Sept., 6 to 10 in.

Zinnia—Half-hardy annuals which thrive in light, rich soil. The dwarfer hybrid varieties are valuable for warm, sunny beds; the taller kinds for borders and the cool greenhouse. For culture, *see* Annuals, p. 123. *Greenhouse Plants*—Pot seedlings up singly in small pots in a compost of two-thirds fibrous loam and one-third dry, well-rotted manure and sand. Give ample light and ventilate freely, but do not let the temperature drop below 60° F., and avoid draughts. Re-pot before the plants get pot-bound, and as soon as the plants are re-established, reduce the temperature by about ten degrees and, as the buds appear, water weekly with weak manure-water and dress with bonemeal. *Species—Z. elegans* (Various, 20–30 in.); *Z. Haageana* (Orange, 12 in.); *Z. pauciflora* (Red, 20 in.). All July to Sept.

CHAPTER 17

Principles of Vegetable Culture

If it is at all possible, the rectangular form of garden plan is by far the most satisfactory and economical to run. The paths should be straight, strong and solid, and the garden should be well drained and sheltered. The shadier parts of the garden should be the home of vegetables that do not primarily require warmth, such as, rhubarb, seakale, Scotch kale, and the many varieties of salad. The pulses, potatoes and cabbages require more sun, and it is a safe rule to follow that where the cabbage will grow to perfection almost any vegetable will do well. The sides of any available walls which face east and south and west should have borders at their base in which fruit trees may be placed, and here also, owing to their more genial situation, early crops of all kinds may be nursed. The width of such borders depends upon the amount of sunlight that visits them, and while they should in no case be so wide as to render cultivation difficult, those which get most sun may be wider than those whose aspect is less sunny. A bed should be given up to herbs, and since so many of these are beautiful in form and sweet-smelling, the strip they occupy may be placed as near the house as is convenient.

Selecting Varieties

It is, of course, impossible to say definitely what are the best varieties to grow, as some kinds thrive on a moderately heavy soil, but do poorly on light soils and *vice versa*. Certain varieties are best for the early crop, others for the main crop, others are preferable for late sowing. At the end of the articles devoted to the individual vegetables, we have given varieties suitable for the various crops; some of the selections loving a light soil, others thriving in heavy soils.

Crop Rotation

With a few exceptions only, it will always be found a good plan to vary the crops taken from any given plot, never growing the same kind of plant on it for two seasons running. Each crop takes out of the soil certain elements and leaves it enriched by others. Thus, for example, leguminous crops, as peas, are able to extract nitrogen from the air, and besides using a part of it themselves, leave the soil richer in nitrogenous constituents than they found it. The nitrogen is stored in the roots which, for this reason, should always be left in the soil. This is a good moment to sow in this soil plants such as the onion, which demand a good supply of nitrogen in the soil ready for their use. It is a good

Catch-Crops

rough rule that tuberous or bulbous-rooted plants should come after fibrous-rooted ones, and *vice versa*. Crops so similar in habit and nature as cabbages, broccoli, sprouts and kale should not follow one another. Plants with shallow roots as the pea, the lettuce and the cabbage should be grown alternately with deep-rooted plants like the beet, the carrot or the parsnip. The soil should not be freshly manured for root-crops, manuring for the previous crop being sufficient. If manure has not previously been given, it must be dug in very deeply to encourage good straight roots. Fresh manure should never come in contact with the roots. Related crops usually suffer from the same diseases; this is another reason for a rotation, as the contaminated soil would be likely to infect a plant of similar kind. (*See* Table, p. 272.)

It will be found that much time will be saved if the rotation is worked out and decided upon well before the planting time. The following table, showing a strip of land divided into three plots, with a rotation on each covering three years, is a useful guide. It can, of course, be extended indefinitely both with regard to the number of plots used or the successive number of years.

THREE-YEAR ROTATION PLAN

Plot.	1st Year.	2nd Year.	3rd Year.
A	Cabbage crops	Root crops	Leguminous crops
B	Root crops	Leguminous crops	Cabbage crops
C	Leguminous crops	Cabbage crops	Root crops

Succession of Crops

Space is valuable, and it is, therefore, essential to plant another crop as soon as the previous one has been cleared. The chief crops that are over early and permit of second cropping are early turnips, onions, cabbages, potatoes and early peas. Quickly maturing crops useful to form the second crop to follow these are spinach, lettuce, onions, shorthorn carrots, turnips, cabbages or broccoli for use the following spring. In selecting these crops, consideration must be given to the correct rotation of crops. (*See* Table, p. 272.)

Catch-Crops

These are fast-maturing crops that may be planted between the rows of slower-growing vegetables or even in the rows between the individual plants. Before the main crop has matured and claimed its full space these " catch-crops " will have matured and have been cleared. Suitable catch-crops are shown in Table, p. 272.

247

When to Sow

On fairly dry soil, in warm situation, the sowing in the open may begin about the end of February—a few early peas, early beans, early horn carrots, and lettuce may then be sown. In March some parsnips, onions, beets, turnips and more peas, beans and carrots may be sown. In order to obtain a succession of vegetables through the year and not gluts at one time and none at another, it is desirable to sow the seeds of most vegetables in successive small quantities so that crop may follow crop.

Always sow in drills, not broadcast; it is then possible to keep the hoe busy between the rows. (*See also* sowing in the open and under glass in chapter 8.)

Thinning and Planting-out—Where crops are sown thinly, little thinning will be necessary, but as soon as the plants can be handled thin out to the distances advised for each vegetable.

Watering

Seedlings—Late in April and early in May while many seedlings are still tender we often experience hot, dry weather that would scorch up many of the seedlings unless they are watered. The hoe should be used unsparingly among the seedlings after watering. This will help to keep the earth moist and will let the air into the ground. It is almost always essential to water transplanted seedlings thoroughly to make the soil firm about their roots.

Maturer Plants—Crops whose roots spread out near the surface of the soil and do not descend very deeply will need liberal watering every day should the summer be very dry; lettuce is a good example of this type of plant.

There are several other crops which, in spite of the fact that their roots run down fairly deeply, need copious supplies of water in dry weather; beans, peas and celery may be instanced in this case.

On the other hand root crops and many plants of the cabbage tribe, provided they are planted in deeply-dug, well-worked soil, will rarely need watering or mulching, even in the driest seasons. (*See also* Watering in chapter 2.)

Blanching and Mulching

For these important garden operations, *see* chapter 2.

Culture of Vegetables

(Arranged in Alphabetical Order)

ARTICHOKE

Chinese Artichoke requires space and a well-drained, well-manured, deeply-dug soil. The tubers should be planted in Mar., in drills 6 in. deep, allowing 12 in. between the plants in the rows and 12 to 24 in. between the rows. The surface of the ground between the rows should be kept well hoed, and early in July a liberal top-dressing of manure should be given. During July and Aug. water should be freely afforded. In light soil the tubers may remain in the ground through the winter, and be dug as required. Or they may be raised about the middle of Nov. and stored under sand or fine soil covered with litter.

Globe Artichoke. Full exposure to the sun is desirable, and frost is less harmful than damp. The ground should be trenched and heavily manured in the autumn, and the planting should be done about the beginning of Apr. The best method of propagation is by root division or suckers, as seed cannot be counted on to come true. No plants should be kept after three or four years old, and it is well to make a small fresh plantation each year. The flower-heads should be picked when about half-grown and closed. Liberal watering and mulching, and, if necessary, staking, are the principal parts of its summer treatment. At the approach of winter some ashes or sand should be banked round the plant, and before frosts are expected the plant should be covered with litter or leaves. About the middle of Mar. this should be removed, and the earth between the rows lightly forked and dressed with manure.

Jerusalem Artichoke does best in a somewhat light soil, deeply dug, and in an open situation. The tubers should be planted early in Mar. in drills 3 in. deep, 18 in. being allowed between the tubers, and 3 ft. between the drills. In very heavy soil it is well to plant only just below the surface and to mix plenty of ashes with the soil.
Storing—The leaves should be cut down early in Nov. and the tubers may be left in the ground through the winter and dug as required.
Varieties—Good varieties are *Old Red* and *White*.

ASPARAGUS

Soil and Site—On clay soils the cultivation of asparagus presents somewhat of a problem, though even here, by throwing up the soil into ridges, placing broken bricks and rubble for drainage, by the addition of burnt rubbish and leaf-mould, and by surface manuring, asparagus of no mean quality can be raised. Where, however, the soil is of a more sandy nature, and the natural drainage is efficient, everyone, with a little care and attention, may easily grow this excellent vegetable. A warm situation should be selected, preferably with a southern aspect. Protection from the prevailing winds must be afforded. The soil, whether light or heavy, should be deeply dug, and while in the case of heavy soils it is well only to enrich the top foot or so of soil so as to keep the roots near the surface; in the case of medium and light soils the ground should be heavily enriched with decayed farmyard manure, preferably to a depth of 4 ft. or more.

249

Planting—The ground being dug and levelled, divide it into 5-ft. beds, with alleys 2 ft. wide between each bed. Strong one-year-old plants, without tops, should be selected and in Apr. planted 1½ to 2 in. deep in three rows in each 5-ft. bed, the rows a foot from each side of the bed, and the plants 2 ft. apart in the rows. Water well after planting if the weather is dry. Throughout the summer the principal work must consist in keeping the surface of the ground broken up by means of the hoe, and in destroying weeds as soon as they appear. Under no circumstances should any other crop be raised between the plants. About the end of Jan. a mulch of stable manure may be laid on the surface and a sprinkling of earth used to cover it; or alternately a little nitrate of soda or guano may be applied in May. About the second week of Feb. each crown should be covered with a few inches of soil or preferably sand, or sand mixed with soil. Shoots may be cut, or better, broken, as low as possible, when about 8 in. in length, being careful not to injure young shoots not yet fit for cutting. No cutting should be done for the first two years at least. In the case of older plantations it is unwise to cut asparagus after the middle of June. Cut down all stems in autumn.

Forcing—See p. 118.

Varieties—*Perfection; Connover's Colossal;* and *Early Giant Argenteuil.*

BEAN, BROAD

Soil—Broad beans like best a deep, somewhat heavy soil, which should be deeply dug and moderately heavily manured in the autumn before sowing.

Sowing—The earliest sowing may be made in a warm and sheltered situation at the end of Oct. or early in Nov. Seed should be sown in the open for main crop purposes in Feb. and Mar., successional crops being obtained by sowing a few each month right up to May or June. About 9 in. should be allowed from seed to seed, and 2 ft. between the rows. A little earth drawn up to the roots when the seedlings are 3 to 4 in. high induces them to put out fresh roots. When the stem is covered with about 18 in. of flowers the top should be pinched off to encourage the growth of the pods. All laterals should be removed as they appear. Should the black fly attack the beans, immediately pinch-back all young shoots; this may arrest the pests. If this is not successful the plants must be syringed with a solution of soft soap.

Varieties—Earliest crop, *Mazagans* or *Early Green* and *Exhibition Longpods;* Main crop, *Giant Green* and *White Windsors.*

Dwarf Broad Beans grow some 12 to 18 in. high, are bushy in form, and occupy no more space than the tall varieties. *Little Marvel* and *Dwarf Fan* are popular varieties.

BEAN, FRENCH OR KIDNEY

Soil—Dwarf Kidney Beans or French Beans like a deep, rich soil, which should be deeply dug and manured in the autumn. They should be grown in an open, unshaded situation

Sowing—By sowing partly in the open and partly under glass, French Beans may be obtained during practically every month of the year. In the open the first sowing should be made under a south wall about the middle of Apr., sheltering the young plants as soon as they come up with a little loose litter. The principal outdoor sowing should be made early in May, but it is well to sow a few seeds at weekly intervals right on to the beginning of July. Seed should be sown 6 in. apart in drills 2 in. deep, 2 to 3 ft. being allowed between the rows.

Thinning and Transplanting—When the young plants appear they should be thinned or transplanted so as to allow at least a foot from plant to plant in the rows. The pods must be gathered before the seeds are formed and the period of bearing will be prolonged if the pods are picked as soon as they are fit.

Varieties—Early sowing, *Masterpiece, Ne Plus Ultra;* followed by *Negro Longpod,* followed again by *Canadian Wonder* and *Perfection;* latest sowing the *Newington.*

BEAN, RUNNER

Soil—The Runner Bean does best in a deep, moderately retentive soil, which has been well manured and deeply dug in the autumn.

Sowing—The earliest seed should be sown in a sheltered situation about the middle of May. Successional crops may be obtained by sowing in the open until the middle of June. Sow in drills, 2 in. deep, 5 in. being allowed from seed to seed in the rows and 6 ft. from row to row. Water and syringe liberally in hot weather.

A weekly soaking with liquid manure as soon as some of the pods have set will increase the crop.

Training—As soon as the plants have formed their first leaves, tall poles 8 ft. in height and firmly set in the ground should be provided. Dust the young plants liberally with soot to keep away slugs. The pods should be gathered as soon as ready, or they will become hard and stringy.

Varieties—Earliest planting, *Earliest of All* and *Tender and True;* later, *Prizewinner, Scarlet Emperor, Streamline,* and *Mammoth White.*

BEETROOT

Soil—The soil should be deep and of medium texture. No manure should be added just before sowing, but the beet should follow a crop, preferably leeks, for which the ground has been heavily manured.

Sowing—For early use, the turnip-rooted kind, of which *Sutton's Globe* and *Crimson Ball* are good varieties, may be sown on a mild hot-bed in a frame from the beginning of Jan. to the end of Mar., or about the first week in Apr., in a warm border in the open, in drills 1 in. deep and 15 in. apart. A little salt dusted into the drills at the time of sowing, and sprinkled between the plants occasionally during June and July, will materially improve the roots. The soil should be made firm after sowing, and the young plants should be thinned to about 9 in. apart. Dust the young shoots with soot or lime to protect them from the birds. The turnip-rooted kinds may also be used for later supplies, where the soil is too poor or shallow for the long-rooted kind. Where the soil is suitable, however, the long-rooted kind are to be preferred for all but the earliest crops. These should be sown in May under similar conditions to those suggested for the turnip-rooted kinds. *Cheltenham Green-top* or *Galloway Purple* are perhaps the best varieties of all this group. *Pineapple* and *Nutting's Old Dwarf Red* are excellent.

Storing—Any roots that remain in the ground should be lifted before the middle of Oct., the leaves should be twisted off, the roots dried and carefully packed away in dry sand in a cool but frost-proof place. If carefully and periodically looked over the roots will remain in good condition until the following Apr.

BORECOLE

The Borecole or Kale is one of the most popular of our vegetables, and is in season from Oct. till Apr.

Soil—A rather stiff, deeply-dug, and well-enriched soil is desirable. The manure should be added some time previously to planting.

Sowing—The seeds should be sown from Mar. to May in drills about 1 in. deep. The seedlings should be thinned out to 4 in. apart where necessary as soon as they appear.

Planting out—The plants may be planted out when about six to eight weeks old, about 2½ ft. being allowed from plant to plant in all directions. Water liberally until the roots are firmly established.

Varieties—Autumn supply, *A1.* and *Dwarf Green Curled;* for Christmas, *Curled Scotch, Drumhead* and *Read's Improved Hearting;* for early spring, *Asparagus Kale, Welsh Kale,* and *Cottager's Kale.* The spring varieties, instead of being sown the previous May, may be sown in early autumn, often with advantage.

BROCCOLI

With care, the broccoli will supply a succession of heads from Nov. till June.

Soil—A well-tilled rich soil is necessary, as rapid growth is essential.

Sowing—The seeds should be sown in an open position in drills ½-in. deep, 1 ft. being allowed between the drills. The ground should previously be finely prepared, dressed with soot and rendered very firm.

Thinning and Transplanting—Thin out to 6 in. apart as soon as possible, and finally to 2½ ft. apart. Broccoli flourish in ground that has been used for another crop and not retrenched. If the soil has been well manured, it should be beaten down hard round the roots. This will encourage hard stems and prevent too much leaf forming. The plants should be kept well supplied with water until properly established, especially the autumn-flowering varieties, and these must also be liberally watered in all stages of their growth during dry hot weather. Before severe weather sets in, the spring kinds should be laid over, with their heads facing the north. This operation checks the action of the roots and the plants consequently become less succulent and better able to resist frost. They are also put in the best possible position for covering with stable litter or any other litter when such protection becomes necessary.

Varieties—Mid-winter, *Self-protecting, Snow's Winter White, King's Large* and *Superb Early White;* to succeed these *Purple* and *White Sprouting Broccoli, Leamington, Late Queen, Model* and *Nine Star.*

BRUSSELS SPROUTS

Soil—Brussels Sprouts require a deeply-dug and previously heavily manured soil, well-trodden before planting.

Sowing—The seed may be sown in a warm situation in drills about ¾-in. deep, and about 10 in. apart, at the end of Feb. or the beginning of Mar. Cover the surface with loose litter until the plants are well up.

Planting out—Late in Apr. the young plants should be moved either to their permanent quarters, or to fresh ground, about 8 in. apart, so that they can easily be again transplanted 3 ft. apart. Water well after transplanting. For the earlier supplies seed may also be sown very thinly early in Aug., the young plants being moved to their permanent quarters the following Apr., having been once transplanted in Oct. For a late supply seed may be sown in rather rich soil about the end of Apr. If the plants are developing too quickly a few of the leaves should be cropped back to stumps in the autumn. This also greatly encourages the production of sprouts. The top growth should be left intact until all the sprouts are cleared, when the top may be cut and used as greens. Should some of the lower leaves turn yellow in autumn they must be removed or the sprouts may rot. Do not cut the tops or heads till late winter or the stems will stop growing and the production of sprouts will cease.

Varieties—Early sowing, *Dwarf Gem* and *Matchless;* general crop, *Aigburth, Cambridge No. 1* and *No. 5, Exhibition, Market Favourite.*

CABBAGE

Soil—The ground should be deeply dug and moderately enriched a few months previous to planting. Cabbages should be liberally supplied with water at all stages of their growth.

Sowing—For an early spring supply, seeds should be sown about the end of July, and again about the middle of Aug. Sow a little seed at frequent intervals, so that the crop may mature successionally. The seeds should be sown thinly in rows 8 in. apart and about 1 in. deep. Keep the beds moist and give a liberal dusting of lime, salt, or soot now and then.

Planting out—About six weeks from the time of sowing the plants may be placed in firm ground which has not been newly dug but has been prepared some two or three months earlier. 15 in. should be allowed from plant to plant in the rows, and 20 in. between the rows. Thoroughly soak the ground after planting and give liberal supplies of water, especially for the first few days.

Varieties—*Ellam's Early, Greyhound, Harbinger, Primo, Velocity.*

For a summer supply, such kinds as *Main Crop, Sutton's Favourite,* and *Miniature Marrow* may be sown at intervals during the second half of Apr. and the whole of May. They should be treated much as advised in the case of spring cabbages, but they should be planted out into somewhat richer soil, as their growth is much more rapid.

For autumn crops we may rely largely on the Coleworts. They may be sown in May and the first two weeks of June, and treated very much as recommended for spring cabbage.

For late autumn, winter and early spring use, savoys and hardy winter cabbages may be sown at the end of May and first half of June. The small-headed kinds have the best quality, though the drumheads are large and hardy. Good winter cabbages are *Winnigstadt, St. Martin* and *St. John's Day.* For later use *New York, January King* and *Bijou* may be grown. Do not cut savoys before Nov.

Red cabbages are grown almost entirely for pickling, although they can be used as second vegetable just as the natural green variety is. The cultivation resembles that of other cabbages. Seed is best sown in Mar.; good compact heads may then be obtained ready for pickling in the autumn. The red cabbage should only be gathered when the head is thoroughly formed, the stem being thrown away as valueless. Useful sorts are *Dutch Blood-red* and *Dwarf Blood-red.*

CARDOON

The prickly Tours cardoon, the red-stemmed Marseilles, and the large-growing Puvis are all much better than the Spanish variety.

Sowing—Seed should be sown in a cold frame or under glass without heat early in Apr. Seed may also be sown early in June in the open.

Planting out—Early in May trenches, some 18 in. apart, should be dug to a depth of not less than 18 in., about 6 in. of thoroughly decayed manure being placed at the bottom of the trench and dug in and thoroughly incorporated with the soil. Plant out the seedlings about the end of May.

Blanching—When the plant is 18 in. high fasten it to a stake, and tie the leaves lightly to it, earthing up the stem at the same time like celery. Throughout the summer water copiously and frequently with soft water and a little guano to prevent flowering. In Sept. the early crop will be fit for use.

CARROT

Soil—A rather light, sandy soil which has been recently enriched by the liberal incorporation of well-rotted manure suits carrots best.

Where the soil is cold and heavy it may be greatly improved by being well trenched and by the liberal addition of wood-ashes, leaf-mould or old potting soil. If these ingredients are not available, the soil may be broken up and then drawn with the rake into ridges a foot high, on which the seeds may be sown.

Sowing—The first sowing may be made in a warm border at the end of Feb., *Early Shorthorns* or *Gem* being chosen. They are best sown about 1 in. deep in drills 15 in. apart, thinning to about 8 in. from plant to plant. Further seed may be sown in Apr. and May, the *Scarlet Horn, Nantes Horn, Scarlet Perfection,* and *James's Intermediate* being selected for this sowing. It is worth while to make a small sowing of *Early Nantes* about the end of June with a view to obtaining some nice small roots in the early months of the year. In all cases, but especially in the case of June-sown carrots, it is wise to add a fairly liberal dressing of soot and lime to the soil in order to reduce the attacks of insect pests to a minimum.

Storing—Carrots may be drawn for the table as soon as large enough; but the main crop for storing should not be taken up till the end of Oct., or even later, unless severe frosts set in. Remove the carrots carefully so as not to damage the roots and store in a frost-proof and fairly dry place. A covering of straw or sacking should be given against severe frosts.

CAULIFLOWER

The cauliflower, a many-purpose vegetable, is in season from June to Nov.

Sowing—In order to maintain a succession, three or four sowings should be made, the first being made on a slight hot-bed (*see* p. 117) in Feb. or very early in Mar. Good kinds for this crop, which is ready about June, are *Early London, All the Year Round,* and *Snowball.* The seedlings should be thinned out, hardened off and planted out in the open in Apr. Early in Apr. a second and larger sowing should be made in the open ground. For this crop such varieties as *Dwarf Mammoth, Autumn Giant, Erfurt, Pearl, Purity,* and *Favourite* may be sown, young plants being planted out in May and June. A third sowing should be made about the middle of Aug. to stand through the winter. For this third sowing such kinds as *Walcheren* will be found best.

Planting out—When the plants are large enough to be handled they should be transplanted 4 in. apart in rich and well-manured soil. In June the Apr. sowings will be fit to plant out where they are to grow; in Sept. they will be heading, and will continue to improve until the frosts of early winter. When the heads begin to appear, shade them from sun and rain by breaking down some of the larger leaves so as to cover them. Water well in dry weather.

Wintering—On the approach of winter, the plants in flower may be taken up with as much earth at their roots as possible and laid in by the roots on their sides in a light sandy soil, in some frost-proof place.

Celery

Autumn-sown plants are generally pricked out under frames for protection during winter, giving plenty of air in fine weather.

CELERIAC

Celeriac is hardy and of easy culture, growing well in almost any rich, well-prepared garden soil.

Sowing—Seed should be sown in Mar., over moderate heat. The seedlings should be pricked out as soon as capable of being handled, and should be potted in 3-in. pots.

Planting out—About the end of May the plants should be transferred to the open. The ground intended for their reception should have been deeply dug and well enriched and should have been made firm previous to planting. Planting should be shallow, as at no stage should any earthing-up take place. Rather, indeed, should the soil be gradually drawn from the bulbs so that they may almost stand on the surface as do onions. Liberal supplies of water should be given throughout the summer, and it is well to keep the surface of the ground between the plants covered with a little leaf-mould or litter. From 12 to 15 in. should be allowed from plant to plant in the rows, and about 18 in. between the rows.

Storing—At the approach of winter the roots should be taken up and stored like beetroots (p. 251).

CELERY

Soil—Celery prefers a soil not too light. In any case, deep or trench cultivation is a necessity, and manure and water must be liberally afforded.

Sowing—Seed should be sown under glass over a heat of about 70° F. Mar. is the month for the principal sowing, but a pan of early seed may be sown in Feb. As soon as the seedlings are able to be handled, about 2 in. high, the young plants should be pricked out singly into 3-in. pots, containing soil rich with well-rotted manure. From this time bottom heat is unnecessary, and the pots may be placed in a cold frame. Later the plants may be transplanted into bigger pots preparatory to the final planting in beds or trenches.

Planting out—The ultimate planting out, when about 6 in. high, takes place for the main crop about the end of June, the earliest plants from the Feb. sowing being put out about the end of May and the late crop about the end of July.

The trench system of growing celery is that usually adopted. A common mistake is to make the trenches too deep. They should, it is true, be deeply dug, and even the subsoil should be broken up to some extent, but it should be left in position, covered with a layer of manure, and manure should be liberally incorporated with the soil itself. When actually ready for planting, the trenches should be 4 ft. apart, about 16 in. wide, and 4 in. deep. In the trenches the young plants should be placed at intervals of about a foot and firmly trodden in. In addition to the stable manure, celery will do all the better if a dressing of ½ oz. each of ammonium sulphate and potash salts to every square yard of soil is well dug into the ground before planting. Water should be liberally given at once, and some shade afforded. The soil between the plants should be kept mulched with old manure so as to afford additional nourishment and to check evaporation. As growth proceeds, earth should be gradually hoed up round the plants, about 4 in. at a time, and potted down firmly to keep out the rain, though the principal earthing-up, which must be done in dry weather, should take place about a month before the celery is required. The leaves should be held together while the earthing-

255

up is in process, so that no soil may be allowed to enter between the stalks. The hearts must be kept well above the earthing-up, and any side growths should be removed. The last earthing-up in the case of the general crop should take place about the end of Oct.

Varieties—For early use, *White Gem*. For main crop, *Superb White* and *Champion White*. *Reds—Standard Bearer*, *Sulham Prize* and *Mammoth Red*.

CHICORY

Apart from its uses as a salad, Chicory affords two possibilities for culinary use. Its early growth may be forced and blanched after the manner of seakale (p. 261), and its unforced green leaves may be used in spring much as spinach is used.

Sowing—Seed may be sown from the middle of Apr. to the middle of June in fine soil which has been well manured for a previous crop, in rows 15 in. apart, the seedlings being thinned to about 9 in. apart in the rows.

Forcing—About the end of Oct. the roots should be lifted, packed in deep boxes in moist light soil, and blanched in perfect darkness. A little forcing should be applied if an early supply is wanted. Discard the roots after forcing. The *Witloof* and *Christmas Salad* are good kinds.

COLEWORT

(*See* Cabbage, p. 253.)

COUVE TRONCHUDA

The culture and treatment of this variety of cabbage are the same as for the ordinary cabbage. It is fit for use, like savoys, after frosty weather sets in.

ENDIVE

(*See* Salads, p. 265.)

KALE

(*See* Borecole, p. 251.)

KOHL-RABI

Soil—The Kohl-rabi is especially useful as an alternative to the turnip where the soil is light, as it will stand severe drought—frost has no effect upon it. The roots are most palatable if eaten when half grown.

Sowing—For a summer supply, sow the seed in Mar. in drills about $\frac{1}{4}$ in. deep, and 18 in. apart. The young plants should be thinned as soon as possible to about 10 in. apart. Transplanting is undesirable. For autumn and winter supplies seed should again be sown towards the end of July. (Store as for Turnips, p. 264.)

Varieties—Short Top Green, *Earliest White* and *Early Purple*.

LEEK

Soil—Very deep, rich soil is essential.

Sowing—For an early crop the seed may be sown in boxes early in Feb. (with a layer of rotted manure at the bottom of the boxes) and kept in moderate heat. When some 2 in. high the seedlings must be pricked off 2 in. apart. Keep in a moderate heat till the middle of Apr. then transfer to a cold frame, harden-off and plant out in May. Seeds may be sown thinly in the open successively in a warm border from the end of Feb. till the end of Mar., $\frac{1}{4}$ in. deep in drills about 6 or 8 in. apart. The seeds should be soaked in lukewarm water for about 12 hrs. previously to being sown.

Saxifrage Aizoon   Phlox subulata var.

PLATE 17 ROCK GARDEN PLANTS

Oxalis enneaphylla   Iris innominata

PLATE 18 STAKING STANDARD ROSES When planting they must be firmly tied to a stake at the top and bottom using sacking to prevent the bark being chafed, *above*.   Never plant too deep; firm the soil round the roots of the plant with the aid of the feet, *below left*.   Pruning should be done, *below right*, in the spring (March or early April)

Planting out—As soon as they are large enough to handle the young plants should be thinned out, and may be transferred to their permanent sites when about 1 ft. high about June. They must be planted firmly with their lower leaves just resting on the ground. If the ground is rich and moderately heavy, the leeks may be planted on the flat in rows, 2 ft. apart, about 12 in. being allowed from plant to plant. When the soil is not so rich and heavy it is desirable to grow leeks in trenches. These should be about a spade's width wide, about 2 ft. apart, and about 15 in. deep, and at the bottom of each should be placed a liberal dressing of well-rotted manure. On this should be placed a little soil, in which the plants should be planted. Give liberal dressings of liquid manure in late summer; and at all times keep the roots moist.

Blanching—As they grow, earth is to be thrown into the trench so as to keep an increasing portion of the stem buried and consequently blanched. When grown on the flat they must be kept well earthed-up by means of the hoe. (*See* p. 19.)

Storing—The leeks can remain in the ground through the winter and be dug as needed, or they may be stored in sand in a dry shed.

Varieties—London Flag, Monarch, Musselburgh, and *The Lyon*.

MUSHROOM

Soil and Site—Mushrooms merely require a supply of horse manure and a certain degree of warmth and moisture. If the manure when crushed in the hand binds, but no excess liquid is pressed out, it contains the required proportion of moisture. During the months of summer and autumn, mushrooms may, perhaps, most conveniently be grown in the open air, but during late autumn, winter and spring, some building or frame is necessary.

Making the Bed—As a rule, about six to nine weeks must be allowed from the commencement of operations to the gathering of a crop. The longest litter should first be shaken out of the manure, retaining all up to the length of about a foot. This should then be made up into a heap about 2 or 3 ft. high and from 4 to 6 ft. wide, and is best made on a gentle slope. In winter-time this heap should be made up under cover, or the heat will too quickly evaporate. Every second day the heap should be thoroughly turned, so as to bring the central portion to the surface and the surface to the centre, and during this process all lumps should be broken up. This turning should be continued for about a week in winter and about two weeks in summer. The manure should then be placed in position and well trodden down. The temperature of the heap should be taken by means of a thermometer plunged to a depth of about 8 in.

Sowing the Spawn—As soon as this temperature gets to about 75° or 80° F., the spawn, which must be fresh and which is bought in bricks composed of a mixture of manure and soil, containing dry mycelium of the mushroom, should be inserted in pieces about 2 in. square. These pieces should be firmly planted by means of a trowel about 2 or 3 in. deep in the manure, and about 8 in. apart. The heap of manure is then at once to be covered with about 2 in. of well-sieved sandy loam. Old garden soil is totally unsuitable for the purpose. This soil should be just, and only just, moist enough to hold together, and should be beaten firm with the flat of the spade.

The whole must then be covered over with a layer of straw, 15 in. in thickness, or with other material to exclude all light. Additional protection should be afforded by mats or sacking, if the spawn is planted in winter.

Care of the Bed—Little or no water should be given to the bed until the mushrooms begin to come up. As soon as the mushrooms appear, however, a moderate supply of tepid water may be given once a week, and it will be found that a little common salt, or, better still, saltpetre, will be beneficial.

So far as possible, the temperature of the air of the building in which mushrooms are being grown should be kept at from 55° to 60° F.

If the bed is to retain its health, mushrooms should not be cut but should be twisted off, separating the stalk as near the base as possible. Fresh soil must be added to fill the holes made by picking, and the bed must again be covered with straw.

Pests—Woodlice play great havoc in mushroom beds. Traps baited with carrot or potato will do much to keep this pest within bounds.

ONION

Soil and Site—Onions require a sunny, open position, and prefer a rather strong, deep and rich friable loam, though they grow quite well in any good light soil. Clay is not very suitable, while a newly-broken soil is impossible as the foliage grows at the expense of the bulbs which are also open to attack by insect pests, always present in freshly-broken soil. The ground should be liberally dressed with lime and with plenty of well-rotted manure buried deeply, trenched deeply, and ridged in early autumn. Dress the top spit liberally with soot or wood-ashes (4 cwt. to the acre). On a light soil kainit (3 cwt. to the acre) and ammonium sulphate (1½ cwt. to the acre) are the most suitable manures.

Sowing in the Open—The main crop should be sown as soon as the ground is in working condition, between Jan. and mid-Mar. Make the seed bed (*see* p. 62) and sow thinly in drills ¼ in. deep and 12 in. apart. Seed may also be sown under glass in a temperature of 60° F. early in Jan. Harden-off in Apr., and plant out early in May.

As soon as possible after appearance of the plants the surplus should be pulled out, without loosening those which remain. At least 3 in. should, at the first thinning, be left from plant to plant. Water well during the summer if the weather is dry.

A sowing in the open should also be made about the middle of Aug. to furnish young onions during the winter, and for use in summer before the main crop is ready. The seedlings are allowed to remain where sown until the end of February, when they should be planted out in a moderately but not too rich soil.

Storing—Towards the end of Sept. the bulbs should be well formed and the tops show indications of ripening. Where this is not the case, go over the crops, bending or breaking them down with the back of a wooden rake, and repeat this as often as may be necessary to check the growth of the tops. As soon as the bulbs seem to be properly matured, which will be known by the decay of the leaves, take them up, spread in a sunny situation in the open air until thoroughly dried. Store in an airy shed or tie them up in what are called ropes; hang them on a shady outside wall and protect them from wet.

Varieties—Spring Sowing: *Bedfordshire Champion, James' Long Keeping,* and *Up-to-Date;* Autumn Sowing: *Autumn Queen* and *Giant Rocca;* Winter Sowing: *Ailsa Craig* and *Excelsior.*

PARSNIP

Soil—To grow the parsnip properly, deeply dug, rich, sandy soil, which

Peas

has been previously well manured, is desirable. If manure is used it should be well rotted, short farmyard manure, well buried to draw the long tap roots deep down and to discourage the production of side roots encouraged by the use of manure on the surface. The ground should be trenched 2 ft. 6 in., and ridged up as long as possible before sowing.

Sowing—Seeds may be sown at intervals from Feb. to May, the best-flavoured, though not the largest roots, being obtained by sowing at the later date. Drills should be made ¾ in. in depth and 18 in. apart. In these seeds should be sown thinly, lightly covered, and well trodden in, and when the young plants appear thinning should be begun, until ultimately not less than 6 in. remain between plant and plant. As soon as they are large enough, they may be pulled.

Storing—During the winter the roots are best left in the ground as when growing, but any that remain over should, after having had their tops trimmed off, be lifted and stored in sand in the dark early in Mar. before growth restarts.

Should the winter frosts prove very severe, the crowns should be protected by a layer of ashes, bracken or straw.

Varieties—*Student, Tender and True,* and *Hollow Crown.*

PEAS

Soil and Site—Peas require deep loam, which has been well enriched and deeply dug or trenched in the autumn. It is a good plan to dig a shallow trench on each side of the rows, so that during the summer months manure and water can be easily supplied. A handful of potash salts to every twelve plants, dug into the soil just before planting, will materially help the crops.

Sowing under Glass—The very earliest peas are obtained by sowing early in Dec. at the rate of nine or ten seeds in a 5-in. pot in a cold frame. The plants should be thinned to six per pot. They must have little or no artificial heat, abundance of light, and free ventilation on every possible opportunity. These plants, after being hardened-off, should be planted out in a warm, south border about the second week in Mar., in deep drills.

Sowing in the Open—The first sowing in the open may be made towards the end of Feb., providing the land is not too wet. To secure a succession sow once a fortnight from this time up till the end of May, or even the middle of June. The seeds should be sown 2 to 3 in. apart in flat-based drills 3 in. deep and 4 in. wide. Before sowing, the drills should be dusted with wood-ashes. Dwarf peas should be planted in rows about 2 ft. apart; medium, 4 ft.; and tall, 12 ft.

Sticking—Stick the peas when 3 in. high, and between the main sticks small twiggy sticks should be inserted to give the peas a start. After sticking, they should be well mulched. In hot, dry weather, peas require a copious supply of water, and syringing overhead.

The peas should be gathered directly they are fit, and if it is wished to prolong the fruiting period no pods should be allowed to remain on the vine beyond this stage.

Varieties—For earliest sowings: *Foremost* and *Little Marvel;* for early sowing in the open: *Kelvedon Wonder, Marvellous, Peter Pan* and *The Pilot.* To follow these: *Giant Stride, Onward,* and *Stratagem.* These may be followed by *Best of All, Matchless Marrowfat* and *Veitch's Perfection.* These should carry us well into Aug. Following these the so-called late peas, such as *Autocrat, British Empire* and *Ne Plus Ultra* may be grown in favoured localities.

POTATO

Soil—Potatoes do best in a deep, sandy, well-drained loam. Before Christmas farmyard manure should be applied at the rate of about 20 tons per acre. This manure may well be supplemented by a mixture of 1½ cwt. ammonium sulphate applied in the drill at the time of planting, and 3 cwt. basic slag and 1½ cwt. potash salts when preparing the soil.

Sprouting—Tubers which are intended to be used for "seed" should be selected at the time of lifting. They should be evenly shaped and should weigh from 2 to 3 oz. each. They should be spread on the floor in an open shed until the skin is set and hard, and should then be packed in single layers in trays and stored in a room inaccessible to frost, where, nevertheless, they are fully exposed to air and light. In the case of very early potatoes these trays may be placed under the stage in the greenhouse or other warm place. A little fine soil may also be sprinkled over the potatoes, which should be slightly watered. By this means a certain amount of growth results and the potatoes, if carefully planted out without damage to the new rootlets, will be more forward than others not treated in this way. In all cases seed potatoes placed in boxes should be arranged with their crowns upwards. The eye in the centre of the crown is that from which growth should be encouraged, as it is much the more prolific, and makes the strongest plant. Only three or four shoots should be encouraged, the others should be rubbed off as soon as they appear.

For the earliest potatoes a south border, preferably sheltered by a wall, should be chosen. The potato is peculiarly susceptible to frost, and it is therefore generally useless to plant before the middle of February even in such a situation. In heavy soils it is generally better to plant after the middle of Mar. For the main crop Mar. is the best month to plant, but some late kinds should also be planted in Apr.

Planting—The soil having been prepared and levelled, drills should be drawn about 5 in. deep and 3 ft. between the rows. The tubers should be laid at the bottom of the drills, about 15 in. apart, and should then be covered by the hoe. When planting the early kinds only 2 ft. need be left between rows. When the plants are 5 to 6 in. high the first earthing-up should take place, and this should be continued every three or four weeks until nearly full grown.

Digging and Storing—Except in the case of early potatoes for immediate use, which are dug up as required, the tubers should not be dug up until the tops are quite dead. One plant should be dug up as a trial; if the potatoes are ripe the skin of the tubers will be set and the potatoes ready for eating. If they are to be stored they should be left in the ground three weeks to a month longer. They are best lifted with a fork inserted deeply under the tubers, which will then not be likely to be damaged. They should be cleared of earth, dried by exposure to the sun for a day or two, then stored in a dry cellar or other dark frost-proof building. Where no building is available, they may be piled up, interspersed with layers of straw, on some raised site, and covered with straw and then a thick layer of earth.

Varieties—Early: *Arran Pilot, Duke of York, Home Guard* and *Ulster Chieftain;* Mid-season: *Arran Banner, Arran Comrade, Great Scott;* Main Crop: *Arran Chief, Dunbar Standard, Kerr's Pink, King Edward, Majestic, Red King.*

RHUBARB

Soil and Site—To produce really good stems a deeply-dug soil somewhat heavily manured with farmyard manure or, if not obtainable, with bone manure, is required. The situation should be sheltered from east winds.

Planting—Carefully selected roots should be planted 5 ft. apart in spring with the top bud 2 in. below the surface. Cut no stems during the first season. Do not weaken the plants by pulling too many stems from any one plant in any one year. Any flower heads should, however, be immediately cut away.

Forcing—A mild degree of forcing can be effected by covering the young shoots (of plants at least two years old) in the early spring with seakale pots or drain-pipes, and surrounding these with a heap of fermenting manure. A large dressing of well-rotted manure should be dug in about the roots as soon as one has finished pulling the leaves. The roots should be lifted and divided every three to four years. Propagate by division of roots.

Varieties—Daw's Champion; Victoria (for summer use); *Champagne* (for early use) and *Stott's Monarch.*

SALSIFY

Soil—Salsify does best in a deep, sandy soil. The manure should be buried 9 or 10 in. deep, the surface only having been enriched either for a previous crop such as celery or peas or by the addition of some well-spent hot-bed soil or old manure.

Sowing—Sow thinly about the end of Apr. in drills 1 in. deep and 12 in. apart. As soon as the seedlings are about 2 in. high they should be thinned to 5 or 6 in. apart. They will be ready for use in the early part of Nov.

Lifting and Storing—The roots are best left in the ground throughout the winter and pulled as required for use. If the frosts are severe the roots should be protected with ashes, straw or bracken. Any roots that remain in Feb. must, however, be lifted before the growth recommences, and stored under sand or earth and straw as advised in the case of beetroot.

Varieties—Giant French, Improved Mammoth, Sandwich Island.

SAVOY

(*See* Cabbage, p. 253.)

SCORZONERA

Scorzonera requires similar treatment to that advised for Salsify.

Variety—Giant Russian.

SEAKALE

Soil—The ground intended for a permanent plantation should be deeply dug, and a very liberal dressing of manure should be incorporated, the top of the subsoil being broken up and left *in situ.*

Sowing—Sow thinly in Mar. or Apr. in drills about 2 in. deep, 18 in. being allowed between the drills. As soon as the seedlings have made six leaves they may be transplanted to rows 18 in. apart, allowing 9 in. from plant to plant. Water liberally and apply liquid manure frequently in hot weather. The following spring about 2½ ft. should be allowed from plant to plant in every direction.

Propagation by Root Cuttings—Far better than propagation by means of seed is propagation by root cuttings. Small roots, or rather pieces of root, about the size of the little finger, 5–6 in. long and ½ in. thick, should be planted vertically about the end of Mar., bud-side upwards, the bud or the top of the piece of root—where there is no bud—being cut straight and planted just on a level with the surface of the ground. The bottom end of the cuttings should be cut slantwise. 18 in. should be allowed between the rows in which these are planted, about 15 in. being allowed from set to set. The surface between the rows should be kept broken up by the hoe, and 2 or 3 in. of manure may be used as a top-dressing. On light soil a dressing of salt, about ½ lb. to the square yard, may also be given with advantage. Early in May all weak growths should be cut away and any flower stems must be removed, so that strong crowns may be formed for forcing in the winter. Water should be given liberally throughout the summer.

Forcing and Blanching—If intended for early use the roots should be lifted about the end of Nov., as soon as the leaves part readily from the crowns. These roots can be packed closely together in light soil, the crowns being on a level with, or just below, the surface. They should be placed in a dark cellar or darkened part of the greenhouse, a large case placed under the staging being excellent for this purpose, and exposed to a continuous temperature of about 60° F. or a few degrees less. The soil in which the roots are packed should be gently watered and then covered with a layer of dry leaves or straw. The kale should be cut when about 7 in. long, and for a continuous supply it is important to place a fresh lot of roots under the forcing conditions weekly. The roots which have been lifted for purposes of forcing and which are not wanted for the moment may be stored away in soil, crown uppermost, so that they can be placed in the forcing-house as required. Forcing takes about three weeks.

If it is intended to force seakale where it stands in the open the plants should be covered with seakale pots (or large drain-pipes covered with slates) about the second week in Nov., and the space between the pots piled up with leaves, or, if these are unobtainable, with fresh manure. Enough leaves should be used to cover the pots. They should be lightly trodden down. Every fortnight a fresh supply of plants should be subjected to this process so as to yield a continuous supply. As soon as the crop has been cut the bulk of the heating material should be cleared away, but a little should be left as protection against frost.

Seakale should be cut when about 7 in. in length and care should be taken to remove not less than ¼ in. of the old wood at the same time. *Lily White* is a good variety.

SHALLOT

Soil—Shallots do best in an open situation, and in a medium, well-drained soil that has been deeply dug and well manured for previous crops. The ground should have ¼ lb. of superphosphate to every square yard forked into it and must be made fairly firm before planting.

Planting—The bulbs, which should be of medium size, should be planted in Feb. or early in Mar. just deep enough to make them firm, but should not be quite covered with soil. 6 to 9 in. should be allowed from bulb to bulb and 12 in. between the rows. At the beginning of July the soil should be drawn away from the bulbs so that they may ripen and about the end of July or early in Aug., when the stems begin to die down, the bulbs should be pulled up and dried, after which they should be stored in a dry, moderately light room.

Varieties—*Russian* is a good variety, and *True Shallot* for pickling.

SPINACH

Soil—A deeply-dug, rather moist soil is to be preferred, a sandy, gravelly soil or sloping situation being unsuitable. If the soil is not moderately rich, a light dressing of well-decayed manure should be applied, but this should be kept some distance under the surface.

Sowing—It is a good plan to soak the seed in water for twenty-four hours before sowing. Sow thinly in the permanent quarters, in drills 1 in. deep and 1 ft. apart. When some 3 in. high the seedlings should be thinned out to 6 to 8 in. apart. Sowing in the open may take place at three-weekly intervals from the end of Feb. to early in May. The *Victoria Roundleaved* and *New Zealand Spinach* are as good varieties as any. In gathering spinach, pick only the largest leaves; do not pick the whole of the leaves from any one plant.

If winter supplies of spinach are desired the *Prickly Spinach* should be sown early in Aug., 3 in. apart in drills and 18 in. between the rows, and must be liberally watered. Of this variety the shoots and not the leaves are used. For a winter crop a light, sandy soil is the most suitable. Early in Feb. use the hoe among the winter spinach and give a liberal dressing of liquid manure.

Varieties—Autumn supply: *New Zealand* and the *Carter;* winter supply: *Prickly* or *Long Standing.*

TOMATO

In most parts of southern England tomatoes of good quality can, in favourable seasons, be grown in the open air, preferably against a south wall or fence. But in most districts of England, and in average seasons in almost all districts, some kind of glass structure is necessary if early, ripe fruit is to be obtained.

Soil—The soil required for the successful growing of tomatoes is fibrous loam, mixed with a little sharp sand, together with leaf-mould and some well-decayed manure. Do not give too much soil at first, start the plant in a small mound of soil, well up near the light, and add to it as the roots grow and demand fresh compost. Over-manuring definitely tends to unfruitfulness, and no manure must be used which has not fully fermented. It is desirable to add a pinch or two of kainit or nitrate of potash at intervals through the growing season.

Sowing—Sow at weekly intervals through Feb. and Mar., sowing ¼ in. deep and 1 in. apart in pans covered with glass and paper and placed close to the glass in a warm greenhouse or moderately warm frame. (Night temperature, 60° F.; day temperature, 70° F.) They should be shaded from the strong sun till the seeds germinate. Seed sown in Feb. should produce fruit in July. As soon as two leaves appear on the seedlings they should be pricked-off singly into thumb pots, a good half of the stem being buried in the soil. In a small greenhouse it is well that these young seedlings should be kept near the glass, to keep them short-jointed. As they grow they should be moved on into larger pots, and in about 10 or 12 weeks they should be ready for planting out into borders, 18 in. apart in the row, or into the final pots, some 10 in. in diameter, in which they are to be fruited. The first truss of bloom must be formed before the plants are finally planted out. Potting must be very firm.

Cultivation under Glass—Generous watering is essential at every period of growth, though a permanently saturated condition of the soil is, of course, undesirable. Under glass, 3 ft. should be allowed from plant to plant. Wires 9 or 10 in. from the glass may be employed to run the plants along under the glass. All side shoots must be nipped off, only the flower trusses being allowed to break from the main stem. The plants should have their heads pinched out as soon as they reach the top of the wires. To "set" the fruit pass a rabbit's tail over the flowers each day. Although warmth is necessary, over-heating is to be avoided. A night temperature of 55° to 60° F. and a day temperature of 60° to 70° or 75° F. should mark the extremes. Ample ventilation should be given. Seeds may be sown in June and July to furnish tomatoes through the winter.

Cultivation in the Open—When it is proposed to grow tomatoes in the open air, seeds should be sown in Mar. under conditions similar to those already suggested. Suitable varieties, such as *Essex Wonder, Market King, M.P.* or *Stonors,* should be selected for the purpose. The young plants, when some 15 in. high, should be cautiously hardened, and should be planted out about the end of May. A medium loam is the most suitable soil, and good drainage is essential. The best situation for tomato plants is against a south wall fully exposed to the sun. For the first week or so the plants should be protected at night by means of seakale pots or drain-pipes. They should be well watered with liquid manure to keep up a rapid growth. As soon as the blossom-buds appear watering should cease. Stop the side-shoots by nipping off the tops, and throw out all those sprays that show little signs of fruit, and do not allow the plant to grow much over 3 ft. high. Water only to prevent a check in case of very severe drought. In dry weather a mulching with manure is very beneficial.

If the fruit will not ripen, cut off the branches on which full-grown fruit is found and hang them in a warm, dry greenhouse to mature.

Varieties—*Best of All, Harbinger, Money Maker,* and for early sowing *Early Market* and *Sunrise.*

TURNIP

Soil—The most suitable soil for this vegetable is a sandy loam which has been deeply dug and well manured for a previous crop.

Sowing—Successional sowings may be made in the open in Mar., Apr., and May, the *Red* and *White Milan* varieties, the *Early Paris Market* and the *Snowball* being chosen. The plants should be thinned to at least 6 in. apart as soon as possible. Turnips intended for autumn and early winter use should be sown in an open situation in July, the *Redtop Mousetail* and *Veitch's Red Globe* are most suitable. Sown the first week in Aug. for mid-winter crops, *Orange Jelly* and *Golden Ball* are good mid-winter kinds.

Storing—When frost sets in the turnips should be covered with a few inches of leaves or litter and left in the ground. In the spring any roots left will send up a crop of young green shoots—" turnip-tops "—which have considerable value as a green vegetable.

VEGETABLE MARROW

Soil and Site—This vegetable requires a deep, light, rich soil, and a fairly sheltered position, where ample water can be supplied in dry weather.

Early marrows can be grown in frames after the manner of cucumbers, but as they require less heat, it is well to let the fermenting mass consist half of leaves and half of stable manure. The temperature at which these early frame marrows should be kept should vary from 55° F. to about 75° F. When the plants begin to bear fruit 1 oz. each to the square yard of super-phosphate and sulphate of ammonia should be applied and well watered in. If slugs are tiresome, a dressing of soot over the soil will keep them away. But the majority of marrows will naturally be grown in the open air.

Sowing—Two seeds should be sown 1 in. apart early in Apr. in each 3-in. pot or pan, filled with light, sandy soil, covering the seeds about 1½ in.

Cucumber

The seeds are placed flat, on their sides, not vertically in the soil. Place near the glass in gentle heat and keep fairly moist, and as soon as the plants are sufficiently strong to handle pot them off into 7-in. pots, putting two plants in each, and replace them near the glass in the warmth. When well established, remove to a cold frame, and gradually harden-off. Towards the end of May, or as soon as the weather is warm and appears to be settled, plant them out and protect them for a time by hand-glasses or other means and water well until the roots get hold of the soil. Train and regulate the shoots, so as to prevent them from growing too closely together, and stop them, if necessary, to forward the growth of the fruit. After a few of the marrows have set, but not before, a weekly dressing of liquid manure should be given, or artificial manures may be applied as advised for frame marrows. If it is impracticable to sow under glass, seeds may be sown in May on the bed itself. Three seeds are usually planted 1½ in. deep and 9 in. apart in the form of a triangle, each seed or patch of seeds being covered with an inverted flower-pot, the hole being covered with a piece of tile. When the young plants are up they should gradually be hardened by the removal of the pots for increasing periods during the daytime. Two of the three seedlings in each group should be removed as soon as the rough leaves have appeared.

Making the Bed—The bed for marrows grown in the open should be made up in about the second week in May. A shallow trench about 4 ft. wide should be dug, and about 18 in. depth of an equal mixture of leaves and half-rotten stable manure should be laid in this. This fermenting mass should then be covered with the soil taken out from the trench.

Cutting—Marrows should be cut while the skin can still be broken by the thumb-nail, the earliest to be cut usually being little more than 9 in. long.

Varieties—*The Melon, Moore's Cream, Table Dainty, Tender and True, Long Green* and *Long White*.

SALADS

CORN SALAD

Sow in drills about 3 to 6 in. apart, in light, rich soil in a warm situation. Successional sowings between Feb. and Sept. will give a supply almost all through the year. Water liberally. The leaves should be eaten when they are young and tender; that is when the plant has about four leaves. Protect from severe frost with a covering of hay or straw.

CRESS

Sow four days earlier than the mustard in order to have both ready at the same time. Sow thickly and cover very lightly with soil in the open in Mar. or Apr. in a sunny spot and every fortnight for a succession from Apr. to Sept. in a moist and sheltered position. The seed leaves only are eaten. For winter use, sow from Oct. to Mar. in boxes placed in a greenhouse or window.

CUCUMBER

Soil—Early in Mar. a hot-bed should be prepared. Liberal dressings of guano are very beneficial. (*See* pp. 117 and 118.)

Sowing—In a few days, when the steam generated by the hot-bed has been allowed to escape, seeds may be sown in the bed, rather more being sown than plants are required. The seedlings will make their appearance above ground in two or three days.

Cultivation and Training—·As soon as the plants appear, a day temperature of about 80° F. and a night temperature of 60° F. should be aimed at. The temperature should be regulated by the opening of the lights so as to admit air. Should the night temperature much exceed 60° F., it is well to wedge up the lights about ½-in. when shutting for the night and during hot weather this amount of night ventilation may be increased. When the plants are grown in a frame and have made two leaves pinch out the point above the second; each plant will then send out two lateral shoots above the second leaf on each shoot; pick off the top. After that, stop them above every fruit, and as the plants grow add fresh soil to keep the roots covered till the whole bed is level, taking care that the soil is of the same temperature as that in the bed. If the cucumbers are grown in the greenhouse, stakes should be placed to lead the stems up to the first wire and until this is reached all side-shoots must be pinched out. The main-stems must be stopped when the top of the roof is reached. The laterals are run along the wires until they are some 2 ft. in length when they must also be stopped. Liberal supplies of tepid water are essential, but the leaves should be watched, as should they turn yellow it is an indication either that too much water is being given or that the temperature is too cold. Twice, or, in hot weather, three times a day, the plants and bed should be well wetted, either from the watering-can by means of a fine rose, or by means of a garden syringe. In cold weather the lights should be covered with matting at night to exclude the frost.

From two to four plants will be sufficient for a two-light frame.

The cucumbers should be gathered as soon as they have attained adequate size, and malformed ones should at once be removed to encourage the formation of fresh fruit.

Varieties—Challenger, Improved Telegraph, and *Tender and True.*

DANDELION

Sow from Mar. till June in drills a foot apart, the seedlings being thinned to 9 in. apart in the rows. In Nov. the roots may be lifted and stored in sand until they are wanted, when by planting in boxes and the application of a little heat in a dark place, nice blanched growths are obtainable (*see* Forcing Seakale, p. 262.) When used as a vegetable the plant may be left out of doors, and the young leaves gathered from Mar. till June. The improved thick-leaved and broad-leaved are both good varieties.

ENDIVE

Soil—Endive thrives in light moderately rich soil. The ground should be trenched to a depth of 2 ft. and thoroughly manured.

Sowing—The first sowing should be made about the middle of May. For the main crop sow in the middle of June, and again about the middle of July. Plants to stand the winter should be sown early in Aug. Sow thinly, 1 in. deep, in drills 12 in. apart and the plants, when ready, should be thinned out to 9 in. Plenty of water should be given in dry weather, and liquid manure occasionally.

Blanching—When nearly full-grown, the plants should be blanched. In the case of the earlier crops and the broad-leaved kinds tie them up loosely when dry, after the same fashion as Cos lettuce, and draw the soil up about each plant. But as late crops intended for winter use are liable to be injured by frost these and the curly-leaved kinds should be blanched by covering the plants with inverted pots, the hole in which should be closed with a cork. Blanching should be done at intervals, so as to have a continuous supply. The Aug. sowing should be planted out in some sheltered situation. In many localities these plants require the protection of glass to winter them safely.

Varieties—Large Ruffec, Green Curled, and *Green and White Batavian.*

LETTUCE

Lettuces are of two kinds—those coming under the heading of Cabbage lettuces, which are short and globular in shape, and the Cos kind, which have long leaves.

Soil—Both kinds like a light, rich and deep soil. For the main crop of summer lettuces a piece of ground that has already been well cultivated should again be trenched, incorporating in the process plenty of good fresh stable manure. The layer of manure should be placed a spade's depth below the surface. This process will prevent many of the lettuces from "bolting", as is so apt to occur in hot, dry weather. Abundance of moisture at the roots and ample room for leaf growth are essentials.

Sowing—Lettuces may be sown under glass any time from Jan. to Mar., but it is unsafe to sow them in the open until after this date, when successive sowings once a fortnight until Aug. should be made in the bed in which the majority of them are to remain. Transplanting is necessary in the case of part of the crop, but the best plants are obtained by sowing in the permanent position.

Sowing in the Open, Thinning and Planting Out—Early in Mar. the seed should be sown thinly in drills a foot apart and ¼ in. deep on the bed prepared as above, and when the plants are big enough to handle they should be thinned to about 6 in. apart, the thinnings being themselves planted out at the same interval elsewhere in the plot. Final thinning to 12 in. apart must be made if good lettuces are to be grown, and it is better to leave too few plants than too many. For two or three weeks after planting out the young seedlings must be well dusted with soot to keep off the slugs. Ample moisture will now be required.

Winter Lettuces—Winter lettuces are obtained partly from special sowings and partly by the preservation of part of the late summer crop. Sow in successive lots from Aug. to the latter part of Oct., the earlier sowings being made both in the open and in frames, but the later ones—those sown in Oct. —in frames only. Fine soil, well mingled with old rotted manure, is necessary for the seedlings when pricked out. Of these seedlings, some should be planted in frames on light soil, not too far from the glass, at 3-in. intervals, and when the young plants touch each other they should be thinned out by pulling for use and for planting out. These thinnings may be planted out in warm border at 6-in. intervals, leaving a crop still in the seed bed. All the crop in frames needs careful handling, plenty of moisture being allowed, or warm, bright weather will cause the plants to bolt. Slight protection given to the outdoor crop will keep them safe through the hard weather, and it is probable that the plants will be crowded enough to need the removal and transplanting of every other one, a process which needs extreme care. If placed in Mar. in a warm sunny border, the lettuces will be useful in early summer.

Tying and Blanching—Tie the leaves of Cos lettuces with raffia just above the centre when nearly ready for cutting, so as to blanch their hearts. Cabbage lettuces do not need tying.

Varieties—Paris White (Cos), *Trocaders* (Cabbage), *Giant White Cos,*

Black Bath Cos (Winter), *Arctic King* and *Imperial* (both good Winter Cabbage), *May King* and *Chestnut Early* (Cabbage, for frame).

MUSTARD

Mustard is grown in the same manner as cress. (*See* p. 265.)

RADISH

The radish may be grown successfully all the year round by sowing the seed in a hot-bed (*see* p. 117) in frames from Oct. to Feb., and in the open ground at fortnightly intervals during the remainder of the year.

Soil—Radishes thrive best in a light and slightly limed loam, manured for a previous crop.

Sowing—Sow thinly in drills 1 in. deep, from 3 to 4 in. apart for long radishes, and from 4 to 6 in. apart for the larger sorts, as the *Spanish*. Any seedlings that press on their neighbours should be at once thinned out. Early sowings, about Feb., will require to be protected from frost by a covering of litter, but this must be removed every mild day as soon as the plants appear above ground. Sheltered positions facing south are best for the early crops. When the weather is hot and the ground dry, water before sowing; some days before drawing, water the. beds well and keep the soil moist until the crop is finished.

Varieties—*Red Globe Short Top* (early use), *French Breakfast* (summer use), *Turnip Red, Turnip White* and *Black Spanish* (winter use).

RAMPION

Sow in drills about 10 in. apart in Mar. or Apr. for use in autumn, and in May for a winter supply. Thin out to 4 to 8 in. apart in the rows. Lift all remaining roots in Nov. and store in sand in a dry frost-proof shed. A rich soil in a shady position is necessary.

WATERCRESS

This salad plant is best grown in a stream of pure running water with a good gritty bed. Vigorous shoots, 15 in. long, should be placed evenly over the surface of the bed in Mar. If the water is then gradually admitted these shoots will form roots in a few days, when more water can be let in as the plants become established, but care must be taken not to admit the water too rapidly or the plants will be torn from their young roots. The watercress will be ready for cutting about Aug. Provided the soil is kept very moist watercress can be grown in deep trenches, the seed being sown in May. By growing *Brown Winter Cress*, which is planted in Aug or Sept., watercress may be had almost all the year round.

HERBS

BORAGE

This is a good plant for bee-keepers, whilst its flowers are used in claret-cup and its young leaves in salads. It grows in any good, ordinary soil, and should be sown in Mar. or April, in shallow drills 15 in. apart, the seedlings being thinned subsequently to 10 in. apart.

CHERVIL

Chervil well repays careful cultivation, deep digging, and moderate enrichment of the soil. In the warmer parts of the country seeds may be sown early in Sept. in a warm, dry situation, the seedlings being thinned to about 6 or 7 in. apart. This crop will need the protection of mats fastened on bent sticks when the nights are frosty. In other parts of the country the seed may be mixed with fine soil or sand in the autumn, and the boxes containing the mixture may be placed in a frost-proof room for the winter. About the end of Feb. seed and soil may be sown together in drills in the situation that they are permanently to occupy.

CHIVES

Chives are of the onion tribe, and its shoots are used in soups and salads. It likes a good garden soil, and is propagated by division in Mar. or Oct. The plants should be in rows a foot apart, with 6 in. between the plants. Seed may be sown in the open in Apr.

FENNEL

Fennel likes a rich soil, and is propagated by seed and root division. Sow in Apr. in drills an inch deep, the drills being 18 in. apart, and when the plants are about 3 in. high they should be transplanted and set 9 to 12 in. apart. Root division is done in Mar., the plants being replaced a foot apart in rows at the distance of a foot. The flower stalks should be cut off as soon as they appear.

GARLIC

Garlic requires to be treated in the same manner as shallots (*see* p. 262).

HORSERADISH

Trench the ground in late autumn to a depth of 2 to 3 ft., applying very little manure, as a heavy dressing encourages a tendency to fork. Then take up some old roots, cut off the crowns about 1½ in. long, and remove all fibrous roots. Next, with a dibble, which is marked 2 ft. from the lower end —that being the depth the crowns are to be planted—make holes 10 to 12 in. apart in rows 18 in. apart. This done, take a lath-stick split at the end, insert the crown in the slit, thrust it down to the bottom of the hole, and push it out by another stick which is thrust down for the purpose. It is unnecessary to fill up the holes, as they gradually fill as the horseradish nears the surface. If a fresh row is planted every spring, and another taken up, the crop will be kept in good condition, and a fresh piece of improved ground offered every year for other crops. The roots will be ready for digging in Nov. two years hence, when the roots should be dug up and stored in sand until required.

MARJORAM

Marjoram likes a sunny spot and good soil. It is of two kinds, sweet marjoram, which is the most common kind, an annual, which should be raised from seed sown in gentle heat in Mar. and planted out in May 9 to 12 in. from plant to plant, and pot marjoram, which is a hardy perennial and is raised from seed in the same way or increased by root division. Both kinds can also be sown out of doors in Apr., the seedlings being thinned later to their proper intervals of 9 to 12 in., the plants increased by root division needing an interspace of a foot. The pot marjoram, as it outlives the winter, needs a dry soil and a warm position, or a cold winter may injure it.

MINT

Mint will do well in a not too sunny corner of the garden, though not in full shade. Lift the roots in Mar., divide them, and replant 9 in. apart in trenches about a couple of inches deep. Liberal supplies of water are needed.

PARSLEY

Parsley requires light, rich, deeply-dug loam, with a good admixture of leaf-mould, sand and a little old mortar. Two sowings should be made, one for the summer crop, sown in Apr., the other for winter and spring, sown in July. Sow thinly in drills 15 in. apart and an inch deep. Not until about seven or eight weeks after sowing will the seed begin to show above ground, when it must be kept carefully weeded and well watered. The seedlings should be thinned out when old enough to handle to 6 to 9 in. apart. Any flower-buds should be nipped off at once. The crop required for winter use should be picked close in Sept. when a fresh crop of leaves will shoot up. If a frame is available the plants for the winter supply should be transferred to it in Aug. or Sept.; plant about 5 in. apart, and cover the frame with matting in frosty weather. Parsley runs to seed in the second year, and it is therefore necessary to make a sowing every year. Parsley needs semi-shade.

ROSEMARY

Rosemary likes much the same conditions as does lavender, and may be propagated by cuttings taken in Apr., and planted in a semi-shaded situation. They may be transplanted from the nursery bed in Sept. or the following Apr.

RUE

Sow in gentle heat in Apr., or take slips in June and Sept. The rows should be 18 in. and the plants 12 to 18 in. apart.

SAGE

Sow in a sunny, sheltered spot in late Mar. or early Apr., the seedlings, when large enough, being transplanted to a nursery bed about 4 in. apart, and later re-transferred to their final bed: this at about a year old. Cuttings with a "heel" may also be taken in Apr.

SAVORY

Savory likes a rich but not too heavy soil, and the summer kind should be sown in Apr. in drills 12 in. apart, subsequently thinning the seedlings to 9 in. apart. The winter savory may be raised in the same way, or the old plants may be divided and replanted in Mar. The winter savory is the simplest to grow, as it does not need yearly renewal; but both kinds should be grown for a continuous supply.

TARRAGON

A sheltered position and a light loam are needed. The plants are propagated by root division in Mar., the little plants being put in drills 3 in. deep and 18 in. apart. There should be 9 to 12 in. from plant to plant. The surface of the bed should receive a dressing of well-rotted manure, and another dressing again each year in autumn, when the stems should be cut down.

THYME

Thyme enjoys full sun and a light, rich soil. It is best raised by division in Apr., setting the roots at intervals of a foot in each direction. Seed may also be sown in Mar. or Apr., or cuttings taken in summer. It is advisable to remake the beds each year.

The following table shows what seeds should be sown during the various months of the year. Full cultural details will be found in the paragraphs on the particular plants.

Seed or Tubers	Jan.	Feb.	Mar.	April	May	June	July	Aug.	Sept.	Oct.	Nov.	Dec.
Artichokes,												
Chinese	–	–	*	–	–	–	–	–	–	–	–	–
Globe	–	–	–	*	–	–	–	–	–	–	–	–
Jerusalem	–	–	*	–	–	–	–	–	–	–	–	–
Asparagus	–	–	*	–	–	–	–	–	–	–	–	–
Beans,												
Broad	–	*	*	*	*	–	–	–	–	–	–	–
Kidney or												
French	–	–	–	–	*	*	–	–	–	–	–	–
Runner	–	–	–	–	*	*	–	–	–	–	–	–
Beetroot	–	–	*	*	*	–	–	–	–	–	–	–
Borecole or Kale	–	–	*	*	*	–	–	–	*	–	–	–
Broccoli	–	–	–	*	*	–	–	–	–	–	–	–
Brussels Sprouts	–	*	*	–	–	–	–	–	–	–	–	–
Cabbages	–	–	*	*	–	–	–	*	–	–	–	–
Cardoons	–	–	–	–	–	*	–	–	–	–	–	–
Carrots	–	*	*	*	*	–	–	*	–	–	–	–
Cauliflower	–	*	–	*	–	–	–	*	–	–	–	–
Celery	–	*	*	–	–	–	–	–	–	–	–	–
Colewort	–	–	–	–	–	*	*	*	–	–	–	–
Kohl-rabi	–	–	*	–	–	–	*	–	–	–	–	–
Leeks	–	*	*	–	–	–	–	–	–	–	–	–
Onions	*	*	*	–	–	–	*	*	*	–	–	–
Parsnips	–	*	*	*	*	–	–	–	–	–	–	–
Peas	–	*	*	*	*	*	–	–	–	–	–	–
Potatoes	–	*	*	*	–	–	–	–	–	–	–	–
Salsify	–	–	–	*	–	–	–	–	–	–	–	–
Savoys	–	–	–	*	–	–	–	–	–	–	–	–
Seakale	–	–	*	*	–	–	–	–	–	–	–	–
Shallots	–	*	*	–	–	–	–	–	–	–	–	–
Spinach	–	–	*	*	*	*	*	*	*	–	–	–
Swedes	–	–	*	*	*	*	–	–	–	–	–	–
Turnips	–	–	*	*	*	*	*	*	–	–	–	–
Vegetable												
Marrows	–	–	–	–	*	–	–	–	–	–	–	–

In the above table, the *'s denote when to sow or plant.

CROP ROTATION AT A GLANCE

The following table shows what crops a certain vegetable may follow and what it may *not* follow. It also shows what crops a vegetable may be followed by and the crops that should not come after it.

Principal crop	Crops it may follow	Crops it may not follow	Crops it may be followed by	Crops it may not be followed by	Catch-crops which may be planted between rows
Beans	Asparagus, borecole, broccoli, cabbages, turnips, parsnips, carrots, potatoes	*Leguminous plants of its own family, *i.e.*, peas, etc.	Beet, c a r r o t s, celery, leeks, lettuces, parsnip, salsify, turnip, and any of the Cabbage tribe	*Leguminous plants of its own family, *i.e.*, peas, etc.	Borecole, Brussels sprouts
Beet	Cabbage tribe, and any crops but those specified in n e x t column	Spinach, turnips, parsnips, carrots, salsify, and scorzonera	Peas, beans, cabbages, cauliflower, lettuces, onions and any spring-sown crop except those in next column	Spinach, turnips, parsnips, a n d carrots	Nothing
Borecole and Brussels Sprouts	Peas, beans, lettuces, potatoes	*Cruciferous plants of own order, *i.e.*, any of Cabbage tribe, turnips, etc.	Peas, beans, beet, carrots, parsnips, onions, potatoes, k i d n e y beans, celery, salsify, leeks, lettuce, endive, spinach	*Cruciferous plants of own order, *i.e.* any of Cabbage tribe, turnips, etc.	Beans
Broccoli	Peas, beans, kidney beans	*Cruciferous plants of own family	Any crop to be sown or planted when cleared off	*Cruciferous plants of own family	Nothing
Cabbages	Peas, beans, kidney beans, potatoes, lettuces, onions, leeks, celery, etc.	*Cruciferous plants of own family	Peas, beans, k i d n e y beans, potatoes, lettuces, carrots, parsnips, beet, salsify, celery, seakale, onions, leeks, radishes, endive, shallots, etc.	*Cruciferous plants of own family	Coleworts
Carrots and Parsnips	Cabbage tribe and any crops, except those in next column	Any crops except root crops and *Umbelliferous plants	Any crops except those in next column	Any crops except root crops and *Umbelliferous plants	Nothing
Cauliflower	Peas, beans, potatoes, celery, kidney beans, onions, carrots, lettuces, beet	*Cruciferous plants of own family	Peas, beans, potatoes, celery, onions, carrots, salsify, endive, leeks, lettuces, beet, parsnip	*Cruciferous plants of own family	Spinach, lettuces, endive

272

Brussels Sprouts

Cauliflower, early

PLATE 19 VEGETABLES

Marrow, Long Green

Parsnips

PLATE 20 PROTECTION OF SHRUBS IN WINTER To protect tender young shrubs during winter insert four canes round the plant, *above left*. Place straw round the base, *above right*, and then cut the sacking and tie it round the canes to form a screen from the wind, *below*.

Principal crop	Crops it may follow	Crops it may not follow	Crops it may be followed by	Crops it may not be followed by	Catch-crops which may be planted between rows
Celery	Any crop except those in next column	Parsnips, carrots, parsley	Peas, beans, kidney beans, onions, potatoes, turnips, and any of the Cabbage tribe	Parsnips, carrots, parsley	Lettuces, endive, dwarf early peas, French beans
Endive and Lettuce	Asparagus, potatoes, peas, beans, and any of the Cabbage tribe	Chicory, salsify, scorzonera, artichokes, cardoons, and any plants of the family *Compositæ	Peas, beans, potatoes	Chicory, salsify, scorzonera, artichokes, cardoons, and any plants of the family *Compositæ	Nothing
Kidney Beans and Peas	Potatoes, carrots, parsnips, turnips, broccoli, and any of the Cabbage tribe	Beans, and *Leguminous plants of own family	Broccoli, cabbages of any kind, spinach, late turnips, potatoes, beet, celery, parsnips, onions, leeks, salsify, endive, shallots	Beans, and *Leguminous plants of own family	Summer spinach, radishes, lettuce, broccoli, turnip, early carrots; borecole and Brussels sprouts between dwarf sorts
Leeks, Onions, Shallots, etc.	Cabbage tribe, celery, potatoes, peas, beans, kidney beans, lettuces, endive, spinach	Garlic, chives, and any crop of the onion tribe	Cabbages, carrots, coleworts, celery, cauliflower, parsnips, potatoes, peas, beans, beet	Garlic, chives, and any crop of the onion tribe	Nothing
Potatoes	Any crop except those specified in the next column	Carrots, parsnips, beet, salsify, scorzonera	Any crop requiring a loose, clean, well-worked soil, and all *Cruciferous plants, peas, beans, etc.	Root crops generally, as carrots, parsnips, beet, etc.	Brussels sprouts, cabbages, borecole, broccoli, and late celery if there is space enough for trench
Seakale	Potatoes, peas, beans, carrots, parsnips, beet, celery, etc.	*Cruciferous plants of own family	Potatoes, peas, beans, carrots, parsnips, beet, celery, etc.	*Cruciferous plants of own family	Nothing
Spinach	Peas, beans, kidney beans, cabbage, cauliflower, lettuces, etc.	Beet	Peas, beans, kidney beans, cabbage, cauliflower, lettuces, etc.	Beet	Nothing
Turnips	Potatoes, spinach, peas, beans, lettuces, etc.	*Cruciferous plants of own family	Potatoes, spinach, peas, beans, lettuces, beet, carrot, parsnip	*Cruciferous plants of own family	Nothing

*NOTE.—*Cruciferæ*—Cabbage, cauliflower, broccoli, colewort, turnip, radish, cress, seakale, mustard, horseradish; *Leguminosæ*—Peas, beans; *Umbelliferæ*—Carrot, parsnip, parsley, celery, fennel, carraway; *Compositæ*—Globe artichoke, Jerusalem artichoke, scorzonera, salsify, endive, chicory.

NOTE.—A dressing of 3 qrs. per ¼ acre is equal to 2 lb. to the square rod, or 1 oz. to the farmyard manure which is applied in the Autumn or Spring

Name of Vegetable	Farmyard Manure	Artificial Fertilizers *	
Beans	Moderately heavy, 3-4 tons	Basic slag	3 qrs.
		Vegetable or wood-ashes	3 qrs.
Beetroot . . .	Organic manure for preceding crop only	Ammonium sulphate	1½ qrs.
		Potash salts	1½ qrs.
		Peruvian guano	2 qrs.
Cabbage (including Broccoli, Brussels Sprouts, Cauliflower, Kale, etc.)	Moderately, 3 tons	Salt	2½ qrs.
		Steamed bone flour	2½ qrs.
		Nitrate of lime	1½ qrs.
		Sulphate of potash	1 qr.
Carrots . . .	Organic manure for preceding crop only	Ammonium sulphate	1½ qrs.
		Kainit	3 qrs.
		Salt	2½ qrs.
Celery	Moderately, 3 tons	Ammonium sulphate	1½ qrs.
		Potash salts	1½ qrs.
		Salt	2½ qrs.
Leeks	Moderately, 3 tons	Ammonium sulphate	1½ qrs.
		Potash salts	1½ qrs.
		Steamed bone flour	3 qrs.
Lettuce . . .	Moderately, 3 tons	None necessary	
Onions . . .	Moderately, 3 tons	Ammonium sulphate	1½ qrs.
		Kainit	3 qrs.
		Soot	1 cwt.
Parsnips . . .	Organic manure for preceding crop only	Ammonium sulphate	1½ qrs.
		Kainit	3 qrs.
Peas	Moderately, 3 tons	Basic slag	3 qrs
		Potash salts	1 qr.
		or wood or veg. ashes	3 qrs.
		Nitrate of soda	1½ qrs.
Potatoes . . .	Fairly heavily, 5 tons	Ammonium sulphate	1½ qrs.
		Basic slag	3 qrs.
		Potash salts	1½ qrs.
		or wood or veg. ashes	3 qrs.
Radishes . . .	Moderately, 3 tons	None necessary	
Spinach . . .	Moderately, 3 tons	(a) Ammonium sulphate (heavy soil) or	1½ qrs.
		(b) Nitrate of soda (light soil)	1½ qrs.
Turnips . . .	Organic manure for preceding crop only	Ammonium sulphate	1½ qrs.
		Kainit	3 qrs.
		Steamed bone flour	3 qrs.

* In each case, all the fertilizers quoted should be used if the best

FOR VEGETABLE CROPS

¼ ACRE)

to the square yard. Unless otherwise stated, the artificial manures are given in addition according to the soil; heavy in Autumn, light in early Spring.

When to Apply Artificial Fertilizer	Remarks
Autumn and Winter Spring	No farmyard manure is needed unless the soil is exhausted. On heavy soil substitute 2 qrs. of superphosphate for the basic slag, and apply when the crop is maturing.
Spring. When sowing Spring. When sowing Before sowing When growing When growing When grown, as top-dressing Early Spring	Soil should have been well manured with organic matter for previous crop, which crop should not have been a root one. Farmyard manure should be well dug in in Autumn in heavy soil, or in early Spring in light soil. On light soil nitrate of soda should be substituted for the nitrate of lime.
Spring. When sowing Spring or Autumn, according to soil When growing	Soil should have been well manured with organic matter for previous crop, which crop should not have been a root one. On heavy soil substitute 1 qr. of sulphate of potash for the kainit and apply early in Spring.
When sowing When growth commences When growing When sowing When growth commences When growing	Farmyard manure should be well dug in in Autumn in heavy soil or in early Spring in light soil. Farmyard manure should be dug in in Autumn in heavy soil or in Spring in light.
When sowing Spring or Autumn, according to soil When growing	The farmyard manure should be well dug in in Autumn in heavy soil or in Spring in light soil. On heavy soil 1 qr. sulphate of potash should be substituted for the kainit, and applied in early Spring.
When sowing Spring or Autumn, according to soil Autumn and Winter Spring, when sowing	Soil should have been well manured for previous crop, which should not be a root one. No farmyard manure is needed unless soil is exhausted. On heavy soils 2 qrs. superphosphate should be substituted for the basic slag, and applied when the crop is maturing.
When growing When planting Autumn or Winter When preparing soil	Soil should be deeply worked and the farmyard manure incorporated in the Autumn. On heavy soil 2 qrs. superphosphate should be substituted for the basic slag, and applied when the crop is maturing.
(a) When sowing	No artificial should be necessary if the farmyard manure has been dug in.
(b) When growing	
When sowing Autumn or Spring, according to soil When growth begins	Soil should have been well manured for previous crop, which should not have been a root one. On heavy soil substitute 2 qrs. superphosphate for the steamed bone flour and apply when the crop is maturing.

results are desired. One fertilizer is, however, better than none.

275

CHAPTER 18

The Herbaceous Border

Its Siting, Planting and Care

One of the most attractive features of a garden can, with skilful and careful design and planning, be the herbaceous border. It entails very little labour as compared with the upkeep of beds filled with annuals, or with the laying out of the more severe bedding designs. Once planted the herbaceous border lasts for many years, merely requiring weeding, staking, occasional mulching, and forking over annually. The width of the border must naturally vary according to the size of the garden and many other considerations. But where possible it should be not less than 4 feet wide, and where there is plenty of space it should be at least double that width.

Site and Background

The herbaceous border may occupy almost any position in the garden, but the best results will be obtained if it faces due south and has some protection in the form of a wall or a hedge from the cold winds from the north and east, though care should be taken that the hedge is far enough away for its roots not to take nourishment from the flowers in the border.

Much thought should be given to the choice of a good background, as it can make or mar the border. A wall or trellis covered with roses is good, so also is a wall planted with fruit trees, but the dark green background provided by a yew hedge is very hard to beat.

Most perennials will grow in almost any soil, but a deep, rich, well-drained loam is preferred by most.

Preparing the Border

The ground intended to be devoted to this purpose should be thoroughly prepared in advance. This is even more important than in the case of beds for annuals or for tender plants, which will occupy the ground for a single season only. For the properly-prepared and properly-planted border should not require thorough remaking or replanting for several years to come; for one of its chief charms consists in the " settled-down " appearance, which is only possible with plants which have occupied the same ground for some time.

The border may be prepared either in September or in early January. In the first case the plants should be put in in October or November and in the second in March or April.

Gradation of Flowering Plants

The ground should be well drained and then thoroughly trenched to a depth of 2 to 3 feet, care being taken not to bring any sour or heavy subsoil to the top. With the bottom spit should be mixed good stable manure when the soil is heavy, or cow or pig dung if the land should be light, while some substance such as ashes of burnt vegetable matter, bonemeal, or basic slag—in fact anything that will help to break up and lighten the soil—should be added to the top spit. If the soil is too light it may be improved by the addition of leaf-mould and a little thoroughly pulverized clay. Should the earth prove too heavy, coarse sand and wood-ashes will serve to lighten it.

The border should be left for a month or so after trenching in order that it may settle down before the plants are put in.

Time and Planting

As a general rule the best time to plant the border is in October or November, but in the north and very exposed positions it is often advisable to defer the planting until March or April. The plants that bloom early should of course, if possible, be planted in the autumn so that the roots may get well established before they have to bear the strain of flowering. This applies to such plants as lupins and peonies. Autumn planting is also advisable in light soils, as very dry weather in late spring may prove disastrous to plants newly inserted in a light soil that will soon dry and parch the unestablished roots. In wet, cold soils spring planting is best; if plants must be put in in the autumn, let it be done in September. Thick succulent-rooted plants are more apt to decay if planted in autumn; these should be spring-planted whenever possible.

In planting, holes should be dug sufficiently deep to allow the roots to be placed in without being doubled up, and wide enough to admit of the roots being well spread out, and covered with fine soil which should be pressed firmly round the crowns. Firm planting is essential and care must be taken that the crowns are not placed lower than ground level, as there is every possibility of their rotting off if this is done; the plants should be so inserted that the crowns are just on the surface of the soil. Some herbaceous plants are "tap-rooted", as the anchusa and sunflower, and these demand an extra deep hole for planting, otherwise their long roots will be bent up and prevented from penetrating deeply into the soil and so obtaining the necessary nourishment and moisture. When planting, study the habits of the roots, and allow them to follow what seems to be their natural course, rather than direct them in one special way. Some roots want to run perpendicularly downwards, others grow horizontally; each should be assisted and humoured.

Gradation of Flowering Plants

As a general rule the taller-growing plants, as the rudbeckia, sunflower, hollyhock and delphinium should be placed at the back of the border and there should be a gentle gradation down through plants of medium height, as the phloxes, campanulas and carnations, to the violas, daisies, silenes and dwarfer species in front, but this procedure must not be adopted invariably or a stiff and severe effect will ensue, and the freedom and irregularity which are the chief charms of a herbaceous border will be lost. Here and there clumps of the taller flowers should be grouped in outstanding positions well to the front of the border, and some small-growing and creeping plants should seem to find their way right to the back, at the base of the taller ones, so as break up the general outline and to introduce some element of surprise, for a border loses much of its charm if it can all be seen at a glance from one end. The flowers should be planted in groups of from four or five to eight or nine of each kind in a clump, but not too closely together; the dwarfer the plants the more in a group. It is one of the greatest mistakes to plant perennials singly in various parts of the border, as this gives a patch-work effect which is not at all pleasing; the ideal to aim at is masses of striking but well-harmonized colours.

The distance at which plants should be planted from one another depends on the height to which the plants may be expected to grow, and on their "bushiness". But as a guiding principle it can be taken that the dwarfer kinds should be planted about 8 inches apart, the medium sorts 15 inches apart; and the tallest kinds some 2 feet from one another. So far as space provision is concerned, the aim should be to show practically no bare earth during the period of active growth, and at the same time to avoid any overcrowding which interferes with individual development. There is thus great scope for knowledge of the habits of plants, as well as for taste in arrangement of colours and forms.

Each plant should be clearly labelled as it is planted, or confusion either in the colour scheme or in the gradation of height will be sure to ensue. When all the plants are in, the soil around them should be neatly forked over, so that the border may have a tidy and "finished" appearance.

Colour Grouping

We now come to colour grouping; this is perhaps the most difficult problem that has to be solved in the construction of the border. So much depends on the correct solution, and infinite pains will have to be expended in order that the best result may be obtained. Aim at large splashes of colour; do not go out for contrasts, but let the tints merge gently from the one into the other and with a gentle crescendo lead up from the paler shades to the most vivid colours at the summit. Let us first of all plan our red group. Start with the pale pinks, next to them put the deeper shades, and so on until the most vivid and powerful reds are reached; from this zenith of colour work gradually back to the palest of pink.

The purples, blues, and yellows can be arranged in the same way as described for the reds. We cannot, however, place these groups up against one another indiscriminately or we shall have hard lines and in places clashing colours, but we know that pink harmonizes delightfully with pale yellow so we may join our red group to the yellow group.

Similarly pink is exquisite alongside lilac so we can link these up with our purple group, and our blue group with our yellows, for pale yellow blends delightfully with pale blue.

We should also remember that tints may be made to lead the one from the other so as to blend harmoniously. The yellows will run into orange, the orange through orange-scarlet to scarlet, thence to the deepest crimson. Similarly through the pale blues we reach dark blue, then purple and down again through lilac to pale blue or lavender grey or white. Plants with ample green foliage must not be neglected, as nature uses green very liberally in her colour schemes. White, if not used to excess, is invaluable as it will always help us out of difficulties, for it may be placed next to the strongest colours equally as well as against the palest; if too much white is used the border will present a "patchy" effect.

Many of the strong colours may be associated without going through a gradation of their paler tints. Deep blue or purple, for instance, blends well with gold, orange or yellow, but care must be taken not to use any clashing colours in close proximity. The ultra vivid colours should be held in check, as they strike the eye so quickly and are apt, if used too freely, to submerge the more delicate tints.

Do not fall into the common mistake of placing all the bright colours at the back and middle of the border, let there be some groups of vivid colouring well to the front; there are innumerable edging plants such as aubrietas, dianthus (pinks), and saxifrages that afford brilliant tints for this purpose. These groups of colour must not be bounded by hard straight lines, each group must be irregular in shape and should merge gradually and imperceptibly into the group next to it.

The novice must not feel disheartened if the colour scheme is not perfect the first year; few, if any, are infallible in their colour grouping, and there are the subsequent years in which errors may be corrected.

Flowers from April to October

In this we have a problem nearly as difficult as that provided by the colour scheme. Our aim is to secure a continuity of bloom from early spring until late in the autumn. Thus the plants we choose for the border must be not only brilliant in their colours, but should have as long as possible a period of bloom. If the border is wisely planned, there is no reason why there should not be plenty of colour from the beginning of April right up to the end of October.

Bulbs such as the snowdrop, the crocus, the tulip, the scilla, the chionodoxa, and the anemone, and such early-flowering plants as the alyssum, the anchusa, the aubrieta, and the earlier delphiniums will give a good show in spring. During May, June and July pæonies, lupins, delphiniums, irises, inulas, erigerons, antirrhinums, and many others will furnish all the colour needed; there is no trouble at this period. In August and September we have sweet peas, thalictrums, phloxes, sunflowers, penstemons, antirrhinums, and late delphiniums; while gladioli, red-hot pokers, aconitums, rudbeckias, dahlias, sunflowers, chrysanthemums, and Michaelmas daisies will carry on the bloom well to the end of October.

Replacements

The designer of the herbaceous border has still other things to think about. He must remember that by midsummer, or even before, the early-flowering plants will have finished blooming and will be beginning to look untidy however carefully dead flowers have been picked off. He must, therefore, endeavour to plant later-flowering and taller-growing flowers which, as they grow up, will screen these. This, however, is more difficult than it at first appears, for a plant that will grow tall enough totally to obscure the plant behind it, but not until that plant has flowered, must be chosen. It will not do to plant *any* later-flowering plant to replace an early bloomer, even though it grows to the correct height to continue the uniformity of the scheme and flowers at the right time, for it must be remembered that the substitute plant must also fulfil the requirements of the colour scheme; it being necessary to replace a yellow flower by a yellow one or by one whose flowers will harmonize with yellow.

Annuals may be used to fill vacant spaces, and for this purpose alyssum, asters, centaurea, clarkia, stocks, mignonette and nemophila are hard to rival.

Care of the Border

Let us say that the border has been constructed and planted in the autumn. Through the winter little attention will be necessary, but it will be wise to cover the crowns of the less hardy perennials, such as penstemons and aquilegias, with fibre or small mounds of ashes to protect them from hard frosts in case the weather should be too severe. In the winter too, when there is little foliage and most pests are dormant, is the time to wage war on slugs and other pests infesting the borders. (*See chapter on* Diseases and Pests.)

At the beginning of spring, weeds will have begun to grow and a great deal of labour later on will be saved if these are kept down from the beginning. During the spring and summer it is necessary to keep the hoe busy, not only to keep down the weeds, but to keep the soil well turned and conserve the moisture in hot, dry weather. When the buds are forming the plants should be assisted by the application of a little artificial manure, applied just before rain, if possible: if no rain comes the chemicals should be well hoed in. A suitable mixture is one of 1 part of sulphate of ammonia to 2 parts of nitrate of soda, and applied at the rate of 2 oz. to the square yard. If preferred, a top-dressing of two-thirds well-decayed stable manure and one-third leaf-mould may be given in spring in lieu of the artificial manure. Staking, *see* p. 22.

Watering and Manuring

During the very dry weather, the plants will benefit if watered about every other day. Dead flowers should be cut off at once as this will prolong the flowering; once a plant is allowed to go to seed, it soon stops flowering. As the plants die and turn yellow, they must be cut down to within 3 inches of the ground; this keeps the border tidy and gives room to other plants; and in November when all flowers are over, all the plants should be cut down like this and be clearly labelled. Evergreen plants, such as red-hot pokers, should, of course, not be cut down. At this time, or late in February, dig some well-decayed manure and leaf-mould in between the plants, but do not let the manure cover the crowns or they may rot off, and mind that the digging fork does not injure the roots.

Renewing the Border

About every three to four years the border will be all the better for a thorough retrenching and manuring; many of the plants, too, will be getting over-bulky and will need dividing, partly because they will overcrowd less vigorous neighbours and partly because their flowers will have deteriorated both in size and colour. The border is best renewed in November, when all the plants, with the exception of such as pæonies, delphiniums, lilies, daffodils, and irises, should be removed, carefully labelled as to colour, height, species, etc., and laid aside in a warm and sheltered position. If they are to be left out of the border for more than a couple of days or so, they should be " heeled-into " the reserve garden. The border must be thoroughly trenched, digging as close as possible up to the plants left in position, and the subsoil should be well manured. If the soil is at all sour it should be dressed with lime at the rate of 10 oz. to the square yard. The plants should be divided, the inner and older stems being discarded, and the outer and younger crowns being replanted as when the border was first made.

This work may also be done in February or March; this is wiser in colder localities where the plants might not stand an extra severe winter directly after replanting.

Propagation of Herbaceous Perennials

Herbaceous perennials may be propagated from seeds, cuttings, offsets, layers, and root divisions. The latter method is the most generally used. The use of seeds, however, is becoming increasingly popular, especially in the case of new species, although it is a somewhat lengthy process, as the plants do not attain to their best for three years. Seed is best sown in the open in May or June, or if preferred, in shallow boxes in a cold frame. First-year plants must not be allowed to flower at all; second-year plants may be permitted to bloom in moderation, but they must not be allowed to go to seed. In the chapter on *The Propagation of Plants*, p. 62, will be found full instructions for the various methods of propagation mentioned above.

HARDY HERBACEOUS PERENNIALS

NOTE.—For details as to Colour, Height, Season of Flowering, Culture, and the best Species and Varieties, *see* the Alphabetical List of Flowering Plants and Shrubs, page 147.

Acanthus latifolius
A. mollis and spinosus
Achillea clypeolata, A. fili-pendulina
A. Ptarmica fl. pl.
Aconitum Carmichaelii, A. japonicum and A. Napellus
Adonis amurensis and A. vernalis
Agastache mexicana
Alstromeria aurantiaca
Althæa rosea (Hollyhock)
Anchusa italica (Dropmore, Opal and Pride of Dover)
Anemone alpina
A. apennina, A. coronaria, A. fulgens, A. Hepatica, A. hybrida, and its vars.
Anthemis tinctoria vars.
Anthericum Liliago, "St. Bernard's Lily"
Aquilegia cœrulea (Rock Columbine)
A. longissima
Armeria latifolia, A. plantaginea and varieties
Artemisia lactiflora
Asphodelus lutea and A. ramosus ('King's Spear')
Aster Amellus and vars.
Aster novi-belgii and vars.
Astilbe Davidi
Aubrieta deltoidea vars.
Bellis perennis (Daisy)
Bergenia cordifolia
Bocconia (*see* Macleaya)
Buphthalmum salicifolium
Campanula lactiflora, C. latifolia
Catananche cœrulea
Centaurea hypoleuca, and C. macrocephala
Cephalaria tatarica
Cheiranthus Cheiri (Wallflower)
Chelone Lyoni and C. obliqua
Chrysanthemum arcticum, C. uliginosum and others
Cimicifuga cordifolia
Coreopsis lanceolata
Corydalis nobilis

Delphinium hybrids
Dianthus barbatus (Sweet William)
D. Caryophyllus (Carnation)
D. plumarius (Pink)
Dicentra spectabilis
Dictamnus albus
Dodecatheon Hendersonii, D. Meadia, etc.
Doronicum plantagineum var. excelsum, etc.
Dracocephalum sibiricum
Echinacea purpurea
Echinops Ritro and others
Eremurus (various)
Erigeron speciosus
Erodium Manescavi
Eryngium (various)
Erysimum Perofskianum
Filipendula palmata
Gaillardia grandiflora
Galega officinalis, etc.
Gaura Lindheimeri
Geranium (various)
Geum (various)
Gypsophila paniculata
Hedysarum (various)
Helenium (various)
Helianthus (Sunflower)
Helleborus niger
Hemerocallis flava
Heuchera sanguinea
Horminum pyrenaicum
Hosta Fortunei
Hypericum olympicum
Iberis sempervirens
Incarvillea Delavayi
Inula ensifolia
Iris germanica and vars.
Kentranthus ruber and vars. (Valerian)
Kniphofia (various)
Lathyrus grandiflorus
Leptandra (Veronica) virginica
Ligularia clivorum
Linaria dalmatica
Linum flavum, L. narbonense, and L. perenne
Lobelia (various)
Lupinus (various) (Lupin)
Lychnis chalcedonica
Lysimachia clethroides

Lythrum (various)
Macleaya cordata, M. microcarpa
Malva moschata
Meconopsis cambrica
Mimulus luteus
Monarda didyma
Myosotis scorpioides (Forget-Me-Not)
Nepeta Faassenii
Œnothera glauca var. Fraseri, etc. (Evening Primrose)
Pæonia lactiflora
Papaver orientalis vars.
Penstemon (various)
Phlox barbartus vars. and hybrids
Physalis Franchettii, etc.
Physostegia virginiana Vivid
Polemonium cæruleum and vars.
Poterium obtusum
Primula elatior, P. vulgaris and many garden vars.
Rudbeckia laciniata and many garden vars.
Salvia haematodes, S. superba
Saponaria officinalis, S. o. var. flore plena, etc.
Saxifraga (various)
Scabiosa caucasica vars.
Sedum spectabile and S. s. var. variegatum, etc.
Sidalcea candida, S. neo-mexicana, S. spicata
Smilacina racemosa
Solidago canadense
Stokesia cyanea, and S. c. var. alba
Thalictrum aquilegiifolium, T. Delavayi
Tradescantia virginiana and vars.
Trillium grandiflorum
Trollius asiaticus, T. europæus and vars.
Veronica incana, V. spicata and V. longifolia (Speedwell)
Viola (various) garden vars.

282

CHAPTER 19

The Rock Garden

With Sections on Moraine Garden and Alpine House

The chief uses of the rocks and stones in a rock garden are the provision of coolness for the roots and the storing of moisture in crevices for the use of the plants. But the idea that rock plants grow best in practically nothing but rock is a mistaken one. A generous allowance of good soil between, amongst, and beneath the stones is essential for the healthy growth of the plants. As the function of the rocks is to provide shelter for roots, it is clearly useless to plant slabs of rock or stone perpendicularly in the soil. No protection is afforded in this way: the roots cannot get beneath them, and they do not preserve any moisture. Large masses of stone, two or more feet in length, should be used, where possible, and should be sunk well and firmly in the earth in a slightly slanting direction —tilted backwards, not forwards, so that the rain may trickle down to the roots of the plants. If the rocks lean forward, over the plants, the roots will be sheltered from the rain and probably parched. Although the visible portions of the rocks in the garden should be as pleasing as may be to the eye, and should all slant in the same direction to represent a natural outcrop or stratum of stone, it should never be forgotten that they are not there for the sake of picturesque effect, but to protect the roots of the plants growing among them. The slopes of the mounds in which the boulders are set must not be too steep and should be as natural in appearance as possible; there should be miniature ranges and mountain peaks and dividing them valleys into which spurs from the hills project. Winding paths, 18 inches to 2 feet in width, with stepping stones, should be cut through these gorges so that every part of the rock garden is easily accessible. The pockets in which the alpines are to be planted should be irregular in shape and may vary from a few inches in diameter to as many feet across; they must be from a foot to 18 inches in depth, and so constructed that the soil will not wash out of them. If there is any chance of the soil in the pockets becoming sodden, clinker and rubble drainage must be provided.

Fig. 19. It is essential to have soil-filled spaces or crevices between the rocks. A is a vertical crevice and B a horizontal space made by placing stones between the rock surfaces.

Fig. 20. How to build a rock garden. The rocks should be bedded into the site and set at a uniform angle to give the appearance of natural outcrop of rock strata. Each rock should be slightly inclined backwards and staggered; that is, there should be no overhang, otherwise no moisture will find its way into the horizontal fissures. This section shows clearly the position of the brick and/or rubble for drainage purposes.

Soil for Alpines and Rock Plants

The great majority of alpines and rock plants like a rich soil, containing a large portion of coarse sand or grit, leaf-mould and other decayed vegetable matter. As a whole these plants are not faddy as to soil and most thrive well in the compost mentioned above. However, there are some which thrive and only grow best in certain soils. (*See Alphabetical List of Flowering Plants*, p. 147). For these it is quite easy to scoop out a hollow and to substitute a little special compost in which the rock plant may be inserted.

Alpine plants in their native habitat receive a yearly top-dressing of vegetable matter from the material carried down by the melting snows, and alpines in a rock garden are all the better for a top-dressing artificially applied in imitation of this natural process.

Where rock plants are studied in their natural conditions it will be found that in most cases the soil around the roots is completely covered by the stalks and leaves, each plant touching its neighbours, and that practically no soil is left exposed. This arrangement is of the greatest use to the plants, as by preventing the exposure of the soil to the action of sun and wind, its natural moisture is preserved, so that so far as we can we should provide this protection. This is, however, rather difficult to do at first, as while the plants are still small and most need protection they are unable to cover the surface of the ground, and to plant them closer together would merely mean starving and overcrowding them. In such a case the best thing to do is to cover the intermediate surface of the soil with chips of stone, small enough to be easily pushed aside by a shoot, but sufficient to prevent the over-drying of the earth.

Site and Selection of Stones

As regards the situation of the rock garden, it should, where possible, have an open, sunny position, preferably facing all aspects, for the benefit of various plants, and away from walls and overhanging trees. The rock garden always looks best where it has not to bear contrast with any formal arrangement of garden or shrubbery; a wild and "natural-looking" site, and, where possible, one where the natural rock of the district crops up here and there, is the most favourable, where there is choice. In making the garden the stone of the district should always be used if it can, but any stone will do, except, perhaps, the very crumbling slates or magnesian limestone. Two of the best are weathered limestone and sandstone.

It is essential that there be no spaces and hollows under and around the stones, and that the earth be well bedded round them, or the air within the hollow spaces will dry up the soil and drain the moisture from the roots of the plants, while the stones may also subside and upset the general effect of the rock garden.

Plants for the Rock Garden
When making a selection of plants for the rock garden there are several points to be borne in mind. The first is that we should aim at having bloom over the longest possible period of the year. In this connection some of the smaller-growing bulbs (*see* List of Bulbs, p. 145) which bloom in the winter and early spring are invaluable, while those later autumn-flowering alpines, such as *Astilbe simpliciflora, Saxifraga Fortunei* and *Zauschneria californica* furnish colour long after the great majority of rock plants have finished blooming.

Some of the stronger growers soon over-run the rock garden and smother other plants less luxuriant, perhaps, but more beautiful and useful.

These vigorous growers must, therefore, be limited in number and those that are chosen must be sternly cut back from time to time and kept in check.

To add interest to the rock garden as many of the various genera as possible should be selected, but the garden must never be overcrowded. Bulbs are often overlooked when planting the rock garden. This should not be, for few sights are more lovely than some of the smaller-growing bulbs blooming above a carpeting of Acæna microphylla, Arenaria balearica, or other dwarf trailer.

For a selection, *see* list on p. 289.

Times and Methods of Planting
Rock plants should be planted out either in the spring or, better still, in the early autumn, but not later than September, since the roots make but little growth after that month and the plant is liable to be washed out of the earth by heavy rain, or lifted from the soil by the action of the frost. If care is taken, however, all alpines can be planted out at any time between early April and the end of September. Plants from pots may, of course, be planted at any time, providing the weather is neither too dry nor too wet.

When planting in a crevice, it is essential that there shall be no airpocket at the bottom; this would drain all moisture from the roots and in some cases may cause them to shrivel. To avoid this, first ram plenty of good gritty soil well into the crevice and make sure that the bottom is well filled, then scrape out some of the soil at the top and set the plant in firmly, pressing the soil well down round the root, and fix it in tightly by means of a smaller wedge of stone. Care should be taken that shade-lovers, like the ourisias and shortias, are given congenial situations, such as a sheltered position at the base of a rock facing north or east, while sun-loving plants such as alyssum, arabis, onosma, aubrieta, etc., should be planted in crevices where they can hang over and furnish the face of the rocks while, on the flat parts and damp low-lying situations, gentians, primulas of the japonica types and all the more luscious plants will thrive. When planting do not overcrowd. An occasional dwarf evergreen shrub, in accordance with the position it occupies, will accentuate or detract from the heights and will add naturalness to the landscape.

THE MORAINE GARDEN

Many of the more fastidious of the alpines will not prosper in the ordinary rock garden. The plants to which we refer grow on mountain slopes covered with loose stones, where the melting of the snow during summer provides them with plenty of ice-cold water and where a blanket of snow protects them during the winter.

The conditions we have to endeavour to reproduce are, therefore, adequate moisture for the roots in summer while the plants are growing, but at the same time good drainage, and secondly protection from damp and excessive cold in winter.

Siting and Constructing Moraine

An ideal and natural position for the moraine would be at the lower end of a valley between two rocky spurs, the gorge gradually expanding into a flat bed of scree with occasional boulders strewn over it. To make a moraine, dig out about 2½ feet of the soil and make the bottom of the basin or trench slope slightly towards the front: the slope must not be too steep or the moraine will become over-dry in summer. The lower 10 inches of this basin must be made watertight by means of puddling with clay or cement. Make an outlet in front, which when closed keeps about 10 inches of water, but not more, in the lowest part of the basin, while, when the outlet is open, none at all remains. Now cover the bottom of the trench with about 10 inches of rubble, stones or any material that will afford good drainage. Above this place another 3 inches or so of smaller stones roughly 1 inch in diameter; these will fill the gaps between the larger stones and prevent the small grit above from sinking through and blocking the drainage. The hollow must then be filled up with a mixture of stone chips and gravel, good loam, leaf-mould, and small stone chips similar to those used in frosty weather for sprinkling on wood-paved roads. Cover this, again, with a 2-inch layer of chips. Granite or limestone chips are excellent and easily obtained; flint chips should not be used as they do not conserve moisture. Place a few boulders in the moraine in order to break up the surface and to give the plants some protection. A natural trickle of water may be led into the top of the moraine, or sufficient moisture given from a watering-can each day to cause an overflow from the outlet at the bottom. From November to May, when no additional moisture is needed in the moraine, the outlet should be left open. Many plants that have proved failures in the rock garden proper will, on transplantation to the moraine, flourish beyond all expectations.

Protection in Winter

Silver foliage plants and others whose leaves are covered with fluff or down are, when in their natural haunts, usually protected from frost and damp during the winter by a coat of snow. When they are grown out of doors in this country, they must be given a covering of glass during the winter months. When the plant is a small one nestling in a crevice between the rocks, it is often possible to cover it with a sheet of glass resting on the surrounding rocks, but when this cannot be done, four pieces of stiff galvanized wire should be inserted firmly in the ground and bent over at the top to hold the glass firmly in position over the plant. If the weather is especially severe or the plant very delicate, four other pieces of glass may be firmly set in the soil and supported by the wires so as to form four walls protecting the plant. Sufficient space between the glass roof and the tops of the four walls should be left for adequate ventilation (but not enough to admit the rain or snow) or the plant will be liable to damp-off. The frost will often raise the plants from the soil, especially those planted the previous autumn. In spring each plant should be carefully scrutinized and, if necessary, gently pressed down into the soil.

Care of the Rock Garden

All through the summer months the rock garden must be periodically weeded and all dead flower heads should be cut away. Water the choicer species during dry spells and in May top-dress with a thin layer of sandy loam and leaf-mould. By July most of the plants will have borne the best of their bloom, and many of the most vigorous will now be pushing forth new growth and will commence to overcrowd the less rampageous inmates. These plants, including the shrubby subjects, should, therefore, be trimmed back and at the same time the older portions of the plants and all dead stems and foliage should be removed. Do not, however, trim the plants back so evenly that they have the symmetrical and formal aspect of shrubs in a topiary garden; rather endeavour to foster the wild and natural appearance of the rock garden, and where a plant is not throttling its neighbours and has ample space let it ramble over the rocks at will.

Propagation of Rock Plants

Rock plants may be increased by seed sown as soon as ripe or, failing this, in early spring. Sow in pots or pans under glass. Some germinate better if the pots are plunged out of doors where they are exposed to all weathers and in spring removed to a warm house or frame. Propagate also by cuttings or by division of roots in April or September. It is better to raise alpines from cuttings or by means of division of the roots rather than from seed, which is a lengthy and, in some cases, a difficult process.

If seedlings are raised from a plant which is a variety or of hybrid origin, the chances are that they will not come true to the original plant. In such cases increase by means of cuttings, division or root cuttings. *See* also Propagation, chapter 8.

THE ALPINE HOUSE

There are some choice alpines that cannot be cultivated in the open to the best advantage in our uncertain climate. To say that they are choice does not necessarily mean that they are delicate, but that the blooms of many are apt to be spoilt by inclement weather, and it is to these subjects that the alpine house affords protection while they are in bloom; it will also prolong their season of flowering. Most of the inmates can be brought on in pans sunk to their rims in ashes in the open or in frames until they are about to flower, when they should be transferred to the alpine house to be removed again to the open after flowering.

After the beginning of October all the plants should be housed in a frost-proof frame and must be removed to the house as the blooms become visible.

The alpine house does not require artificial heating and is best of the low span-roofed type, so situated that in runs north and south; both sides then get their fair share of the sun. For management, *see* The Cold House, p. 114.

Compost and Potting

Two-thirds fibrous loam and leaf-mould with one-third coarse, gritty sand makes an excellent compost for most of these plants. Many of the finer saxifrages like a little splintered limestone in their soil, which plants, of course, require a peaty compost.

Individual tastes must be studied as far as possible. Pot-up in pans from 6 to 9 inches in diameter and about 5 inches deep, and as ample drainage is required place 1 to 2 inches of broken crocks in the bottom of the pots for plants like androsaces and saxifrages. For plants of a more vigorous nature and for bulbs 1 inch of crocks will suffice. Re-potting is only needed every second or third year. The stagings should be covered with a 2-inch layer of shingle or ashes so that the atmosphere may be kept moist.

For the treatment of bulbs, *see* Potted Bulbs, p. 143.

PLATE 3

Above left, apple, Worcester Pearmain, and *right*, plums, Victoria
Below left, Mealy Aphis (pest) and Raspberry Beetle (pest)

SELECTION OF ROCK PLANTS

NOTE.—For details as to Colour, Height, Season of Flowering, Culture and the best Species and Varieties, *see* the Alphabetical List of Flowering Plants and Shrubs, p. 147.

*Acæna species
†Achillea clavenae, A. rupestris, A. tomentosa
Adonis vernalis
†Aethionema pulchellum
Alyssum montanum, etc.
†Androsace lanuginosa, etc.
*†Anemone pulsatilla
*Aquilegia glandulosa
Arabis caucasica fl. pl.
*Arenaria species
†Armeria cæspitosa
*Brunnera macrophylla
*†Campanula species
Cerastium tomentosum
Codonopsis clematidea
Corydalis cheilanthifolia
Cotyledon oppositifolia
*Cyclamen (Hardy vars.)
Cytisus kewensis and C. Beanii
†Dianthus (various) (Pink)
†Draba species
Dryas octopetala
Erica carnea (Heath)

†Erodium species
Erysimum rupestre
Gaultheria procumbens
Genista sagittalis
†*Gentiana species
Geum species
Gypsophila repens
*Haberlea rhodopensis
Helianthemum (Sun Rose)
Heuchera sanguinea vars.
†Hypericum species
*Iberis species
Iris (Dwarf Bearded, Hybrid, and Bulbous)
†Lewisia Tweedyi
†Linaria alpina
Linum (Flax) species
Lithospermum diffusum, etc.
Lychnis alpina (Campion)
Macrotomia echioides
Megapterum (Œnothera) missouriense
†*Mertensia primuloides

†Morisia monantha (hypogœa)
Nierembergia rivularis
†*Omphalodes verna, etc.
Onosma albo-roseum, etc.
*Ourisia coccinea
Oxalis enneaphylla, etc.
†Papaver alpinum
Penstemon Scouleri, etc.
Phlox (Dwarf) Species
†Potentilla species
†*Primula species
*Ramonda Myconi
†*Ranunculus alpestris
Saponaria ocymoides
†*Saxifraga species & vars.
Sedum species
Sempervivum species and hybrids
Silene species
Soldanella alpina, etc.
Thymus species
*Viola species
†*Waldsteinia sibirica
Zauschneria californica

NOTE.—In addition to the flowers named in this list there are many dwarf annuals which, though not rock plants in the true sense, deserve a position in the rock garden. It should not be forgotten that hardy bulbs afford masses of colour in the early spring; and suitable species are shown on p. 145; many ferns are also suitable. For dwarf shrubs for the rock garden, *see* List of Flowering Shrubs and Trees.

Those plants that will grow in semi-shade are marked *; those suitable for the Moraine Garden are marked †.

CHAPTER 20

Dry Wall and Paved Garden

The type of garden construction known as a "dry wall" can form an attractive feature of a planned garden. It is built of stones, usually sandstone or limestone, from 2 to 8 inches in thickness, of any size within reason, rectangular and more or less untrimmed. Stones are better than bricks as they provide cooler and moister root-beds for the wall plants. They should be bonded, that is laid in layers, so that lateral extremities of a stone lie over the centres of the two stones in the row immediately below it. This structure serves to keep the wall secure and firm. The stones are best when their upper surfaces are flat, or even cupped, and when placed in position they should be inclined slightly backwards so that they are lower at the back than at the front; the rain will then be collected and drained into the soil at the back of the wall to furnish moisture for the roots. No cement is used, but earth is rammed firmly into the crevices between the stones, sufficient soil being used to keep the stones about an inch apart, vertically. This soil must be rammed well into the back of the wall so that there is soil from the very front to the earth supporting the wall at the back. The soil should be well "firmed" after each row of stones has been laid and no "air-pockets" must be left in the crevices or the roots of the plant will quickly be dried up.

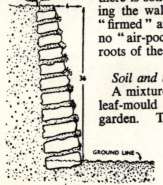

FIG. 21. Section showing the construction of a "dry" wall. The bank should be inclined as shown; that is, for a 36-inch "dry" wall the incline should be about 6 in. at the top. Note the soil-filled spaces between the stones forming the wall.

Soil and its Treatment

A mixture of good loam, decayed cow-manure, and leaf-mould makes the best compost for the wall garden. The first essential is to make a good foundation for the wall. This should be about 10 inches deep and a shade wider than the base of wall. Here the soil is rammed well down till a solid footing is provided. Now lay the first layer of stones, using the largest available, and place them so that their upper sides form one straight horizontal line. If the stones are of moderate size, the gaps left laterally between them may be about 3 inches, the smaller the stones

290

the smaller the gaps between them. Next pack the crevices between the stones tightly with the compost of good loam, leaf-mould and decayed cow-manure. On this is placed the next layer of stone, properly bonded in the manner already explained (*see also* diagram, Fig. 21); and the process is repeated over and over again until the wall has reached the required height. If a stone is occasionally inserted length-wise from back to front, the wall will be secure. The wall should not be built exactly vertical but the top should incline slightly back at an angle of about 1 in 6, that is to say, in a wall 4 feet high the base will project 8 inches further forward than the top. The top of the wall is best left flat so that the rain may soak through to the roots beneath.

How to Plant and When

It is, of course, easiest to plant the wall as it is constructed; the roots may then be spread out as they should be, and can be well covered with soil. Larger plants may thus be employed than when the planting is done when the wall is completed. March and April, when root growth is very vigorous, are the best months in which to construct and plant the wall garden. Seed may be sown in the crevices in spring. The best way to do this is to mix the seeds with a little well-sieved moist sandy soil and to press it into the chink in the wall. A small piece of moss inserted into the crevice will keep the seed moist and will prevent it from being dislodged.

Plants for Sun and Shade

It will be noted that the great majority of the plants given in our list (p. 292) as suitable for the wall garden thrive best in the sun. A wall garden situated in the shade, however, can be made anything but drab and uninteresting, as the names of the shade-lovers will testify. For the shady wall in a cool position such hardy ferns as the asplenium, polypodium, or the scolopendrium must not be overlooked.

In planting, every effort should be made to insert the plants with their roots well spread out, and so that they may penetrate well into the soil at the back of the wall. A little well-rotted cow-manure inserted with the roots will prove beneficial. A plant should never be placed at the *top* of a vertical joint between the stones; its roots would then be likely to become dried up. Rather should it be planted in the crevice just above the centre of a stone.

A good 6 inches of compost should be firmly rammed down on to the top of the wall, and in this soil, at intervals, should be placed large stones; these will help to keep the soil in place and will furnish moist, cool sites for the roots of such plants as rock roses, wallflowers, geraniums, snapdragons, sedums and saxifrages—all ideal plants with which to crown the wall garden.

291

SELECTION OF PLANTS FOR THE DRY WALL AND PAVED GARDEN

NOTE.—For Cultural Details and for Colour, Height, and Time of Flowering, *see* the Alphabetical List of Flowering Plants, p. 147.

DRY WALL

*Acæna adscendens, A. Buchananii and A. microphylla
Acantholimon glumaceum
Achillea species
Æthionema grandiflorum
Alyssum alpestre, A. saxatile, and its vars.
Amarcus Dictamnus, etc.
Androsace primuloides and vars.
Antirrhinum (various)
Aquilegia species
Arabis caucasica fl. pl. and A. androsacea
*Arenaria balearica
Armeria corsica, A. maritima, etc.
Asperula Gussonii
Aubrieta deltoidea vars.
Campanula cæspitosa, C. portenschlagiana
Cerastium tomentosum
Cheiranthus (Wallflower)
*Corydalis lutea

Cotyledon Umbilicus
Dianthus alpinus
Dianthus cæsius, D. deltoides, D. plumarins
Erigeron mucronatus
Erinus alpinus
Eriogonum flavum, etc.
Erodium macradenum
Gypsophila prostrata and G. repens
Helianthemum vars.
Helichrysum bellidioides
Heliosperma alpestre (syn. Silene)
Hypericum fragile and H. polyphyllum
Iberis sempervirens
Leontopodium alpinum
Lewisia species
Linaria alpina and L. Cymbalaria
Linum alpinum, L. salsoloides
Morisia monantha (hypogœa)

Nepeta Faassenii
Onosma albo-roseum
Penstemon Menziesii, P. Scouleri
Phlox amœna, P. subulata vars.
Phyteuma comosum
Polygonum affine
*Primula Allionii, P. Auricula, and P. viscosa
*Ramonda Myconi
Santolina incana
Saponaria cæspitosa and S. ocymoides
*Saxifraga species
Sedum species
Sempervivum species
Silene Schafta
Teucrium Polium
Thymus Serpyllum coccineus
Tunica Saxifraga
Veronica Guthrieana
Zauschneria californica

NOTE.—Those plants suitable for growing in the shade are marked *

PAVED GARDEN

*Acæna Buchananii, A. microphylla and A. myriophylla
Achillea rupestris and A. tomentosa
Alyssum montanum
Antennaria dioica, A. d. var. tomentosa
Anthyllis montana
Arabis bellidifolia variegata
*Arenaria balearica, A. laricifolia
Armeria maritima
Aubrieta deltoides, var.
Bellium minutum
Calamintha alpina
Campanula cæspitosa, C. cochlearifolia, C. garganica, and C. Portenschlagiana
Cerastium arvense and C. tomentosum

*Corydalis lutea
Dianthus deltoides
Dryas octopetala
Erinus alpinus vars.
Erodium chamædryoides
Geranium Pylzowianum
Globularia cordifolia
Gypsophila cerastioides, G. repens
Helianthemum vars.
Herniaria glabra
Hutchinsia alpina
Hypericum nummularium and H. reptans
Linaria alpina, L. repens
Lippia nodiflora
Lotus corniculatus fl. pl.
*Mazus Pumilio, M. radicans
*Mentha Requienii
*Mimulus radicans
Minuartia laricifolia

Morisia monantha (hypogœa)
Oxalis corniculata var. atropurpurea and O. Acetosella rosea
Paronychia argentea and P. serpyllifolia
Penstemon Menziesii
Potentilla alba and nitida
Saponaria ocymoides
*Saxifraga species and vars.
Sedum acre, S. album, S. anglicum
Sempervivum montanum and S. tectorum
Silene acaulis
Thymus Serpyllum, and T. S. var. lanuginosus
Tunica Saxifraga
Veronica alpina, V. repens
*Viola cornuta

NOTE.—Those plants suitable for growing in semi-shade are marked *.

Only certain plants are suitable to the paved garden; these are dwarf in nature and many of them will thrive although trodden on and walked over to a considerable degree, for it must be remembered that the prime reason for a path is its utility as a means of progress. A limited number of plants only, therefore, must be planted in the interstices of the paving, and these must appear to have seeded naturally from surrounding borders or from the rock garden and must in no way impede the pedestrian, although the paved garden should not be subjected to constant traffic. More paved gardens are spoiled by indiscriminate and excessive planting than by any other cause.

If rock work of any kind forms the boundary to the path or the paved garden, allow the plants covering it to encroach a little way and in an irregular manner over the flagstones; this informality will add a touch of nature and help to erase the traces of the handiwork of man.

As to the stones used, the majority should not be less than about 10 inches in diameter or the paving will have a patchy appearance. Stones rectangular in shape are best for paths, but for squares, circles, and ovals, the flags may be of any shape and size provided they are irregular.

The site of the paved garden must, of course, be well drained, in fact the foundation should be similar to that of any ordinary pathway. Over this base is placed a layer of sand some 3 to 6 inches in thickness and on this the flags are laid in an irregular pattern and so that there are gaps of some 2 or 3 inches between the stones. (*See* Crazy Paving, p. 39.) These spaces should be filled with good loamy soil mixed with an eighth part of old mortar, and in this are inserted the plants in small groups or in isolated tufts.

CHAPTER 21

The Water Garden

With Section on the Bog or Marsh Garden

A water garden can be constructed if a source of water is available, i.e. a natural or artificial supply. A very small supply, even a trickle artificially laid on, will suffice, provided it is continuous, but a water garden which is liable to dry up in the summer is a sure source of disappointment. A low-lying piece of land should be selected, preferably one where a natural depression already exists; one should look down on the plants, not have to look up at them. The pond—assuming that one does not already exist—should be made about 3 feet in depth at the deepest point.

Siting and Design

The aim is to copy nature as nearly as possible. Let the pond, therefore, occupy the lowest-lying part of the ground, and to assist in this striving for natural surroundings the water garden may often be advantageously associated with the wild garden, or the rock garden. Size can be made to suit requirements and the surrounding conditions. Shape is dependent upon space and the other features of the garden; naturalness must again be the aim and it should be remembered that a series of sharp and erratic curves will never produce a pleasing and natural outline. The design must be simple; curves may be used, of course, but they must be long, sweeping and natural. On the other hand, not a single curve need be used; the severely simple square or rectangular pool has a charm all its own. In such cases the garden becomes more formal; the pool may well be bordered by a paved walk, and in the crevices between the stones may grow small wall or rock plants. Where the more informal shape has been chosen the grass can well be allowed to clothe the gently sloping banks right down to the water's edge, and marsh plants can be planted in groups from the very brink up to the higher slopes, where bamboos and other shrubs should be used to form a screen and background.

Construction of Pond

Few water plants, except very strong growers, which are better excluded even from the moderately large water garden, require a greater depth of water than 2½ feet. To allow for the thickness of the pond lining and for the inclusion of soil to nourish the roots, it is necessary to excavate to a depth of somewhat over 3 feet. The actual walls of the pond itself are best cut perpendicularly if concrete is to be used (they must be left sloping if the pond is to be "puddled" with clay), but the earth should be thrown well back several feet from the pond so that the banks, on which the marsh plants are to grow, may slope very gently right down to the water's edge.

Now as to the impervious lining to keep the water in the pond. There are three materials that can be used, puddled clay, bricks, mortar, or concrete and cement. We recommend the last as being the easiest to work and the most lasting. Where the subsoil consists of a stiff, sticky, impervious clay, puddling, provided it is well done and is carried to a depth of about 10 inches, is a cheaper and equally successful process.

It must be remembered that all constructional work will have to be hidden and that a permanently moist margin of soil some 2 to 3 feet wide round the pond to accommodate marsh plants will be desirable. It will, therefore, be necessary to excavate to a width sufficient to allow for this; that is to say, supposing it has been decided that the pond shall be 10 feet wide, a hole 3 feet deep all over and 16 feet wide will have to be dug; this allows for a $2\frac{1}{2}$ foot margin of moist earth, as well as 6 inches for the thickness of the wall on each side, if concrete is used. The bottom of the pond need not be more than 5 inches in thickness.

When the excavation is complete all loose soil must be dug out and the bottom made thoroughly firm by pounding with a heavy beater. If the soil over which the concrete is to be laid is left loose, it may shrink away and cause the concrete to crack.

A useful mixture consists of one part of cement, two parts of sand, and five parts of gravel, broken stone, or brick. Whilst still in the dry state, the material should be turned over two or three times. The heap is then wetted with water poured over it from a large water-pot fitted with a fine rose, and the whole is mixed by again turning it over once or twice, so that the materials may be thoroughly amalgamated.

When well mixed and in a semi-liquid condition, place a layer of concrete 6 to 9 inches thick over the bottom of the pond and smooth it down firmly; next build a retaining wall of boards parallel to the earth walls, but 6 inches nearer the centre of the pond. The gap between

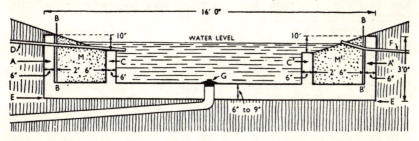

FIG. 22. Sectioned and dimensioned drawing of a pond for a medium-sized garden. M and M¹ are sections for bog plants; D the inflow pipe; F the overflow pipe; G main plug for emptying pond for cleaning.

the wood and the earth sides, when filled up with concrete, will form the two walls A and A'. The supporting boards B'B' and BB are, of course, not removed until the concrete is thoroughly dry. Now construct the two inner walls C and C', each 2½ feet from the outer retaining walls, but 10 inches shorter than them.

An inflow pipe D and an outlet pipe F should be inserted before the concrete work is completed. As soon as the concrete is quite dry it should be roughed over, wetted, and then thoroughly worked over with cement-wash, 2 inches in thickness, care being taken to see that the corners E and E' are perfectly watertight. A word of warning may here be given—it is unwise, apart from the shade cast and the dead leaves and twigs that will fall into the water, to construct a pond under or near trees, as their roots run a considerable distance underground, and are in time likely to crack the concrete unless it is very strong.

Water Supply and Level

For the great majority of aquatic plants a constant flow of water is not a necessity, although it is essential to have a water circulation of some kind in order to prevent stagnation. It should be said that, if the border of marsh plants around the pond is to prove successful, the water must never be allowed to fall below the tops of the inner walls C and C', or the marshy conditions of the banks within the outer containing walls will not be maintained. Likewise the water level must be kept just below the tops of the walls A and A' or too much of the surrounding ground will become marshy. The outflow pipe F is, therefore, a necessity to carry off superfluous rainwater. A plug and outflow G at the bottom of the pond is a useful feature. the water may then periodically be drained away so that the pond can be thoroughly cleaned and rearranged.

When the concrete is thoroughly dry, the spaces M and M' between the retaining walls A and C and A' and C' are filled with a compost of loam and peat, or loam and leaf-mould, and banked up so that the tops of the walls A and A' are covered with soil and hidden from sight. The surrounding ground should slope up gently from this point so that turf may, in places, run right down to the water's edge whence the water and marsh plants may best be surveyed.

At other points rocks may be firmly cemented on the tops of the walls A and A', and sometimes just below the water level. These shelves under the water will form ledges on which aquatics can be planted, and the rocks, which can be built up as miniature cliffs on one side of the pond, will present an excellent contrast to the smooth turf running down to the water's edge on the other.

Plants for the Water Garden

In the moist pockets M and M' are planted the bog or marsh plants, those requiring 4 to 6 inches of water over their crowns being planted under water lower down the bank, while a shade higher up the moist shelf should be grouped those plants flourishing on cool, moist, swampy

296

banks. The bottom of the pond should be covered with a layer of soil some 12 inches deep, in which plants may root.

The best method of planting water plants in a pond or lake is in pans, small tubs, or flat baskets, in which the plants are placed in fibrous loam and a little well-decayed cow-manure, the pans or baskets then being gently lowered into the water in the desired situation. A layer of en-riched mud should cover the bottom of the pond, the baskets resting in this so that the roots of the plants can work out and ramble at will.

The borders of the pond should be hidden with such plants as spread out on the surface of the water, while rooting in the firm soil at the margin. Among these are the water forget-me-not, *Myosotis scorpioides, Comarum palustre, Calla palustris,* and *Veronica Beccabunga.* These, prettily-grouped, will clothe the actual margin, while beyond them the taller-growing plants, such as astilbes, irises, marsh marigolds, with the sedges, grasses, and rushes, thrive on the slightly swampy bank. Many of the ferns love such a situation as this, among them the beautiful *Osmunda regalis.*

Care of Water Garden

Once planted, many aquatic and marsh plants are better if left un-disturbed and only lifted and replanted when they appear to be unhealthy and ailing. Others, however, are much like hardy perennials in their requirements and thrive best if lifted, divided and replaced every third or fourth spring, or when they appear overcrowded. Some of the water lilies make tremendous leaf growth, and consequently little bloom, cover the surface of the water, and prevent the sun's rays from warming it; a function so essential to most aquatics. This strong growth must be periodically cut away, and the roots should be divided if necessary.

Many people are troubled with an objectionable slimy green growth called Blanket weed. This covers the surface of the water in hot, dry weather, usually in spring and summer. It may be disposed of by adding 4 oz. of copper sulphate or 1 oz. of potassium permanganate to each 25,000 gallons of water contained in the pond. A second application should be made in a week's time, should the first be unsuccessful. This will harm neither plants nor fish.

Note.—To obtain the capacity of a pond, multiply the length, breadth and average depth in feet, then multiply by 6 and this will give the approximate number of gallons of water contained in the pond.

Propagation of Aquatic Plants

Aquatic plants, as they are termed, are propagated some by seed and some by division of the roots, which is best carried out in early spring just before growth commences. The seeds, when sown, must be placed under water. In other respects aquatic plants require the same general treatment as other herbaceous plants.

(*See also* the Alphabetical List of Plants, chapter 16, for the culture of individual aquatics.)

THE BOG OR MARSH GARDEN

The site of the bog garden must be low-lying and where the surface drainage will naturally collect. If the subsoil is of sticky clay, a mere trickle of water will keep the soil in a swampy condition. Should the subsoil be light and well drained, a certain amount of excavation will be necessary.

Dig out about 2 feet of the top-soil and introduce a little clay to form a basis; over this stretch a 5-inch bed of rubble or large stones and then a layer of coarse soil. Now fill the hollow, almost to the level of the surrounding land, with a compost of half loam and half leaf-mould or peat. Unless a natural flow of water is available, an artificial trickle,

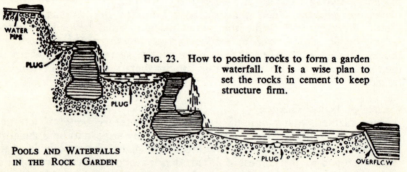

FIG. 23. How to position rocks to form a garden waterfall. It is a wise plan to set the rocks in cement to keep structure firm.

POOLS AND WATERFALLS IN THE ROCK GARDEN

The rocks forming the pools in the above diagram must be set in cement to keep the structure firm; the pools are of concrete and lined with cement. A continuous trickle, artificially fed if necessary, will keep the miniature falls running.

just sufficient to keep the bog swampy, must be introduced. As bog plants should never suffer from drought, the marsh garden should be kept quite moist but must not become stagnant, and for this reason slight bottom drainage is introduced. The bog should never be more than 2 feet in depth; its extent, of course, will depend on space available and taste. Make paths of rough stones or bricks through the bog, and over these place flat stepping-stones so as to make every part of the bog accessible.

Selecting the Plants

Almost any moisture-loving plant may be used, so may all the plants loving the margins of streams and ponds. Do not overcrowd the plants, rather group together three to five plants of the same kind, leave a space, and again plant a group of some different colour, type, and height. If the area is small, greater variety and beauty can be obtained by the use of small-growing species; while among extensive surroundings full rein may be given to the freer-growing varieties, many of which are invaluable as a background where space permits. It is always necessary, however, to bear in mind the size to which the plants will grow in two to three years' time, and to arrange them accordingly.

SELECTION OF PLANTS FOR WATER AND BOG GARDENS

Note.—For Cultural Details, and notes as to Colour, Height and Time of Flowering, *see* the Alphabetical List of Flowering Plants, p. 147.

WATER GARDEN

Alisma Plantago
Aponogeton distachyus
Butomus umbellatus
Calla palustris
Cyperus longus
Hottonia palustris
Limnanthemum nymphæoides
Menyanthes trifoliata
Nuphar advena

Nymphæa alba plenissima
N. Attraction
N. Ellisiana
N. Gladstoniana
N. James Brydon
N. Laydekeri fulgens
N. Marliacea vars.
N. odorata maxima
N. odorata minor

N. odorata sulphurea grandiflora
N. Robinsonii
N. Sunrise
N. tuberosa Richardsonii
Pontederia cordata
Ranunculus Lingua
Sagittaria japonica, S. latifolia
Stratiotes aloides

BOG OR MARSH GARDEN

Acorus Calamus and A. C. var. variegatus
Anagallis tenella
Aruncus sylvester
Arundinaria (Bamboo) species
Arundo Donax
Astilbe species and hybrids
Caltha palustris fl. pl.
Cimicifuga racemosa
Cypripedium spectabile
Filipendula palmata
Gentiana Pneumonanthe
Geum rivale

Gunnera manicata and G. chilensis
Hemerocallis vars.
*Hosta species and vars.
Iris aurea, I. fulva, I. Kæmpferi, I. Monnieri
Leucojum æstivum
Ligularia clivorum
Lysimachia clethroides, L. Nummularia
Lythrum Salicaria roseum
Mimulus cardinalis, etc.
Osmunda regalis
Parnassia palustris

Peltiphyllum peltatum
Phormium tenax
Pinguicula vulgaris
Polygonatum multiflorum
*Primula Beesiana, P. Bulleyana, P. Juliæ, P. rosea florindae, etc.
Rodgersia æsculifolia
Scirpus lacustris
Thalictrum species
Trollius species and vars.
Typha angustifolia and T. minima

Note.—Those plants marked * will grow in semi-shade.

CHAPTER 22

Flowering and Ornamental Shrubs and Trees

Shrubs and trees have not only an intrinsic beauty which adds to the attractiveness of a garden, but they provide shade, backgrounds for herbaceous borders, and a means of dividing the garden into two or more parts. These are only three of countless uses to which shrubs and trees may be put, but they are sufficient to show the importance that must be given to these when a garden is being planned. The variety which is now available of flowering and of evergreen shrubs is enormous. Yet to look at many gardens, one would think that the privet, the laurel, the elder, the euonymus and the rhododendron constituted the whole race.

Before planting, the ground should be deeply dug or trenched to a depth of 2 feet, enriched with well-rotted old manure and leaf-mould, and sufficient space should be allowed to each individual plant for the free and full development of its own peculiar habit of growth. The turf within a radius of 3 to 4 feet round bushes planted on lawns should be permanently removed so that the earth may be thoroughly broken up and exposed to the air.

Methods of Planting

As a general rule, plants of medium size for their kind should be planted rather than fully-grown specimens. They more readily take root and the proportion of losses is much smaller. While there is no hurry, and planting is done with an eye to an effect which is to be produced several years later, it is often wise to plant even younger bushes. In this case it is possible either to fill the space with small bushes and to remove a proportion when they become overcrowded or each shrub may be allotted the full space it will require in later years, the bare soil in between being temporarily decorated by herbaceous plants. Usually the best time to plant deciduous shrubs is from the middle of October, when the leaves begin to fall, to the middle of November, or in February and March. Evergreens are best planted in September and early October, or better still, perhaps, in April and the beginning of May. Never plant evergreens in the depth of winter when their vitality is at the lowest, nor when cold, drying winds are prevalent. Plants that have been grown in pots may, of course, be planted out at almost any time during the year. In the case of both deciduous and evergreen shrubs it is usually wise, at the time of planting, to thin out and reduce the length of the branches by about one-third; this will somewhat relieve the strain put upon the roots, at this time themselves considerably reduced. For details as to how to plant, *see* Planting Fruit Trees, p. 310.

Purpose and Design

The arrangement of shrubs naturally varies according to the purpose which they are to fulfil. If they are to serve as individual specimens on a lawn or similar situation, clearly no " arrangement " is required. If planted in groups it is usually desirable that several plants of a kind should be placed together, though even here full space should be allowed for each individual to develop. This grouping together of, say, three to half a dozen specimens is not only more effective than scattering single plants about indiscriminately, but it makes it easier to give each group of shrubs the special soil in which they thrive best. (For soils suitable to each species, *see* the Alphabetical List of Flowering Plants and Shrubs, p. 147.) The fact that we can have a continued sequence of bloom from flowering shrubs almost all through the year, provided they are carefully selected, is often overlooked. It is necessary, therefore, to select shrubs not only for the colour of their flowers, their suitability for their situation, but also for the time of year at which they flower. Care must be taken that specimens whose colours clash and which bloom simultaneously are not placed together. Associate shrubs whose blooms harmonize in colour and time of flowering, and allow the blooms of the specimens in flower to be set off and enhanced by the foliage of shrubs whose flowers are over or still to come. The stronger growers must be kept in check by periodical pruning or they may overpower the more beautiful, but perhaps less vigorous plants. As backgrounds to borders too great a regularity is usually to be avoided, and their fronts should not present a straight forbidding line. Rather should they afford projections and bays, now pressing out into the border, now forming recesses into which vigorous plants from the border may find welcome shade and shelter. During the summer the soil round the shrubs should be kept well hoed and should be forked over each winter, and where a shrub is seen to be doing badly or to be exhausted, well-decayed manure should be thoroughly worked into the soil round the roots.

Conifers

These are all handsome and graceful trees and among them will be found many species that may well be planted singly as specimen trees on the lawn. Among the best for this purpose are: *Abies homolepis, A. nobilis,* or *A. alba; Cedrus atlantica; Cryptomeria japonica; Chamaecyparis Lawsoniana; C. obtusa* and *Cupressus macrocarpa; Picea Abies, P. Smithiana,* or *P. pungens glauca; Pinus Griffithii (P. excelsa); P. nigra,* and *P. sylvestris; Pseudolarix amabilis; Pseudotsuga taxifolia; Taxodium distichum; Thuja plicata* or *T. orientalis*; and *Tsuga Albertiana.*

Coloured Foliage in Autumn

In planting trees and shrubs it is well worth while to consider their appearance not only in the spring and summer, but in the late and early autumn also, for when the garden is at its most sombre, trees and shrubs may be made to give notes of cheerful and striking colour. A useful selection of these foliage trees and shrubs will be found noted on the list, p. 304.

Pruning—Time, Aim and Method

The time for pruning depends on the season of flowering, and the method is dependent upon whether the bloom is borne on the new or the old wood. Where the new shoots, that is to say those of the current year, bear the flowers, some of the old and weak growth has to be cut in order that the new shoots may be encouraged. This may be done any time from October to November as the flowers are usually borne in late spring or early summer. Where, however, the plants flower on the old wood, generally in late winter or early spring, only the decayed and useless old wood must be cut away, which is usually done in late spring or early summer directly after flowering, as it is of vital importance to give the plants as much time as possible to form and ripen new wood before the winter sets in, as on this wood the flowers will be borne the next spring. Many such plants are only pruned sufficiently to keep them tidy and trim.

April is the best time to trim evergreens, except conifers, which are best trimmed in September or October. Conifers, however, except when grown as hedge-plants, are not usually pruned. When such conifers as the cupressus or yew are used as hedges, they can be pruned back to any height desired; the lateral branches also being trimmed in.

The aim of pruning is, firstly to let air and light to the wood so as to ripen it and thus encourage bloom on flowering shrubs; secondly to train the plant into the shape and size required; and thirdly to keep it tidy. There are also several ways of pruning, the most usual being the cutting back of the shoots. Side shoots are often "spurred" or cut right back leaving only three or four buds; plants requiring this treatment are usually later flowerers, such as the *Buddleia*. Again, the strong main shoots may be "topped" or cut back by about one-third to encourage sturdy growth, or may be only just "tipped" to keep the plant tidy and the growth within bounds; at the same time all old and weak wood is cut out. Another method of pruning, often required, is the removal of the seed-heads from such plants as the rhododendron. If these seed-heads are allowed to remain in position, a poor crop of bloom will result in the following year. Disbudding, the removal of superfluous buds, is also looked upon as pruning, for it increases the size of the flowers left on the plant.

More or less tender shrubs grown in the open in sheltered positions should never be pruned in autumn. This would lay them open to attacks by frost; they should be pruned in April, or even later when danger of severe frosts is past. The reader is referred to the *Alphabetical List of Flowering Plants and Shrubs*, p. 147, where instructions for the pruning

Propagation from Seeds

When sowing seeds saved from the garden, they should not be gathered too early, but must be allowed ample time to ripen, and must be cleaned before being sown. The seeds of such trees as the chestnut, oak or walnut are oily in nature and unless carefully stored in slightly moist sand or fibre are apt to shrivel. They are, therefore, best sown in the open, in the shelter of a wall or hedge, as soon as they are ripe, but the seeds of most shrubs are better sown under glass, in well-drained boxes of sandy soil, in February or March, and when germinated and sufficiently high, should be thinned out to 1½ to 2 inches apart, the less hardy kinds being hardened-off in a cold frame and the hardy kinds planted out in nursery beds in the open. The seeds of most shrubs and trees germinate in a month or two; some, however, like the rose and thorn, take a year and even more.

The seeds of most conifers must be allowed to ripen in their cones on the trees for about a year; some, indeed, require to hang for quite two years.

When the cones have been gathered they are stored in a warm and dry place; the dryness opens the cones and seed are liberated and should be sown thinly in the open in March or April, and be only just covered with a thin layer of fine sandy soil, seeds from healthy trees only being used.

Transplant from the seed-beds to rows in the nursery garden as soon as the seedlings are large enough to handle. It is wise to shelter the young seedlings from the sun.

Propagation from Cuttings

This is undoubtedly the most popular method of propagating shrubs. It provides larger plants in a much shorter time, and ensures that the new plants shall be true to type, which cannot always be relied upon when raising from seed. This method is resorted to especially when propagating dwarf, variegated or rare shrubs. Strong sturdy shoots varying from 3 to 6 inches in length should be taken. During the spring, summer and autumn most shrub cuttings may be struck in a close propagating frame in the greenhouse, preferably with slight bottom heat. During August and September a bed of sandy soil, in a cold frame or under handlights, provides a medium for rooting cuttings of brooms, double gorse, heaths, etc. During October and November cuttings of many shrubs may be inserted in a sheltered border outside. These, as a rule, should be longer than cuttings inserted under glass. They should average 9 to 12 inches.

The cuttings of most conifers, golden privet, and many evergreens always require the protection and moist atmosphere that glass provides.

Cuttings inserted in the autumn remain inactive through the winter and do not usually form roots until the following spring. They must, therefore, not be disturbed until the next autumn, when they may be planted out 12 to 18 inches apart in a nursery bed.

Division, Grafting, Budding and Layering

All the so-called "tufted" shrubs, or those that throw out suckers from their crowns or base, may be propagated by division at the time of year when they are best transplanted.

If the shrubs are grafted, it is usually effected by grafting under glass between January and early June, but many of them may be grafted in the open in April and May.

Budding is usually effected in the open in July and August.

Layering is usually employed in the spring or early summer.

Full information regarding these methods of propagation will be found in chapter 8.

The reader is advised to consult the *Alphabetical List of Flowering Plants and Shrubs,* p. 147, where he will find the best methods of propagating each individual shrub, the most suitable time, whether it is effected in the open or under glass.

HARDY ORNAMENTAL TREES AND SHRUBS

EVERGREEN

Abies (Fir)	Cupressus (Cypress)	Pinus (Pine)
Artemisia Abrotanum [r]	Elæagnus macrophylla [s]	Pseudotsuga taxifolia
Arundinaria metake [s]	*Ilex Aquifolium and	Quercus Ilex
Arundo Donax	vars [s]	Sequoiadendron gigantea
Bambusa Fortunei, etc.	†Juniperus (Juniper)	Taxus baccata and vars. [s]
(Bamboo)	Ligustrum (Privet) [s]	Thuja (various) [s]
Cedrus (Cedar)	Picea Abies, etc.	Tsuga heterophylla

DECIDUOUS

†Acer (Maple)	Fraxinus excelsior pen-	Populus alba Bolleana
Alnus glutinosa, etc.	dula (Weeping Ash)	†Pseudolarix amabilis
Betula verrucosa, etc.	†Ginkgo biloba	Quercus Cerris
Elæagnus angustifolia, syn.	*Hippophæ rhamnoides	†Q. coccinea splendens
hortensis (Oleaster)	Larix decidua (Larch)	†Taxodium distichum
*Euonymus latifolius	†Nyssa sylvatica (Tupelo)	Ulmus Louis van Houttei
†Fagus sylvatica (Beech)	Platanus acerifolia	U. glabra pendula
	P. orientalis	

NOTE.—* denotes Berry-bearing shrubs; † Coloured Foliage in Autumn; r=Shrubs for the Rock Garden, and s=Shrubs that will grow in the shade.

PENDULOUS OR WEEPING TREES

Betula verrucosa (alba) pendula (Birch)	Fraxinus excelsior pendula (Ash)	P. subhirtella pendula (Japanese Cherry)
B. v. pendula purpurea (Purple Birch)	Ilex Aquifolium pendula (Holly)	Quercus robur pendula (Oak)
Cratægus monogyna pendula (Thorn or May)	Populus tremula pendula (Aspen)	Salix babylonica (Willow)
Fagus sylvatica pendula (Beech)	Prunus Mahaleb pendula (St. Lucie Cherry)	Ulmus montana pendula (Wych Elm)

HARDY FLOWERING TREES AND SHRUBS

NOTE.—For Colour of Flowers, Time of Blooming, Heights, Cultural Details, and the best Species and Varieties, *see* the Alphabetical List of Flowering Plants and Shrubs, p. 147.

Abelia triflora (D) and A. grandiflora (E)
Æsculus species (D)
*Ailanthus altissima (D)
†*Amelanchier canadensis
Andromeda polifolia (E)
*Arbutus Unedo, etc. (E)
*Aucuba japonica (E) [s]
Azalea vars. (E or D)
*Azara dentata, etc. (E)
*Berberis Darwinii (E), etc.
Buddleia vars. (D)
Buxus sempervirens (E) [s]
Calluna vulgaris (E) [r]
Calycanthus floridus (D) [s]
Cassinia fulvida (E) [r]
Castanea sativa (D)
Catalpa bignonioides (D)
Ceanothus species (E)
Chænomeles lagenaria (D)
Chimonanthus præcox var. grandiflorus (D) [w]
Chionanthus retusus (D) [s]
Choisya ternata (E) [s]
Cistus (Rock Rose) (E) [r]
†*Clerodendron trichotomum (D)
*Colutea arborescens (D)
*Cornus (D) [w, r, s]
Cotinus Coggygria (D)
*†Cotoneaster (E or D) [r, s]
†*Cratægus (Thorn) (D)
Cytisus (D or E) [r]
Dabœcia polifolia (E) [r]
*Daphne species (E or D) [r]
Deutzia species (D)
Diervilla (Weigela) (D) [s]
†Enkianthus species (D)
Erica species (Heath) (E) [r]
Escallonia species (E or D) [s]
Euonymus japonicus (E)
Exochorda grandiflora (D)
Forsythia species (D) [s]
Fraxinus Ornus (D)

Fuchsia magellanica and vars.
Garrya elliptica (E) [w]
*†Gaultheria procumbens and G. Shallon (E) [r, s]
Genista species (D) [r]
Grevillea rosmarinifolia [r]
Halesia carolina (D)
Halimium lasianthum
†Hamamelis mollis (D) [w]
Hebe (Speedwell) (E) [r]
Hedera Helix (Ivy) (E) [s]
Hibiscus syriacus (D) [s]
Hydrangea species (D) [s]
Hypericum (E or D) [s]
Itea virginian (D) [s]
Jamesia americana (D) [s]
Jasminum species
Juglans regia (D)
Kalmia latifolia, etc.
Kerria japonica fl. pl. (D)
Laburnum (various) (D).
Laurus nobilis (E)
Lavendula Spica (E)
Ledum latifolium (E) [r]
Leiophyllum buxifolium
*Leycesteria formosa (D) [s]
*Ligustrum (Privet) (E) [s]
†Liriodendron Tulipifera
Lonicera (Honeysuckle) (D)
Lupinus arboreus (D)
Magnolia (E or D) species
†*Malus species (D)
Morus nigra (D)
Myrtus communis (E)
Olearia Haastii (E) [r, s]
Osmanthus Aquifolium
†Parrotia persica (D)
*Pernettya mucronata (E)
Philadelphus species (Mock Orange) (D) [s]
*Phillyræa media (E) [s]
Pieris floribunda and P. japonica (E)

Prunus Amygdalus (D)
Prunus avium fl. pl. (D)
P. cerasifera (Cherry Plum) (D)
Prunus Persica (Peach) (D)
P. serrulata vars. (Japanese Cherry)
*Pyracantha Lalandei (E)
Rhododendron (E)
†Ribes aureum, R. sanguineum (D) [s]
Robinia hispida (D)
Romneya Coulteri (D)
*Rosa Hugonis (D)
*†R. rugosa (D)
Rosmarinus officinalis (E)
Rubus ulmifolius (D) [s]
Salix babylonica (D)
*Sambucus canadensis maxima (E) [r]
Santolina Chamæcyparissus (D) [s]
*Skimmia japonica (E) [s]
Spartium junceum (E)
Spiræa species (D) [s, r]
Staphylea colchica (D) [s]
*Symphoricarpos racemosus lævigatus (D) [s]
Syringa vars. (Lilac) (D) [s]
Tamarix pentandra (syn. hispida æstivalis (D)
Tilia dasystyla (D)
Ulex europæus fl. pl. (E)
Veronica (Speedwell), *see* Hebe
†*Viburnum Opulus var. sterile, etc.
†*V. Tinus (E) [w, s]
Vinca major elegantissima (Periwinkle) (E) [s, r]
Weigela (*see* Diervilla)
Yucca gloriosa (E)
Y. recurvifolia (E)

NOTE.—* Denotes best Berry-bearing shrubs; † Coloured Foliage in Autumn; w, Winter-flowering shrubs; r, Shrubs for the Rock Garden; and s, Shrubs that will grow in the Shade; E=Evergreen; D=Deciduous.

CHAPTER 23

Climbing Plants

Among the most attractive flowering plants are the clematis, honeysuckle, Traveller's Joy, etc., all of which are climbing plants and generally, from a cultural point of view, just left "to grow". Such neglect soon reduces the plants to a low quality, for climbing plants need and deserve proper care.

Siting and Supporting

First as to site; nearly all creepers do better if the air can circulate freely round their stems and shoots, but this does not mean that they enjoy cold draughts from the north or east. Most climbers will thrive better on a wooden trellis, provided it is sheltered from these cold blasts, than they will against a brick wall which throws back the sun's rays and is apt to scorch them. Many of less hardy nature, of course, demand the shelter of a wall and several require that this wall shall also face south to catch all available sunlight and warmth. In chapter 16 we have pointed out the preference as to aspect shown by each plant.

Methods of Planting

A creeper must not be planted with its roots right up against a wall, the roots should be placed some 18 inches from the wall, so that they may receive adequate air and moisture. In dry weather a good watering should occasionally be given to all wall plants, even though correctly planted with their roots some way from the wall. The creosote or paint used on the wooden supports of a pergola may be very harmful if it comes into contact with the roots, and this is another reason why the climber should not be planted too close to its support. *See also* the instructions for planting deciduous and evergreen shrubs in the chapter on Shrubs, *also* Planting Fruit Trees, p. 310.

The most valuable of our garden climbing plants are perennials, but annuals also furnish us with a number of beautiful climbers which, by their quick growth and easy culture, are often of the greatest value. *See* list, p. 307.

Full cultural details of the climbers mentioned in this chapter are given in the *Alphabetical List of Flowering Plants and Shrubs*, p. 147; for Pruning and Propagating, *see* chapter on Ornamental and Flowering Trees and Shrubs, p. 300.

SELECTION OF CLIMBING PLANTS

For Cultural Details, and for Colour of Flowers, Time of Flowering, Height, and the best Species and Varieties, *see* the Alphabetical List of Flowering Plants and Shrubs, p. 147.

Ampelopsis
Aristolochia macrophylla (syn. A. Sipho), S.W.
Azara microphylla (Warm Sheltered), S.
*Berberidopsis corallina (Southern Counties only), S.W.
Calycanthus occidentalis, S.W.
*Campsis grandiflora (Trumpet Flower), S.
*Carpenteria californica (Southern Counties), S.
Ceanothus dentatus, S.
C. Gloire de Versailles, S.
C. rigidus, S.
*C. Veitchianus, S.
Celastrus scandens, N.E.
Chænomeles lagenaria vars., C. japonica, E.W.
Chimonanthus præcox (Winter Sweet), S.W.
*Choisya ternata, S.
Clematis flammula, E.W.
C. florida vars., E.W.
C. Jackmannii vars., E.W.
C. lanuginosa vars., E.W.
C. montana vars., N.E.W.
C. patens vars., E.W.
C. Vitalba (Traveller's Joy), N.E.W.
C. Viticella vars., E.W.
Cotoneaster horizontalis, N.E.
C. Henryana, N.E.W.
Cratægus Pyracantha. See Pyracantha coccinea, N.E.
*Eccremocarpus scaber, S. Treat as an annual
Escallonia exoniensis, S.

E. langleyensis, S.
E. macrantha, S.
E. montevidensis, S.
Forsythia suspensa, S.W.
Garrya elliptica, N.E.W.
Hedera dentata, N.
H. Helix (Common Ivy)
Humulus Lupulus aureus (Golden Hop)
*Hydrangea petiolaris (Scandens), N.W.
Jasminum nudiflorum, N.E.W.
J. officinale, N.E.
J. primulinum, S.W.
J. revolutum, S.W.E.
Kerria japonica, S.W.
Lathyrus grandiflorus, S.W.   [Pea), S.W.
L. latifolius (Everlasting
Lonicera Caprifolium, E.
L. japonica flexuosa, N.E.
L. japonica aureo reticulata, N.E.
L. Periclymenum, N.E.
L. P. belgica (Early Dutch), N.E.
L. P. serotina (Late Dutch), N.E.
L. sempervirens (Trumpet Honeysuckle), N.E.
Lycium chinense
Magnolia denudata, W.
M. grandiflora, S.W.
M. Soulangiana
Mutisia decurrens (Sheltered), S.W.
Myrtus communis, S.
M. tarentina, S.
Parthenocissus Henryana (Sheltered), S.

P. quinquefolia (syn. Ampelopsis hereracea) (Virginia Creeper), N.S.E.W.
P. tricuspidata, var. Veitchii (syn. Ampelopsis Veitchii), N.S.E.W.
Passiflora cærulea and P. c. Constance Elliott (Passion Flower), S.W.
Polygonum baldschuanicum
Pyracantha angustifolia, N.S.E.W.
P. coccinea (Fire Thorn), N.S.E.W.
P. c. Lalandei, N.S.E.W.
Rosa. See Rose cultivation.
Rubus laciniatus (Parsley-leaved Blackberry)
R. thyrsoideus fl. pl. (Double - flowered Blackberry)
R. ulmifolius var. bellidiflorus
*Solanum crispum, S.W.
*S. jasminoides (Sheltered), S.W.
Trachelospermum jasminoides
Tropæolum speciosum (Flame Nasturtium), N.
Vitis Coignetiæ (Crimson Glory Vine), S.
V. vinifera purpurea Sheltered, S.W.
Wisteria multijuga and alba, S. or S.W.
W. sinensis, S. or S.W.
W. s. alba, S. or S.W.

ANNUAL

*Calonyction aculeatum (Moon Flower)
*Cobæa scandens (grown as annual)
*Cucurbita (Gourd)

Humulus japonicus
*Ipomœa purpurea (Morning Glory)
Lathyrus odoratus (Sweet Pea)

Quamoclit coccinea, Q. lobata, Q. pennata (Cypress Vine)
*Tropæolum aduncum (Canary Creeper)
T. majus (Climbing Nasturtium)

NOTE.—N.S.E. or W. indicates the most suitable position, e.g. Wall facing North, South, East or West. * denotes Half-hardy.

307

Index

Index

314

Notes

Notes